Valuing Recreation and the Enviromment

NEW HORIZONS IN ENVIRONMENTAL ECONOMICS

General Editors: Wallace E. Oates, *Professor of Economics, University of Maryland, USA* and Henk Folmer, *Professor of Economics, Wageningen Agricultural University, The Netherlands and Professor of Environmental Economics, Tilburg University, The Netherlands*

This important series is designed to make a significant contribution to the development of the principles and practices of environmental economics. It includes both theoretical and empirical work. International in scope, it addresses issues of current and future concern in both East and West and in developed and developing countries.

The main purpose of the series is to create a forum for the publication of high quality work and to show how economic analysis can make a contribution to understanding and resolving the environmental problems confronting the world in the twenty-first century.

Recent titles in the series include:

Global Environmental Change and Agriculture
Assessing the Impacts
Edited by George Frisvold and Betsey Kuhn

The Political Economy of Environmental Policy
A Public Choice Approach to Market Instruments
Bouwe R. Dijkstra

The Economic Valuation of Landscape Change
Theory and Policies for Land Use and Conservation
José Manuel L. Santos

Sustaining Development
Environmental Resources in Developing Countries
Daniel W. Bromley

Valuing Recreation and the Environment
Revealed Preference Methods in Theory and Practice
Edited by Joseph A. Herriges and Catherine L. Kling

Designing Effective Environmental Regimes
The Key Conditions
Jørgen Wettestad

Environmental Networks
A Framework for Economic Decision-Making and Policy Analysis
Kanwalroop Kathy Dhanda, Anna Nagurney and Padma Ramanujam

The International Yearbook of Environmental and Resource Economics 1999/2000
Edited by Henk Folmer and Tom Tietenberg

Valuing Environmental Benefits
Selected Essays of Maureen Cropper
Maureen Cropper

Controlling Air Pollution in China
Risk Valuation and the Definition of Environmental Policy
Therese Feng

Valuing Recreation and the Environment

Revealed Preference Methods in Theory and Practice

Edited by

Joseph A. Herriges

Associate Professor of Economics, Iowa State University, USA

and

Catherine L. Kling

Professor of Economics, Iowa State University, USA

NEW HORIZONS IN ENVIRONMENTAL ECONOMICS

Edward Elgar

Cheltenham, UK • Northampton, MA, USA

Published by
Edward Elgar Publishing Limited
Glensanda House
Montpellier Parade
Cheltenham
Glos GL50 1UA
UK

Edward Elgar Publishing, Inc.
6 Market Street
Northampton
Massachusetts 01060
USA

A catalogue record for this book
is available from the British Library

ISBN 1 85898 646 X

Printed and bound in Great Britain by Bookcraft (Bath) Ltd.

Contents

List of Figures

List of Tables

List of Contributors

Nancy E. Bockstael
Professor of Agricultural and Resource Economics, University of Maryland, College Park, Maryland

Trudy Ann Cameron
Professor of Economics, University of California, Los Angeles

Heng Z. Chen
Economist, American Express Travel Related Services, Phoenix, Arizona

W. Michael Hanemann
Professor of Agricultural and Resource Economics, University of California, Berkeley, California

Daniel Hellerstein
Economist, Economic Research Service, United States Department of Agriculture, Washington, D.C.

Joseph A. Herriges
Associate Professor of Economics, Iowa State University, Ames, Iowa

John P. Hoehn
Professor of Agricultural Economics, Michigan State University, East Lansing, Michigan

Catherine L. Kling
Professor of Economics, Iowa State University, Ames, Iowa

Frank Lupi
Visiting Assistant Professor of Agricultural Economics, Michigan State University, East Lansing, Michigan

Kenneth E. McConnell
Professor of Agricultural and Resource Economics, University of Maryland, College Park, Maryland

Edward R. Morey
Professor of Economics, University of Colorado, Boulder, Colorado

Daniel J. Phaneuf
Assistant Professor of Agricultural and Resource Economics, North Carolina State University, Raleigh, North Carolina

Shannon R. Ragland
Economist, Hagler Bailly, Inc., Boulder, Colorado

W. Douglass Shaw
Associate Professor of Applied Economics and Statistics, University of Nevada, Reno, Nevada

J.S. Shonkwiler
Professor of Applied Economics and Statistics, University of Nevada, Reno, Nevada

Ivar E. Strand
Professor of Agricultural and Resource Economics, University of Maryland, College Park, Maryland

Kenneth E. Train
Adjunct Professor of Economics and Chair, Center for Regulatory Policy, University of California, Berkeley

Quinn Weninger
Assistant Professor of Economics, Utah State University, Logan, Utah

Preface

This book contains a series of papers about valuing the environment using observed behavior on usage of the environment. This type of data is generally referred to as "revealed preference data" and models that employ this data as "revealed preference methods." Thus, traditional travel cost models, random utility models of recreational use, hedonic models, and averting behavior models all fall under the rubric of revealed preference methods. However, the papers in this volume focus on the first two types of models since they have seen the most use in environmental valuation.

The first three chapters of this volume deal with the theory of welfare measurement when the analyst has some form of revealed preference data related to use of the environment. The remaining seven chapters focus on a variety of issues in the empirical implementation of these methods. In the empirical arena, analysts must put these theoretical constructs to use while addressing the econometric and data problems specific to the available data sets.

Two trends in applied economics have provided the impetus for us to put together this volume of papers. First, as most environmental economists are acutely aware, there has been an explosion in the number of papers fitting into the general area of "valuing the environment". There is clear interest among policy makers and environmental economists in putting monetary values on access to, or changes associated with, environmental amenities so that the tradeoffs inherent in development or destruction of these resources can be more systematically understood.

At the same time as general interest in environmental valuation has grown, it is our sense that there has been an increase in the importance of stated preference approaches relative to revealed preference models for estimating these values. The reasons for this are likely numerous, but here we speculate on three. The popularity of the approach is undoubtedly due, at least in part, to the ability of stated preference models to value a wide variety of environmental goods. Additionally, a fertile research agenda was spawned by the controversy surrounding the validity of the contingent valuation approach (the now famous NOAA Blue Ribbon panel report being the most visible input to the debate). The challenge of investigating such a fundamental issue may have brought numerous intellectual resources into this arena. Finally, a number of excellent survey and/or "state-of-the-art" presentations of stated preference methods exist (e.g., Mitchell and Carson, 1989; Cummings *et al.*, 1986; Bjornstad and Kahn, 1996; Kopp, Pommerehne, and Schwarz, 1997; and Bateman and Willis, 1998) which may reduce the costs of entry to researchers interested in that line of research.

It is this third reason that provides a motivation for this collection of papers. In contrast to the ample number of reference volumes on stated preference approaches, no such state-of-the-art volume exists regarding revealed preference approaches. The lack of such a volume strikes us as a potential market failure. Regardless of which "side" one comes down on in the contingent valuation debate, we believe that there continues to be much to learn about preferences for environmental goods from reported behavior concerning environmental use.

Thus, the first of our motives for asking authors to contribute to this volume was to provide a reference source on revealed preference methods, analogous to those already available in the stated preference literature. Collectively, the papers in this volume provide an introduction to economists interested in careful behavioral and econometric modeling of the demand for the environment using observed behavior. Although we do not expect to see a dramatic rise in the proportion of stated to revealed preference applications as a result of this book, we hope that the present volume will reduce barriers to entry and possibly increase interest in these methods.

A second trend that prompted us to collect these papers is the rapid and sizable improvement in computing capabilities that most researchers have experienced in the past decade. Econometricians have been quick to take advantage of these improvements in computational ability and have rapidly developed new algorithms and models that allow the estimation of more complex econometric models. Thus, even environmental economists who have worked in the field of revealed preference methods may find keeping up with the latest modeling advances somewhat daunting. Thus, our second goal for this volume is to provide a single source where revealed preference modelers can find presentations of current, state-of-the-art applications.

In short, we hope that this volume serves as a beneficial starting point for those interested in "tooling up" on revealed preference approaches and a useful presentation of current modeling and estimation techniques for long time practitioners of the trade. To this end, we, as noted earlier, invited authors to contribute papers in two areas: the theory of welfare measurement in revealed preference models and revealed preference models in practice.

Rather than have authors prepare "literature reviews" or "summaries," we felt our goals would be better met by first providing papers that present the basic theory and follow those chapters with state-of-the-art presentations of empirical work that demonstrate how this theory can be translated into empirical estimates. Nancy Bockstael and Ted McConnell (Chapter 1) provide an excellent assessment of the basic welfare theory underlying revealed preference methods as well as an insightful discussion of why revealed preference methods are used less often than their stated preference counterparts. Following their paper, we are fortunate to be able to include two papers that are already well known among environmental economists despite not having been previously published. The first of these is a revision of Michael Hanemann's often cited paper on welfare measurement in random utility models as applied to the environmental arena. The second, another often cited paper, is authored by Edward Morey and provides a rigorous, but readily accessible, description of nested logit models and their properties. Nested logit models have become a mainstay tool in analyzing both recreational site selection and participation.

The topics considered in the "practice" section of the book (Chapters 4 through 10) represent a wide range of the complex empirical issues related to the estimation of revealed preference methods. All of these applications relate to estimating the demand for recreation goods using variants of traditional travel cost methods or random utility models. The first three of these chapters examine various specification issues associated with random utility models.

Kenneth Train lucidly presents a description of mixed logit models, a random parameters generalization of the standard logit specification. As Train argues, the mixed logit offers several advantages over its multinomial logit counterpart. First, like nested logit, mixed logit models do not impose the independence of irrelevant alternatives assumption imbedded in multinomial logit models and can capture correlation patterns across choice alternatives. Second, in applications involving panel data, the mixed logit specification can be used to model correlation among an individual's site selections across choice occasions. Third, the mixed logit model allows the analyst to characterize the distribution of household preferences for specific site attributes. In the following chapter, Heng Chen, Frank Lupi, and John Hoehn present one of the first empirical estimates of a multinomial probit model for recreation demand. This undoubtedly represents a major "growth area" in recreation demand modeling and we expect that both Train's and Chen *et al.*'s work will prompt others to explore the richer error structure and increased flexibility that their models allow.

In Chapter 6, we team up with Dan Phaneuf to present and contrast two primary approaches to estimating revealed preference models for recreation demand when there are multiple sites available and an abundance of corner solutions. We investigate both the relatively unexplored Kuhn–Tucker model and the "linked model" where a random utility model of site selection is combined with a participation decision by recreationists.

Next, Ted McConnell, Quinn Weninger, and Ivar Strand develop and estimate a simple and conceptually compelling model that combines data from both revealed and stated preference sources. This is an area that also strikes us as a "growth area" in environmental valuation; if nothing else, common sense suggests that two sources of information on underlying preferences should be better than one.

An issue in both revealed and stated preference methods that has received too little attention is the probable biases associated with sample nonresponse. Trudy Ann Cameron, Douglass Shaw, and Shannon Ragland (Chapter 8) address this question in the context of a survey concerning water-based recreation within the Columbia River system. Survey responses are combined with zip-code level Census data to simultaneously model the decision to return the original survey and the household's recreation pattern. The authors find that nonresponse can substantially distort models of recreation usage and the welfare implications derived from them.

The last two papers both address the issue of controlling for the count nature of trip data in traditional recreation demand models. Scott Shonkwiler's Chapter 9 introduces a flexible, multivariate count data model adapted from the generalized linear models of the biometrics literature. The resulting generalized estimating equations are relatively simple to apply, while permitting exact welfare analysis. Dan Hellerstein concludes the book in Chapter 10 with a discussion of the behavioral foundations of count data models.

In closing, we would like to thank Wally Oates for supporting the idea of this book in the first place, Elgar Publishing Co. for publishing it, and John Miranowski and the Department of Economics at Iowa State University for providing financial support for the project. In addition, we would like to thank Kerry Smith, Skip Crooker, and Chris Azevedo for valuable review and editing and Donna Otto and Ruth Bourgeois for their excellent technical assistance. Finally, a sincere thanks to each of the authors who were patient with us throughout the editing and revising process and who provided us with good-natured (if not always timely!) responses to our requests.

Joseph A. Herriges and Catherine L. Kling

REFERENCES

Bateman, I.J., and K.G. Willis, eds., *Contingent Valuation of Environmental Preferences*, Oxford University Press: New York, 1998.

Bjornstad, D.J., and J.R. Kahn, *The Contingent Valuation of Environmental Resources: Methodological Issues and Research Needs*, Edward Elgar Publishers: Aldershot, England, 1996.

Cummings, R.G., D.S. Brookshire, and W.D. Schulze, eds., *Valuing Environmental Goods: A State of the Arts Assessment of the Contingent Method*, Rowman and Allanheld: Totowa, N.J., 1986.

Kopp, R.J., W.W. Pommerehne, and N. Schwarz, *Determining the Value of Non-Marketed Goods: Economic, Psychological, and Policy Relevant Aspects of Contingent Valuation Methods*, Kluwer Academic Publishers: Boston, 1997.

Mitchell, R.C. and R.T. Carson, *Using Surveys to Value Public Goods: The Contingent Valuation Method.* Washington, DC: Resources for the Future, 1989.

1. The Behavioral Basis of Non-Market Valuation

Nancy E. Bockstael and Kenneth E. McConnell

1.1 INTRODUCTION

This chapter, and indeed this book, deals with the use of observations on individual behavior to infer the economic value of changes in public goods in general, and environmental goods in particular. Our point of departure concerns the relative infrequency of studies that use behavioral methods to infer the values of changes in the quality of the environment. Given the long debate about contingent valuation versus behavioral methods, it is all the more surprising to realize that in fact there are comparatively few studies which use the latter to infer economic values for environmental goods. The debate pits the intuitive appeal of behavioral revelations of willingness to pay against the contrary notion (at least to economists) that hypothetical questions can provide useful information about preferences. The *practice* of revealed preference valuation is far more difficult than the *concept*, and it is in the *practice* that contingent valuation has taken the advantage. In this chapter we try to explain intuitively what makes behavioral methods hard to apply and why some particular types seem to work.

The appeal of contingent valuation is often attributed to its ability to assess existence value. But contingent valuation is popular even when the goal is the estimation of use values, because even in these cases it is sometimes the *only* method that works. Unexpected oil spills or sudden increases in fecal coliform may influence behavior, but even if the pollution event is severe, if it is also short-lived, it may leave few behavioral traces. Two specific models —hedonic models and random utility models of recreational site choice— account for most of the behavioral studies aimed at environmental valuation. These models tend to track chronic environmental effects, such as long run changes in air pollution for hedonic models or steady declines in fish stocks for random utility models of recreational fishing. Averting behavior studies have also addressed chronic problems, such as air pollution and radon contamination. To some extent, nature conspires against the use of behavioral methods. But even in the confines imposed by nature, it seems reasonable to explore additional behavioral alternatives.

Our purpose in this chapter is to identify the basic elements that are required to infer the economic value of changes in the environment using behavioral methods. This will engage us in a discussion of the links between public and private goods in a spirit different from the current literature. Much of the current revealed preference literature assumes that the links between public and private goods are clear, and concentrates instead on econometric issues. There are certainly interesting and important questions in that realm, but it is odd that, by focusing on precise scenario depiction and careful probing of what respondents know, contingent valuation exhibits more concern with these links than does research using behavioral methods.

We will attempt to provide an intuitive appreciation for environmental valuation based on revealed preference. This involves two questions: what kinds of assumptions about preferences and technology are helpful and what kinds of observable circumstances are needed? We have some faint hope that a more general and intuitive approach will lead to insights that produce innovations in behavior-based methods to valuation, advances that are badly needed.

The following analysis is limited to the household sector of the economy. This leaves out the production sector, which is also naturally damaged by declines in environmental quality. We concentrate on the household sector because it seems the more problematic of the two for valuation. Among households, non-market valuation means that both the pollution and the activities impaired by pollution are non-market. Hence for households, non-market valuation requires modeling the link between households' activities and pollution as well as valuing the changes in activities. For firms modeling the link is the principal issue, because the impaired activities are by their nature market activities.

1.2 A GENERAL THEORY?

The starting point for valuing environmental amenities is the theory of public goods. The most basic tenet of this theory is that the social value of public goods is the summation of individuals' private values. This definition of social value implies the existence of an individual's marginal value function. In concept an individual's valuation of increments of the public good is given by differentiating his indirect utility function with respect to the public good. While it is useful to distinguish between marginal values and demand curves, one may think of the summation of private marginal value functions as containing information about the demand for public goods. The fundamental issue in environmental valuation is that the demand curve for public goods is not observable. We can never completely determine from behavior how the services of public goods are consumed; we can only learn about them by observing behavior towards goods and services that are linked with public goods. But no 'general method' exists for exploiting observations on private behavior to infer the value of public goods.

Our discussion will focus on the value of discrete changes in environmental amenities, because these are more relevant for economic policy. This relevance stems from the discrete nature of policy. While there is a great deal of literature on marginal values of environmental quality, the usefulness of these marginal values is limited to pedagogical purposes and to extended national income accounting, where linearized marginal values are employed. In the general theory of the consumer, it is so easy to go from marginal values to the values of discrete changes that this distinction is frequently lost. But in the public good case, the total value of a change can often be revealed only with hard work and under special circumstances, even when the marginal valuation is apparent.

While there may be no general theory of environmental valuation, there are key requirements of models that should hold for welfare changes to be measurable. These elements are:

1. a way to link changes in the observable behavior of people with changes in the level of a public good or environmental amenity;
2. a plausible approach for ensuring that the changes in observed behavior constitute most of the response to the change in the public good (and not the behavioral response to other stimuli);
3. paired observations on behavior influenced by the environmental amenity, and levels of the environmental amenity; and for some models, parametric prices, such that some relevant demand curve can be estimated as a function of the amenity and typically the price.

The first requirement is that there be a reason to believe that changes in the environmental good will influence some observable behavior. Even this can not be taken for granted, but where it is evident it provides direction for the econometric work. For example, one might expect that swimming in a lake will decline with increases in fecal coliform (but only if experience or publicity informs the recreationist). As a counter-example, people may care about the diversity of life in tropical forests, but it seems unlikely that changes in this diversity will bring about changes in some specific behaviors.

The second requirement is as critical but in most instances untestable. To continue the fecal coliform example, the researcher might adopt the maintained hypothesis that households would not value the levels of this pollutant if they do not use the lake. Such a hypothesis would support the revealed preference measure as an approximation of the full value of the change in the environmental good to the individual, equivalent to the statement that there is no existence or non-use value present and the environmental amenity does not influence the consumption of other household goods and services.[1] As a counter-example, it is reasonable to believe that use of air conditioning would increase during a high ozone period in a metropolitan area. And with proper econometric work, one could perhaps isolate the influence of ozone levels on air conditioning use. Yet exposure to high ozone levels cannot be completely mitigated by air conditioning and considerable other services are provided by an air conditioner, so that an attempt to value changes in ozone by estimating the shift in the demand for air conditioning would miss in several ways.

The final element is that we observe the relevant behavior in conjunction with levels of environmental quality and, for some models, parametric prices associated with that behavior. For almost all models, it is necessary to estimate how behavior changes with levels of environmental quality. For most classes of models, it is also necessary to manipulate demand curves in price–quantity space. The need for parametric prices relates to evaluating discrete rather than marginal changes in the environment. Pairs of marginal values of the environmental quality and behavior, or even marginal values of the environmental quality and levels of the environmental quality, will typically not permit the estimation of values of discrete changes in the environment. For example, the hedonic model permits the estimation of the marginal value of an environmental attribute, such as air pollution, but only fairly restrictive assumptions about preferences allow these marginal values to be translated into values of discrete changes.

We approach valuation from the point of view of general restrictions, rather than the usual taxonomy of travel cost, averting behavior, hedonics, etc., in order to expose the underlying structure of the problem and the parallels that exist across the commonly delineated "valuation methods". What emerges from this approach is a sense that these "methods" are somewhat artificial molds into which too many problems have been forced. Thinking in terms of these molds unnecessarily limits the possibilities for retrieving empirical welfare measures. Many environmental valuation problems can be set up in more than one way, where the choice among contending methods depends on the nature of the observable behavior and the credibility of the restrictions necessary to recover information about preferences.

---

[1] Revealed preference methods also can work if there is a set of goods, rather than one good, which exhibits this relationship with the environmental good (see Bockstael and Kling, 1998).

1.3 MODELS OF BEHAVIOR AND RESTRICTIONS NEEDED TO VALUE CHANGES IN ENVIRONMENTAL GOODS

We begin by considering an environmental good, which we will call b, and will interchangeably refer to b as an environmental amenity or a public good. For simplicity of exposition, b is considered a "good" environmental quality, rather than a pollutant. There are any number of ways in which b might affect the individual. Some will leave behavioral footprints and others will not. By definition, values associated with the latter cannot be recovered using revealed preference methods. For the most part we are concerned with b's that can be controlled through environmental policy, the more common forms of air and water pollution. Properly handled, however, the models could also apply to environmental accidents such as oil spills as well as other types of environmental amenities.

In any event, if a change in the environmental amenity matters to the individual then it must show up either in his preference function or in a constraint. That means that, however the problem is structured, both the indirect utility function and the expenditure function will include b. One can express the compensating variation of a discrete change in the environmental good, from b^0 to b^1 for example, in either implicit form as:

$$v\left(p^0, b^0, y^0\right) = v\left(p^0, b^1, y - CV\right) \tag{1.1}$$

or in explicit form as:

$$CV = m\left(p^0, b^0, u^0\right) - m\left(p^0, b^1, u^0\right) \tag{1.2}$$

where v is the indirect utility function, m is the expenditure function, p^0 is the current vector of prices, y^0 is the current level of income, and u^0 is the reference level of utility.[2]

The problem is not in stating this Hicksian measure of welfare but in finding some observable manifestation of it. In conventional welfare economics, observable approximations to compensating variation measures of price changes are possible because $\partial m / \partial p$ is a function which, under many circumstances,

---

[2] Throughout we adopt the convention of signing compensating variation consistently with the sign of the welfare change. Thus if b is an amenity and b increases then compensating variation will be positive.

is closely approximated by a behavioral function—the consumer's demand curve. In environmental valuation, $\partial m / \partial b$ has no closely related behavioral function; there is no useful analog to Shepherd's lemma. Further, simple observation of $\partial m / \partial b$ may not be sufficient to uncover information on preferences, and in most instances, marginal values are *not* relevant for policy. Revealed preference methods for valuing environmental goods must rely on exploiting information about private decisions to reveal individuals' preferences for the public good.

At this point the "General Theory" of environmental valuation ends, for there is no foolproof way to tackle the problem such that approximations for individuals' valuations of the public good will emerge. In fact, in some problems there may be no way to reveal these preferences. A notable example is the case in which existence value or passive use value is present. In such a case, b will still appear in the objective function (and in the indirect utility and expenditure functions), but there will be no observable behavior related to it.[3] To obtain welfare measures for changes in b, further restrictions are necessary (although not necessarily sufficient), and for the most part these restrictions are not testable. Since they depend on a commonsense assessment of the circumstances, the verdict will vary with the problem (and, alas, possibly with the researcher).

1.3.1 The Weak Complementarity Restriction in its Simplest Form

Suppose we begin with a basic model of the form:

$$\max_{q} u(q,b) \qquad \text{subject to } y = p'q \tag{1.3}$$

where q is a vector of market goods with corresponding price vector p and y is income; b is environmental quality or a proxy for it which we introduce into the utility function to indicate that the individual has preferences over levels of b. Without additional restrictions, this model is too general to allow valuation of changes in b from observed behavior. The plausible stories one can tell about the relationship between the public good and private decisions generate the choice of restrictions on preference functions and technology.

While the application of revealed preference methods is not necessarily restricted to this interpretation, in most cases the environmental amenity is most plausibly viewed as having something to do with the *quality* of a privately

---

[3] Occasional creative attempts to infer passive use values of b through behavior have been made (e.g., Farrow and Larson, 1995), but it is one thing to recognize that b remains in the preference function and quite another to try to value it.

consumed good, and the most commonly invoked link is that of weak complementarity. The specific preference restriction maintained in this construct is that changes in the level of *b* have no effect on the individual unless he consumes some specific q_i.

Using p_{-i} to denote the vector of prices for goods other than q_i and p_i^* to denote the "choke" price for q_i, we can write the expression for the area behind a Hicksian demand curve, conditioned on a given level of *b*, as

$$\int_{p_i^0}^{p_i^*} \frac{\partial m}{\partial p_i}(p_i, p_{-i}^0, b^0, u^0)dp_i = m(p_i^*, p_{-i}^0, b^0, u^0) - m(p_i^0, p_{-i}^0, b^0, u^0) .$$

The difference in such areas, evaluated at two levels of *b*, can be written as

$$\begin{aligned} &\left\{m(p_i^*, p_{-i}^0, b^1, u^0) - m(p_i^0, p_{-i}^0, b^1, u^0)\right\} \\ &-\left\{m(p_i^*, p_{-i}^0, b^0, u^0) - m(p_i^0, p_{-i}^0, b^0, u^0)\right\} \end{aligned} \qquad (1.4a)$$

which, given weak complementarity assumptions, must equal

$$m(p^0, b^0, u^0) - m(p^0, b^1, u^0) . \qquad (1.4b)$$

This follows because $m(p_i^*, p_{-i}^0, b^1, u^0) = m(p_i^*, p_{-i}^0, b^0, u^0)$ by the definition of weak complementarity. The equality derives from the belief that when the good that is complementary to *b*, in this case q_i, is not consumed, increases in *b* need not be compensated. "Belief" is used advisedly here because preferences that conform with weak complementarity are inherently untestable.

The link to behavior comes from recognizing $\partial m / \partial p_i$ as the Hicksian demand for q_i so that the expression in (1.4a) yields the difference between the areas under two Hicksian demand functions. The result is extremely useful, since this restriction on preferences leads to the critical expression in (1.4b), which equals the original definition of compensating variation in (1.2).

An additional restriction is implicit in (1.4a,b). The good, q_i, must be a non-essential good; it must be one for which there is a finite compensation for its elimination. If this is not the case, then there exists no Hicksian choke price because there is no way to drive the demand for q_i to zero and still maintain the original level of utility. This is typically an innocuous restriction. Only when we find ourselves attempting to value too broad a category of goods, do we face even the potential of encountering essential goods.[4]

Whether the difference in (1.4a) can be approximated by differences in areas behind the Marshallian counterpart is another question. We can not rely on Willig's bounds (Willig, 1976) for price changes to establish this approximation, since we seek a substantively different equivalence from that sought in Willig's analysis. We need a measure of the area between two compensated curves rather than the area behind one curve between two prices, and there is no guarantee that the Marshallian measure will bound the Hicksian one in its usual way (Bockstael and McConnell, 1993). All that can be said at this point is that there is, so far, little evidence that the income effect and the influence of b on individual behavior are generally sufficiently strong to cause a significant divergence between the change in the area behind Hicksian and Marshallian demand curves. But the evidence is not entirely impartial, because it arises in part from the kinds of methods successfully estimated. Random utility models are typically estimated with linear-in-income utility functions, so that income effects are not revealed. Hedonic price functions by their nature do not include income. The one behavioral model where income might reasonably show up would be travel cost demand functions, but there the correlation between time costs and income often stymies efforts to estimate a plausible value for the income effect.

The necessity of imposing restrictions is revealed in a converse way by those efforts that have sought bounds for the marginal value of b, $-\partial m / \partial b$, in the absence of restrictions on preferences. Neill (1988) showed that, without any restrictions on preferences, the marginal value of a change in b can be bounded by the resulting change in the expenditure on goods that are Hicksian complements with b and on those that are Hicksian substitutes. But this result is effectively void of empirical content, because it is not possible to observe whether a good is a Hicksian substitute or a complement and we can have no intuition about this. The one case in which we can deduce the Hicksian effect—when the good is a Marshallian substitute—is of no particular use. It merely confirms the obvious; the bound conveys the "non-information" that some number less than zero is a lower bound on the value of b. Even if the bounds were meaningful, only bounds on marginal values, rather than values of discrete changes, would be obtainable. The moral of the story is that without specific restrictions on preferences, behavioral methods will not provide useful information about the value of public goods.

[4] This is one of the many reasons why trying to value the world's ecosystems is a ludicrous endeavor.

1.3.2 Introducing Household Production Technology

Despite its central position in the environmental valuation literature, the basic construct of weak complementarity *as outlined above*, is rarely applicable. In the above construct, p_i is assumed fixed and no market intervenes to cause p_i to vary with b. When b is weakly complementary to a marketed good, though, we would expect that the price of those units of the good embodying higher levels of b would be bid up. Circumstances in which the prices of marketed goods vary with quality are widely observed.

There are a few plausible cases that fit the basic weak complementarity construct. Consider the case of public drinking water in the U.S. some twenty years ago, before bottled water or home water filters were prevalent. Each local government supplied public water according to a price structure, driven by the costs of supplying this public utility. For a variety of technical reasons, different jurisdictions supplied different quality water in terms of taste, tendency to stain clothes, and other non-health-related characteristics. A household's demand for water would likely have been a function of these quality characteristics, since for drinking purposes other beverages could be substituted and laundry services could be substituted for washing clothes at home. Both quality and price varied over jurisdictions but price did not signal the variation in quality, since public water supply is not locationally fungible and pricing is not competitive. Here is a case that fits the simple weak complementarity model. Drinking water quality varies over the populace, it only matters to those who use it, and the variation in quality of drinking water does not induce variation in prices.

More often than not, though, the weak complementarity restriction is associated not with a marketed good, but with a commodity produced by the household; and the environmental amenity is most easily viewed as a quality characteristic of that commodity. For this reason, no market intervenes to cause the price of the commodity to vary with the level of b.

Because there is considerable household production in all non-market behavior, this story seems to fit many situations quite well and explains why the weak complementarity model can so adventitiously ignore the potential effect of changes in b on price. Suppose that x is purchased and produces z according to the function $z = z(x)$. In such cases, instead of (1.3) above, we might frame the problem in the following terms:

$$\max_{q,x} u\big(q, z(x), b\big) \qquad \text{subject to } y = p'q + r'x \tag{1.5}$$

where the household purchases inputs x at prices r to produce z, the household produced good. Other goods, q, are purchased on the market at prices, p. The indirect utility function is $v(p,r,b,y)$ and the minimum expenditure function is $m(p,r,b,u)$. Now, the necessary preference restrictions link b and one or more of the z's.

To obtain welfare measures in this context, however, requires that the marginal cost of producing an associated commodity (call it z_i) be treated as its price, which is possible only if the marginal cost of production is constant. An example is the usual travel cost model that treats the cost of a trip as constant over trips. The problem that arises when the marginal cost of z_i varies with z_i is the well-documented nonlinear price problem (Epstein, 1981; Bockstael and McConnell, 1981). Two difficulties emerge when the marginal cost is a function of the endogenous quantity. Marginal value still equals marginal cost, but the solution of the first order conditions for quantity may not provide a standard Marshallian demand curve, which relies on prices as parameters.[5] Further, using the first order conditions to estimate marginal value and marginal cost functions is especially difficult in demand systems, where the exclusion restrictions required for identification are difficult to justify.

Because there are strong welfare results associated with production theory, an added restriction on production technology can sometimes extricate us from the nonlinear price problem. If an essential input (x_j) into the production of z_i can be identified, then the change in demand for x_j will reveal information that will help value the change in b (Bockstael and McConnell, 1983). The welfare change due to a change in b will be

$$CV = m(r,p,b^0,u) - m(r,p,b^1,u)$$

and the equivalent of (1.4a,b) will be

$$\begin{aligned}&\{m(r_i^*,r_{-i}^0,p^0,b^1,u^0) - m(r_i^0,r_{-i}^0,p^0,b^1,u^0)\}\\ &-\{m(r_i^*,r_{-i}^0,p^0,b^0,u^0) - m(r_i^0,r_{-i}^0,p^0,b^0,u^0)\}\end{aligned} \quad (1.6a)$$

$$= m(r^0,p^0,b^0,u^0) - m(r^0,p^0,b^1,u^0) \quad (1.6b)$$

where r_j^* is the choke price for the demand for input x_j, and (1.6a) is an expression for the area between two compensated input demand functions. The equivalence between (1.6a) and (1.6b) exists when two conditions hold. At the

[5] The Marshallian demand function is the solution of all n+1 first order conditions including the budget constraint, where the first n are functions of marginal costs and the last is a function of total costs.

choke price for x_j the demand for x_j will be 0, but this implies that $z_i = 0$, since x_j is an essential input in the production of z_i. This restriction together with weak complementarity between b and z_i ensures the equivalence. In this case, two restrictions are employed: one on the relationship between the input and the commodity, and one on the relationship between the environmental service and the commodity. In the absence of essentiality, $z(r_j^*)$ will not be zero, and in the absence of weak complementarity $m(r_j^*, r_{-j}^0, p^0, b^1, u^0)$ will not equal $m(r_j^*, r_{-j}^0, p^0, b^0, u^0)$.

This result allows us to see the similarity in the underlying structure of the models, and the prevalence of weak complementarity. The household production model mathematically collapses to the original weak complementarity model of equation (1.3) but provides a more compelling story.

1.3.3 The Environmental Quality Viewed as an Input

There is an almost indistinguishable line between viewing the environmental good as a quality characteristic of a household-produced commodity and viewing it as an input into the production of such a commodity. Sometimes one interpretation seems to fit better and sometimes the other. For example, we might view the stock of wildlife as a quality characteristic of a wilderness experience, where the wilderness experience is the commodity produced by the household by combining its time, travel costs, and services from a wilderness area. However, if we were to redefine the commodity, then perhaps the stock of wildlife would be better viewed as an input into the production of wildlife sightings. In other cases, an environmental amenity may be an input into the household production of one non-marketed good and a quality characteristic of a distinctly different one. For example, reductions in suspended particulate matter in the air might raise the quality of a recreational trip, where visibility of scenic vistas plays an important part in the enjoyment. Alternatively, such reductions might be viewed as entering positively into an individual's health production function. By treating b as an *input* in a household production process, we are essentially retelling the story and redefining the commodity of interest. In so doing we are allowing new possibilities for connections between the public good and private decisions.

Interpreting b as an input into the production of some household-produced commodity, such as "personal environmental quality" as suggested by Bartik (1988a), can be reflected in the model as a slight reformulation of (1.5):

$$\max_{q,x} u(q, z(x,b)) \quad \text{subject to } y = p'q + r'x \,. \tag{1.7}$$

The problem in (1.7) can be written as a two step optimization. First

$$\min_{x} r'x \quad \text{subject to } z = z(x,b).$$

This yields the cost function $C(z,b,r)$, which reflects the costs of achieving different levels of z, given levels of the environmental quality, b. Second

$$\max_{q,z} u(q,z) \qquad \text{subject to } y = p'q + C(z,b,r).$$

If the cost function can reasonably be assumed linear (or approximately linear) in z, then $C(z,b,r)$ becomes $C_z(b,r)z$. Now z has a parametric price that varies with b.[6] If this restriction is plausible, we have the equivalence of a welfare measurement problem where a change in *price* is being evaluated. We know all about those kinds of welfare problems. We can now map changes in b directly into changes in a parametric price for z. Observing behavioral responses in the consumption of z, brought about by changes in b, yields Marshallian welfare measures, and these will be related to the preferred Hicksian measures according to the usual Willig formula.

Should the researcher feel comfortable with this apparently straightforward model, he need only be reminded of the complications introduced by *time*. The household production literature grew out of the recognition that an important input in the household production process is almost always the time of one or more household members. When the most appropriate story is one in which the household produces both a commodity of interest and the quality of that commodity, the role of time in both production processes makes it virtually impossible to pose logically consistent household production functions in which the marginal costs of these two outputs are constant. Joint production is the culprit (Pollak and Wachter, 1975). This case, and others without relevant parametric price, precludes valuation in a straightforward way. But once again there are additional restrictions that can, if plausible, come to the rescue.

The simplest restriction that gives easily obtained welfare measures requires that an element of the x vector, again call it x_j, be a substitute for b in the production of the household commodity z. The dual to (1.7) requires

$$\min_{q,x} p'q + r'x + \mu\left(u^0 - u\left(q, z(x,b)\right)\right). \tag{1.8}$$

---

[6] This specification of preferences is the first case analyzed by Courant and Porter (1981) in models of defensive expenditures and averting behavior.

This yields the expenditure function $m(r,p,b,u)$. In this case, $-m_b = \mu u_z \partial z / \partial b$. But at the optimum, the individual sets $r_j = \mu u_z \partial z / \partial x_j$ for all j, which implies that at the optimum,

$$-m_b = \mu u_z \partial z / \partial b = r_j dx_j / db \tag{1.9}$$

where dx_j / db is the rate of technical substitution between b and x_j in the production of z. In (1.9) we have the marginal value of b.

Occasionally this result has been taken to mean that if b is an input into household production, then welfare measures, even for discrete changes in b, can be obtained purely from information about household technology, with no knowledge about preferences. This is true only if x_j and b are perfect substitutes in the sense that one can be substituted for another at a fixed and constant rate to achieve the same level of z. To find the value of a *discrete* change in b, the expression must be integrated over the range of b, holding utility rather than z constant. However, if x_j and b are perfect substitutes, the integral over the change in b, holding z constant, will equal the integral over the same range, holding utility constant (Bartik, 1988a).

It is easy to see this with a simple example. If x and b produce z according to the production function, $z = (ax + b)^2$, which exhibits perfect substitution between x and b, then the rate of technical substitution between b and x will be constant (in this case, $1/a$). From equation (1.9) the marginal value of b will also be constant, $-m_b = r / a$. But to find the compensating variation of a discrete change in b, it is useful to derive the cost function for z, $C(z,r,b) = r\{(\sqrt{z} - b) / a\}$. One can see that b has the effect of supplying the individual with "free" units of z. Although the cost function is nonlinear in z, the price ratio between z and q (the numeraire) is not affected by the level of b. Since b does not enter the utility function directly, returning the individual to the same level of utility after a change in b requires returning him to the same consumption bundle as before the change, and the only way to do that is to compensate him with the amount $(b^1 - b^0)r_j / a$, the amount of money necessary to make up, directly, for the change in b.[7]

Implicit in the above approaches that use information about household technology to value b is an additional hidden restriction, somewhat analogous to the non-essentiality restriction discussed in conjunction with weak complementarity. In order to value a change in b using information about a substitute input, changes in the level of that input must be able to mitigate

[7]The exception is when the original bundle represents a corner solution where $z = b$ and $x_j = 0$. At this solution, the slope of the indifference curve will not necessarily be equal to the price ratio between z and q.

completely all losses in b. Using the air conditioning example again, it is clear that air conditioning cannot entirely mitigate the effects of changes in ozone (especially over the possible range of such changes) both because air conditioners could not necessarily filter extreme ozone levels and because the individual is not always protected by air conditioning. In contrast, degradation in the quality of a public drinking water supply can be completely mitigated by options such as bottled water.

The assumption of perfect substitutes is one of the few "magic bullets" available in non-market valuation. It allows the estimation of the value of discrete changes in b without any knowledge of preferences. It might seem that minor departures from the perfect substitutes assumption would also provide good approximations but caution is warranted. Any departure from perfect substitutes means that the preference function as well as the production function is involved in valuation.[8]

It frequently happens that we are unable to identify a continuous input that is a perfect substitute to the environmental amenity. More often, we will have some general notion of a cost function $C(z,b,r)$, which we cannot easily argue is linear in z. Nonetheless, if we are willing to admit the usefulness of bounds, additional welfare measures are obtainable that again depend only on information about technology.

Bartik (1988a) has shown that the "defensive expenditures" necessary to hold z (rather than utility) constant with the change in b will be a lower bound on the compensating variation of the change in b. That is, "defensive expenditures" defined in this way will understate gains from improvements in environmental quality and overstate losses from environmental degradation. Following Bartik's proof but in our notation, the change in defensive expenditures (holding z constant) is equivalent to

$$m(r,p,b^0,u^0)-m(r,p,b^1,u^0;z^0)$$

where the second term is the expenditure necessary to achieve the initial utility level after the change in the public good, but holding the quantity of the household produced commodity constant. First, by definition,

$$\begin{aligned} &m(r,p,b^0,u^0)-m(r,p,b^1,u^0;z^0) \\ &\quad = pq(p,b^0,r^0,u^0)+C(z^0,b^0,r^0)-pq(p,b^1,r^0,u^0;z^0)-C(z^0,b^1,r^0). \end{aligned}$$

---

[8] For example, suppose that z is produced with a constant elasticity production function: $z=(ax^\theta+b^\theta)^{1/\theta}$ so that $dx/db=a(b/x)^{\theta-1}$. The problem again becomes complicated because x also depends on b and simple approximations are not available.

But $q(p,b^0,r^0,u^0)$ must equal $q(p,b^1,r^0,u^0;z^0)$; since both utility and z are equal in the two cases, q must also be equal. Therefore,

$$m(r,p,b^0,u^0)-m(r,p,b^1,u^0;z^0)=C(z^0,b^0,r^0)-C(z^0,b^1,r^0)$$

which is Bartik's definition of defensive expenditures—the change in the costs of producing z^0 when b changes. Compensating variation can be written as:

$$CV=m(r,p,b^0,u^0)-m(r,p,b^1,u^0;z^0)+m(r,p,b^1,u^0;z^0)-m(r,p,b^1,u^0)$$

where the first two terms are the defensive expenditures associated with a change in b and the third term must exceed the fourth by the Le Chatelier Principle. The last expression is Bartik's result. When $b^1>b^0$, defensive expenditures fall short of the exact compensating variation by the amount $m(b^1,u^0;z^0)-m(b^1,u^0)$.

This result is particularly easy to see in the special case when the cost function is linear in z, since changes in b map directly into changes in the price of z. The compensating variation is the area behind the Hicksian demand function for z, between the two parametric prices, $C_z(b^0,r)$ and $C_z(b^1,r)$. An increase in b means a decrease in price, which produces a positive compensating variation measure (according to our signing convention). A lower bound on this welfare gain is given by the change in expenditures necessary while still consuming the original level of the commodity (z^0). This lower bound is the rectangle $[C_z(b^0,r)-C_z(b^1,r)]z^0$.

It is easy to confuse Bartik's lower bound welfare measure (the change in expenditures holding z constant) with a measure equal to the *observed* change in expenditures on z (that is, allowing z to change and holding income constant.) The amount by which an individual actually changes his expenditures on z does not, in the general case, tell us much about the welfare effect.

1.4 MODELS THAT IMPLICITLY TREAT ENVIRONMENTAL QUALITY AS A CHOICE VARIABLE

Consider the inherent difficulty of estimating the behavioral models, described in the previous section, as functions of b. Sufficient observations on combinations of varying b, associated prices (or costs) and behavior must be available in order to estimate some relevant demand function. A few attempts have been made to pool data either over time or over geographical location in order to obtain the necessary variation in b. For example, in an early study, Brown, Singh and Castle (1964) estimated the quantity of fishing trips from different distance zones as a function of the catch of steelhead salmon.[9] However, these attempts are of limited usefulness, in part because it is difficult to hold other important factors constant, and in part because relevant data on non-market behavior must usually be collected through surveys. It is expensive to sample several geographically separate populations, and it is impossible to accomplish this at different points in time when the need for valuation estimates is pressing, such as in damage assessment cases.

Instead of a natural experiment in which we assess different households' responses to different levels of the public good, we can examine the same household's choice among geographically dispersed alternatives. When these alternatives embody different levels of b, certain modeling approaches allow inferences about valuation. Although the distinction appears moot, the public good is now an array of qualities associated with different alternatives (e.g. at different locations) and the change in the public good is now a change in that array—that is, a change in the level of the public good at some locations. In the type of problems dealt with in this section, the individual appears to be choosing an ambient level of b. This is because the individual chooses his location and the level of the public good varies over location. But it is important to remember that the vector of levels of the public good at different locations is given and can be changed only by policy (or accident) and not by the individual. If we did not make this distinction, it would look as though we were trying to derive a welfare measure for a change in a choice variable, which is not a meaningful question (at least in the absence of rationing). Welfare questions are only well defined if they relate to changes in the parameters that individuals face in optimizing over their choice sets.

Where circumstances of this sort exist, we can sometimes observe the tradeoff an individual is willing to make between money and levels of the public good. However, the policy questions of interest may be subtly different. The question: "how does an individual value a change in b?" may no longer be quite relevant. Instead the relevant welfare change will depend on the actual change in b to which the individual is exposed. This will depend, in turn, on his choice of alternative before and after the exogenous change in b. These models make explicit how much the context of the valuation problem, and the availability of substitutes, matters.

---

[9] The Brown *et al.* study basically entailed the estimation of two equations, one for catch as a function of total trips from the zone, and the other for trips as a function of catch and other exogenous variables. As a behavioral model, the idea of total trips as a function of the total quantity of fish caught in the zone is not an intuitively plausible story.

1.4.1 When Markets Intervene

In the models represented by (1.3) and (1.5), the price or marginal cost of the associated commodity was not expected to vary systematically with levels of the public good, except by chance, since no market intervened between the supply of b and its consumption. But suppose a market does intervene to cause the price of a good to vary with its quality level. This distinction is an important one and has caused researchers to reframe the welfare problem. Although never explicitly mentioned, the problem still must retain the property that b does not matter if the related good is not consumed, but attention is now turned to extracting information about preferences from market prices.

The residential housing market is one of the few places in which environmental quality is actually traded. The fact that the price of a residential location can be expected to be bid up when it possesses higher levels of b or other good attributes such as bedrooms, lot size, etc. (denoted by the vector w), and bid down when the location has undesirable attributes, insures that the hedonic price function, denoted $P_h(w,b)$, is well behaved. Substantial experience with hedonic price functions for housing provides evidence of these well-behaved properties. See, for example, Smith and Huang (1993, 1995) for evidence on air pollution and housing prices.

The hedonic price analysis would *appear* to afford an ideal means of exploiting a private decision to value a public good. An individual maximizes utility, which is a function of the quantity of market goods, q, the level of the public good embodied in the hedonic good, b, and the quantity of other characteristics of the hedonic good, w, subject to a budget constraint that includes the cost of purchasing the hedonic good as well as the normal marketed goods:

$$\max_{q,w,b} u(q,w,b) \qquad \text{subject to } y = p'q + P_h(w,b)\,.$$

$P_h(w,b)$ is the price of the hedonic good that varies with the level of characteristics embodied in it. In most applications, each individual purchases only one unit of the hedonic good, and each is a price taker of the hedonic price function which is the locus of equilibrium points determined by the offer and bid curves of market participants. First order conditions imply that an individual chooses his location along the hedonic function such that

$$(\partial u / \partial b)/(\partial u / \partial q_k) = \partial P_h / \partial b$$

where q_k is a numeraire good. This condition produces a marginal valuation of the public good. The slope of the hedonic function at the chosen level of b equals the marginal value of b.

Very little in the way of structure of the utility function need be specified in order to derive marginal values for b. But the hedonic price function cannot give back marginal value *functions*, and thus cannot tell us how an individual values a discrete change in an attribute. The hedonic locus yields information about only one point on each individual's marginal value function. Other points on the hedonic locus are associated with other individuals who possess other characteristics and thus have other marginal value functions. Only when all individuals are identical can information about an individual's marginal valuation function be extracted directly from the hedonic locus, for the simple reason that in this case the hedonic locus is the *common* valuation function (or bid function, as it is called in the hedonic literature).

The original notion was to estimate a demand function for the public good by first estimating a nonlinear hedonic price function and then estimating a second stage demand function using $\partial P_h / \partial b$ evaluated at the individual's choice as his price for b. But this has been shown in numerous papers to be incorrect (see Brown and Rosen, 1982; Palmquist, 1991; Bartik, 1988b; Diamond and Smith, 1985). In order to identify the marginal value function one must either impose restrictions, including considerable separability of the preference function (Epple, 1987), or one must find a way to observe more than one point on any given marginal value function (Ohsfeldt and Smith, 1985). After a good deal of work, the first approach has been largely abandoned, since only some combinations of functional forms for the preference and hedonic price functions will allow identification and the imposition of these functional forms is entirely arbitrary.

The second approach involves estimating hedonic models across multiple markets. For multiple market hedonic price functions to identify preferences, the marginal value functions must be constant across markets, after controlling for known socio-demographics. At the same time, the hedonic price functions must differ significantly across markets for there to be any hope of identifying the underlying preference parameters (Ohsfeldt and Smith, 1988). If preferences are similar across markets, then, for the hedonic price function to be significantly different, the supply of characteristics must be dramatically different across markets. But if that is the case, then individuals are likely to have been influenced by those differences in selecting the market in which to live, and we cannot allow this endogeneity if we wish to identify marginal values using cross-market information.

Practically speaking, there may be few cases in which marginal value *functions* can be extracted from hedonic markets. The hedonic case is one in which two problems are confounded in the first order conditions: the marginal costs of the environmental services are not constant to the consumer (i.e. the nonlinear price problem) and, without quite strong assumptions, only marginal values are recoverable.

Yet in a sense the hedonic model is one of the success stories for behavioral methods. In some plausible circumstances, approximate discrete welfare measures can be obtained directly from estimating the hedonic price function, which itself is a relatively easy analysis to perform and does not require strong assumptions about preferences or technology.[10] Bartik (1988b) and Palmquist (1991) have argued persuasively for the use of the hedonic price function to calculate an approximate welfare measure for a discrete change in an environmental amenity where that change is localized enough such that the hedonic equilibrium locus is unlikely to shift as a result. In such a case one can argue that the small number of properties that experience the change in b are revalued. As long as moving is costless, everyone can costlessly return to equilibrium, and only the original owners of those properties where a change in b took place experience any welfare effects. Specifically, if a house experiences a discrete increase in b, then the original owner enjoys a windfall gain equal to the change in the value of the house predicted by moving the house along the hedonic price function. Given that moving is not costless, the welfare measure calculated in this way is an upper bound, but probably not a bad approximation.

Oddly, this welfare measure—while a good approximation of the welfare effect of the change in environmental quality at a location—is *not* an approximation of anyone's willingness to pay for a discrete change in b. In fact, a measure of an individual's willingness to pay for a change in b is not the correct answer to the policy question. The market intervenes. As a result, if the public sector undertakes a policy that changes the level of b at a few locations, then the seller will gain more than his own valuation of the change in b because the property can be sold to some one who has a higher value for this quality.

The existence of the market may make valuation of a localized change in b easier, but it makes the valuation of a more pervasive change in b more difficult. If the changes in the array of levels of the environmental amenity are large enough, the hedonic equilibrium price function can be expected to move, and in a way that cannot easily be predicted. In this case, even if we were able to estimate individuals' marginal bid functions, this information would not be enough. To value a policy change that alters the b vector, we would also need to be able to predict the location of the new hedonic price function.

1.4.2 Framing the Decision Problem in a Discrete Choice Setting

The success of discrete choice models requires special attention. These models have been used not only for recreational choice, where they have become the norm, but also in housing market settings, where they compete with hedonic

[10] This ignores the difficulties in choosing functional form, etc. but these difficulties are common to most welfare measurement problems.

models, and in models of averting behavior. In most cases, discrete choice modeling is simply a strategic option that works, in part because it better characterizes the decision environment and in part because it aligns itself more closely with realistic policy questions. But it also allows us to sidestep some of the obstacles that arise in the extraction of welfare measures from continuous models of behavior. Understanding the success of discrete choice models may yield some insights into the difficulties encountered in other settings.

In practice, the set of alternatives embodying different levels of the public good available to an individual at a point in time is finite and thus the available levels of the public good that can be chosen are discrete. All previous models could be framed in terms of choices among discrete goods, either market or household produced, that are associated with different levels of the public good. Once cast in a discrete choice framework, there are no inherent differences in the behavioral model and its ability to produce welfare measures, whether the choice is among houses, recreational sites, or mitigation technologies as long as differing costs and different levels of environmental quality are associated with these choices.

Like all behavioral methods of valuation, discrete choice models ultimately succeed by analyzing household behavior in the face of varying levels of environmental attributes. But there are significant differences. The most obvious difference is that when making discrete choices, individuals are assumed to choose among a finite and known set of alternatives. The second difference between continuous models and discrete choice approaches is the way in which the latter take account of the actual *distribution* of environmental quality and thus explicitly recognize the context in which a choice is made. The third difference is in the definition of the choice occasion. The typical neoclassical factor or commodity demand function explains the number of units consumed of the good per period of time, and derives welfare measures from the fact that an individual will increase the *quantity* of his consumption of a good, during that time period, up to the point where its marginal value equals its marginal cost to him. The discrete choice framework seeks to explain the choice among alternatives at a point in time, and thus the quantity dimension of the choice is suppressed. For recreational models the choice occasion may occur at any time and be replicated over time under different circumstances. For mitigation technology, choice occasions may be infrequent, and for housing decisions, approximately unique events. In any case, welfare measures depend on observing individuals being willing to pay at least a given differential in cost to achieve an observed increment in quality.

The most common discrete choice construct in the literature is the extension of the weak complementarity model where the environmental amenity is a quality characteristic of a household-produced commodity. In this model, individuals are viewed as choosing among a finite set of alternative commodities they could produce and consume on a specific choice occasion, where each of these commodities has a different, exogenous level of quality. As they choose which of the finite set of mutually exclusive commodities to produce, they are inherently choosing the environmental quality they will enjoy.

Expressing the individual's decision in the discrete choice framework involves recasting the problem presented in (1.5) as a random utility model (McFadden). If the individual makes the discrete choice of alternative i, then his utility will be given by

$$\max_{q,x} U(q,z_i,b_i) \quad \text{subject to } y^* = p'q + c_i z_i \qquad (1.10)$$

where q is a vector of other goods, z_i is the quantity of the alternative commodity chosen, c_i is the constant marginal cost of producing z_i, b_i is its quality and y^* is income available for this choice occasion. Since the discrete choice is among mutually exclusive alternatives on a given choice occasion, the quantity of the chosen commodity is usually a single unit so that z is dropped from the problem. Defining $V(p,y^*,c_j,b_j)$ as the conditional indirect utility function on a choice occasion, conditional on the individual choosing alternative j, the optimality problem of interest is the discrete comparison of the V's. The individual chooses commodity i if

$$V(p,y^*,c_i,b_i) \geq \max\left(V(p,y^*,c_1,b_1),\ldots,V(p,y^*,c_N,b_N)\right). \qquad (1.11)$$

By observing an individual's choice among the alternatives, we can deduce the implicit tradeoffs he is making between the level of the environmental amenity and expenditures of money. But, once again, typical welfare measures extracted from these models are not the answer to "how much does an individual value a change in environmental quality?" Instead they measure the welfare effect of a change in environmental quality at a given location (or set of locations) taking explicit account of the context, i.e. the levels of environmental quality at substitute locations. If a policy alters the quality level associated with alternative j, then only those individuals who currently consume alternative j, or who would choose to consume this alternative after the change, will be affected. Consequently, this approach tells us how people are affected by a specific change in some b_i, given the available substitutes.

The distinction between continuous models and discrete choice models is a matter of modeling strategy. Each approach takes an array of qualities, typically given geographically, and constructs a model and a story for individual behavior. In the discrete case, an individual chooses among a choice set of alternatives by finding the alternative that gives maximum utility. The elemental indirect utility function derived from (1.11), conditional on the choice of the ith alternative, is frequently assumed to be linear in arguments,

$$v_i = \alpha b_i + \beta(y - c_i) + \varepsilon_i$$

where α and β are parameters of the utility function, and ε is the part of preferences known to the household but not the researcher.[11] Since this part of preferences is not known, behavior is described in terms of probabilities. When the unknown terms have extreme value distributions, the resultant probabilities have quite tractable properties for estimation and welfare. Perhaps even more important, welfare measures make a great deal of sense. The calculation of welfare effects for changes in *b* requires that the researcher describe the geographical distribution of the changes—that is, which alternatives experience the changes in *b*. As a result, the model provides considerable flexibility in describing policy scenarios.

The hedonic travel cost model is an alternative approach that uses the same type of information but attempts to exploit the hedonic concept in the recreational context. The first hedonic travel cost models attempted to model both demand for trips and demand for quality, but more recent formulations (Englin and Mendelson, 1991) restrict the analysis to a single choice occasion, similar to the random utility model. The concept upon which welfare measures are obtained, however, has not changed. Hedonic travel cost models attempt to relate the cost of a household-produced recreational trip associated with each site, c_i, directly to the level of quality, b_i, at the site (and to the level of other attributes, w_i) and do so by estimating separate regressions of c_i as functions of b_i and w_i for each origin of residence in the sample. But if recreational sites with different qualities are distributed randomly across a region, then there may be no regularity in the relationship between costs and attributes. For some people, the best attributes may just happen to be the closest, and the worst farthest away. This can happen because the commodity in question is produced by the household and there is no market that intervenes to bid up the price of these household-produced commodities with high qualities. The con-

[11] The typical functional form has some drawbacks, however. If we were to take the known part of the preference function, then we could do welfare analysis for any change in *b*—the value of a discrete change in *b* is simply $\alpha\Delta b/\beta$, where Δb is the observed change in *b*. This is a fairly unrealistic model however, because it gives a constant marginal value of *b* no matter how big the changes in *b*. When the randomness of preferences is accounted for, the value of a finite change in *b* becomes a convex rather than linear function of Δb. This unrealistic situation is easily remedied by assuming a concave function of *b* in the deterministic part of the preferences.

sequence of this irregular relationship between costs and attributes is that we cannot estimate a general relation between c and b and insure that "marginal prices" will all be positive. This is in fact what one finds in the early efforts to estimate the hedonic travel cost model.

Even if nature were cooperative and distributed the qualities and sites in such a way that we could observe an increasing function, $C(b)$, we would still face the same difficulties found in hedonic models of housing prices: endogeneity of the b's and hence marginal cost of the b's.

There is, however, useful information when an individual chooses among an array of sites with differing access costs and qualities. But it may not be best captured by attempting to estimate a continuous function, $C(b)$. Smith, Palmquist and Jakus (1991) attempt to rationalize the hedonic travel cost model by estimating a Farrell production frontier from the dominant (c_i, b_i) pairs for each individual. When looked at in this way, the underlying intuition of the problem is not substantially different from that underlying the discrete choice framework. In both cases we seek information about the tradeoffs people make between expenditures and quality, and we only learn about those tradeoffs if nature presents us with enough variation in those pairs such that more than one alternative lies on the potential frontier. In other words, if one alternative has both lower costs and higher quality than all others, then it will dominate, and no information can be obtained using either the random utility model or the Farrell production frontier. The two models use the information quite differently, however. In the hedonic travel cost model of Smith *et al.* (1991), information about the costs of acquiring higher quality (i.e. the costs of moving along the frontier) is used in subsequent continuous demand estimation. The outcome is a marginal value function for environmental quality, which, unlike the random utility model results, gives no way of deducing what the welfare effects would be of a change in environmental quality at any specific location, holding the others constant.

The discrete choice framework has also been used to solve some of the practical problems that arise when the public good is best viewed as an *input* into the household production function. To frame the problem in the way presented earlier, we need to view quality as an approximately continuous set of alternatives available at different prices. More often than not, this continuous construct just doesn't fit. If there is no continuum of alternatives then it is impossible to calculate the defensive expenditures necessary to hold z constant after the environmental change.

Ideally, we would like to think of changes in b as changing the marginal cost of producing z, but there appear to be few useful cases in which this story is appropriate. In many, a contamination incident might cause an individual to seek a means of mitigating the change in his personal environmental quality. As a result, he may choose an alternative technology for achieving this, one that relies on purchases of market goods. But once having resorted to the market for alternative technologies, he may end up with a higher z (a higher level of his personal environmental quality) not a lower one, even though he is having to pay for it. This is because the quality level often increases in discrete steps and he is unable to adjust his choice of quality at the margin.

As an example, consider the drinking water quality case again. To measure the welfare effects of a contamination incident, we want to cast the incident as an increase in the price of drinking water quality. But in reality, the water quality possibilities are discrete and few, and the contamination incident is more logically viewed as lowering the quality of one of the discrete alternatives. A contamination incident typically alters the quality, but not the price, of the tap water alternative. After behavioral adjustments have been made, the individual may actually consume better water quality than before the spill if there is no technology that produces water of a lesser quality at a lower cost, except for the contaminated water supply.

To use the expenditures on these alternative technologies as a lower bound on compensating variation is a mistake since personal environmental quality z is not being held constant. Nonetheless, observations on peoples' behavior can produce information about welfare effects. The individuals' choice among discrete alternatives with different costs and different qualities is fundamentally the same as is represented in the random utility model (1.11), except now the quality of only some of the alternatives need necessarily be in the control of the public sector. If we can accurately measure both the quality and the costs for all alternatives, as well as peoples' choices among these alternatives, then a discrete choice model may allow us to extract the welfare effects of a policy change that alters publicly supplied drinking water.[12]

Even when the market intervenes, as in the housing market, the choice problem can be cast in either a continuous or discrete framework. Once again, the basic information from which we infer values comes in the form of bundles of prices and attributes (P_j,b_j). The modeling choices are whether the researcher views the household as choosing the optimal bundle by trading off higher prices with different b's continuously or simply choosing different houses, and therefore different bundles, discretely. In the traditional hedonic case, the assumption of continuity and interior solutions for the b's creates econometric problems, and very strong assumptions are required to identify and estimate the marginal value functions in such a way as to recover information about preferences. Cropper *et al.* (1993) show that the same observable behavior, essentially a set of hedonic data augmented by household demographic information, can be used to estimate the parameters of the utility function by discrete choice he-

---

[12] For efforts in this direction, see Abdalla, Roach and Epp (1992) and Humplick, Madanat and Kudat (1993).

donic models. The natural advantage of the discrete choice model is the absence of problems of endogeneity or identification. Households do not move along continuous price gradients. Instead the tradeoffs between environmental and other amenities are manifested when households choose among different bundles.

1.5 WHY IS THIS WELFARE ANALYSIS SO DIFFICULT TO DO IN PRACTICE?

There are far more contingent valuation studies than there are revealed preference analyses in the environmental literature. Contingent valuation studies cover the spectrum of environmental issues, while behavioral methods are limited to recreational demand studies, hedonic models and an occasional averting behavior study. So what makes welfare measurement of changes in public goods so difficult in the revealed preference setting?

Perhaps the most difficult problem in trying to use behavioral models to value environmental policy changes is finding a link between the government action or environmental insult and the environmental characteristic perceived and valued by the individual. Contingent valuation surveys have the luxury of explaining this link to respondents. In a sense, contingent valuation resembles experimental science in its ability to design studies, while behavioral methods must await experiments provided by nature. Even so, the former is often faulted for the way in which it provides the information that links policy with things people care about. But methods of revealed preference cannot even take such a liberty, for there is no way of knowing whether individuals are actually responding to a particular environmental change. Even when we find a statistically significant relationship between behavior and an environmental measure, we cannot know for certain that this relationship isn't really due to a third factor which happens to be correlated in space or time with environmental quality.

1.5.1 Linking Changes in the Environment to Changes in Behavior

There are three generic reasons why there might be no response to changes in the public good. The first is that it doesn't matter to individuals. Determining whether this is indeed true is, in itself, of interest for public policy. And a number of papers have undertaken simply to estimate the revealed preference type models, without attempting any welfare analysis, in order to test this hypothesis. There are numerous hedonic studies that seek only to establish that housing values vary with environmental amenities and increasing numbers of studies that seek to document defensive expenditures in the face of environmental hazards, without in either case attempting to value the change in the environment.

However, the absence of a behavioral response is not sufficient evidence that the change does not matter to an individual (even if we exclude from consideration the existence of "passive use" values). Individuals will not change their behavior if they cannot adjust at the margin and if their next best alternative generates less utility than their current choice, even with environmental degradation. This is another way of saying that a continuum of environmental quality alternatives rarely exists for the individual. More often than not, there is a finite set of cost/quality alternatives (where quality here designates all the quality characteristics important to an individual, not just environmental quality). A localized water quality incident may not provoke a change in behavior if the next best alternative recreational site is still less desirable. A radon reading above recommended levels may not trigger defensive expenditures if the only technology that can redress the problem is exceedingly costly. An individual may not incur the transactions costs of relocating as a result of air quality degradation, unless the deterioration in air quality is quite large. In each case the individual may, instead, suffer in (behavioral) silence.

Finally, it may be the case that individuals would care and would change their behavior if they knew about the environmental quality change and its implications, but this knowledge, for one reason or another, is not available. These circumstances exist most commonly where the link between the change in the environmental good and the individual is health-related. This link, requiring knowledge beyond what is immediately available to the senses, typically involves changes in risks. A change in an environmental good can also have an effect, unknown to the individual, on the likelihood of other uncertain events as well—such as his property suffering storm damage or on his recreational fish catches. When outcomes materialize fairly quickly, this knowledge can be gained with experience, but then the researcher has the added burden of modeling the learning process. For other types of environmental changes (e.g. elevated levels of exposure to carcinogens), the outcome can never be known with certainty, and the individual does not have the expertise to determine his risk without publicly supplied information.

In many cases of interest, the b that affects an individual is really an uncertain outcome for which the individual possesses some crude probability distribution. In this case, our models described above can still work, but b, even at a given location, is now more appropriately thought of as a vector of parameters of a probability distribution. A policy change or some unexpected incident may change the mean and the variance of the distribution, and may also truncate it in some way. It will be the revealed preference researcher's job to guess at how the individual perceives this change in risk and include in his model a measure of this change.

It is beyond the scope of this chapter to give adequate treatment to risk and uncertainty. However, one aspect of this problem is worthy of particular emphasis because it relates so directly to using behavioral methods to measure damages. When environmental degradation is invisible to people, then there will be no behavioral change. Using an example from Foster and Just (1989), a contamination of the milk supply by pesticides will not induce behavioral changes if people are not informed of the contamination. Revealed preference methods measure damages through their effect on behavior, so if there is no behavioral change, it looks as though there is no damage. However, if people are ultimately given the information about the threat, they will, in reaction to the information, change their behavior and generate revealed preference measures of damage.

Following revealed preference theory to its apparently logical conclusion, it would seem that it is the information that causes the damage not the environmental degradation. Put another way, how do we use revealed preference methods to value the information without coming to the counter-intuitive conclusion that information is a "bad"? An insightful way of thinking about this problem was offered by Foster and Just, who use the concept of compensating surplus to aid in measuring the loss to individuals who are not immediately informed of the change in risk. The individual is seen as suffering greater losses when ignorant of the effect, because his losses are measured as if he knew about the effect but was prevented from adjusting his behavior in response. Using this logic we can measure two things. The loss due to the environmental degradation is measured as the change in the expenditure function under full information. The value of the information about the degradation is the difference between the expenditure function evaluated at (a) the degraded quality and the old choices and (b) the degraded quality and the new, adjusted choices.

1.5.2 When Utility Generating Effects Are Not Separable

The difficulty in detecting behavioral response to an environmental change is further confounded because phenomena in the real world are not always separable. The air quality problem discussed earlier is a good example. We may observe individuals using their air conditioners more often in ozone alert periods. But since these periods are almost always correlated with periods of high temperature, we have no way of knowing whether individuals perceive the ozone health hazard and, more important, whether they respond to it by increasing expenditures on air conditioning. In any event, they are getting another benefit from these expenditures besides ozone reduction. In terms of our earlier notation, we want a situation in which the preference function takes the form $u(q,z(x,b))$ but the actual preference function motivating behavior is

$u(q, z(x, b), t(x))$, where x is air conditioning services, $z(x, b)$ is ozone content of the air, and $t(x)$ is ambient temperature.

To some degree the problem of non-separable effects is always present in behavioral analysis. For example, when z is trips and x is travel time, expression (1.5) gives rise to the travel cost model. But a quite reasonable way to write this preference function is $u(q, z(x, b), b, x)$ in cases where the travel itself generates utility. Resolution of the problem is left to the judgement of the researcher, who typically weighs the relative contributions of services for different motivations. It has become commonplace, for example, to ignore the value of travel time created by producing a recreational trip. On the other hand few have ventured to assume that ozone reduction dominates in the use of air conditioning.

1.5.3 Obtaining the Right Data

Despite the facile discussion of 'observed behavior', such data is only slightly less difficult to measure than the valuation itself. Whether the variable is recreational trips, choice of recreational site, water filter purchases, or miles driven, these data are not easily obtainable under ordinary circumstances, even without pollution events. Such data require careful surveying, just as in contingent valuation.

The data requirements necessary to exploit revealed preference relationships can be unobtainable, if circumstances do not generate the right natural experiments. In the models discussed in the first section, it is often necessary to estimate demand functions for goods or inputs, which means observing enough price–quantity variation for continuous demand function estimation. And in some cases one must also observe this variation under at least two quality regimes. In practice this variation in price has most easily been found in hedonic markets or by exploiting the natural price variation that arises in travel cost models. To make use of discrete choice models, the individual must be presented with pairs of price/quality alternatives such that his choice will convey some information. That means that the particular price/quality pairs must be useful; there must be enough variation and that variation cannot be such that one alternative will obviously dominate.

1.5.4 Exploring Behavioral Connections

Revealed preference analyses are not controlled experiments. More than most think, they rely for their success on the good judgement of the researcher. When *no* behavioral effect is econometrically found, is it because people don't care? Or because we used the wrong proxy for the environmental change? Or because we looked at the wrong kind of behavior? When a significant behavioral response *is* found, is it because people do care? Or because people are responding to a different stimulus, that just happens to be correlated with the environmental change we wish to value? Most revealed preference studies that seek to value an environmental change are, in a sense, reduced form analyses. The link between the environmental change and the behavior is never made explicit; the researcher just prays that whatever b he is able to measure is, on the one hand, adequately related to the environmental change being valued, and, on the other hand, a sufficiently good proxy for what people perceive and care about.

These sorts of "sloppy" connections would not be tolerated in contingent valuation experiments. Presumably they are accepted in the analysis of revealed preference for the very reason that the experiment cannot be controlled. Yet perhaps something can be learned from the methods regularly used in stated preference valuation. It seems obvious to borrow from those methods, such as focus groups, that help the researcher learn about perceptions, motivations, and reasoning processes. Would it improve hedonic models if we could establish in some systematic way that people do indeed consider the air quality when choosing residential location in a given city? If we were to ask people how they cope with ozone alert periods, we might learn of a different way in which they behaviorally respond. Might it not be wise to explore how people react to risk so that we include the right parameters of probability distributions when seeking a reaction to health-related environmental damages? These kinds of tools can be turned around for behavioral methods to ascertain how households might respond to observable variables rather than conceptually correct variables. For example, for exposures to risk, it seems reasonable that households are interested in dispersion as well as central tendency. Yet it may be that only central tendencies are available. Focus groups might reveal that households would respond if they could only learn about the central tendency.

Revealed preference studies may not be experiments, but they still almost always require survey work since they depend on non-market behavior. Traditionally this survey work has been restricted to asking people "what they have done". Only a few researchers have thought to ask people "what they would do". One of the most vexing problems in behavioral studies is observing enough natural variation in price/quality pairs for which behavior can be recorded. Perhaps an obvious solution is to combine questions about what individuals have done with questions about what they would do were circumstances somewhat different. Such contingent behavior studies might not suffer from many of the problems encountered when asking values and they would be targeted towards people who "behave" in the context of the problem and who would presumably not find it difficult to imagine the behavioral changes they would make when faced with different prices, different qualities, different alternatives.

Researchers have begun to combine stated behavior and revealed choices to improve valuation. McConnell, Weninger and Strand (1999) demonstrate one such study and discuss several others and Englin and Cameron (1996) provide another example. But we are suggesting an additional link—the kinds of preparations that go into a stated preference approach. It would be useful to find out before the study is undertaken how people say they behave.

1.6 CONCLUSIONS

In this chapter we have focused on the common elements of behavioral methods. We have chosen this path out of the belief that the most productive research in the future will be at the extensive margin—extending current ways of thinking about the underlying welfare economics to new problems, rather than econometric refinement of existing methods. That new uses of valuation methods would be utilized, one needs only to look at the global use of contingent valuation to ascertain. New developments are more likely when one confronts a problem with general notions of how behavioral methods work, rather than with the specific toolkit of travel cost models, defensive expenditures, etc.

While the development of new methods is more likely to be serendipitous than planned, some general problems need to be solved. And for their solution, we argue that the application of revealed preferences can fruitfully adopt some of useful methods practiced by contingent valuation analysts. Better understanding of the underlying perceptions and motivations of "subjects" would certainly strengthen revealed preference studies. In addition, where nature does not provide sufficient data to estimate revealed preference models, combining contingent behavior with actual behavior may be a useful alternative.

REFERENCES

Abdalla, C.W., Roach, B.A., and Epp, D.J. (1992), "Valuing Environmental Quality Changes Using Averting Expenditures: An Application to Groundwater Contamination." *Land Economics* 88(2):163–70.

Bartik, T.J. (1988a), "Evaluating the Benefits of Non-Marginal Reductions in Pollution Using Information on Defensive Expenditures." *Journal of Environmental Economics and Management* 15(1):111–27.

Bartik, T.J. (1988b), "Measuring the Benefits of Amenity Improvements in Hedonic Price Models." *Land Economics* 64(2):72–83.

Bockstael, N. E. and Kling, C.L. (1988), "Valuing Environmental Quality Changes When Quality is a Weak Complement to a Set of Goods." *American Journal of Agricultural Economics* 70(3), 654–62.

Bockstael, N. E. and McConnell, K. E. (1981), "Theory and Estimation of the Household Production Function for Wildlife Recreation." *Journal of Environmental Economics and Management* 8(3): 199–214.

Bockstael, N.E. and McConnell, K. E. (1983), "Welfare Measurement in the Household Production Framework." *American Economic Review* 73(4):806–14.

Bockstael, N.E. and McConnell, K. E. (1993), "Public Goods as Characteristics of Non-Market Commodities." *Economic Journal* 103:1244–57.

Brown, J.N. and Rosen, H.S. (1982), "On the Estimation of Structural Hedonic Price Models." *Econometrica* 50(3):765–68.

Brown, W.G., Singh, A., and Castle, E. (1964), "An Economic Evaluation of the Oregon Salmon and Steelhead Sport Fishery." Oregon Station Technical Bulletin 78, Corvallis, Oregon (September).

Courant, P. and Porter R. (1981), "Averting Behavior and the Cost of Pollution." *Journal of Environmental Economics and Management* 8:321–29.

Cropper, M.L., Deck, L., Kishor, N., and McConnell, K.E. (1993), "Valuing Product Attributes Using Single Market Data: A Comparison of Hedonic and Discrete Choice Approaches." *Review of Economics and Statistics* 75(2):225–32.

Diamond, D.B. and Smith, B.A. (1985), "Simultaneity in the Market for Housing Characteristics." *J. Urban Economics* 17: 280–92

Englin, J. and Cameron, T.A. (1996), "Augmenting Travel Cost Models with Contingent Behavior Data: Poisson Regression Analyses with Individual Panel Data." *Environmental and Resource Economics* 7: 133–47.

Englin, J. and Mendelsohn, R. (1991), "A Hedonic Travel Cost Analysis for Valuation of Multiple Components of Site Quality: The Recreation Value of Forest Management." *Journal of Environmental Economics and Management* 21(3):275-90.

Epple, D. (1987), "Hedonic Prices and Implicit Markets: Estimating Demand and Supply Functions for Differentiated Products." *Journal of Political Economy* 95(1):59–80.

Epstein, L.G. (1981), "Generalized Duality and Integrability." *Econometrica* 49(3): 655–78.

Farrow, S. and Larson, D.M. (1995). "Behavior and Total Valuation" Association of Environmental and Resource Economists' Newsletter, Fall.

Foster, W. and Just, R.E. (1989), "Measuring the Welfare Effects of Product Contamination with Consumer Uncertainty" *Journal of Environmental Economics and Management* 17(4): 266–83.

Humplick, F., Madanat, and Kudat, A., (1993), "Modeling Household Responses to Water Supply: A Service Quality Approach", Working Paper, TWURD WP #4, The World Bank, August.

McConnell, K.E., Wenninger, Q. and Strand, I.E. (1999), "Joint Estimation of Contingent Valuation and Truncated Demands." Chapter 7 in J.A. Herriges and C.L. Kling (eds.) *Valuing Recreation and the Environment*, Aldershot: Edward Elgar pp. 199–216.

Neill, Jon R. (1988), "Another Theorem on Using Market Demands to Determine Willingness to Pay for Non-traded Goods" *Journal of Environmental Economics and Management* 15: 224–32.

Ohsfeldt, R. L. and Smith, B. A. (1985), "Estimating the Demand for Heterogeneous Goods." *Review of Economics and Statistics* 67:165–71.

Ohsfeldt, R. L. and Smith, B. A. (1988), "Assessing the Accuracy of Structural Parameter Estimates in Analyses of Implicit Markets." *Land Economics* 64: 135–46.

Palmquist, R. B. (1991), "Hedonic Models". Chapter IV in Braden and Kolstad (ed), *Measuring the Demand for Environmental Quality*. pp77–122.

Palmquist, R. B. (1992), "A Note on Transactions Costs, Moving Costs, and Benefit Measurement" *Journal of Urban Economics* 32: 40–44.

Pollak, R.A. and Wachter, M.L. (1975), "The Relevance of the Household Production Function and Its Implications for the Allocation of Time." *Journal of Political Economy* 83(2):255–77.

Smith, V.K. and Huang, J.C. (1993), "Hedonic Models and Air Pollution: Twenty-five Years and Counting." *Environmental and Resource Economics* 3:378–94.

Smith, V.K. and Huang, J.C. (1995), "Can Markets Value Air Quality: A Meta-Analysis of Hedonic Property Value Models." *Journal of Political Economy* 103:209–27.

Smith, V.K., Palmquist, R.B., and Jakus, P. (1991), "Combining Farrell Frontier and Hedonic Travel Cost Models for Valuing Estuarine Quality." *Review of Economics and Statistics* 73(4):694–99.

Willig, Robert. (1976), "Consumer Surplus without Apology." American Economic Review 66:589–97.

2. Welfare Analysis with Discrete Choice Models*

W. Michael Hanemann

2.1 INTRODUCTION

A major accomplishment in recent years has been the development of statistical models suitable for the analysis of discrete dependent variables. This has enabled economists to study behavioral relationships involving purely qualitative variables that are not amenable to conventional regression techniques. In Amemiya's (1981) terminology, the multi-response qualitative response (MRQR) model involves a dependent variable taking N distinct values, $\tilde{y} = 1, 2, \ldots,$ or N, which is related to vectors of independent variables, W_j, and parameters, β_j, by some functions of the general form[1]

$$\pi_j \equiv \Pr\{\tilde{y} = j\} = H_j(W_1\beta_1, \ldots, W_N\beta_N) \qquad j = 1, \ldots, N. \tag{2.1}$$

Specific examples are the polychotomous probit model (Daganzo, 1979),

$$\pi_1 = \int_{-\infty}^{\infty}\int_{-\infty}^{W_1\beta_1 - W_2\beta_2 + \varepsilon_1} \cdots \int_{-\infty}^{W_1\beta_1 - W_N\beta_N + \varepsilon_1} n(\varepsilon_1, \ldots, \varepsilon_N; 0, \Sigma)\, d\varepsilon_1, \ldots, d\varepsilon_N \tag{2.2}$$

where $n(\cdot)$ is a multivariate normal density with zero mean and covariance matrix Σ, and the generalized logit (GEV) model (McFadden, 1978, 1981),

$$\pi_j = \frac{\exp(W_j\beta_j)G_j\left[\exp(W_1\beta_1), \ldots, \exp(W_N\beta_N)\right]}{G\left[\exp(W_1\beta_1), \ldots, \exp(W_N\beta_N)\right]} \qquad j = 1, \ldots, N \tag{2.3}$$

---

* This chapter appeared earlier as Hanemann (1985); it extends research initiated in Hanemann (1982).

[1] Throughout the paper a tilde will be used to denote random variables.

where G is a positive, linear homogeneous function, and G_j denotes its partial derivative with respect to the jth argument.[2]

These statistical models have been used to analyze many types of economic behavior. Aitchison and Bennett (1970) and McFadden (1974) have offered a theoretical derivation of these models which applies whenever the events whose probabilities are given by (2.1) represent the outcome of a decision by a maximizing agent. Suppose an agent is choosing among N courses of action and π_j = Pr{jth act chosen}. Assume that the payoff or utility associated with the jth act, $\tilde{u}_j$, is a random variable with mean $W_j\beta_j$. Equivalently, $\tilde{u}_j = W_j\beta_j + \tilde{\varepsilon}_j$, where $\tilde{\varepsilon}_j$ is a random variable with zero mean. The agent chooses that act which has the highest utility. This yields a MRQR model of the form (2.1):

$$\pi_j = \Pr\{W_j\beta_j + \tilde{\varepsilon}_j \geq W_i\beta_i + \tilde{\varepsilon}_i, \forall i\} \equiv H_j(W_1\beta_1, \ldots, W_N\beta_N) \qquad j = 1, \ldots, N. \qquad (2.4)$$

Let $\tilde{\eta}_{(j)} = (\tilde{\eta}_{1j}, \ldots, \tilde{\eta}_{j-1,j}, \tilde{\eta}_{j+1,j}, \ldots, \tilde{\eta}_{Nj})$ where $\tilde{\eta}_{ij} \equiv \tilde{\varepsilon}_i - \tilde{\varepsilon}_j$. It follows from (2.4) that

$$H_j(W_1\beta_1, \ldots, W_N\beta_N) = F_{(j)}(W_j\beta_j - W_1\beta_1, \ldots, W_j\beta_j - W_N\beta_N) \qquad j = 1, \ldots, N, \qquad (2.5)$$

where $F_{(j)}$ is an (N-1) dimensional joint cumulative distribution function associated with the random vector $\tilde{\eta}_{(j)}$. As Daly and Zachary (1970) have shown, the converse is also true. Any MRQR model (2.1) in which the probability functions $H_j(\cdot)$ can be cast in the form of an (N-1) dimensional joint cumulative distribution function as in (2.5) is derivable from a utility maximization choice model such as (2.4). For this reason, a MRQR model satisfying (2.5) is said to be a random utility maximization (RUM) model.

This link between statistical models for discrete dependent variables and the economic concept of utility maximization is potentially very valuable because it raises the possibility of applying the conventional apparatus of welfare theory to empirical models of purely qualitative choice. Suppose the statistical model satisfies (2.5) and some subset of the variables in W_j represents attributes of the jth discrete choice. Can one derive from the fitted model an estimate of the effect on the agent's welfare of a change in these attributes analogous to the compensating and equivalent variation measures of conventional utility theory?

[2] The standard independent logit model (McFadden, 1974) is a special case where

$$G(t_1, \ldots, t_N) \equiv \sum t_j \text{ and } \pi_j = \exp(W_j\beta_j)\left[\sum \exp(W_i\beta_i)\right]^{-1}.$$

This issue was first raised in connection with RUM models of transportation mode choice by Domenich and McFadden (1975), Williams (1977), and Daly and Zachary (1978) but, until recently, it has received relatively little attention in other branches of applied economics. An exception is the papers by McFadden (1981) and Small and Rosen (1981) which explore the relationship between RUM models and conventional deterministic models of consumer behavior. However, both of these papers impose special restrictions on the underlying random utility function which have the effect that the discrete choice probabilities are independent of the consumer's income. Not only does this limit the applicability of their analysis, but it also obscures some important distinctions between alternative approaches to welfare measurement in the random utility context that happen to vanish when there are no income effects. When income effects *are* present, there are at least three distinct ways to formulate measures of compensating variation for RUM models (and three ways to formulate measures of equivalent variation) that can differ significantly in numerical value. In this paper I explain these different approaches to welfare measurement and analyze the relationships among them. I also provide formulas for computing the welfare measures, together with some numerical examples. Furthermore, I show that the same approaches to welfare measurement carry over to RUM models involving *mixed* discrete/continuous choices of the type analyzed by Dubin and McFadden (1984) and Hanemann (1984).

The paper is organized as follows. Sections 2.2 and 2.3 focus on the most common type of logit and probit models involving what I will call an additively random utility function and purely discrete, budget-constrained choices. In section 2.2, I analyze the relationship between this type of RUM model and the more conventional, deterministic model of consumer choice. In section 2.3, I explain the alternative approaches to measuring welfare changes in the random utility setting and investigate the relationships among them. In section 2.4, this analysis is extended to other forms of RUM models including those with a more general stochastic structure and those involving mixed discrete/continuous choices. Section 2.5 deals with the practical problems of calculating the welfare measures and analyzes their properties in the case of some simple price/quality changes.

2.2 BUDGET-CONSTRAINED DISCRETE CHOICE

2.2.1 Deterministic Utility Models

The general setup of a purely discrete choice model is as follows. An individual consumer has a quasi-concave, increasing utility function defined over the commodities $x_1, \ldots, x_N$, and z, where z is taken as the numeraire. In addition, the individual's utility may depend on some other variables, $q_1,\ldots,q_N$, which he takes as exogenous; these are, for example, quality attributes of the nonumeraire goods.[3] He chooses (x, z) so as to maximize

$$u = u(x_1,\ \ldots,\ x_N, q_1,\ \ldots,\ q_N, z) \tag{2.6}$$

subject to a budget constraint,

$$\Sigma p_j x_j + z = y, \tag{2.7}$$

and two other constraints which introduce an element of discreteness into his choice. First, for logical or institutional reasons, the x_j's are mutually exclusive in consumption,

$$x_i x_j = 0 \qquad all \quad i \neq j. \tag{2.8}$$

Secondly, the x_j's can only be purchased in fixed quantities,

$$x_j = \bar{x}_j \ or\ 0 \qquad j = 1,\ \ldots,\ N. \tag{2.9}$$

An example might be where the x_j's are different brands of an indivisible durable good, and the consumer needs only one of these brands. Since the quantities of the x_j's are limited by (2.9), the choice among them is a qualitative choice. Moreover, although the numeraire is inherently a divisible good, once one of the x_j's has been selected the quantity of z is fixed by the budget constraint (2.7).[4] Thus, the model (2.6)–(2.9) represents a purely discrete utility-maximizing choice.

To obtain the demand functions implied by this model, first suppose that the individual has selected good *j*. His utility conditional on this decision, denoted by u_j, is

$$\begin{aligned} u_j &= u(0,\ldots,0,\bar{x}_j,0,\ldots,0,q_1,\ldots,q_N,\ldots,y - p_j\bar{x}_j) \\ &\equiv v_j(q_1,\ldots,q_N,y - p_j\bar{x}_j) \end{aligned} \tag{2.10}$$

where v_j is increasing in $(y - p_j\bar{x}_j)$. I will refer to the $v_j(\cdot)$'s as conditional indirect utility functions. At this point it is common to make an additional

[3] For simplicity, I treat the q_j's as scalars, but they could be vectors.

[4] I assume that $y \geq \max[p_i, \bar{x}_i]$, so that $z \geq 0$.

assumption about the utility function (2.6) that the consumer does *not* care about the attributes of a good unless he actually consumes that good, i.e.,

$$x_j = 0 \Rightarrow \frac{\partial u}{\partial q_j} = 0 \qquad j = 1, \ldots, N. \tag{2.11}$$

This assumption was introduced by Mäler (1974), who named it "weak complementarity." Given (2.11), the conditional indirect utility functions (2.10) take the special form[5]

$$u_j = v_j(q_j, y - p_j\bar{x}_j) \qquad j = 1, \ldots, N. \tag{2.12}$$

The solution to the consumer's problem can be represented by a set of binary-valued indices, $\delta_1, \ldots, \delta_N$, where $\delta_j \equiv 1$ if $x_j > 0$ and $\delta_j \equiv 0$ if $x_j = 0$. These indices are related to the conditional indirect utility functions by

$$\delta_j(p,q,y) = \begin{cases} 1 & \text{if } v_j(q_j, y - p_j\bar{x}_j) \geq v_i(q_i, y - p_i\bar{x}_i) \quad \forall i \\ 0 & \text{otherwise.} \end{cases} \tag{2.13}$$

Accordingly, the unconditional ordinary demand functions associated with the utility model (2.6)–(2.9) can be expressed as

$$x_j(p, q, y) = \delta_j(p, q, y)\,\bar{x}_j \qquad j = 1, \ldots, N. \tag{2.14}$$

Substitution of these demand functions into the direct utility function (2.6) yields the unconditional indirect utility function,

$$v(p,q,y) = \max\,[v_1(q_1, y - p_1\bar{x}_1), \ldots, v_N(q_N, y - p_N\bar{x}_N)]. \tag{2.15}$$

This purely discrete choice model may be compared with the conventional utility maximization model where (2.6) is maximized subject only to the budget constraint (2.7) and a nonnegativity constraint on x and z that is assumed not to be binding. The point to be emphasized is that all the constructs of conventional, continuous choice models—the ordinary demand functions, the indirect utility function, and consumer's surplus—carry over to the discrete

[5] If and only if $u(\cdot)$ is increasing in q_j, then $v_j(\cdot)$ in (2.10) and (2.12) is increasing in q_j.

choice model. Duality relationships also carry over, including Roy's Identity (see Small and Rosen, 1981) and the duality between expenditure minimization and utility maximization (see below). The discrete choice model serves to provide a theoretical underpinning for the statistical MRQR model. However, in order to generate the statistical model, it is necessary to add a stochastic element and introduce the notion of random utility.

2.2.2 Random Utility Models

A random utility model arises when one assumes that, although an individual's utility function is deterministic for *him*, it contains some components which are unobservable to the econometric investigator and are treated by the investigator as random variables. This combines two notions which have a long history in economics—the idea of a variation in tastes among individuals in a population and the idea of unobserved variables in econometric models. These components of the utility function will be denoted by the random vector $\tilde{\varepsilon}$, and the utility function will be written $\tilde{u} = u(x, q, z, \tilde{\varepsilon})$. More specifically, throughout the remainder of this section I assume that the random elements enter additively as follows:[6,7]

$$u(x, q, z, \tilde{\varepsilon}) = u(x, q, z) + \Sigma\zeta(x_j)\,\tilde{\varepsilon}_j \qquad (2.6')$$

where $\zeta(x_j) = 1$ if $x_j > 0$ and $\zeta(x_j) = 0$ otherwise. For the individual consumer $\tilde{\varepsilon}_1, \ldots, \tilde{\varepsilon}_N$ is a set of fixed constants (or functions); but for the investigator, it is a set of random variables with some joint cumulative distribution function, $F_\varepsilon(\varepsilon_1, \ldots, \varepsilon_N)$, which induces a distribution on $\tilde{u}$.

In the budget-constrained random utility discrete choice model, the individual is assumed to maximize (2.6′) subject to the constraints (2.7)–(2.9). In addition, I will assume that the nonstochastic component of (2.6′) satisfies (2.11). This maximization yields a set of ordinary demand functions and an indirect utility function which parallel those developed above except that they now involve a random component from the point of view of the econometric investigator. Suppose that the individual has selected good *j*. Conditional on this decision, his utility is $\tilde{u}_j$ where, from (2.6′), (2.7), (2.8), (2.9), and (2.11),[8]

---

[6] This additive specification is employed by Domenich and McFadden (1975), Williams (1977), Daly and Zachary (1978), McFadden (1981), Small and Rosen (1981), and many others. More general formulations of $u(x,q,z,\tilde{\varepsilon})$ will be considered in section 2.4.1.

[7] With no loss of generality, I assume that $E\{\varepsilon_j\} = 1, \forall j$.

[8] It follows from the weak complementarity assumption, (2.11), that the elements of W_j include the attributes and price of good *j* but not those of the other goods. Without this assumption, $\tilde{u}_j = v_j(q_1, \ldots, q_N, y - p\bar{x}_j) + \tilde{\varepsilon}_j$, and the vector W_j includes $q_i, i \neq j$. In the case of the inde-

$$\tilde{u}_j = v_j(q_j, y - p_j\bar{x}_j) + \tilde{\varepsilon}_j \qquad j = 1, \ldots, N, \tag{2.12$'$}$$

the nonstochastic component being identical to (2.12). The discrete choice indices,

$$\tilde{\delta}_j = \delta_j(p, q, y, \tilde{\varepsilon}) = \begin{cases} 1 & \text{if } v_j(q_j, y - p_j\bar{x}_j) + \tilde{\varepsilon}_j \\ & \quad \geq v_i(q_i, y - p_i\bar{x}_i) + \tilde{\varepsilon}_i \;\; \forall i \\ 0 & \text{otherwise,} \end{cases} \tag{2.13$'$}$$

are now random variables. Their mean, $E\{\delta_j\} \equiv \pi_j$, is given by

$$\begin{aligned} \pi_j &= \Pr\{v_j(q_j, y - p_j\bar{x}_j) + \tilde{\varepsilon}_j > v_i(q_i, y - p_i\bar{x}_i) + \tilde{\varepsilon}_i \;\; \forall i\} \\ &= F_{(j)}[v_j(q_j, y - p_j\bar{x}_j) - v_1(q_1, y - p_1\bar{x}_1), \\ &\qquad \ldots, v_j(q_j, y - p_j\bar{x}_j) - v_N(q_N, y - p_N\bar{x}_N)], \end{aligned} \tag{2.16}$$

where $F_{(j)}$ is the joint cumulative distribution function of the (N-1) differences $\tilde{\eta}_{ij} = \tilde{\varepsilon}_i - \tilde{\varepsilon}_j$. When $v_j(\cdot)$ can be cast in the form $v_j = W_j\beta_j$, (2.16) constitutes a RUM as defined in (2.5). I refer to it as a budget-constrained discrete choice RUM because of the restrictions on the regressors W_j and coefficients β_j implied by (2.12′), namely, that the variables y and p_j enter in the form $(y - p_j\bar{x}_j)$ and that v_j is increasing in this term.

The requirement that the arguments of $F_{(j)}$ in (2.16) take the form of utility differences may be regarded as the analog of the integrability conditions in conventional demand theory. It provides a criterion for determining whether a given statistical MRQR model is compatible with the economic hypothesis of utility maximization. In addition, it offers a practical procedure for specifying a statistical model in empirical applications: First postulate some parametric function for $v_j(q_j, y - p_jx_j), j = 1, \ldots, N$, and then form the differences

---

pendent logit model where the $\tilde{\varepsilon}_j$'s are independent extreme value variables, the resulting discrete choice possibilities,

$$\pi_j = \frac{\exp\left[v_j\left(q_1, \ldots, q_N, y - p_j\bar{x}_j\right)\right]}{\sum \exp\left[v_i\left(q_1, \ldots, q_N, y - p_i\bar{x}_i\right)\right]}$$

do not possess the Independence of Irrelevant Alternatives (IIA) property. (This is a version of what McFadden (1981) calls the "universal logit" model.) Thus, there is some connection between weak complementarity and the IIA property.

$v_j - v_1, \dots, v_j - v_N$ and substitute these into $F_{(j)}$. Another analog with conventional demand theory is worth mentioning. Suppose that the utility function (2.6′) is replaced by some monotonic transformation, $\hat{u}(x, q, z, \tilde{\varepsilon}) \equiv T[u(x, q, z) + \Sigma\zeta_j \tilde{\varepsilon}_j], T' > 0$. The discrete choices indices (2.13′) and, hence, the discrete choice probabilities (2.16) are invariant with respect to this transformation since

$$\begin{aligned} &v_j(q_j, y - p_j \bar{x}_x) + \tilde{\varepsilon}_j \geq v_i(q_i, y - p_i \bar{x}_i) + \tilde{\varepsilon}_i \\ \Leftrightarrow\ &T[v_j(q_j, y - p_j \bar{x}_j) + \tilde{\varepsilon}_j] \geq T[v_i(q_i, y - p_i \bar{x}_i) + \tilde{\varepsilon}_i]. \end{aligned} \tag{2.17}$$

Thus, when one estimates the MRQR model (2.16), he recovers the underlying utility function (2.6′) only up to an arbitrary monotonic, increasing transformation.

The unconditional ordinary demand functions associated with the budget-constrained discrete choice RUM model are

$$\tilde{x}_j = x_j(p, q, y, \tilde{\varepsilon}) = \delta_j(p, q, y, \tilde{\varepsilon})\bar{x}_j \qquad j = 1, \dots, N, \tag{2.14′}$$

and the expected quantity demanded is $E\{\tilde{x}_j\} = \pi_j \bar{x}_j$. Substituting the demand functions (2.14′) into the discrete utility function (2.6′) yields the unconditional indirect utility function

$$\tilde{u} = v(p, q, y, \tilde{\varepsilon}) \equiv \max[v_1(q_1, \bar{y} - p_1 x_1) + \tilde{\varepsilon}_1, \dots, v_N(q_N, y - p_N \bar{x}_N) + \tilde{\varepsilon}_N]. \tag{2.15′}$$

Recall that $v(\cdot)$ gives the utility attained by the individual maximizing consumer when confronted with the choice set (p, q, y). This is a known number for the consumer; but for the econometric investigator, it is a random variable with a cumulative distribution function $F_v(\omega) \equiv \Pr\{v(p, q, y, \tilde{\varepsilon}) \leq \omega\}$ derived from the assumed distribution $F_\varepsilon(\cdot)$ by a change of variables

$$F_v(\omega) = F_\varepsilon(\omega - v_1, \dots, \omega - v_N). \tag{2.18}$$

In section 2.3, I show how the unconditional utility function is used to measure the welfare effects of a change in p or q. But first I identify a special family of utility models in which this welfare analysis is considerably simplified.

2.2.3 The Case of No Income Effects

Dual to the above utility maximization is an expenditure minimization problem: minimize $\sum p_i x_i + z$ subject to (2.6′), (2.8), and (2.9). This generates a set of compensated demand functions and an expenditure function which, like the ordinary demand functions and the indirect utility function, involve a random component from the econometrician's viewpoint. Suppose that the individual has selected good j. Assuming that his utility function satisfies the weak complementarity condition (2.11), his expenditure conditional on this decision is $\tilde{e}_j = g_j(q_j, u - \varepsilon_j) + p_j \bar{x}_j$, where $g_j(\cdot)$ is the inverse of $v_j(\cdot)$ in (2.12′), i.e., $g_j[q_j, v_j(q_j, t)] \equiv t$. The unconditional compensated demand functions can be written as $x_j(p, q, u, \tilde{\varepsilon}) = \delta_j(p, q, u, \tilde{\varepsilon})\, \bar{x}_j$, where

$$\delta_j(p,q,u,\tilde{\varepsilon}) \equiv \begin{cases} 1 & \text{if } g_j(q_j, u - \tilde{\varepsilon}_j) + p_j \bar{x}_j \\ & \leq g_i(q_i, u - \tilde{\varepsilon}_i) + p_i \bar{x}_i \quad \forall i \\ 0 & \text{otherwise,} \end{cases} \tag{2.19}$$

and the unconditional function is

$$\begin{aligned} \tilde{e} &= e(p,q,u,\tilde{\varepsilon}) \\ &= \min\,[g_1(q_1, u - \tilde{\varepsilon}_1) + p_1 \bar{x}_1, \ldots, g_N(q_N, u - \tilde{\varepsilon}_N) + p_N \bar{x}_N]. \end{aligned} \tag{2.20}$$

An important class of utility models, to which Small and Rosen (1981) and McFadden (1981) have drawn attention, is that for which the unconditional ordinary and compensated demand functions coincide. In the Appendix the following result characterizing this class of utility models is proved:

PROPOSITION. The unconditional ordinary and conditional demand functions coincide if the direct utility function (2.6′) is some monotonic transformation of

$$\tilde{u} = h(x, q) + \gamma z + \Sigma \zeta(x_j)\, \tilde{\varepsilon}_j \tag{2.21a}$$

for some function $h(\cdot)$ and positive constant g. Assuming that $h(\cdot)$ satisfies (2.11), the corresponding form of the conditional indirect utility function is

$$\tilde{u}_j = h_j(q_j) + \gamma\, y - \gamma\, p_j \bar{x}_j + \tilde{\varepsilon}_j \qquad j = 1, \ldots, N, \tag{2.21b}$$

where $h_j(q_j) \equiv h(0,\ldots,\bar{x}_j,0,\ldots,0,q)$.

In order to motivate the proof of this proposition, it is useful to introduce an alternative method of representing the unconditional ordinary and compensated demand functions. Consider the demand for the first good. Given $(p_2,\ldots, p_N, q, y)$, one can write the ordinary demand function as a step function

$$x_1(p,q,y,\tilde{\varepsilon}) = \begin{cases} 0 & \text{if } p_1 \geq \tilde{p}_1^* \\ \bar{x}_1 & \text{otherwise,} \end{cases} \tag{2.22}$$

where the switch price, $\tilde{p}_1^*$, is a function of $(p_2, \ldots, p_N, q, y, \tilde{\varepsilon})$. Suppose that the actual price of the good is p_1^0; accordingly, the utility attained by the consumer is $\tilde{u}^0 = v(p_1^0, p_2, \ldots, p_N, q, y, \tilde{\varepsilon})$. The compensated demand function evaluated at $\tilde{u}^0$ is also a step function

$$x_1(p,q,\tilde{u}^0,\tilde{\varepsilon}) = \begin{cases} 0 & \text{if } p_1 \geq \tilde{p}_1^{**} \\ \bar{x}_1 & \text{otherwise,} \end{cases} \tag{2.23}$$

where the switch price, $\tilde{p}_1^{**}$, is a function of $(p_2, \ldots, p_N, q, \tilde{u}^0, \tilde{\varepsilon})$.

By construction $x_1(p_1^0, p_2, \ldots, p_N, q, y, \tilde{\varepsilon}) \equiv x_1(p_1^0, p_2, \ldots, p_N, q, \tilde{u}^0, \tilde{\varepsilon})$. However, the entire graphs of the two demand functions coincide, $x_1(p_1, p_2, \ldots, p_N, q, y, \tilde{\varepsilon}) \equiv x_1(p_1, p_2, \ldots, p_N, q, \tilde{u}^0, \tilde{\varepsilon})$ for *all* p_1, if and only if $\tilde{p}_1^* = \tilde{p}_1^{**}$. In the appendix, I show that this occurs nontrivially only when the direct utility function takes the form in (2.21a). The assertion about the conditional indirect utility functions (2.21b) follows directly from (2.21a) by application of (2.10).

There is an important corollary to this proposition which enables one to test whether an empirical MRQR model satisfies (2.21). Observe from (2.21a) that the income variable drops out of the utility differences

$$\tilde{u}_j - \tilde{u}_i = h_j(q_j) - h_i(q_i) - \gamma\ (p_j\bar{x}_j - p_i\bar{x}_i) + \tilde{\varepsilon}_j - \tilde{\varepsilon}_i. \tag{2.24}$$

Since it is these utility differences that enter into the formula for the discrete choice probabilities (2.16), it follows that the choice probabilities are *independent* of the consumer's income when the utility function satisfies (2.21)—there are no income effects.[9]

---

[9] The marginal utility of income, γ, can still be estimated because it appears as the coefficient of the price difference term in (2.24). The point is that income itself cannot appear as an explicit variable in a MRQR model satisfying (2.21).

The utility function in (2.21a) satisfies the quasilinearity property that one finds when there are no income effects in conventional, continuous choice models—for example, see Katzner (1970, p. 93). As will be shown in the next section, it has the same implications for welfare analysis in discrete choice RUM models as in conventional, continuous choice models, namely, that the compensating and equivalent variations coincide and can be measured by areas under ordinary demand functions.

2.3 COMPENSATION MEASURES

In this section I show how one can perform welfare evaluations with statistical MRQR models that satisfy the integrability condition (2.16) and, hence, are derivable from the utility maximization model (2.6′)–(2.9). Suppose that the set of prices and qualities available to the individual changes from (p^0, q^0) to (p^1, q^1). Thus his utility changes from $\tilde{u}^0 \equiv v(p^0, q^0, y, \tilde{\varepsilon})$ to $\tilde{u}^1 \equiv v(p^1, q^1, y, \tilde{\varepsilon})$. By analogy with welfare analysis in conventional, continuous choice models, this utility change could be measured in money units by the quantity $\tilde{C}$ which satisfies

$$v(p^1, q^1, y - \tilde{C}, \tilde{\varepsilon}) = v(p^0, q^0, y, \tilde{\varepsilon}) \tag{2.25}$$

or the quantity $\tilde{E}$ which satisfies

$$v(p^1, q^1, y, \tilde{\varepsilon}) = v(p^o, q^o, y + \tilde{E}, \tilde{\varepsilon}). \tag{2.26}$$

The problem in the RUM context is that $\tilde{C}$ and $\tilde{E}$ are random variables since they depend on $\tilde{\varepsilon}$. Although the compensation required to offset the price/quality change is a fixed number for the individual consumer, for the econometric investigator it is a random variable since the individual's utility function is known only up to a random component. How, then, to obtain a single number representing the compensating or equivalent variation for the price/quality change?

In fact, the existing literature contains hints of up to three different approaches to welfare evaluation in the random utility context, but the conceptual distinction between these approaches does not appear to have been recognized. One approach is to derive the probability distribution of the quantity $\tilde{C}$ and calculate its mean, $C^+ \equiv E\{\tilde{C}\}$. As shown below, this calculation is sometimes difficult because of the complexity of the distribution of $\tilde{C}$. A second approach is to employ the expectation of the individual's indirect utility function, $V(p, q, y) \equiv E\{v(p, q, y, \tilde{\varepsilon})\}$ and define the compensating variation in terms of this function.[10] The resulting welfare measure, $C^{\bullet}$, satisfies

$$V(p^1, q^1, y - C^{\bullet}) = V(p^0, q^0, y). \tag{2.27}$$

The distinction between C^+ and $C^{\bullet}$ is subtle but important. C^+ is the observer's expectation of the maximum amount of money that the individual could pay after the change and still be as well off as he was before it. By contrast, $C^{\bullet}$ is the maximum amount of money that the individual could pay after the change and still be as well off, in terms of the observer's expectation of his utility, as he was before it. The third welfare measure is derived as follows. One might want to know the amount of money such that the individual is just at the point of indifference between paying the money and securing the change or paying nothing and foregoing the change. For the observer, this could be taken as the quantity C^* such that

$$\Pr\{v(p^1, q^1, y - C^*, \tilde{\varepsilon}) \geq v(p^0, q^0, y, \tilde{\varepsilon})\} = 0.5, \tag{2.28}$$

i.e., there is no more than a 50:50 chance that the individual would be willing to pay C^* for the change.

Although these three welfare measures are conceptually distinct, several relationships can be established among them. First, it is simple to show that, while C^+ is the *mean* of the distribution of the true but random compensation $\tilde{C}$, C^* is the *median* of this distribution.[11] Thus, if the distribution were symmetric, C^+ and C^* would coincide. In practice, however, this may not occur: the distribution of $\tilde{C}$ may be highly skewed, and its mean, C^+, may differ by an order of magnitude from its median, C^*. Some circumstances in which this can occur are described in Section 2.5.

The second point is that, whereas C^+ and C^* are both invariant with respect to a transformation of the utility function, the welfare measure $C^{\bullet}$ is *not* invariant. As noted earlier, the statistical MRQR model allows one to recover the underlying utility function (2.6′) only up to an arbitrary monotone transformation. Consider the transformation $\hat{u}(x, q, z, \tilde{\varepsilon}) \equiv T[u(x, q, z, \tilde{\varepsilon})], T' > 0,$

---

[10] Table 2.1 provides formulas for calculating $V(\cdot)$ for the GEV model, (2.3), the independent logit model, and binary and trichotomous probit models.

[11] The median of the distribution of $\tilde{C}$, C_M, has the property that $\Pr\{\tilde{C} \geq C_M\} = 0.5$. But, since $v(p, q, y, \tilde{\varepsilon})$ is increasing in y,

$\tilde{C} \geq C_M \Rightarrow v(p^1, q^1, y - C_M, \tilde{\varepsilon}) \geq v(p^1, q^1, y - \tilde{C}, \tilde{\varepsilon}) = v(p^0, q^0, y, \tilde{\varepsilon})$ from (2.28), $C^* = C_M$.

introduced in connection with (2.17), and let $\hat{v}(p, q, y, \widetilde{\varepsilon}) \equiv T[v(p, q, y, \widetilde{\varepsilon})]$. Then

$$v(p^1, q^1, y - \widetilde{C}, \widetilde{\varepsilon}) = v(p^0, q^0, y, \widetilde{\varepsilon})$$
$$\Leftrightarrow \hat{v}(p^1, q^1, y - \widetilde{C}, \widetilde{\varepsilon}) = \hat{v}(p^0, q^0, y, \widetilde{\varepsilon}). \qquad (2.29)$$

It follows that $\widetilde{C}$ and therefore, both C^+ and C^* are unaffected by the utility transformation. This is not true for $C^\bullet$ because, if one defines $\hat{C}^\bullet$ by

$$E\{\hat{v}(p^1, q^1, y - \hat{C}^\bullet, \widetilde{\varepsilon})\} = E\{\hat{v}(q^0, q^0, y, \widetilde{e})\}. \qquad (2.30)$$

In general $\hat{C}^\bullet$ does not satisfy (2.27). Thus, $\hat{C}^\bullet \neq C^\bullet$. In effect, the welfare measure $C^\bullet$ implies a cardinal concept of utility.

This general result notwithstanding, there *are* some circumstances in which $C^\bullet$ is invariant with respect to a utility transformation. The most important is when there are no income effects. In this case, from (2.21b) the unconditional indirect utility function takes the following form:

$$v(p, q, y, \widetilde{\varepsilon}) = \gamma y + \max[h_1(q_1) - \gamma p_1 \overline{x}_1 + \widetilde{\varepsilon}_1, \ldots, h_N(q_N) - \gamma p_N \overline{x}_N + \widetilde{\varepsilon}_N]$$
$$\equiv \gamma y + s(p, q, \widetilde{\varepsilon}). \qquad (2.31)$$

Hence

$$V(p, q, y) = \gamma y + E\{s(p, q, \widetilde{\varepsilon})\} \equiv \gamma y + S(p, q), \qquad (2.32)$$

and from (2.27)[12]

---

[12] $S(p, q)$ can be constructed from the formulas given in Table 2.1. For example, with the GEV model one obtains

$$C = \frac{1}{\gamma}\left\{\ln G\left[\exp(v_1^0), \ldots, \exp(v_N^0)\right] - \ln G\left[\exp(v_1^1), \ldots, \exp(v_N^1)\right]\right\}$$

while, with the binary independent probit model where Σ is diagonal and normalized so that σ = 1, one obtains

$$C = \frac{1}{\gamma}\left\{\Delta^0\Phi(\Delta^0) + v_2^0 + \phi(\Delta^0) - \Delta^1\Phi(\Delta^1) - v_2^1 - \phi(\Delta^1)\right\}$$

where $v_j^t \equiv v_j(q_j^t, y - p_j^t \overline{x}_j) = h_j(q_j^t) + \gamma(y - p_j^t \overline{x}_j)$ and $\Delta^t \equiv v_1^t - v_2^t, t = 0,1$.

$$C^{\bullet} = \frac{1}{\gamma}[S(p^1, q^1] - S(p^0, q^0)]. \tag{2.33}$$

However, on substituting (2.31) into (2.25), one obtains

$$\tilde{C} = [s(p^1,\ q^1, \tilde{\varepsilon}) - s(p^0, q^0, \tilde{\varepsilon})] / \gamma. \tag{2.34}$$

It follows, therefore, that when there are no income effects [13]

$$C^{+} \equiv E\{\tilde{C}\} = C^{\bullet}. \tag{2.35}$$

What about measures of equivalent variation? By working with (2.26) rather than (2.25), one obtains three alternative measures of equivalent variation, which I denote E^{+}, E^{*}, and $E^{\bullet}$.[14] These are related to one another in the same ways as C^{+}, C^{*}, and $C^{\bullet}$. Moreover, it follows directly from (2.31) and (2.32) that, when there are no income effects, $E^{+} = C^{+}$, $E^{*} = C^{*}$,, and $E^{\bullet} = C^{\bullet}$. When there *are* income effects, however, the corresponding equivalent and compensating variations differ. The similarity with welfare analysis in conventional, continuous choice models is evident.

Another result that carries over from conventional, continuous choice models is the relationship between compensation measures and areas under ordinary demand curves when there are no income effects. To show this, I need to employ the following result about $V(\cdot)$, which applies regardless of whether or not there are income effects[15]

$$\frac{\partial V}{\partial v_j} \equiv \frac{\partial E\{\max[v_1 + \tilde{\varepsilon}_1, \ldots, v_N + \tilde{\varepsilon}_N]\}}{\partial v_j} = \pi_j \qquad j = 1, \ldots, N. \tag{2.36}$$

Now suppose that there are no income effects and, for simplicity, the only change is in p_1 and q_1, with $p_2, \ldots, p_N$ and $q_2, \ldots, q_N$ remaining constant. In this case, using (2.36),

---

[13] When there are no income effects, C^* satisfies:

$$\Pr\{s(p^1, q^1, \tilde{\varepsilon}) - s(p^0, q^0, \tilde{\varepsilon}) \geq \gamma C^*\} = 0.5\ .$$

[14] The equivalent variation for a change from (p^a, q^a) to (p^b, q^b) is equal to the negative of the corresponding compensating variation measure for the change from (p^b, q^b) to (p^a, q^a).

[15] This is proved by Williams (1977), Daly and Zachary (1978), and Sheffi and Daganzo (1978).

$$C^{\bullet} = \frac{1}{\gamma}[V(p^1,q^1,y) - V(p^0,q^0,y)]$$
$$= \frac{1}{\gamma}\int_{v_1^0}^{v_1^1} \frac{\partial V}{\partial v_1} dv_1 \qquad (2.37)$$

or

$$C^{\bullet} = \frac{1}{\gamma}\int_{v_1^0}^{v_1^1} \pi_1(v_1,\dots,v_N)dv_1 \qquad (2.38)$$

In particular, if only p_1 changes, (2.38) becomes[16]

$$C^{\bullet} = \frac{1}{\gamma}\int_{p_1^0}^{p_1^1} \frac{\partial V}{\partial v_1}\frac{\partial v_1}{\partial p_1} dp_1$$
$$= -\bar{x}_1 \int_{p_1^0}^{p_1^1} \pi_1(p_1)dp_1$$
$$= -\int_{p_1^0}^{p_1^1} E\{x_1(p,q,y,\tilde{\varepsilon})\}dp_1. \qquad (2.39)$$

Thus, when there are no income effects, the expected compensating variation for a price change is given by the area under the expected ordinary demand function.

It may be useful to relate the foregoing analysis to the papers by McFadden (1981) and Small and Rosen (1981), which also deal with welfare evaluations in RUM models. Both of these papers focus on the case where there are no income effects and employ the welfare measure $C^{\bullet}$.[17] Thus they do not consider the distinction between $C^{\bullet}$ and the other two welfare measures introduced above. McFadden derives the formula for $C^{\bullet}$ in (2.37) from the utility function (2.21)[18], and in his Theorem 5.1 he proves the converse: if the formula for $C^{\bullet}$

[16] The second line follows from the fact that $\partial v / \partial p_1 = -\gamma \bar{x}_1$ using (2.21b). The third line follows from the fact that $E\{\tilde{x}_1\} = \bar{x}_1 \pi_1$.

[17] McFadden (1981) and Small and Rosen (1981) interpret $V(\cdot)$ as the average indirect utility function over a population of individuals and $C^{\bullet}$ as the average compensation. I interpret $V(\cdot)$ and $C^{\bullet}$ as the observer's expectation of a single individual's utility function and compensation. I would calculate $C^{\bullet}$ (or C^{+}, or C^{*}) for each individual separately and then aggregate over the entire population, perhaps using weights derived from some social welfare function.

[18] McFadden (1981) actually derived (2.37) for a more general additively random RUM model involving continuous as well as discrete choices. This type of model is discussed further in section 2.2.

is given by (2.37), the utility function is (2.21).[18] Small and Rosen obtain the formula for $C^{\bullet}$ in (2.39) but with some additional assumptions. However, their analysis appears to be defective: given the additively random utility specification, the no-income-effects utility function (2.21) is both necessary and sufficient for (2.39) to hold.[19]

2.4 OTHER RANDOM UTILITY MAXIMIZATION MODELS

2.4.1 Random Coefficients Models

In the discrete choice model studied in sections 2.2 and 2.3, the random element representing differences in tastes among individuals and/or unobserved variables was introduced in a very specific way, namely, additively as in (2.1′). In some circumstances, however, this may seem unduly restrictive, and one may prefer to introduce the random element in a different manner. For example, one may wish to specify the no-income-effects utility model (2.21a, b) as

$$u(x, q, z, \tilde{\varepsilon}) = h(x, q) + \tilde{\gamma} z + \Sigma \xi(x_j)\, \tilde{\varepsilon}_j \qquad (2.40a)$$

$$\tilde{u}_j = h_j(q_j) + \tilde{\gamma} y - \tilde{\gamma} p_j \bar{x}_j + \tilde{\varepsilon}_j, \qquad (2.40b)$$

where $\tilde{\gamma}$ is now a random variable, uncorrelated with $\tilde{\varepsilon}_1, \dots, \tilde{\varepsilon}_N$, with a mean of $\tilde{\gamma}$ and a variance of σ_γ^2. Equivalently, $\tilde{\gamma} = \bar{\gamma} + \tilde{\varepsilon}_o$ where $E\{\tilde{\varepsilon}_o\} = 0$ and var $\{\tilde{\varepsilon}_0\} = \sigma_\gamma^2$. An interpretation of this formulation could be that consumers vary in the weight they place on the numeraire good, *z*, relative to the *x*'s; in addition, because of (our) errors of measurement or observation in the attributes of the discrete choices, consumers appear to vary in their preferences for individual *x*'s. I will refer to any RUM model such as (2.40) where the random element enters nonadditively via the slope coefficients as a "random coefficients" model. This type of model was introduced into the MRQR literature by Hausman and Wise (1978).[20]

---

[19] Besides assuming that there are no income effects, Small and Rosen (1981] make two additional assumptions: (1) $\partial v_j / \partial y$ is independent of p_j and q_j and (2) $\partial v_j / \partial q_j \to 0$ as $p_j \to \infty$. It can be shown that (2.21) implies (1) but precludes (2).

[20] It has generally been restricted to probit rather than logit models because the normal distribution is closed under addition, unlike the extreme value distribution. This is less of a consideration if the discrete alternative-specific random terms, $\varepsilon_1, \dots, \varepsilon_N$, are omitted from the model, leaving only the random slope coefficients(s).

Much of the analysis in sections 2.2 and 2.3 carries over to random coefficients models. Given some direct utility function $u(x,q,z,\widetilde{\varepsilon})$, the conditional indirect utility functions are

$$\widetilde{u}_j = u(0,\ldots,0,\overline{x}_j,0,\ldots,0,q,y-p_j\overline{x}_j,\widetilde{\varepsilon}) \equiv v_j(q_j,y-p_j\overline{x}_j,\widetilde{\varepsilon}). \qquad (2.41)$$

The discrete choice indices are

$$\widetilde{\delta}_j = \delta_j(p,q,y,\widetilde{\varepsilon}) = \begin{cases} 1 & \text{if } v_j(q_j,y-p_j\overline{x}_j,\widetilde{\varepsilon}) \geq v_i(q_i,y-p_i\overline{x}_i,\widetilde{\varepsilon}) \ \forall i \\ 0 & \text{otherwise,} \end{cases} \qquad (2.42)$$

and the discrete choice probabilities are

$$\pi_j = \Pr\,\{v_j(q_j,y-p_j\overline{x}_j,\widetilde{\varepsilon}) \geq v_i(q_i,y-p_i\overline{x}_i,\widetilde{\varepsilon}) \text{ all } i\}. \qquad (2.43)$$

Similarly, the unconditional indirect utility function is

$$v(p,q,y,\widetilde{\varepsilon}) = \max\,[v_1(q_1,y-p_1\overline{x}_1,\widetilde{\varepsilon}),\ldots,v_N(q_N,y-p_N\overline{x}_N,\widetilde{\varepsilon})]. \qquad (2.44)$$

Using this function, the welfare measures C^+, C^*, and $C^\bullet$, or E^+, E^*, and $E^\bullet$ can be constructed along the lines indicated above for the additively random utility model.

However, depending on the precise form of the random coefficients specification, some of the relationships among these welfare measures may no longer hold. In particular, it is not necessarily true that $C^+ = C^\bullet$ when there are no income effects. In the case of the model (2.40), the discrete choice probabilities are independent of the consumer's income since they take the form

$$\pi_j = \Pr\,\{h_j(q_j) - \overline{\gamma}\,p_j\overline{x}_j + \widetilde{\omega}_j \geq h_i(q_i) - \overline{\gamma}\,p_i\overline{x}_i + \widetilde{\omega}_i \text{ all } i\} \qquad (2.45)$$

where $\widetilde{\omega}_j \equiv \widetilde{\varepsilon}_j - \widetilde{\varepsilon}_0 p_j\overline{x}_j$, $j = 1,\ldots,N$. But, from (2.40b),

$$\begin{aligned} v(p,q,y,\widetilde{\varepsilon}) &= (\overline{\gamma}+\widetilde{\varepsilon}_0)y \\ &\quad + \max[h_1(q_1) - \overline{\gamma}p_1\overline{x}_1 + \widetilde{\omega}_1,\ldots,h_N(q_N) - \overline{\gamma}p_N\overline{x}_N + \widetilde{\omega}_N] \\ &\equiv (\overline{\gamma}+\widetilde{\varepsilon}_0)y + s(p,q,\widetilde{\omega}); \end{aligned} \qquad (2.46)$$

hence,

$$C^{+} = E\left\{\frac{s(p^{1}, q^{1}, \tilde{\omega}^{1}) - s(p^{0}, q^{0}, \tilde{\omega}^{0})}{\bar{\gamma} + \tilde{\varepsilon}_{0}}\right\} \tag{2.47}$$

while

$$C^{\bullet} = \frac{E\{s(p^{1}, q^{1}, \tilde{\omega}^{1}) - s(p^{0}, q^{0}, \tilde{\omega}^{0})\}}{\bar{\gamma}} \tag{2.48}$$

where $\tilde{\omega}_j^t \equiv \tilde{\varepsilon}_j - \tilde{\varepsilon}_0 p_j^t \bar{x}_j$, $t = 0,1$. Thus, $C^{+} \neq C^{\bullet}$. Similarly, although the relationships in (2.37) and (2.38) still apply to $C^{\bullet}$, the relationship in (2.39) no longer holds. Nevertheless, it still follows from (2.46) that $E^{+} = C^{+}$, $E^{*} = C^{*}$, and $E^{\bullet} = C^{\bullet}$ in the random coefficients, no-income-effects model.

2.4.2 Nonbudget-Constrained and Mixed Discrete/Continuous Choices

The budget-constrained discrete choice RUM model implies that the conditional indirect utility functions have the form given in (2.12′) or (2.41). This imposes substantive restrictions on the manner in which the price and income variables enter the formula for the discrete choice probabilities. However, the literature contains many empirical examples of logit or probit models of consumer choices that violate these restrictions. For example, one finds MRQR models based on conditional indirect utility functions of the form

$$\bar{u}_j = h_j(q_j) - \beta_j p_j + \gamma_j y + \tilde{\varepsilon}_j, \ \beta_j \neq \gamma_j \qquad j = 1, \dots, N \tag{2.49}$$

or

$$\tilde{u}_j = h_j(q_j) - \beta p_j + \gamma y p_j + \tilde{\varepsilon}_j \qquad j = 1, \dots, N, \tag{2.50}$$

which are clearly inconsistent with (2.12′) or (2.41). How can such models occur?

One possible explanation is that the consumer is not actually making a purely discrete choice but rather what might be called a “mixed discrete/continuous” choice. In this case, the utility maximization is *not* constrained by (2.9); instead, the x’s can vary continuously, subject to a nonnegativity constraint. However, there is an element of discreteness in the consumer’s choices which arises either because the x's are mutually exclusive—i.e., the constraint (2.8) applies—or because the consumer's preferences force a corner solution in which some of the x's are not consumed (in effect, the various x's are perfect substitutes). Thus, the consumer faces both a discrete choice—which of the x's to select—and a continuous choice—how much to consume if he selects x_j. The discrete choice may lead to a statistical MRQR model which satisfies (2.5), but the structure of the conditional indirect utility functions is now different; they no longer satisfy (2.12′) or (2.41).

Since these models are described in detail in Hanemann (1984), my discussion here will be brief. They typically involve a random coefficients specification of the utility function rather than the additive formulation in (2.6′). Suppose the consumer has selected good j. Maximization of $u_j(x_j, q_j, z, \tilde{\varepsilon}) \equiv u(0,\ldots,0, x_j, 0,\ldots,0, q, z, \tilde{\varepsilon})$ with respect to x_j (now freely variable) and z subject to a budget constraint, $p_j x_j + z = y$, yields a conditional ordinary demand function $x_j(p_j, q_j, y, \tilde{\varepsilon})$, and a conditional indirect utility function, $v_j(p_j, q_j, y, \tilde{\varepsilon})$. The latter is quasi-convex and decreasing in p_j and increasing in y, but it does not have the same structure as (2.41)—the coefficient of p_j is no longer equal to minus the coefficient of y. Allowing for this difference, the consumer's discrete choice indices are defined as in (2.42), and the discrete choice probabilities are defined as in (2.43). Instead of (2.14′), the unconditional ordinary demand function for the jth good takes the form: $x_j(p, q, y, \tilde{\varepsilon}) = \delta_j(p, q, y, \tilde{\varepsilon})\, x_j(p_j, q_j, y, \tilde{\varepsilon})$. Thus, the probability that one observes an individual who selects, say, the first brand and consumes three units is

$$\begin{aligned} &\Pr\{x_1(p,q,y,\tilde{\varepsilon}) = 3 \text{ and } x_i(p,q,y,\tilde{\varepsilon}) = 0,\ \forall i \geq 2\} \\ &\quad = \Pr\{x_1(p_1,q_1,y,\tilde{\varepsilon}) = 3 \mid v_1(p_1,q_1,y,\tilde{\varepsilon}) \geq v_i(p_i,q_i,y,\tilde{\varepsilon})\ \forall i\} \\ &\quad \times\ \Pr\{v_1(p_1,q_1,y,\tilde{\varepsilon}) \geq v_i(p_i,q_i,y,\tilde{\varepsilon})\ \forall i\}. \end{aligned} \tag{2.51}$$

Substituting the unconditional ordinary demand functions into the direct utility function yields the unconditional direct utility function which also can be defined as in (2.44). From this, the welfare measures C^{+}, C^{*}, and $C^{\bullet}$ can be constructed in the same manner as for purely discrete choices.[21]

Thus, mixed discrete/continuous choices can give rise to formulas for the discrete choice probabilities involving conditional indirect utility functions that violate the restrictions implied in (2.12′) or (2.41)—c.f., the second probability statement on the right-hand side of (2.51). However, precisely because there is

---

[21] An example of an application of welfare analysis in a mixed discrete/continuous choice RUM model is given in Hanemann (1984).

also a continuous choice in these models, it is inefficient to estimate the parameters of the utility model from data on the discrete choices alone: the continuous choices contain information about the individual's preferences that should not be overlooked. Accordingly, if one really is dealing with a mixed discrete/continuous choice, the estimation should be based on (2.51) rather than on (2.41) as in conventional MRQR models. Once the model has been estimated, the three approaches to welfare evaluation described in section 2.3 carry over directly.

Another explanation for MRQR models which violate the restrictions in (2.12′) or (2.41) is that the individual genuinely faces a purely discrete choice but one that is not bound by the budget constraint (2.7). An example where this occurs is discrete choices among actions with uncertain consequences by a von Neumann–Morgenstern expected-utility-maximizing individual. Suppose an individual has wealth y and a utility-of-wealth function whose nonstochastic component is denoted by $\psi(y)$. The individual must choose among N actions whose consequences depend on the state of the world, $s = 1, \ldots, S$. Associated with act j are a vector of state probabilities, $\rho_j = (\rho_{j1}, \ldots, \rho_{jS})$, and a vector of monetary consequences, $z_j = (z_{j1}, \ldots, z_{jS})$. Using an additively random formulation, the individual's utility conditional on the choice of act j is

$$\tilde{u}_j = \sum_s \rho_{js} \, \psi(y + z_{js}) + \tilde{\varepsilon}_j, \tag{2.52}$$

and the discrete choice probabilities are

$$\pi_j = \Pr\{\Sigma \rho_{js} \psi(y + z_{js}) + \tilde{\varepsilon}_j \geq \Sigma \rho_{is} \psi(y + z_{is}) + \tilde{\varepsilon}_i, \ \forall i\} \quad j = 1, \ldots, N, \tag{2.53}$$

which is a statistical MRQR model that differs from (2.12′). Given that the individual has chosen optimally, his utility is $v(\rho, z, y, \tilde{\varepsilon}) \equiv \max[\tilde{u}_1, \ldots, \tilde{u}_N]$. Suppose that the state probabilities and/or payoffs change from (ρ^0, z^0) to (ρ^1, z^1). In order to measure the welfare effects of this change, the quantities C^+, C^*, and $C^\bullet$, or E^+, E^*, and $E^\bullet$ can be constructed from $v(p, z, y, \tilde{\varepsilon})$ along the lines indicated above. For example, $C^+ = E\{\tilde{C}\}$ where $\tilde{C}$ satisfies $v(\rho^1, z^1, y - \tilde{C}, \tilde{\varepsilon}) = v(\rho^0, z^0, y, \tilde{\varepsilon})$ and, similarly, with the other welfare measures.[22]

[22] In Hanemann (1979) this type of discrete choice model is employed to infer the value of life (i.e., the value of changes in mortality probabilities) from data on individual risk-taking behavior.

2.5 APPLICATIONS

In this section I show how one actually computes the welfare measures once the parameters of the RUM model have been estimated. For simplicity, I deal with measures of compensating variation; but, with appropriate changes, everything carries over to measures of equivalent variation. I will concentrate mainly on the calculation of C^+ and C^*: the formulas in Table 2.1 should usually suffice for calculating the expected indirect utility function, $V(\cdot)$, from which $C^\bullet$ can be obtained via (2.27). If there are no income effects, one obtains a closed-form expression for $C^\bullet$ [see (2.38) and (2.48)]. If there are income effects, however, numerical techniques, such as Newton's method, will be required to solve (2.27).[23]

In order to cover both additively random and random coefficient specifications, I write the conditional indirect utility functions as $v_j(p_j, q_j, y, \varepsilon)$, $j = 1, \ldots, N$, where ε is a vector of *all* the random elements in the model, with joint density function $f_\varepsilon(\cdot)$. I focus on the special case where there is a change in the prices and/or quality attributes of only *one* good, say x_1. Furthermore, I assume that the change is unambiguously an improvement, i.e., $\tilde{u}_1^1 \equiv v_1(p_1^1, q_1^1, y, \tilde{\varepsilon}) > \tilde{u}_1^0 \equiv v_1(p_1^0, q_1^0, y, \tilde{\varepsilon})$. In addition to presenting computational formulas, I will develop some bounds on the magnitudes of C^+ and C^* and identify the circumstances in which $C^+ \lesseqgtr C^*$. When there are more complex price/quality changes, the analysis becomes more complicated, but it follows the same basic logic as that presented here.

To simplify the exposition, it is convenient to present the formulas for the case when $N = 3$; however, with appropriate changes everything carries over to the case of an arbitrary $N \geq 2$. Define $\tilde{u}_i \equiv v_i(p_i, q_i, y, \tilde{\varepsilon})$ $i = 2,3$, $\tilde{u}^{0\theta} \equiv \max[\tilde{u}_1^0, \tilde{u}_2, \tilde{u}_3]$, and $\tilde{u}^1 \equiv \max[\tilde{u}_1^1, \tilde{u}_2, \tilde{u}_3]$. The trick in computing C^+ in this case is to recognize that there are five possible events which partition the domain of $f_\varepsilon(\cdot)$ into five disjoint regions. I denote these events (1/1), (2/1), (2/2), (3/1), and (3/3) and the corresponding regions A(1/1), A(2/1), etc. The events are as follows. The event (1/1) is that the individual originally chose good 1; since good 1 improves while there is no change in goods 2 and 3, it follows that he continues to prefer good 1. Another possibility is that the individual originally chose good 2 and, after the change, he either still prefers good 2 (2/2) or switches to good 1 (2/1). The last two events are that the individual originally chose good 3 and either still prefers that good after the change (3/3), or switches to good 1 (3/1). The corresponding regions of ε-space are

---

[23] Some formulas for approximating C^* were presented in Hanemann (1982, 1983).

$$A(1/1) = \{\tilde{\varepsilon} | \tilde{u}_i \leq \tilde{u}_1^0, i = 2,3\}$$
$$A(2/2) = \{\tilde{\varepsilon} | \tilde{u}_1^1 \leq \tilde{u}_2 \text{ and } \tilde{u}_3 \leq \tilde{u}_2\}$$
$$A(2/1) = \{\tilde{\varepsilon} | \tilde{u}_3 \leq \tilde{u}_2 \text{ and } \tilde{u}_1^0 \leq \tilde{u}_2 \leq \tilde{u}_1^1\}$$
$$A(3/3) = \{\tilde{\varepsilon} | \tilde{u}_1^1 \leq \tilde{u}_3 \text{ and } \tilde{u}_2 \leq \tilde{u}_3\}$$
$$A(3/1) = \{\tilde{\varepsilon} | \tilde{u}_2 \leq \tilde{u}_3 \text{ and } \tilde{u}_1^0 \leq \tilde{u}_3 \leq \tilde{u}_1^1\}.$$

The probabilities of the events are

$$\begin{aligned} \Pr\{1/1\} &= \pi_1^0 \\ \Pr\{2/2\} &= \pi_2^1 \\ \Pr\{2/1\} &= \pi_2^0 - \pi_2^1 \\ \Pr\{3/3\} &= \pi_3^1 \\ \Pr\{3/1\} &= \pi_3^0 - \pi_3^1 \end{aligned} \tag{2.54}$$

where π_i^t is the probability that the individual chooses the ith good either before the change ($t = 0$) or after it ($t = 1$).

Observe that, if events (2/2) or (3/3) occur, the individual does *not* gain from the improvement in good 1 because it is still dominated by some other good; if events (1/1), (2/1), or (3/1) occur, he *does* gain, and the improvement in his welfare can be measured in money by the quantities $\tilde{C}(1/1)$, $\tilde{C}(2/1)$, or $\tilde{C}(3/1)$ where

$$v_1[p_1^1, q_1^1, y - \tilde{C}(1/1), \tilde{\varepsilon}] = \tilde{u}_1^0 \tag{2.55a}$$

$$v_1[p_1^1, q_1^1, y - \tilde{C}(2/1), \tilde{\varepsilon}] = \tilde{u}_2 \tag{2.55b}$$

$$v_1[p_1^1, q_1^1, y - \tilde{C}(3/1), \tilde{\varepsilon}] = \tilde{u}_3\,. \tag{2.55c}$$

Thus, the compensation $\tilde{C}$ defined in (2.25) is given by

$$\tilde{C} = \begin{cases} 0 & \text{if } \tilde{\varepsilon} \in A(2/2) \text{ or } \tilde{\varepsilon} \in A(3/3) \\ \tilde{C}(1/1) & \text{if } \tilde{\varepsilon} \in A(1/1) \\ \tilde{C}(2/1) & \text{if } \tilde{\varepsilon} \in A(2/1) \\ \tilde{C}(3/1) & \text{if } \tilde{\varepsilon} \in A(3/1). \end{cases} \tag{2.56}$$

Hence

$$C^{+} = \int_{A(1/1)} \widetilde{C}(1/1) f_{\varepsilon}(\varepsilon)d\varepsilon + \int_{A(2/1)} \widetilde{C}(2/1) f_{\varepsilon}(e)d\varepsilon + \int_{A(3/1)} \widetilde{C}(3/1) f_{\varepsilon}(\varepsilon)d\varepsilon. \quad (2.57)$$

By virtue of the assumption that the change in (p_1, q_1) is unambiguously an improvement,

$$\widetilde{C}(1/1) > 0. \quad (2.58)$$

When the event (2/1) occurs, since $\widetilde{u}_1^0 \le \widetilde{u}_2 \le \widetilde{u}_1^1$, from (2.55) one has

$$v_1[p_1^1, q_1^1, y - \widetilde{C}(1/1), \widetilde{\varepsilon}] \le v_1[p_1^1, q_1^1, y - \widetilde{C}(2/1), \widetilde{\varepsilon}] \le v_1(p_1^1, q_1^1, y, \widetilde{\varepsilon}).$$

Because $v_1(\cdot)$ is increasing in y, this implies that, over the region where $\widetilde{C} = \widetilde{C}(2/1)$, $0 \le \widetilde{C}(2/1) \le \widetilde{C}(1/1)$. Similarly, over the region where $\widetilde{C} = \widetilde{C}(3/1)$, $0 \le \widetilde{C}(3/1) \le \widetilde{C}(1/1)$. Hence, from (2.56),

$$0 \le \widetilde{C} \le \widetilde{C}(1/1). \quad (2.59)$$

Since $\widetilde{C} > 0$ with positive probability (as long as $\pi_1^0 > 0$), and also $\pi_j = \exp(W_j\beta_j)G_j[\exp(W_1\beta_1), \ldots, \exp(W_N\beta_N)]G[\exp(W_1\beta_1), \ldots, \exp(W_N\beta_N)]^{-1}$ with positive probability (as long as $\pi_2^1 + \pi_3^1 > 0$), it may be deduced that

$$0 < C^{+} \equiv E\{\widetilde{C}\} < E\{\widetilde{C}(1/1)\}. \quad (2.60)$$

What about the welfare measure C^*? It follows from (2.26), (2.54), and (2.56) that if $\pi_2^1 + \pi_3^1 = (1 - \pi_1^1) \ge 0.5$, i.e., if $\pi_1^1 \le 0.5$, then $C^* = 0$. If $\pi_1^1 > 0.5$, C^* can be determined in the following manner. Given any constant C^*, define $\widetilde{u}_1^*(C) \equiv v_1(p_1^1, q_1^1, y - C, \widetilde{\varepsilon})$, $\widetilde{u}_i^*(C) \equiv v_i(p_i, q_i, y - C, \widetilde{\varepsilon})$, i=2,3, and $\pi^*(C) \equiv \Pr\{\widetilde{u}^*(C) \ge \widetilde{u}^0\}$. Then, the welfare measure C^* solves

$$\begin{aligned} 0.5 = \pi^*(C^*) \\ &= \Pr\{\widetilde{u}^*(C^*) \ge \widetilde{u}^0 \text{ and } \widetilde{u}_1^*(C^*) \ge \widetilde{u}_1^0\} \\ &= \Pr\{\widetilde{u}_2 \le \widetilde{u}_1^0, \widetilde{u}_3 \le \widetilde{u}_1^0 \text{ and } \widetilde{u}_1^0 \le \widetilde{u}_1^*(C^*)\} \\ &\quad + \Pr\{\widetilde{u}_3 \le \widetilde{u}_2 \text{ and } \widetilde{u}_1^0 \le \widetilde{u}_2 \le \widetilde{u}_1^*(C^*)\} \\ &\quad + \Pr\{\widetilde{u}_2 \le \widetilde{u}_3 \text{ and } \widetilde{u}_1^0 \le \widetilde{u}_3 \le \widetilde{u}_1^*(C^*)\}. \end{aligned} \quad (2.61)$$

These results apply to *any* RUM model. They can be sharpened somewhat if one focuses specifically on additively random models in which $v_j(p_j, q_j, y, \tilde{\varepsilon}) = v_j(p_j, q_j, y) + \tilde{\varepsilon}_j, \quad j = 1, 2, 3.$

In that case (2.55a) becomes $v_1[p_1^1, q_1^1, y - \tilde{C}(1/1)] + \tilde{\varepsilon}_1 = v_1(p_1^0, q_1^0, y) + \tilde{\varepsilon}_1$, or, canceling out $\tilde{\varepsilon}_1$, $v_1[p_1^1, q_1^1, y - C(1/1)] = v_1(p_1^0, q_1^0\ y)$, i.e., $C(1/1)$ is nonstochastic.[24] Accordingly (2.57) becomes

$$C^+ = C(1/1)\pi_1^0 + \int_{A(2/1)} \tilde{C}(2/1) f_\varepsilon(\varepsilon) d\varepsilon + \int_{A(3/1)} \tilde{C}(3/1) f_\varepsilon(\varepsilon) d\varepsilon. \qquad (2.57')$$

Now, the quantity $C(1/1)$ is the compensation measure that one might calculate if he disregarded the random elements in the utility function. For example, Feenberg and Mills [1980] used $C(1/1)$ to measure the benefits from an improvement in the quality of a site after they estimated an additively random logit model of discrete choices among recreation sites. If one knew for sure that an individual would select good 1, then $C(1/1)$ would indeed be the appropriate welfare measure. In the random utility context, however, two adjustments must be made: $C(1/1)$ must be multiplied by $\pi_1^0 < 1$, and the other terms on the right-hand side of (5.57′) must be added which measure the gain to the individual if he originally selected some other good and then switched to good 1. The net effect is that $C(1/1)$ *overestimates* the value of C^+ since, with $C(1/1)$ nonstochastic, (2.60) yields[25]

$$0 < C^+ < C(1/1). \qquad (2.60')$$

As for C^+, it was already noted that, if $\pi_1^1 \le 0.5$, $C^* = 0$. Similarly, from (2.55) and (2.56), if $\pi_1^0 \ge 0.5$, then $C^+ = C(1/1)$. If $\pi_1^0 < 0.5 < \pi_1^1$, C^+ can be obtained by solving (2.61) which, in this case, may be simplified to

$$\begin{aligned} 0.5 &= \pi^*(C^*) \\ &= \Pr\{\tilde{u}_2 \le \tilde{u}_1^0 \text{ and } \tilde{u}_3 \le \tilde{u}_1^0\} + \Pr\{\tilde{u}_3 \le \tilde{u}_2 \text{ and } \tilde{u}_1^0 \le \tilde{u}_2 \le \tilde{u}_1^*(C^*)\} \\ &\quad + \Pr\{\tilde{u}_2 \le \tilde{u}_3 \text{ and } \tilde{u}_1^0 \le \tilde{u}_3 \le \tilde{u}_1^*(C^*)\} \\ &= \pi_1^0 + (\pi_2^0 - \pi_2^*) + (\pi_3^0 - \pi_3^*) \\ &= 1 - (\pi_2^* + \pi_3^*) \\ &= \pi_1^* \end{aligned} \qquad (2.61')$$

---

[24] Equivalently, $C(1/1)$ satisfies $E\{v_1[p_1^1, q_1^1, y - C(1/1)] + \tilde{\varepsilon}_1\} = E\{v_1[p_1^0, q_1^0, y] + \tilde{\varepsilon}_1\}$.

[25] A similar conclusion is reached in Hanemann (1983) where Feenberg and Mills' (1980) welfare measure is compared with C^+.

where

$$\pi_1^* \equiv \Pr\left\{\tilde{u}_2 \leq \tilde{u}_1^*\left(C^*\right) \text{ and } \tilde{u}_3 \leq \tilde{u}_1^*\left(C^*\right)\right\},$$

$$\pi_2^* \equiv \Pr\left\{\tilde{u}_1^*\left(C^*\right) \leq \tilde{u}_2 \text{ and } \tilde{u}_3 \leq \tilde{u}_2\right\}, \text{ and}$$

$$\pi_3^* \equiv \Pr\left\{\tilde{u}_1^*\left(C^*\right) \leq \tilde{u}_3 \text{ and } \tilde{u}_2 \leq u_3\right\}.$$

As an illustration, consider the additively random model derived from the conditional indirect utility functions

$$\tilde{u}_j = \psi_j(p_j, q_j) + \gamma_j(p_j, q_j)\, y + \tilde{\varepsilon}_j \equiv v_j + \tilde{\varepsilon}_j \qquad j = 1, 2, 3, \qquad (2.62)$$

where $\gamma_j(\cdot) > 0$, which is a generalization of (2.49) and (2.50). Applying (2.55a–c), one obtains

$$C(1/1) = \frac{[\psi_1^1 - \psi_1^0 + y(\gamma_1^1 - \gamma_1^0)]}{\gamma_1^1} \equiv \frac{v_1^1 - v_1^0}{\gamma_1^1} \qquad (2.63a)$$

$$\tilde{C}(2/1) = \frac{[\psi_1^1 - \psi_2 + y(\gamma_1^1 - \gamma_2) + \tilde{\varepsilon}_1 - \tilde{\varepsilon}_2]}{\gamma_1^1} \equiv \frac{v_1^1 - v_2 + \tilde{\varepsilon}_1 - \tilde{\varepsilon}_2}{\gamma_1^1} \qquad (2.63b)$$

$$\tilde{C}(3/1) = \frac{[\psi_1^1 - \psi_3 + y(\gamma_1^1 - \gamma_3) + \tilde{\varepsilon}_1 - \tilde{\varepsilon}_3]}{\gamma_1^1} = \frac{v_1^1 - v_3 + \tilde{\varepsilon}_1 - \tilde{\varepsilon}_3}{\gamma_1^1} \qquad (2.63c)$$

where $\psi_1^t \equiv \psi_1(p_1^t, q_1^t), \gamma_1^t \equiv \gamma_1(p_1^t, q_1^t)$, and $v_1^t \equiv \psi_1^t + \gamma_1^t\, y$, $t = 0, 1$. By assumption, $v_1^1 > v_1^0$. Then, C^+ is given by (2.57') where, for $i = 2, 3$,

$$\int_{A(i/1)} \tilde{C}(i/1) f(\varepsilon) d\varepsilon = \left(\frac{v_1^1 - v_i}{\gamma_1^1}\right)\left(\pi_i^0 - \pi_i^1\right) + \int_{v_i - v_1^1}^{v_i - v_1^0} \int_{-\infty}^{v_i - v_j} \frac{\eta_1}{\gamma_1^1} f_\eta(\eta_1, \eta_2) d\eta_1 d\eta_2 \quad (2.64)$$

where $\tilde{\eta}_1 \equiv \tilde{\varepsilon}_1 - \tilde{\varepsilon}_i, \tilde{\eta}_2 \equiv \tilde{\varepsilon}_j - \tilde{\varepsilon}_i, j \neq 1, j \neq i$, and $f_\eta(\cdot)$ is the bivariate density of $(\tilde{\eta}_1, \tilde{\eta}_2)$. Similarly, assuming that $\pi_1^0 < 0.5 < \pi_1^1$, C^* solves

$$0.5 = \int_{-\infty}^{\infty} \int_{-\infty}^{v_1^1 - \gamma_1^1 C^* - v_2 + \varepsilon_1} \int_{-\infty}^{v_1^1 - \gamma_1^1 C^* - v_3 + \varepsilon_1} f(\varepsilon_1, \varepsilon_2, \varepsilon_3)\, d\varepsilon_1\, d\varepsilon_2\, d\varepsilon_3. \tag{2.65}$$

Suppose, specifically, that $f_\varepsilon(\cdot)$ is the extreme value density, so that this is a standard logit model. The integral in (2.64) can readily be evaluated and, on substituting into (2.57′) and simplifying, one obtains

$$C^+ = \frac{1}{\gamma_1^1} \ln\left(\frac{e^{v_1^1} + e^{v_2} + e^{v_3}}{e^{v_1^0} + e^{v_2} + e^{v_3}} \right). \tag{2.66}$$

The corresponding forumula for C^* is

$$C^* = \begin{cases} 0 & \text{if } v_1^1 \le \ln[\exp(v_2) + \exp(v_3)] \\ \dfrac{v_1^1 - \ln[\exp(v_2) + \exp(v_3)]}{\gamma_1^1} & \text{if } v_1^0 \le \ln[\exp(v_2) + \exp(v_3)] \le v_1^1 \\ \dfrac{(v_1^1 - v_1^0)}{\gamma_1^1} & \text{if } v_1^0 \ge \ln[\exp(v_2) + \exp(v_3)] \end{cases} \tag{2.67}$$

Hence,

$$C^* \gtrless C^+ \text{ as } \frac{v_1^1 + v_1^0}{2} \gtrless \ln[\exp(v_2) + \exp(v_3)]. \tag{2.68}$$

Observe from (2.66) that C^* satisfies

$$\ln[\exp(v_1^1 - \gamma_1^1 C^+) + \exp(v_2 - \gamma_1^1 C^+) + \exp(v_3 - \gamma_1^1 C^+)] = \ln[\exp(v_1^0) + \exp(v_2) + \exp(v_3)]. \tag{2.69}$$

By contrast, using (2.27) and the formula in Table 2.1, the welfare measure $C^\bullet$ satisfies

$$\ln[\exp(v_1^1 - \gamma_1^1 C^\bullet) + \exp(v_2 - \gamma_1^1 C^\bullet) + \exp(v_3 - \gamma_1^1 C^\bullet)] = \ln[\exp(v_1^0) + \exp(v_2) + \exp(v_3)]. \tag{2.70}$$

Table 2.1 Formulas for $V \equiv \mathrm{E}\{\max[v_1 + \tilde{\varepsilon}_1, \ldots, v_N + \tilde{\varepsilon}_N]\}$

1. Generalized extreme value

$$F_\varepsilon(\varepsilon_1, \ldots, \varepsilon_N) = \exp\{-G[\exp(-\varepsilon_1), \ldots, \exp(-\varepsilon_N)]\}$$

$$V = \ln\{G[\exp(v_1), \ldots, \exp(v_N)]\} + 0.57722$$

2. Independent logit

$$F_\varepsilon(\varepsilon_1, \ldots, \varepsilon_N) = \exp[-\Sigma \exp(-\varepsilon_j)]$$

$$V = \ln \Sigma \exp(v_j) + 0.57722$$

3. Probit[a]

$$F_\varepsilon(\varepsilon_1, \ldots, \varepsilon_N) = N(0, \Sigma), \quad \Sigma = \{\sigma_{ij}^2\}$$

a. Binary probit, $N = 2$

$$V_2 = (v_1 - v_2)\Phi\left(\frac{v_1 - v_2}{\kappa_2}\right) + v_2 + \kappa_2 \phi\left(\frac{v_1 - v_2}{\kappa_2}\right),$$

$$\kappa_2 \equiv \left(\sigma_{11}^2 + \sigma_{22}^2 - 2\sigma_{12}^2\right)^{1/2}$$

b. Trichotomous probit, $N = 3$[b]

$$V_3 \approx (V_2 - v_3)\,\Phi\left(\frac{V_2 - v_3}{\kappa_3}\right) + v_3 + \kappa_3\,\phi\left(\frac{V_2 - v_3}{\kappa_3}\right)$$

$$\kappa_3 \equiv \left(\sigma_{33}^2 + S_2^2 - 2S_{2,3}^2\right)^{1/2}$$

$$S_{2,3}^2 \equiv \sigma_{23}^2 + \left(\sigma_{13}^2 - \sigma_{23}^2\right)\,\Phi\left(\frac{v_1 - v_2}{\kappa_2}\right)$$

$$S_2^2 \equiv v_2^2 + \sigma_{22}^2 + \left(v_1^2 + \sigma_{11}^2 - v_2 - \sigma_{22}^2\right)\Phi\left(\frac{v_1 - v_2}{\kappa_2}\right)$$
$$+ (v_1 + v_2)\kappa_2\left(\frac{v_1 - v_2}{\kappa_2}\right) - V_2^2$$

[a] ϕ and Φ are, respectively, the standard univariate normal probability density function (p.d.f.) and cumulative distribution function (c.d.f.).

[b] Using Clark's (1961) approximation.

Table 2.2 Welfare Calculations for the Logit Model (2.62)

Case	π_j^0	π_1^1	$C(1/1)$	C^*	C^+	$C^\bullet$	$\pi_1^0 \cdot C(1/1)$
i	0.06338	0.33333	2	0	0.33999	0.35018	0.12676
ii	0,33333	0.78699	2	1.31	1.14093	1.17827	0.66667
iii	0.78699	0.96466	2	2	1.79643	1.81183	1.57397

Thus, $C^{\bullet} < C^{+}$ if $\gamma_1^1 < \min(\gamma_2, \gamma_3)$, and $C^{\bullet} > C^{+}$ if $\gamma_1^1 > \max(\gamma_2, \gamma_3)$, while $C^{\bullet} = C^{+}$ if $\gamma_1^1 = \gamma_2 = \gamma_3$; the last case corresponds to the no-income effects utility model (2.21).

In order to get a feel for these formulas, it may be helpful to resort to a numerical example. Suppose that $v_2 = v_3 = 0$, $\gamma_1^1 = 1, \gamma_2 = 0.5$, and $\gamma_3 = 1.5$. I consider three sets of values for v_1^0 and v_1^1: (i) $v_1^0 = -2$, $v_1^1 = 0$; (ii) $v_1^0 = 0$, (iii) $v_1^1 = 2$, $v_1^0 = 2$, $v_1^1 = 4$. Thus, in each case $C(1/1) = 2$. In the first case, $\pi_1^1 < 0.5$ so that $C^* = 0$, while in the third case $\pi_1^o > 0.5$, so that $C^* = C(1/1)$. The corresponding values of C^{+} and $C^{\bullet}$ are presented in Table 2.2. It will be seen that C^{+} and $C^{\bullet}$ are close in value but they both differ from C^*. As one would expect, in the first two cases the quantity $C(1/1)$ significantly over-estimates all three welfare measures. The last column in the table gives the value of $\pi_1^0 \cdot C(1/1)$, the first term in the formula for C^{+} (2.57′). It can be seen that this yields a very crude approximation of the value of C^{+}, the quality of the approximation becoming worse as π_1^0 gets lower.

To what extent can these formulas be generalized? If $N > 3$ in the logit model (2.62), the term $\left[\exp(v_2) + \exp(v_3)\right]$ in (2.66)–(2.70) is replaced by

$$\sum_{j=2}^{N} \exp(v_j).$$

This is when the change is restricted to good 1. When one is dealing with a more complex change, the formulas are different but they can readily be developed by following the steps that lead to (2.66)–(2.70). For example, if there is an improvement in good 1 combined with a deterioration in good 2, there are now *six* possible events which partition $\tilde{\varepsilon}$ – space—(1/1), (2/2), (2/1), (3/3), (3/1), and (2/3)—and

$$\tilde{C} \begin{cases} < 0 & \text{if } \tilde{\varepsilon} \in A(2/2) \\ = 0 & \text{if } \tilde{\varepsilon} \in A(3/3) \\ > 0 & \text{otherwise.} \end{cases}$$

Alternatively, suppose the only change is in good 1 and the utility function is given by (2.62), but this is now a GEV (generalized logit) or multivariate probit model. In the GEV case, the appropriate formulas are a straightforward extension of (2.66)–(2.70). In the probit case, however, numerical techniques would be required to evaluate the integrals in the formulas for C^{+} and C^*, (2.64) and (2.65). If the RUM model is additively random but *not* linear in *y*, unlike (2.62), this affects the formulas for $\tilde{C}(1/1)$, $\tilde{C}(2/1)$, and $\tilde{C}(3/1)$ in (2.63) as well as

(2.64) and (2.65). Finally, if the RUM model is not additively random, one has to work directly with (2.55), (2.57), and (2.61), and numerical evaluation may well be required.

APPENDIX: PROOF OF PROPOSITION

Here I prove that the consumer's preferences have the form given in (2.21a) if the switch prices $\tilde{p}_1^*$ in (2.22) and $\tilde{p}_1^{**}$ in (2.23) coincide. With no loss of generality, I shall assume that $N = 2$ and $\bar{x}_1 = \bar{x}_2 = 1$. The switch price $\tilde{p}_1 = p_1^*(p_2, q_1, q_2, y, \tilde{\varepsilon})$ is defined implicitly by

$$u(1, 0, q_1, q_2, y - \tilde{p}_1^*) + \tilde{\varepsilon}_1 = u(0, 1, q_1, q_2, y - p_2) + \tilde{\varepsilon}_2. \qquad \text{(A.1)}$$

Suppose that the actual price of good 1 is p_1^0. By virtue of (A.1), one can write

$$\tilde{p}_1^* = p_1^0 - \tilde{A}^*, \qquad \text{(A.2)}$$

where $\tilde{A}^*$ is defined by

$$u(1, 0, q_1, q_2, y - p_1^0 + \tilde{A}^*) + \tilde{\varepsilon}_1 = u(0, 1, q_1, q_2, y - p_2) + \tilde{\varepsilon}_2. \qquad \text{(A.3)}$$

The switch price $\tilde{p}_1^{**} = p_1^{**}(p_2, q_1, q_2, \tilde{u}, \tilde{\varepsilon})$ is defined by

$$g_1(q_1, \tilde{u}^0 - \tilde{\varepsilon}_1) + \tilde{p}_1^{**} = g_2(q_2, \tilde{u}^0 - \tilde{\varepsilon}_2) + p_2 \qquad \text{(A.4)}$$

or

$$\tilde{p}_1^{**} = p_2 + u^{-1}(\tilde{u}^0 - \tilde{\varepsilon}_2 | 0, 1, q_1, q_2) - u^{-1}(\tilde{u}^0 - \tilde{\varepsilon}_1 | 1, 0, q_1, q_2), \qquad \text{(A.5)}$$

where $u^{-1}(u | x_1, x_2, q_1, q_2)$ is the inverse of $u(x_1, x_2, q_1, q_2, z)$ with respect to its last argument.

Observe that $\tilde{p}_1^* = \tilde{p}_1^{**}$ trivially when $p_1^0 \geq \tilde{p}_1^*$; then $x_1 = 0$ from (2.22), $\tilde{u}^0 = u(0, 1, q_1, q_2, y - p_2) + \tilde{\varepsilon}_2$, and so

$$u^{-1}(\tilde{u}^0 - \tilde{\varepsilon}_2 | 0, 1, q_1, q_2) = y - p_2. \qquad \text{(A.6)}$$

Substituting this into (A.5) yields

$$\tilde{p}_1^{**} = y - u^{-1}(\tilde{u}^0 - \tilde{\varepsilon}_1 | 1, 0, q_1, q_2). \tag{A.7}$$

The last two equations together imply

$$u(1, 0, q_1, q_2, y - \tilde{p}_1^{**}) + \tilde{\varepsilon}_1 = u(0, 1, q_1, q_2, y - p_2) + \tilde{\varepsilon}_2, \tag{A.8}$$

and a comparison with (A.1) shows that $\tilde{p}_1^* = \tilde{p}_1^{**}$.

Accordingly, I focus on the nontrivial case where $p_1^0 < \tilde{p}_1^*$. In this case, $\tilde{u}^o = u(1, 0, q_1, q_2, y - p_1^o) + \tilde{\varepsilon}_1$ and, in general, $\tilde{p}_1^* \neq \tilde{p}_1^{**}$. Since

$$u^{-1}(\tilde{u}^0 - \tilde{\varepsilon}_1 | 1, 0, q_1, q_2) = y - p_1^0, \tag{A.9}$$

(A.5) may be written as

$$\tilde{p}_1^{**} = p_1^0 - \tilde{A}^{**}, \tag{A.10}$$

where

$$\tilde{A}^{**} \equiv y - p_2 - u^{-1}(\tilde{u}^0 - \tilde{\varepsilon}_2 \big| 0, 1, q_1, q_2). \tag{A.11}$$

It follows from (A.2) and (A.10) that $\tilde{p}_1^* = \tilde{p}_1^{**}$ iff $\tilde{A}^* = \tilde{A}^{**}$. However, (A.1) implies that

$$u(1, 0, q_1, q_2, y - p_1^o) + \tilde{\varepsilon}_1 = u(0, 1, q_1, q_2, y - p_2 + \tilde{A}^{**}) + \tilde{\varepsilon}_2. \tag{A.12}$$

From (A.3) and (A.12), $\tilde{A}^* = \tilde{A}^{**}$ independently of $(p_1^0, p_2, q_1, q_2, y)$ if and only if the utility function has the quasilinear form given in (2.21a).

REFERENCES

Aitchison, J. and Bennett, J. (1970), "Polychotomous Quantal Response by Maximal Indicant," *Biometrika*, 57, pp. 253–62.

Amemiya, T. (1981), "Qualitative Response Models: A Survey." *Journal of Economic Literature*, 19, pp. 1483–536.

Clark, C.E. (1961), "The Greatest of Finite Set of Random Variables," *Operation Research*, 9, 145–62.

Daganzo, C. (1979), *Multinomial Probit*. New York: Academic Press.

Daly, A. and Zachary, S. (1978), "Improved Multiple Choice Models." In *Determinants of Travel Choice*, ed. by D.A. Hensher and M.Q. Dalvi. Farnborough, England: Saxon House.

Domenich, T.A. and McFadden, D. (1975), *Urban Travel Demand: A Behavioral Analysis*. Amsterdam: North-Holland.

Dubin, J.A. and McFadden, D.L. (1984), "An Econometric Analysis of Residential Electric Appliance Holdings and Consumption," *Econometrica*, 52, No. 2, pp. 345–62.

Feenberg, D. and Mills, E.S. (1980), *Measuring the Benefits of Water Pollution Abatement*. New York: Academic Press.

Hanemann, W.M. (1979), "The Value of Lifesaving Reconsidered." University of California, Agricultural and Resource Economics, Giannini Foundation Working paper no. 113, August.

Hanemann, W.M. (1982), "Applied Welfare Analysis with Qualitative Response Models," University of California, Agricultural and Resource Economics, Giannini Foundation Working paper no. 241.

Hanemann, W.M. (1983), "Marginal Welfare Measures for Discrete Choice Models." *Economics Letters*, 13, pp. 129–36.

Hanemann, W.M. (1984), "Discrete/Continuous Models of Consumer Demand." *Econometrica*, Vol. 52, pp. 541–61.

Hanemann, W.M. (1985), "Welfare Analysis with Discrete Choice Models," University of California, Agricultural and Resource Economics, Giannini Foundation Working paper.

Hausman, J.A. and Wise, D.A. (1978), "A Conditional Probit Model for Qualitative Choice: Discrete Decisions Recognizing Interdependence and Heterogeneous Preferences." *Econometrica*, 14, pp. 403–26.

Katzner, D.W. (1970), *Static Demand Theory*. New York: Macmillan.

Mäler, K. (1974), *Environmental Economics*. Baltimore: Johns Hopkins University Press.

McFadden, D. (1974), "Conditional Logit Analysis of Qualitative Choice Behavior." In *Frontiers of Econometrics*, ed. by P. Zarembka. New York: Academic Press.

McFadden, D. (1978), "Modelling the Choice of Residential Location." In *Spatial Interaction Theory and Planning Models*, ed. by A. Karlquist, L. Lundquist, F. Snickars, and J.L. Weibull. Amsterdam: North-Holland.

McFadden, D. (1981), "Econometric Models of Probabilistic Choice." In *Structural Analysis of Discrete Data,* ed. by C.F. Manski and D. McFadden. Cambridge, MA: MIT Press.

Sheffi, Y. and Daganzo, C.F. (1978), "Another Paradox of Traffic Flow," *Transportation Research*, 12, pp. 43–46.

Small, K.A. and Rosen, H.S. (1981), "Applied Welfare Economics with Discrete Choice Models." *Econometrica*, 49, pp. 105–30.

Williams, H. (1977), "On the Formation of Travel Demand Models and Economic Evaluation Measures of User Benefit." *Environment and Planning*, 9, pp.285–344.

3. TWO RUMs unCLOAKED: Nested-Logit Models of Site Choice and Nested-Logit Models of Participation and Site Choice[1]

Edward R. Morey[2]

3.1 INTRODUCTION

Policy analysts often require the consumer's surplus associated with a change in the costs or characteristics of a group of consumption activities. The consumer's choice of consumption activity generally involves two simultaneous decisions: whether to participate in a given class of activities and, if so, which alternative to choose from that class. For example, one simultaneously decides both whether to participate in a given class of site-specific recreational activities and, if so, which site to visit. Joint decisions of this type can be modeled in either a multinomial logit (ML) framework or a nested-logit (NL) framework.[3]

Use of the NL model, in contrast to the ML model, is increasingly advocated, particularly when the intent is to model simultaneously both the decision to participate and the choice of site.[4] The argument is that the Independence of Irrelevant Alternatives (IIA) assumption, implicit in the ML model, although often reasonable when all the alternatives are recreational sites of a particular

[1] "Thanks" George, Trudy, Cathy, Sally, Michael, Michael, Joe, Dan, Ray, Bill, Don, Karen, Alpna, Miles, Chris, and Maggie, who snored at my feet.

[2] Department of Economics, Campus Box 256, University of Colorado, Boulder, Colorado 80309-0256, Edward. Morey@Colorado.edu, <http://spot.Colorado.edu/~morey/index.html

[3] Joint decisions of this type can also be modeled in other frameworks, but these other frameworks are not the topic of this paper.

[4] See Bockstael *et al.* (1986, 1987 and 1991), Carson *et al.* (1987), Morey *et al.* (1993, 1995 and 1998a), Kling and Thomson (1996), and Hoehn *et al.* (1996). Additional examples of discrete-choice models of recreational demand between 1988 and 1997 are Bockstael *et al.* (1989), Creel and Loomis (1992), Jones and Sung (1992), Hausman *et al.* (1995), Milon (1988), Morey *et al.* (1991), Parsons and Kealy (1992 and 1995), and Parsons and Needleman (1992). Earlier examples are Caulkins *et al.* (1986), Feenburg and Mills (1980), Hanemann (1978), and Morey (1981)

type, can be unreasonable when the sites differ by type or one of the alternatives is nonparticipation. Participation and site choice should therefore be modeled as a two or more stage nested decision that does not impose IIA a priori across all pairs of alternatives. For example, stage one models the participation decision, and stage two models the choice of site given participation. The individual makes the participation and site choice decisions simultaneously. It is common, but unnecessary, to assume that NL models require a sequential decision process.

The intent of this monograph is to lay out in a simple fashion the NL model and then provide rigorous, but straightforward, derivations of its properties.[5] My motivation for creation of this monograph was to increase my own understanding and experience the pleasures inherent in that process.

Section 3.2 derives the probability of choosing an alternative, and then uses it to form some sample-specific likelihood functions. Section 3.3 interprets the parameters in the NL model as they relate to unobserved attributes of the alternatives, and the dependence, or independence, of the random components of utility. In this framework, the IIA assumption is discussed. This section also identifies and discusses special cases of NL. Section 3.4 advocates Full Information Maximum Likelihood (FIML) estimation. Section 3.5 derives expected maximum utility, Section 3.6 discusses budget exhaustion and the other required regularity conditions for conditional indirect utility functions, Section 3.7 derives compensating and equivalent variations, and Section 3.8 expands the nest to three levels. *Example Boxes* are used throughout to link the theory to the application of recreation demand and benefit estimation. *Diversion Boxes* are footnotes that have outgrown the genre.

3.2 THE TWO-LEVEL NL MODEL OF RECREATIONAL DEMAND: ITS CDF, PROBABILITIES, AND LIKELIHOOD FUNCTION

The intent of this section is to use the basics of probability theory to derive the probability of choosing each alternative from the assumptions that form the basis of the two-level NL model of consumer demand. Once derived, these probability equations can be used to form likelihood functions, the specific form of which depends on the properties of one's sample.

The two-level NL model is designed to explain an individual's choice of alternative when there is a two-dimensional choice set from which the individual

---

[5] Those familiar with the 1994 version of this paper will find a few corrections, many more references, and much more elaboration, particularly with respect to the extreme value distribution, regularity conditions, parameter estimation, and consumer's surplus estimation.

must choose one of C distinct alternatives, where one of the dimensions of the choice set can be characterized in terms of M distinct types, and the other dimension in terms of J distinct types: $C \leq M \times J$. The individual chooses an alternative, *ni*, where $n \in M$ and $i \in J$, subject to the restriction that their choice of type in terms of the *J*th dimension is consistent with their choice of type in terms of the *M*th dimension. Without loss of generality, nest the two dimensions such that if the individual chooses an alternative of type $n \in M$, then the individual's choice of alternative in the J dimension is restricted to a subset of the J types. This subset has J_n elements where J_m is the number of J types consistent with a choice of type $m \in M$.

Examples: Consider two different two-dimensional models of recreational demand: a model of participation and site choice, and a model of site choice only, but where the sites are of three distinct types.

A model of participation and site choice: Consider a choice set with C=10 alternatives: visiting one of eight fishing sites, staying at home, and going bowling and all other activities. In this case, one might assume M has two elements; 1=fishing and 2=not fishing; J_1=8 (the number of sites) and J_2=2 (staying home, bowling and all other nonfishing activities).

A model of site choice with saltwater sites, lakes, and rivers: Consider a choice set with C=12 alternatives: three saltwater sites, four lakes, and five rivers. In this case, one might assume that M has three elements; 1= saltwater fishing, 2=lake fishing; and 3=river fishing; J_1=3, J_2=4, and J_3=5.

NL models assume the utility the individual receives if he chooses alternative *mj* is

$$U_{mj} = V_{mj} + \varepsilon_{mj} \quad \forall\ (mj) \in C \qquad (3.1)$$

where V_{mj} is the systematic component of utility and ε_{mj} is a random component.[6] Both terms are known to the individual, but the ε_{mj} are unobserved by the researcher, and so they are random variables from the researcher's perspective. Choice is therefore completely deterministic from the individual's perspective; simply put, each time a choice is made, the individual chooses the alternative that provides the most utility.

---

[6] Two things should be noted about Equation (3.1). First, it is quite general in that it requires only that V_{mj} exist; that is, the variables that determine V_{mj} are separable from ε_{mj}. Second, there are discrete-choice models that fulfill Equation (3.1) that are not NL models, e.g., multivariate Probit models.

Consider, in general, the change in utility and choice resulting from a change in the vector of $\langle V_{mj} \rangle$. Given optimal choice in the new state, the choice in the initial state minimizes the utility change resulting from the change in $\langle V_{mj} \rangle$. If it did not, that alternative would not be maximizing utility in the initial state. But, given optimal choice in the initial state, the choice in the new state maximizes (minimizes) the utility change if the new $\langle V_{mj} \rangle$ is an improvement (deterioration). One maximizes potential gains and minimizes potential losses. Consider an example: alternative 1, 2, and 3 have utility of 5, 10 and 15 in the initial state and 20, 10 and 15 in the new state. The individual will switch from alternative 3 to 1, and the change in maximum utility is 5. Five is the maximum utility gain given that alternative 3 was initially chosen, and the minimum utility gain given that alternative 1 is chosen in the new state. A change in V_{mj}, $\langle V_{mj} \rangle$, might or might not lead to the choice of a different alternative. For example, a decrease in V_{lk} will not result in a different choice if the individual is not currently choosing alternative *lk*, and might not even if he or she is.

Alternatively, the researcher cannot say with certainty which alternative an individual will choose; rather, he or she can merely determine the probability that the individual will choose a particular alternative. Let $\langle \varepsilon_{mj} \rangle$ denote the vector of these *C* random terms; that is

$$\langle \varepsilon_{mj} \rangle = \{\varepsilon_{11}, \varepsilon_{12}, \ldots, \varepsilon_{1J_1}, \varepsilon_{21}, \varepsilon_{22}, \ldots, \varepsilon_{2J_2}, \ldots, \varepsilon_{M1}, \varepsilon_{M2}, \ldots, \varepsilon_{MJ_M}\}$$

Let $f(\langle \varepsilon_{mj} \rangle)$ denote their joint probability density function (PDF), and let $F(\langle \varepsilon_{mj} \rangle)$ denote their cumulative density function (CDF).

The probability of choosing a particular alternative is derived by noting that

$$\begin{aligned} Prob(ni) &= Prob[\mathrm{U}_{ni} > \mathrm{U}_{mj} \ \forall \ mj \neq ni] \\ &= Prob[\varepsilon_{mj} < \mathrm{V}_{ni} - \mathrm{V}_{mj} + \varepsilon_{ni} \ \forall \ mj \neq ni]. \end{aligned} \tag{3.2}$$

Without loss of generality, order the alternatives so that alternative *ni* is the first alternative, i.e., 11. Therefore

$$\begin{aligned} Prob(11) &= Prob[\varepsilon_{mj} < V_{11} - V_{mj} + \varepsilon_{11} \ \forall \ mj \neq 11] \\ &= \int_{\varepsilon_{11}=-\infty}^{+\infty} \int_{\varepsilon_{12}=-\infty}^{V_{11}-V_{12}+\varepsilon_{11}} \cdots \int_{\varepsilon_{mj}=-\infty}^{V_{11}-V_{mj}+\varepsilon_{11}} \cdots \int_{\varepsilon_{MJ}=-\infty}^{V_{11}-V_{MJ}+\varepsilon_{11}} f(\varepsilon_{11}, \varepsilon_{12}, \ldots, \varepsilon_{mj}, \ldots, \varepsilon_{MJ}) d\varepsilon_{MJ} \cdots d\varepsilon_{mj} \cdots d\varepsilon_{12} d\varepsilon_{11}. \end{aligned} \tag{3.3}$$

This is the area under the two-dimensional surface, $f(\langle \varepsilon_{mj} \rangle)$, where $U_{11} > U_{mj} \ \forall \ mj \neq 11$. Although Equation (3.3) is a straightforward representation of *Prob(11)*, it can be represented more compactly in terms of the CDF, $F(\langle \varepsilon_{mj} \rangle)$. Equation (3.3) expresses *Prob(11)* as a *C*-level multiple integral; using the CDF, *Prob(11)* can alternatively be expressed as a single integral. The ability to express *Prob(11)*, and more generally *Prob(ni)*, as a single integral makes evaluation of these probability functions much more tractable—who likes to evaluate multiple integrals?

The area under $f(\langle \varepsilon_{mj} \rangle)$ *can be visualized when C has only two elements (e.g., a trip to site 1 or a trip to site 2).* $f(\langle \varepsilon_{mj} \rangle) = f(\varepsilon_1, \varepsilon_2)$ *and the probability of visiting site 1,* $Prob(1)$ *is the area under* $f(\varepsilon_1, \varepsilon_2)$ *above the shaded area.*

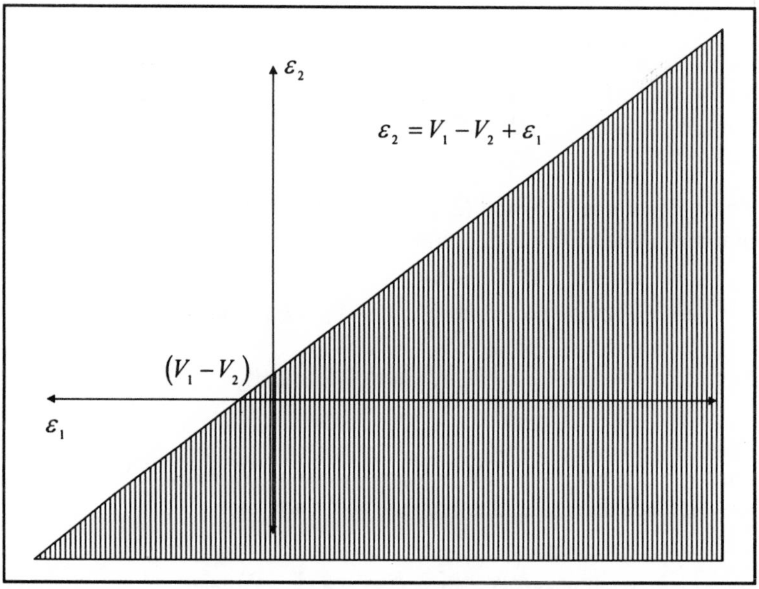

Figure 3.1 The Probability of Choosing an Alternate

The first step in expressing *Prob(11)* in terms of the CDF is to note that, in general,

$$Prob\left[\varepsilon_{mj} < \bar{\varepsilon}_{mj} \ \forall \ mj \neq 11 : \varepsilon_{11} = \bar{\varepsilon}_{11}\right]$$
$$= \int_{\varepsilon_{12}=-\infty}^{\bar{\varepsilon}_{12}} \cdots \int_{\varepsilon_{mj}=-\infty}^{\bar{\varepsilon}_{mj}} \cdots \int_{\varepsilon_{MJ}=-\infty}^{\bar{\varepsilon}_{MJ}} f\left(\bar{\varepsilon}_{11}, \varepsilon_{12}, \ldots, \varepsilon_{mj}, \ldots, \varepsilon_{MJ}\right) d\varepsilon_{MJ} \cdots d\varepsilon_{mj} \cdots d\varepsilon_{12}$$
$$= F_{11}\left(\bar{\varepsilon}_{11}, \bar{\varepsilon}_{12}, \ldots, \bar{\varepsilon}_{mj}, \ldots, \bar{\varepsilon}_{MJ}\right), \quad (3.4)$$

where $F_{ni}(\cdot)$ denotes the derivative of F with respect to its (ni)th argument, and the *bar over a variable*, $\bar{}$, denotes a specific value of that variable. Equation (3.4) tells us that the area under the density function defined in the middle term of Equation (3.4), which is a probability, can be expressed as a derivative of the CDF.[7] The probability that $\left[\varepsilon_{mj} < \bar{\varepsilon}_{mj} \ \forall mj \neq 11\right]$ is then obtained by integrating Equation (3.4) with respect to ε_{11} from minus to plus infinity. That is,

$$Prob\left[\varepsilon_{mj} < \bar{\varepsilon}_{mj} \ \forall \ mj \neq 11\right]$$
$$= \int_{\varepsilon_{11}=-\infty}^{+\infty} F_{11}\left(\varepsilon_{11}, \bar{\varepsilon}_{12}, \ldots, \bar{\varepsilon}_{mj}, \ldots, \bar{\varepsilon}_{MJ}\right) d\varepsilon_{11}. \quad (3.5)$$

Utilizing Equations (3.3) and (3.5), the probability of choosing alternative 11 is, in terms of the CDF,

$$Prob(11) = Prob\left[\varepsilon_{mj} < V_{11} - V_{mj} + \varepsilon_{11} \ \forall \ mj \neq 11\right]$$
$$= \int_{\varepsilon_{11}=-\infty}^{+\infty} F_{11}\left(\left\langle V_{11} - V_{mj} + \varepsilon_{11}\right\rangle\right) d\varepsilon_{11}, \quad (3.6)$$

where $\left\langle V_{11} - V_{mj} + \varepsilon_{11}\right\rangle = \left\{\varepsilon_{11}, V_{11} - V_{12} + \varepsilon_{11}, \ldots, V_{11} - V_{mj} + \varepsilon_{11}, \ldots, V_{11} - V_{MJ} + \varepsilon_{11}\right\}$. However, since there is nothing unique about alternative 11,

$$Prob(ni) = \int_{\varepsilon_{ni}=-\infty}^{+\infty} F_{ni}\left(\left\langle V_{ni} - V_{mj} + \varepsilon_{ni}\right\rangle\right) d\varepsilon_{ni}, \quad (3.7)$$

where $\left\langle V_{ni} - V_{mj} + \varepsilon_{11}\right\rangle = \left\{V_{ni} - V_{11} + \varepsilon_{ni}, \ldots, V_{ni} - V_{ni} + \varepsilon_{ni}, \ldots, V_{ni} - V_{MJ} + \varepsilon_{ni}\right\}$. As noted above, Equation (3.7) is preferred over Equation (3.3) because it is a

---

[7] The second step in Equation (3.4) follows from the fact that

$$F\left(\bar{\varepsilon}_{11}, \bar{\varepsilon}_{12}, \ldots, \bar{\varepsilon}_{mj}, \ldots, \bar{\varepsilon}_{MJ}\right) = \int_{-\infty}^{\bar{\varepsilon}_{21}} \cdots \int_{-\infty}^{\bar{\varepsilon}_{mj}} \cdots \int_{-\infty}^{\bar{\varepsilon}_{MJ}} f\left(\varepsilon_{11}, \ldots, \varepsilon_{mj}, \ldots, \varepsilon_{MJ}\right) d\varepsilon_{MJ} \cdots d\varepsilon_{mj} \cdots d\varepsilon_{12}.$$

Take the derivative of both sides with respect to ε_{11} and evaluate at $\bar{\varepsilon}_{11}$.

single integral, whereas Equation (3.3) is a *C*-level multiple integral. Equation (3.7) is the probability of choosing alternative *ni* for any model that assumes Equation (3.1). Up to this point the model is very general; it is consistent with any $F(\langle \varepsilon_{mj} \rangle)$.

To generate a two-level NL model, specifically assume that the CDF is[8]

$$F(\langle \varepsilon_{mj} \rangle) = \exp\left\{ -\sum_{m=1}^{M} a_m \left[\sum_{j=1}^{J_m} \exp(-s_m \varepsilon_{mj}) \right]^{1/s_m} \right\}$$

$$= \exp\left\{ -\sum_{m=1}^{M} \left[\sum_{j=1}^{J_m} \exp(-s_m [\varepsilon_{mj} - \alpha_m]) \right]^{1/s_m} \right\}, \qquad (3.8)$$

where $a_m = \exp(\alpha_m)$, $a_m > 0$ and $s_m \geq 1\ \forall m$.[9] The condition ($a_m > 0$ and $s_m \geq 1\ \forall m$) is sufficient to guarantee that Equation (3.8) is a globally well-behaved CDF (see *Diversion 1* for more details). The $\langle a_m \rangle$ position the distribution and the $\langle s_m \rangle$ determine its variances and covariances. This CDF is a special case of a multivariate generalized extreme value distribution. The generalized extreme value distribution was first proposed by McFadden (1978). The task at hand is to show that the derivative of the this CDF, when plugged into Equation (3.7), generates the *Prob(ni)* equation for the two-level NL model.

Diversion 1: Equation (3.8) is not a globally well-defined CDF $\forall$ $\langle a_m \rangle$ and $\langle s_m \rangle$, and this often causes problems when the $\langle s_m \rangle$ are estimated.

Simply put, for a function, $F(\langle \varepsilon_{mj} \rangle)$, to be a well-defined CDF its range must be the unit interval and it must be nondecreasing in $\langle \varepsilon_{mj} \rangle$. This second condition can be alternatively stated as $F(\langle \varepsilon_{mj} \rangle)$ must be the integral of a nonnegative density function, $f(\langle \varepsilon_{mj} \rangle)$. Since

$$f(\langle \varepsilon_{mj} \rangle) = \frac{\partial}{\partial \varepsilon_{11}} \frac{\partial}{\partial \varepsilon_{12}} \cdots \frac{\partial}{\partial \varepsilon_{MJ}} F(\langle \varepsilon_{mj} \rangle),$$

continued

[8] Alternatively, if one assumed a multivariate normal CDF, the model would be multivariate Probit.

[9] Those familiar with McFadden (1978) will note that I have not used his notation. My s_m is his $1/(1-\sigma_m)$. I find my notation simpler both in terms of word-processing and comprehension. Note that $s_m \geq 1 \Leftrightarrow 0 \leq \sigma_m < 1$. Alternatively Börsh-Supan (1990), and Kling and Herriges (1995) use the notation θ_m, where $s_m = 1/\theta_m$. They refer to θ_m as a *dissimilarity coefficient*.

the nonnegativity of $f(\langle \varepsilon_{mj} \rangle)$ requires that the mixed partial,

$$\frac{\partial}{\partial \varepsilon_{11}} \frac{\partial}{\partial \varepsilon_{12}} \cdots \frac{\partial}{\partial \varepsilon_{MJ}} F(\langle \varepsilon_{mj} \rangle),$$

is always nonnegative.

Assume $a_m > 0 \ \forall m$. Given this, $s_m \geq 1 \ \forall m$ is necessary and sufficient for Equation (3.8) to be a well-defined CDF. The condition ($s_m \geq 1 \ \forall m$) is typically referred to as the Daly–Zachary–McFadden condition, except that it is often stated $(0 < \theta_m \leq 1 \ \forall m)$. Looking ahead, when $s_m \geq 1 \ \forall m$ the model is said to be globally consistent with stochastic utility maximization.

Sometimes estimated s_m are less than one. For such cases, Börsh-Supan (1990) and Herriges and Kling (1996) consider whether the estimated model is locally consistent with stochastic utility maximization.

A major reason for choosing this particular CDF, Equation (3.8), is that it generates a closed form solution for Equation (3.7). This greatly simplifies estimation of the model, eliminating the need for numerical integration. Most CDFs do not generate closed forms for the *Prob(ni)*. For example, if one assumes the CDF is multivariate normal (the multivariate Probit model), the Equation (3.7) integral will not have a closed-form solution, so estimation of the likelihood function requires complex, numerical, multiple integration. This is why estimated multivariate probit models limit the choice set to a small number of alternatives (e.g.,two, three, four), but NL models can be estimated with large numbers of alternatives.[10]

Examples: Consider the $F(\langle \varepsilon_{mj} \rangle)$ for the two models of recreational demand introduced in the first example box.

The model of participation and site choice where *M* has two elements: 1= fishing and 2=not fishing, J_1=8 (the number of sites) and J_2=2 (staying home and bowling). For this example,

continued

[10] Advances are being made in this area. See, for example, McFadden(1989), Pakes and Pollard (1989), Layton (1996), Chen (1996) and Chen *et al.* (1997).

$$F\left(\left\langle \varepsilon_{mj} \right\rangle\right) = \exp\left\{-\left(a_1\left[\exp(-s_1\varepsilon_{11})+\cdots+\exp(-s_1\varepsilon_{18})\right]^{(1/s_1)}\right.\right.$$
$$\left.\left.+a_2\left[\exp(-s_2\varepsilon_{21})+\exp(-s_2\varepsilon_{22})\right]^{(1/s_2)}\right)\right\}.$$

The model of site choice with saltwater sites, lakes and rivers, where M has three elements: 1= saltwater fishing, 2=lake fishing, and 3=river fishing; $J_1=3$, $J_2=4$ and $J_3=5$. For this example,

$$F\left(\left\langle \varepsilon_{mj} \right\rangle\right) = \exp\left\{-\left(a_1\left[\exp(-s_1\varepsilon_{11})+\cdots+\exp(-s_1\varepsilon_{13})\right]^{(1/s_1)}\right.\right.$$
$$+a_2\left[\exp(-s_2\varepsilon_{21})+\cdots+\exp(-s_2\varepsilon_{24})\right]^{(1/s_2)}$$
$$\left.\left.+a_3\left[\exp(-s_3\varepsilon_{31})+\cdots+\exp(-s_3\varepsilon_{35})\right]^{(1/s_3)}\right)\right\}.$$

To obtain the closed form of the *Prob(ni)* equation, first take the derivative of the multivariate extreme value CDF with respect to its (*ni*)th element. One obtains

$$F_{ni}\left(\left\langle \varepsilon_{mj} \right\rangle\right) = \exp\left\{-\sum_{m=1}^{M} a_m\left[\sum_{j=1}^{J_m}\exp\left(-s_m\varepsilon_{mj}\right)\right]^{1/s_m}\right\}$$
$$\times a_n\left[\sum_{j=1}^{J_n}\exp\left(-s_n\varepsilon_{nj}\right)\right]^{(1/s_n)-1}\exp\left(-s_n\varepsilon_{ni}\right). \tag{3.9}$$

Substituting $\left\langle V_{ni}+\varepsilon_{ni}-V_{mj}\right\rangle$ for $\left\langle \varepsilon_{mj}\right\rangle$ in Equation (3.9), one obtains

$$F_{ni}\left(\left\langle V_{ni}+\varepsilon_{ni}-V_{mj} \right\rangle\right) = \exp\left\{-\sum_{m=1}^{M} a_m\left[\sum_{j=1}^{J_m}\exp\left(-s_m\left(V_{ni}+\varepsilon_{ni}-V_{mj}\right)\right)\right]^{1/s_m}\right\}$$
$$\times a_n\left[\sum_{j=1}^{J_n}\exp\left(-s_n\left(V_{ni}+\varepsilon_{ni}-V_{nj}\right)\right)\right]^{(1/s_n)-1}\exp\left(-s_n\varepsilon_{ni}\right). \tag{3.10}$$

Before substituting the RHS of Equation (3.10) into Equation (3.7) to obtain *Prob(ni)*, simplify Equation (3.10) into terms that do, and do not, involve ε_{ni} so that $F_{ni}(\langle V_{ni} + \varepsilon_{ni} - V_{mj} \rangle)$ in Equation (3.7) will be easy to integrate with respect to ε_{ni}. Factoring Equation (3.10) one obtains

$$F_{ni}(\langle V_{ni} + \varepsilon_{ni} - V_{mj} \rangle) = \exp(-\varepsilon_{ni})\exp\{-\exp(-\varepsilon_{ni})\exp(-V_{ni})B\}A, \quad (3.11)$$

where

$$A \equiv a_n \left[\sum_{j=1}^{J_n} \exp(s_n V_{nj}) \right]^{(1/s_n)-1} \exp(-V_{ni})\exp(s_n V_{ni}), \quad (3.12)$$

and

$$B \equiv \sum_{m=1}^{M} a_m \left[\sum_{j=1}^{J_m} \exp(s_m V_{mj}) \right]^{1/s_m}. \quad (3.13)$$

Note that A and B do not depend on ε_{ni}. Plugging Equation (3.11) into Equation (3.7), one obtains

$$Prob(ni) = A \int_{\varepsilon=-\infty}^{+\infty} \exp(-\varepsilon)\exp[-\exp(-\varepsilon)ZB]d\varepsilon, \quad (3.14)$$

where $Z \equiv \exp(-V_{ni})$. Rather than trying to integrate this with respect to ε, simplify it further by making the change of variables $w = \exp(-\varepsilon)$ $\Rightarrow d\varepsilon = -(1/w)dw$ to obtain

$$Prob(ni) = -A \int_{w=0}^{+\infty} \exp(-wZB)dw = \frac{A}{ZB}. \quad (3.15)$$

Substituting back in for *A*, *B*, and *Z*, one obtains

$$Prob(ni) = \frac{\exp(s_n V_{ni}) a_n \left[\sum_{j=1}^{J_n} \exp(s_n V_{nj}) \right]^{(1/s_n)-1}}{\sum_{m=1}^{M} a_m \left[\sum_{j=1}^{J_m} \exp(s_m V_{mj}) \right]^{1/s_m}}, \qquad (3.16)$$

which is the probability of choosing alternative *ni* in a two-level NL model.

Example: For the **model of site choice with saltwater sites, lakes and rivers,** the probability that the individual will choose the third lake site ($ni = 23$) is

$$\begin{aligned} Prob(23) = &\left\{ \exp(s_2 V_{23}) a_2 \left[\exp(s_2 V_{21}) + \cdots + \exp(s_2 V_{24}) \right]^{(1/s_2)-1} \right\} \\ &\div \left\{ a_1 \left[\exp(s_1 V_{11}) + \cdots + \exp(s_1 V_{13}) \right]^{1/s_1} \right. \\ &+ a_2 \left[\exp(s_2 V_{21}) + \cdots + \exp(s_2 V_{24}) \right]^{1/s_2} \\ &\left. + a_3 \left[\exp(s_3 V_{31}) + \cdots + \exp(s_3 V_{35}) \right]^{1/s_3} \right\}, \end{aligned}$$

Assuming that the elements of $\langle a_{mj} \rangle$ are all positive (see *Diversion 1*), inclusion of the parameters $\langle a_{mj} \rangle$ is equivalent to adding a group-specific constant term, α_m, to each of the V_{mj}, where $\alpha_m = \ln(a_m)$. To see this, replace a_m with $\exp(\alpha_m)(\Rightarrow \alpha_m = \ln(a_m))$; in which case *Prob(ni)* can be rewritten as

$$Prob(ni) = \frac{\exp[s_n(\alpha_n + V_{ni})] \left\{ \sum_{j=1}^{J_n} \exp[s_n(\alpha_n + V_{nj})] \right\}^{(1/s_n)-1}}{\sum_{m=1}^{M} \left\{ \sum_{j=1}^{J_m} \exp[s_m(\alpha_m + V_{mj})] \right\}^{1/s_m}}, \qquad (3.16a)$$

Diversion 2: Conditions on the Prob(ni)

The *Prob*(*ni*) have the following properties for all $\langle V_{mj} \rangle \in R^C$: (i) each *Prob*(*ni*) is greater than zero and less than one; (ii) the *Prob*(*ni*) sum to one;

(iii) $\dfrac{\partial Prob(lk)}{\partial mj} = \dfrac{\partial Prob(mj)}{\partial lk}$

continued

and (iv) the $Prob(ni)$ are invariant to replacing each α_m with $(\alpha+\alpha_m)\ \forall\ \alpha \in R$ ($\Leftrightarrow$adding a positive constant to each of the α_m). Note that the *Prob*(*ni*) possess properties (i)–(iv) even if the s_m are not all ≥ 1, so these properties hold even if Equation (3.8) is not a well-behaved CDF. Given $(a_m > 0\ \forall m)$, $(s_m \geq 1\ \forall m)$ is necessary and sufficient to ensure that these probabilities are consistent with an underlying density function $\forall \langle V_{mj} \rangle \in R^C$. More generally, given probabilities that possess properties (i)–(iv), such probabilities will always be consistent with a well-behaved underlying density function if $\forall$ *mj*, the mixed partial derivative of *Prob(mj)* with respect to the $V_{lk}, lk \neq mj$, is always nonpositive when the mixed partial is of an odd-order and nonnegative when the mixed partial is of an even-order (Herriges and Kling, 1996). For Equation (3.16a), $(s_m \geq 1\ \forall m)$, and these sign restrictions on the mixed partials are equivalent. As noted in *Diversion 1*, when these conditions are fulfilled, the NL model is said to be globally consistent with stochastic utility maximization.

Alternatively, if some of the s_m are less than 1, it is still possible that, for the $\langle V_{mj} \rangle$ of interest, the aforementioned mixed partials all have the correct signs; that is, for all current and proposed levels of the $\langle V_{mj} \rangle$, the mixed partials have the correct signs. In such cases, the *Prob(ni)* are said to be locally consistent with stochastic utility maximization.

If desired, the probability, Equation (3.16), can be decomposed into the probability of choosing an alternative of type *n* multiplied by the probability of choosing alternative *i* from the group of alternatives that are of type *n*; i.e.,

$$Prob(ni) = Prob(i|n)Prob(n), \tag{3.17}$$

where

$$Prob(n) = \frac{a_n \left[\sum_{j=1}^{J_n} \exp(s_n V_{nj}) \right]^{1/s_n}}{\sum_{m=1}^{M} a_m \left[\sum_{j=1}^{J_m} \exp(s_m V_{mj}) \right]^{1/s_m}}, \tag{3.18}$$

and

$$Prob(i|n) = \frac{\exp(s_n V_{ni})}{\left[\sum_{j=1}^{J_n} \exp(s_n V_{nj}) \right]}. \tag{3.19}$$

Equation (3.16) is made explicit by specifying functional forms for the V_{mj}, where V_{mj} is the conditional indirect utility function for alternative *mj*. V_{mj} is assumed to be a function, often linear, of the cost of alternative *mj*, the budget, the characteristics of alternative *mj*, and characteristics of the individual. For example, if *mj* is a fishing site, the variables might be the cost of a trip to site *mj*, the expected catch rate at site *mj*, and other characteristics of the site. The regularity conditions on the V_{mj} are considered in Section 3.6.

Consider now the problem of estimating the parameters in the V_{mj} functions using a random sample of individuals that reports the alternative, or alternatives, chosen by each individual in the sample. Note that the choices can be actual choices, hypothetical choices, or a combination of both.[11]

At this point it is important to make a distinction. Denote each time an individual must choose between the C alternatives in the choice set as a *choice occasion*. An important distinction is whether the sample contains information on the alternative chosen for just one choice occasion for each individual, or whether the data set reports, by individual, the alternative chosen on each of a number of choice occasions. The number of observed choice occasions could vary across individuals. Start with the simpler case where the sample contains the choice on only one choice occasion for each individual. The probability of observing individual h choosing alternative ni on the one choice occasion is *Prob(hni)*. If one further assumes that the choices of the H individuals in the sample are statistically independent, $\operatorname{cov}\left(\varepsilon_{hni},\varepsilon_{kmj}\right)=0,\ \forall n,i,m,j,h\neq k$, the probability of observing the set of observed choices is

$$f\left(\left\langle y_{1mj}\right\rangle,\left\langle y_{2mj}\right\rangle,\ldots,\left\langle y_{Hmj}\right\rangle\right)=\prod_{h=1}^{H}\prod_{n=1}^{M}\prod_{i=1}^{J_n} Prob(hni)^{y_{hni}}, \qquad (3.20)$$

where $y_{hni}=1$ if individual h choose alternative ni, and zero otherwise, C is the number of alternatives in the choice set, *Prob(hni)* is defined by Equation (3.16), and

$$\left\langle y_{hmj}\right\rangle=\left\{y_{h11},y_{h12},\ldots,y_{h1J_1},y_{h21},y_{h22},\ldots,y_{h2J_2},\ldots,y_{hM1},y_{hM2},\ldots,y_{hMJ_M}\right\}.$$

Examples: Consider what constitutes a **choice occasion** for the two models of recreation demand introduced in the first example box.

continued

[11] Examples of ML and NL models of site-specific recreational activities choice estimated using hypothetical choices or hypothetical and actual choices include Adamowicz *et al.* (1994, 1996), Swait and Adamowicz (1996), and Buchanan *et al.* (1998). Morey *et al.* (1997b) uses choices among pairs of hypothetical alternatives to estimate a ML model for monument preservation programs.

In the model of **participation and site choice,** the fishing season can be divided into a finite number of periods and each period is a choice occasion. For example, each week in the season might be defined as a choice occasion, or, more generally, the season might be divided into a fixed number of periods, but with no restriction that each period is of a specified length, just that the sum of the choice occasions equal the season. The critical issue for this simple model of participation and site choice is that no more than one site is chosen on each choice occasion.

In the model of **site choice with saltwater sites, lakes and rivers,** a choice occasion is each time a fishing trip is taken.

Equation (3.20) is the likelihood function for this sample; that is, it is the probability of observing the choices in the sample as a function of the *Prob(hmj)*. The task is to find those values of the parameters in the *Prob(hmj)* that maximize the likelihood function. Since the parameters that maximize the log of the likelihood function also maximize the likelihood function, estimation is simplified by finding those values of the parameters that maximize the log of the likelihood function.

$$L = \sum_{h=1}^{H} \sum_{n=1}^{M} \sum_{i=1}^{J_n} y_{hni} \ln[Prob(hni)] . \qquad (3.21)$$

Estimation of log likelihood functions are discussed in Section 3.4.

Examples: The log likelihood functions for the two models of recreational demand introduced in the first example box when the sample only reports the alternative chosen on one choice occasion for each individual in a sample of H=100 individuals is Equation (3.21), where for:

the model of participation and site choice M has two elements: 1= fishing and 2=not fishing, J_1=8 (the number of sites) and J_2=2 (staying home and bowling).

the model of site choice with saltwater sites, lakes and rivers, M has three elements: 1= saltwater fishing, 2=lake fishing, and 3=river fishing; J_1=3, J_2=4 and J_3=5.

Consider now the case where the data set reports, by individual, the alternative chosen on each of a number of choice occasions, where the number of observed choice occasions may vary across individuals. Such samples are generated by *repeated-choice* problems; that is, the discrete-choice problem faced by each individual repeats, so there are multiple choice occasions. Some discrete choice problems such as what furnace to purchase or what individual to marry do not repeat, or, hopefully, do not repeat often. In contrast, discrete choice problems in recreational demand are characterized by repetition. The problem of where to go on a fishing trip repeats every time one takes a trip. The problem of whether to take a fishing trip also repeats every choice occasion (for example, every day or every week).

Let T_h denote the number of choice occasions observed for individual *h* and ε_{hmjt} the random component in the utility individual *h* receives during choice occasion *t* if alternative *mj* is chosen. Assume, in addition to the previous assumption that choices are statistically independent across individuals, that choices for a given individual are statistically independent across choice occasions. That is, assume $\text{cov}(\varepsilon_{knis}, \varepsilon_{kmjt}) = 0 \ \forall k,n,i,m,j,s \neq t$.[12]

---

[12] One way to generate correlation across choice occasions is to assume individual-specific, alternative-specific random effects that cannot be attributed to observable variations in alternative and individual characteristics. We have assumed $U_{hmjt} = V_{hmjt} + \varepsilon_{hmjt}$, where each $\langle \varepsilon_{hmjt} \rangle$ is a random draw from Equation (3.8). Now consider replacing ε_{hmjt} with the sum of two random components, $v_{hmj} + \varepsilon_{hmjt}$, where, as above, the $\langle \varepsilon_{hmjt} \rangle$ are independent across choice occasions, but the $\langle v_{hmj} \rangle$ remain the same across choice occasions. One might view $\langle v_{hmj} \rangle$ as randomly drawn once a year from some PDF, $f(\langle v_{hmj} \rangle)$, so that $\langle v_{hmj} \rangle$ varies from year to year but not across choice occasions within a year, or one might assume the individual's $\langle v_{hmj} \rangle$ is drawn only once. The $\langle v_{hmj} \rangle$ add individual-specific, alternative-specific constants to the conditional indirect utility functions, and these terms remain constant across choice occasions, so cause the random term to be correlated across choice occasions. $Prob(hnit|\langle v_{hmj} \rangle)$ is the standard nested logit probability after these alternative specific constants have been added to the deterministic component of utility for each alternative. Assuming the $\langle v_{hmj} \rangle$ do not depend on the explanatory variables in the model, $Prob(hnit, \langle v_{hmj} \rangle) = Prob(hnit|\langle v_{hni} \rangle) f(\langle v_{hmj} \rangle)$. Note that this joint probability depends on the unobservable $\langle v_{hmj} \rangle$. Proceed by specifying a functional form for $f(\langle v_{hmj} \rangle)$ such that when one sequentially integrates $Prob(hnit|\langle v_{hmj} \rangle)$ from $-\infty$ to $+\infty$ with respect to each of the elements of $\langle v_{hmj} \rangle$, one obtains a computable form for *Prob(hni)* as a function of the parameters and explanatory variables in the NL model, and the parameters in $f(\langle v_{hmj} \rangle)$. This is not a trivial exercise. Simplifying assumptions include

$$f(\langle v_{hmj} \rangle) = \prod_{m=1}^{M} \prod_{j=1}^{J_m} f(v_{hmj})$$

and some or most of the elements of $f(\langle v_{hmj} \rangle)$ are zero (only some alternatives have individual-specific, alternative-specific random effects).

One can also generate correlation across choice occasions by assuming one or more of the parameters or the characteristics that determine $\langle V_{hmjt} \rangle$ vary across individuals but do not vary across choice occasions for a given individual. See Hausman and Wise (1978). For example, one might assume $\alpha_{hc} = \alpha_c + \gamma_h$, where α_{hc} is individual in *h*'s parameter on characteristic *c* and the $\gamma_h \sim n(0, \sigma^2)$. Two examples of random-parameter models are Layton and Brown (1998) and Train (1998). Morey and Rossmann (1998) generate correlation across choice occasions by estimating a model with individual-specific parameters.

Diversion 3 outlines a different method to allow correlations across choice occasions, a method that allows the variance of the random components to systematically differ across individuals. The method does not allow an individual to have persistent site preferences that are independent of site and individual characteristics included in the model.

For this case, let $Y_{hni} \equiv$ the number of times individual h chooses alternative ni, where

$$\sum_{n=1}^{M}\sum_{i=1}^{J_n} Y_{hni} = T_h .$$

The probability of observing the vector of alternatives $\langle Y_{hni} \rangle$ for individual h is determined by the multinomial density function:

$$f\left(\langle Y_{hmj} \rangle\right) = \frac{T_h!}{\prod_{n=1}^{M}\prod_{i=1}^{J_n} Y_{hni}!} \prod_{n=1}^{M}\prod_{i=1}^{J_n} Prob(hni)^{Y_{hni}} . \tag{3.22}$$

The log of the likelihood function for this sample is[13]

$$L = \sum_{h=l}^{H}\sum_{n=1}^{N}\sum_{i=1}^{J_n} Y_{hni} \ln\left[Prob(hni)\right]. \tag{3.23}$$

Note that it is possible to estimate the number of choice occasions by maximizing Equation (3.23) for different values of *T*. For an example, see Morey *et al.* (1991).

Another common but more complicated type of sample is a sample that contains, for each individual, information on the specific alternative chosen for some choice occasions, but only partial information on the alternative chosen for other choice occasions. For example, one might know the specific alternative chosen for some choice occasions but for others only know which of the *M* groups contains the alternative. The log of the likelihood function for such an "incomplete" sample is

$$L = \sum_{h=l}^{H}\sum_{n=1}^{N}\left\{ Y_{hn} \ln\left[Prob(hn)\right] + \sum_{i=1}^{J_n} Y_{hni} \ln\left[Prob(hni)\right]\right\} \tag{3.24}$$

where *Prob(hn)* is defined in Equation (3.18), Y_{hn} is the number of times we know individual *i* chose an alternative of type *n* but not which one. Note that in this case

$$T_h = \sum_{n=1}^{N}\sum_{i=1}^{J_n} Y_{hni} + \sum_{n=1}^{N} Y_{hn} .$$

[13] The additive term, *ln*(multinomial coefficient), is omitted because it does not depend on the values of the parameters in the *Prob(hmj)*.

For example, in our **model of participation and site choice** one might know for some choice occasions both whether and where an individual fished, but for other choice occasions know that a trip was taken but not have information about the destination.

In the **model of site choice for saltwater sites, lakes and rivers,** one might know for some choice occasions the exact site chosen, but for other choice occasions only that the trip was to a river.

3.3 SPECIAL CASES OF THE TWO-LEVEL NL MODEL

The significance of the a_m and s_m parameters in the CDF, Equation (3.8), is deciphered by remembering that the utility an individual receives if he chooses alternative *ni* is, from the analyst's perspective, a random variable; i.e., $U_{ni} = V_{ni} + \alpha_m + \varepsilon_{ni}$, where $\alpha_m = \ln(a_m)$, $(V_{ni} + \alpha_m)$ is deterministic, and ε_{ni} is the random variable.[14] The V_{ni} are a function of the *attributes* of the alternatives that are observed by the analyst. The $(\alpha_n + \varepsilon_{ni})$ are the impacts of the unobserved attributes. As noted earlier, inclusion of the $\langle a_m \rangle$ parameters is equivalent to adding a group-specific constant term, α_m, to each of the V_{mj}; this will be elaborated on below.

A critical issue in all two-level discrete choice models is whether each element of the vector $\langle \varepsilon_{mj} \rangle$ is **independently** drawn from the same univariate distribution, or whether elements of $\langle \varepsilon_{mj} \rangle$ are drawn from a multivariate distribution and are therefore correlated. The NL CDF, Equation (3.8), allows the ε_{mj} to be correlated by type.

What would cause the random terms, $\langle \varepsilon_{mj} \rangle$, to be correlated by type? If an attribute that is an important determinant of choice is not observed, it influences the magnitude of the $\langle \varepsilon_{mj} \rangle$, the $\langle \alpha_m \rangle$, or both. If this attribute **varies** across alternatives within a group less, or more, than across alternatives in different groups, the random elements in group *n* will be more correlated with each other than they are with the random elements for alternatives that are not in group *n*.[15] If, in addition, the amount the unobserved attribute **varies** within a group varies by group, alternatives in some groups will be more correlated with each other than the alternatives in other groups are correlated with each

---

[14] Note that the α_m can be viewed as either a parameter in the CDF, Equation (3.8), as it is here, or as a possible component of V_{mj}.

[15] For example, if size is an important unobserved attribute of the alternatives, and size varies less within groups than across groups, the random terms for the alternatives that belong to group *n* will be more correlated with each other than they are with the random terms that are not in group *n*.

other. In these two cases, it is inappropriate to assume that the random terms for all C alternatives are independently drawn from the same univariate distribution. The NL CDF, Equation (3.8), allows the random terms to be correlated by groups and for the degree of correlation to vary by group.

For example, in our **model of participation and site choice**, one might expect the random terms in the conditional indirect utility function for the fishing sites $(\langle \varepsilon_{1i} \rangle)$ to be more correlated with one another than they are with the random term for staying at home (ε_{21}) or the random term for bowling (ε_{22}). This would happen if there are important unobserved attributes of the alternatives that vary more, or less, across the fishing sites than they vary across the fishing sites and the other two alternatives. For example, the attribute fish stock varies across fishing sites but is always zero for staying at home and bowling, so omitting it would cause the $(\langle \varepsilon_{1i} \rangle)$ to be more correlated with one another than they are with the (ε_{21}) or (ε_{22}).

Consider our **model of site choice with saltwater sites, lakes, and rivers.** Assume that aquatic vegetation varies significantly across rivers but not as much across lakes sites or saltwater sites. If this attribute of sites is unobserved, the random terms for the river alternatives $(\langle \varepsilon_{3i} \rangle)$ will be more correlated with each other than with the random terms for lakes and saltwater sites.

Alternatively, if the **variation** in the unobserved attributes is not systematic by group type, it is reasonable to assume that each element of $\langle \varepsilon_{mj} \rangle$ is drawn from the same univariate distribution. This is what is assumed by the ML model. It assumes that each element of $\langle \varepsilon_{mj} \rangle$ is independently drawn from a univariate extreme value distribution

$$F(\varepsilon_{ni}) = \exp\left[-a_n \exp(-r\varepsilon_{ni})\right] = \exp\left[-\exp(-r(\varepsilon_{ni} - \alpha_n))\right]. \qquad (3.25)$$

Recollect that $\alpha_m = \ln(a_m)$. The probability of choosing alternative *ni,* Equation (3.16) simplifies to

$$Prob(ni) = \frac{a_n \exp(rV_{ni})}{\sum_{m=1}^{M}\sum_{j=1}^{J_m} a_m \exp(rV_{mj})} = \frac{\exp\left[r(\alpha_n + V_{ni})\right]}{\sum_{m=1}^{M}\sum_{j=1}^{J_m} \exp\left[r(\alpha_m + V_{mj})\right]}, \qquad (3.26)[16]$$

[16] Looking back, Equation (3.19) looks like Equation (3.26) with $a_n = 1\ \forall M$ and $s_n = r$. However, s_n in Equation (3.19) is not r in Equation (3.26). The s_n in Equation (3.19) can be viewed as s_n / r with r set equal to 1.

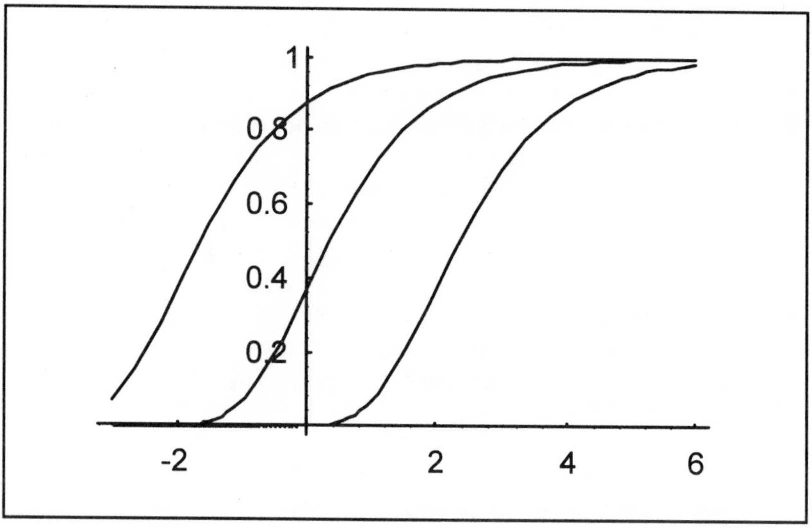

Figure 3.2 The Extreme Value CDF with r=1 and Modes of -2, 0 and 2

Diversion 3: Properties of the extreme value distribution [Equation (3.25)]. Precisely speaking, Equation (3.25) is a type 1 extreme value distribution with mode $=\alpha_n$, mean$=\alpha_n+\gamma/r$, median$=\alpha_n+0.635\gamma/r$, and $\sigma^2=\pi^2/6r^2$, where γ is Euler's constant (≈ 0.57721). Note that σ^2 increases as r decreases; e.g., if $r=1$ and $\alpha_n=0$, 98% of the ε_{ni} are in the interval 0.57721 ± 2.56, whereas if $r=0.1$ and $\alpha_n=0$, 98% of the ε_{ni} are in the interval 0.57721 ± 128.The density function is

$$f(\varepsilon_{ni}) = r\exp[-r(\varepsilon_{ni}-\alpha_n)]\exp\{-\exp[-r(\varepsilon_{ni}-\alpha_n)]\}.$$

It is called an extreme value distribution because it can be derived as a distribution of extreme (largest or smallest) values. The distribution of maximum I.Q. is a distribution of extreme values, so is the distribution of maximum utility across discrete alternatives. However, the fact that the extreme value distribution can be interpreted as a distribution of extreme values has nothing to do with its choice as the appropriate distribution for the random component of utility for each alternative in a discrete choice model. Rather, its appeal is that its adoption leads to a closed form solution for *Prob(ni)*.

continued

Note that with the ML model r can vary across individuals either as a function of the individual's characteristics or by allowing each individual to have a separate r. When there is variation in r, it is possible to estimate them. Estimation of a separate r for each individual requires multiple observations per individual. There are numerous reasons why one might want to allow r to vary: ability to make choices varies, the incentive to make choices can vary (e.g., with hypothetical versus actual choices), and the model includes all of the important explanatory variables for only some individuals. Morey and Rossmann (1998) estimate and discuss individual specific r's in a ML model. The estimated r will be relatively large (σ^2 small) for those individuals whose choices are being correctly predicted by $\langle V_{mj} \rangle$ and small for those individuals whose choice cannot be explained by the $\langle V_{mj} \rangle$. Note that $Prob(ni) \to 1/C \ \forall \ ni$ as $r \to 0$.

Incorporating r's that vary by individual: If $U_{hij} = V_{hij} + \varepsilon_{hij}$ where each ε_{hij} for individual h is an independent draw from $f(\varepsilon) = \exp[-\exp(-r_h\varepsilon)]$, then $\hat{U}_{hij} = rV_{hij} + \hat{\varepsilon}_{hij}$ where each $\hat{\varepsilon}_{hij}$ for individual h is an independent draw from $f(\varepsilon) = \exp[-\exp(-\varepsilon)]$, and the probabilities are Equation (3.26) with r replaced by r_h.

One might also allow r to vary across choice occasions as a function of the complexity of the problem [Swait and Adamowicz (1996)].

Note that with ML models it is typical, but unnecessary, to assume $a_m = 1$ $(\alpha_m = 0)$ $\forall m$; that is, groups (represented by group-specific constants) are consistent with the ML model. If the $\langle V_{mj} \rangle$ are linear in their parameters, one cannot identify r separately from those parameters, so, without loss of generality, r is set to 1.[17] With r =1, Equation (3.26) can be derived from Equation (3.16) by restricting $s_m = 1 \ \forall m$.

As is well known, the ML model imposes the IIA assumption which says that the ratio of any two probabilities is independent of any change in any third alternative; that is[18]

---

[17] For example, $V_{mj} = \mu(I - p_{mj}) \ \forall mj$, where I is income and p_{mj} is the cost of the alternative, then

$$Prob(ni) = \frac{\exp[(r\mu)(I - p_{ni})]}{\sum_{m=1}^{M}\sum_{j=1}^{J_m} \exp[(r\mu)(I - p_{mj})]}$$

and one cannot identify both r and μ.

[18] In what follow r is set equal to 1.

$$\frac{Prob(ni)}{Prob(lk)} = \frac{\exp(V_{ni})}{\exp(V_{lk})} . \tag{3.27}$$

This restriction is correct if the variation in unobserved attributes is not systematic by group type, but inappropriate if it is.

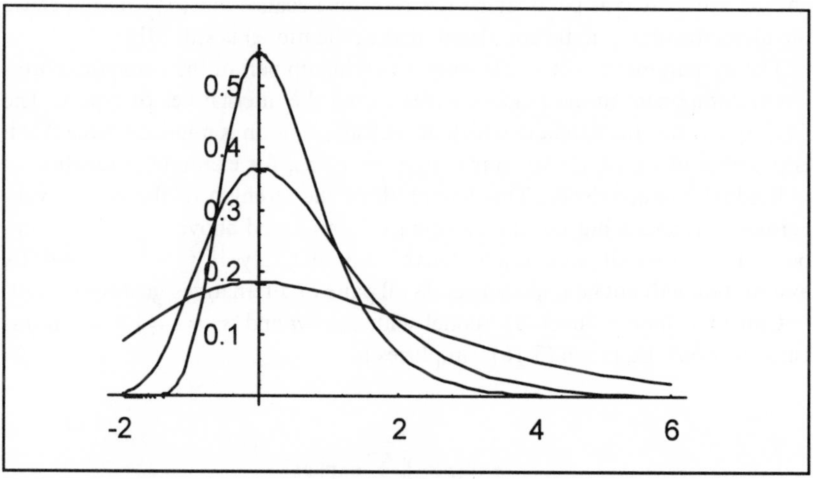

Figure 3.3 The Extreme Value PDF with Mode=0 and r=0.5, 1.0, and 1.5

If an important unobserved attribute has the same magnitude for all the alternatives in a group but differs across groups, this will affect the $\langle a_{mj} \rangle$, but not the $\langle s_{mj} \rangle$. Such attributes cause alternatives within a group to be more similar to one another than they are to alternatives in different groups, but does not influence the correlations of the $\langle s_{mj} \rangle$. Consider the following example: size varies across alternatives, but all alternatives of the same type are the same size. The omission of size will cause the $\langle a_m \rangle$ to vary in magnitude, but will not cause the elements of $\langle s_{mj} \rangle$ to differ from 1.

The a_m and s_m add systematic variation across groups that is in addition to the systematic variation in terms of the V_{mj}; that is, they allow the groups to differ in systematic ways in addition to the differences that can be attributed to variations in the observed attributes that appear as independent variables in the V_{mj}. a_n reflects the relative attractiveness of alternatives of type n. *Ceteris paribus*, a_n will be large, in a relative sense, if alternatives of type n have more of an important, but unobserved, attribute.

Note that allowing a_m to vary, while holding $s_m = 1 \; \forall m$, is not sufficient to weaken the IIA assumption. This can be seen by considering a case where $s_m = 1 \; \forall m$ but a_m varies. In this case,

$$Prob(ni) = \frac{a_n \exp(V_{ni})}{\sum_{m=1}^{M} a_m \sum_{j=1}^{J_m} \exp(V_{mj})} \text{ and } \frac{Prob(ni)}{Prob(lk)} = \frac{a_n \exp(V_{ni})}{a_l \exp(V_{lk})}. \quad (3.28)$$

Thus, the IIA assumption still holds for all pairs of alternatives given that a_n and a_l are treated as parameters. IIA remains because the $\langle a_m \rangle$ do not cause the elements of ε_{mj} to be correlated; that is, the model is still ML.

The s_n parameter, not a_n, is what is picking up part of the common (correlated) component in the random terms for all the alternatives of type *n*. The $\langle s_m \rangle$ determine the extent to which the IIA assumption is imposed. Note that it is possible to let $\langle s_m \rangle$ vary across individuals as, for example, a function of individual characteristics. This would allow the strength of the nest to vary across individuals but not the groupings.[19] As noted above, $s_m = 1 \ \forall m$ imposes IIA across all pairs of alternatives. Alternatively, if $s_m \neq 1 \ \forall m$, the IIA assumption will not be imposed across all pairs of alternatives, just some pairs.

Consider the two-level NL model with $a_m = a$ and $s_m = s \neq 1 \ \forall m$. In this case *Prob(ni)*, Equation (3.16), simplifies to

$$Prob(ni) = \frac{\exp(sV_{ni}) \left[\sum_{j=1}^{J_n} \exp(sV_{nj}) \right]^{(1/s)-1}}{\sum_{m=1}^{M} \left[\sum_{j=1}^{J_m} \exp(sV_{mj}) \right]^{1/s}}, \quad (3.29)$$

If $s_m = s \neq 1 \ \forall m$, the random terms in each group are more correlated with each other than they are with the random terms in other groups, but the degree to which they are more correlated with their fellow group members is constant across groups. In NL models of recreational demand, it is common to assume $s_m = s \neq 1 \ \forall m$.

When $a_m = a$ and $s_m = s \neq 1 \ \forall m$,

---

[19] If the estimated (or specified) $\langle s_{\cdot} \rangle$ were all exactly one for some individuals, for this subset of individuals the nest would collapse and the model would be ML. A model can be NL for some individuals and ML for others.

$$\frac{Prob(ni)}{Prob(lk)} = \frac{\exp(sV_{ni})\left[\sum_{j=1}^{J_n}\exp(sV_{nj})\right]^{(1/s)-1}}{\exp(sV_{lk})\left[\sum_{j=1}^{J_l}\exp(sV_{lj})\right]^{(1/s)-1}}. \quad (3.30)$$

Examining Equation (3.30), one sees that:

- IIA still holds for any pair of alternatives within the same group ($n = l$). If $n=l$, Equation (3.30) simplifies to

$$\frac{Prob(ni)}{Prob(lk)} = \frac{\exp(sV_{ni})}{\exp(sV_{lk})}.$$

- IIA still holds for all pairs of alternatives that are in different groups ($n \neq l$) if the alternative changed is not in the same group as either alternative in the pair. That is, Equation (3.30) is not a function of changes in alternatives that are in other groups.
- But, IIA does not hold for pairs of alternatives that are in different groups ($n \neq l$) if the alternative changed is in the same group as one of the alternatives in the pair. That is, Equation (3.30) is a function of the attributes of alternatives *n* and *l*, so a change in any alternative in either group *n* or *l* will affect the ratio.

For example, if alternative 11 is altered, it will not change

$\frac{Prob(12)}{Prob(13)}$, $\frac{Prob(21)}{Prob(22)}$ or $\frac{Prob(31)}{Prob(42)}$, but it will affect $\frac{Prob(12)}{Prob(22)}$.

In summary, generalizing from ML to NL only partially relaxes the IIA assumption. This is an important but often overlooked point. Generalizing Equation (3.29) by allowing both a_m and s_m to vary buys no more in terms of the IIA; IIA is still imposed to the same degree.

For Example: Consider **the model of site choice with saltwater sites, lakes and rivers,** where *M* has three elements: 1= saltwater fishing, 2=lake fishing; and 3=river fishing; J_1=3, J_2=4 and J_3=5.

$$F(\langle\varepsilon_{mj}\rangle) = \exp\Big\{-\Big(a_1\left[\exp(-s_1\varepsilon_{11})+\cdots+\exp(-s_1\varepsilon_{13})\right]^{(1/s_1)}$$
$$+a_2\left[\exp(-s_2\varepsilon_{21})+\cdots+\exp(-s_2\varepsilon_{24})\right]^{(1/s_2)}$$
$$+a_3\left[\exp(-s_3\varepsilon_{31})+\cdots+\exp(-s_3\varepsilon_{35})\right]^{(1/s_3)}\Big)\Big\}.$$

continued

The ratio of the probabilities for any two sites of the same type will not be influenced by a change in the attributes of any other site or sites. For example, the ratio of probabilities for two of the rivers will not change if the attributes of any of the saltwater sites, lakes, or other rivers change.

The ratio of the probabilities for any two sites that are different water types will not be influenced by a change in the attributes of a site (or sites) that is not of one of those water types. For example, the ratio of probabilities for a lake site and a river site will not change if the attributes of one or more saltwater sites change.

The ratio of the probabilities for any two sites that are different water types will be influenced by a change in the attributes of a site (or sites) that is one of these water types. For example, the ratio of probabilities for a lake site and a river site will change if the attributes of some other lake or river site change.

3.4 ESTIMATION

Although this monograph is not about estimation *per se*, a few comments about estimation are in order. The log of the likelihood function [examples are Equation (3.21), (3.23) and (3.24)] can be maximized in one step by using a numerical algorithm to find the vector of parameters $\{ a_1, a_2, \ldots, a_M,\ s_1, s_2, \ldots, s_M$; and the parameters in the $\langle V_{mj} \rangle$ functions} that maximize it. This approach is deemed Full Information Maximum Likelihood, FIML.[20] Alternatively, one can adopt a two-stage sequential estimation (SE). The parameters in the V_{mj} for group m can be divided into two categories for purposes of estimation, those that just influence the allocation between alternatives in group m (that is, those that appear in the conditional probabilities, Equation (3.19), for group m), and all other parameters. In the first step of sequential estimation, one sets $s = 1$ and for each group one separately estimates just those parameters that determine the allocation amongst the alternatives in that group. This is done by maximizing the log of the likelihood function for the choice of each j in the group conditional on the choice of n.[21] In this first stage, the model for each group is a ML model with J_n alternatives. In the second stage of a sequential estimation, one

[20]Note that identification requires that one of the a_m is set to some positive constant; e.g. 1. If one's intent is to estimate a basic two-level nested model ($a_m = a$ and $s_m = s\ \forall\ m$), the a cancels out and the parameter vector is just {s; and the parameters in the $\langle V_{mj} \rangle$ }.

[21] Note that the data used to estimated the parameters in each nest are typically only a subset of the full data set because they include only those observations that involve a choice in that nest.

estimates the $\langle a_m \rangle$, $\langle s_m \rangle$, and other parameters, given the parameter estimates from the first stage.

Although this two-step estimation procedure is tempting, and it is the easier approach given existing computer hardware and software, I recommend against it. It has been known for a long time that the sequential technique leads to parameter estimates that are not asymptotically efficient, and, without a difficult correction, standard-error estimates that are inconsistent (Amemiya, 1978).[22] Although there is no result that states that FIML estimates always have better statistical properties in finite samples, FIML is both consistent and asymptotically efficient, so it dominates in large samples, and FIML and sequential estimation often produce very different parameter estimates.[23] Monte Carlo studies also indicate that FIML estimates are more efficient than sequential estimation; see, for example, Brownstone and Small (1989).[24] Software programs (e.g., *Gauss* and other such programs) that directly maximize the log of the likelihood function for the full model, Equation (3.21), (3.23) or (3.24), are now widely available for both PCs and mainframes. There are numerous examples of FIML NL estimation both in other fields and in recreational demand. Two recreational examples are Morey *et al.* (1993 and 1998a).

An important issue with FIML estimation of a NL model is the starting values for the parameters. For NL models, the FIML log-likelihood function is not guaranteed to be globally concave, so depending on the starting values for the parameters, one can possibly achieve a local rather than a global maximum.[25] This suggests that one estimate the model with a number of different starting values to increase the probability that the maximum found is the global maximum. Two set of possible starting values are the sequential estimates and the estimates derived by assuming the model is ML ($s_m = 1 \; \forall m$) . The sequential estimates, although not asymptotically efficient, are consistent, so they are one set of reasonable starting values, particularly if the sample size is large.[26]

FIML estimation can often be quite difficult; the ability to find the maximum can be quite sensitive to starting values, the search algorithm, and how the parameters in the model are scaled. The starting values can affect the outcome in two ways: if there are multiple, local maxima, the one found often depends

---

[22] Formula for correcting the standard errors can be found in Amemiya (1978) and McFadden(1981).

[23] See, for example, Cameron (1982 and 1985), Hensher (1986), Brownstone and Small (1989), and Kling and Thompson (1996).

[24] In addition, simulations show that even when data have been generated by a NL model, SE estimates do not always exist.

[25] In contrast, the likelihood function for ML models is globally concave, so with ML models there is less need to worry about starting values.

[26] Hensher (1986) discourages the use of the sequential estimates as starting values for FIML estimation. In my opinion, they should not be used as the only starting values.

on where the search begins, and starting values can cause search algorithms to search in an area of parameter space where small changes in parameter values can generate values of machine zero for components of the likelihood function, in which case the program crashes.[27] Maximum likelihood is invariant to rescaling parameters in the model (e.g., changing the units in which explanatory variables are denoted), but the search algorithms are not. Scaling determines the relative rates at which the parameters change from iteration to iteration. Search algorithms generally converge more quickly when the explanatory variables are scaled such that their parameters are of the same order of magnitude. A characteristic of NL models is that the log likelihood is highly nonquadratic in the $\langle s_m \rangle$ parameters. This makes the $\langle s_m \rangle$ parameters difficult to estimate, and implies that one should avoid search algorithms that rely on quadratic approximations (e.g. BHHH). In addition, it is probably wise to scale the $\langle s_m \rangle$ parameters such that they vary more slowly than the other parameters.

Estimation often leads to an estimate(s) for s (s_m) that is greater than zero but less than one. This result indicates that the estimated NL model is not globally consistent with stochastic utility maximization (⇔ not globally consistent with an underlying density function).[28] For details see *Diversions 1* and *2*. For cases where the s_m are all positive but not all one or greater, Börsh-Supan (1990) and Herriges and Kling (1996) have derived the conditions under which the estimated NL model is consistent with stochastic utility maximization at a specified $\langle V_{mj} \rangle$.[29] If these local conditions hold at every $\langle V_{mj} \rangle$ in the data set and at every $\langle V_{mj} \rangle$ that is being evaluated for policy purposes, the estimated model is locally consistent with stochastic utility maximization. The basics of these conditions are presented in *Diversion 4*, but an example from Kling and Herriges (1995) suggests that if some of the estimated s_m are less than one by a significant amount, the estimated model will not be locally consistent with utility maximization.

Diversion 4: Conditions under which the estimated model is locally consistent with stochastic utility maximization at $\langle V_{mj} \rangle$.

continued

---

[27] One can increase the accuracy of the likelihood function and reduce the probability of encountering machine infinity by coding expressions of the form $\ln[\exp(a)+\exp(b)+\exp(c)]$ as $a + \ln[1+\exp(b-a)+\exp(c-a)]$.

[28] To complicate things more, note that since the estimated s_m are random variables, one should be concerned with whether one can reject the joint null hypothesis that the $\langle s_{mj} \rangle$ are each 1 or greater. Note that this complication also holds when considering local consistency. For more details see Kling and Herriges (1995).

[29] Herriges and Kling (1996) correct a misstatement in Börsh-Supan (1990) and provide second order derivative conditions and some bounds on the consistency region.

A necessary, but generally not a sufficient condition for local consistency is that $Prob(k) \geq 1 - s_k \;\forall k$, where *Prob(k)* is the probability of choosing an alternative in group *k*. Note that this condition will always be fulfilled if $s_m \geq 1 \;\forall\; m$, but if ($0 < s_m < 1$) the probability of the condition being violated increases as *Prob(k)* decreases and as s_k decreases.

If there are J_k alternatives in group *k*, then there are $(J_k - 1)$ conditions for that group, including $Prob(k) \geq 1 - s_k$. For details see Herriges and Kling (1996), and remember that they express the conditions in terms of θ_k, where $\theta_k = 1/s_k$.

When the estimated model is neither globally or locally consistent with stochastic utility maximization, it is an indication that the NL framework is not appropriate, or the assumed nesting structure is incorrect for the population, or the assumed nesting structure is incorrect for some subset of the population, or the $\langle V_{mj} \rangle$ are misspecified. One can impose global consistency by replacing, in estimation, s_m with $s_m = 1 + \exp(\rho_m)$. Not surprisingly, imposing consistency can have a significant effect on the parameter estimates. For more specifics on the implications of different nesting structures, see Kling and Thompson (1996) and Hauber and Parsons (1996).

One must also be cognizant of choice-based samples; that is, samples where individuals are selected into the sample as a function of the alternative(s) they choose. For example, a sample of anglers recruited at fishing sites is choice-based, and the sample anglers will take more trips, on average, than anglers randomly chosen from the population of anglers. Choice-based samples are typically easier to collect than a random sample of the population.

Without weights in the likelihood function to correct for the nonrepresentativeness of the sample in terms of choices made, parameter estimates will be inconsistent. Simply put, choices need to be weighted such that the contribution to the likelihood function is reduced for choices that are over-represented in the sample and increased for choices that are under-represented in the sample. With correct weights choices in the weighted sample have the same proportions as in the population. For details see Manski and Lerman (1977). Morey *et al.* (1995 and 1998a) use weights to correct for the fact that the anglers in their choice-based sample take, on average, more trips than the average angler in their target population. Creation of weights requires independent information on how alternative choices are distributed in the population, and this information is often not available.

One must also be cautious when using the estimated parameters to draw inferences from a sample to the population. If the sample is not representative of the population in terms of the characteristics of its members, sample averages will not reflect population averages, even when one has correctly estimated the parameters.[30] To estimate behavioral changes or consumer's surplus estimates for the target population, one needs to know the joint distribution in the population of the individual characteristics in the model. If this distribution is known, often it is not, one can determine the probability that an individual with certain characteristics appears in the population and compare this to the proportion of individuals in the sample with these characteristics. This information can then be used to weight the estimate for each individual in the sample to obtain a weighted average that reflects the population average.

For example, if the intent is to estimate the average consumer's surplus for a population of anglers, if gender is the only individual characteristics in the model, 60% of anglers in the population are male but 80% of the anglers in the sample are male, then to obtain an estimate of the average consumer's surplus for the population, before averaging, the female consumer's surplus estimates in the model should be multiplied by two and the male estimates by 3/4.

For example, Morey *et al.*(1997), when estimating average consumer's surplus for the population, weight to correct for the fact that low income households, blacks, and certain age groups are under-represented in the sample.

In conclusion, one needs to consider why there should be group constants or a nested model. If all of the important explanatory variables are included in the model, there is no need for group or alternative specific constants, and they should not be included. Including group or alternative specific constants will always improve the fit but can mask the true effects of the included explanatory variables. The more numerous the added constants, the less there is left to be explained by the explanatory variables. The intent of modeling and estimation is to explain observed behavior and how behavior and utility will differ if the values of the explanatory variables change, not to solely predict the sample, so constants should be used with caution.

One should also ask why the random components are likely to be correlated by group. If the answer is an omitted variable that varies more (or less) within a group than across groups, it would be better to try to collect that data and

[30] It is important to distinguish between samples that are not representative in terms of the choices made verus samples that are not representative in terms of important individual characteristics. Samples can be either, neither or both. Nonrepresentative in terms of choice made causes, without weighting, parameter estimates to be inconsistent, nonrepresentative in term of individual characteristics does not.

include the variable in the model than to nest. Nesting can also mask the effect of explanatory variables.

3.5 DERIVATION OF EXPECTED MAXIMUM UTILITY FOR THE TWO-LEVEL NL MODEL

The intent of this section is to use the basics of probability theory to derive expected maximum utility from Equations (3.1) and (3.8). Expected maximum utility often plays an important role in the derivation of compensating variation and equivalent variation. Before proceeding with the derivation of expected maximum utility from the NL model, it is important to point out that the expected maximum utility derived in this section is the expected maximum utility *per choice occasion*, not for the year or fishing season. One must remain cognizant of this if one's intent is to derive the per year compensating variation associated with a change in the attributes of a site or sites.

Let $U \equiv \max\left(\left\langle U_{mj}\right\rangle\right) \equiv \max\left(\left\langle V_{mj}+\varepsilon_{mj}\right\rangle\right)$ denote the largest element in the vector $\left\langle V_{mj}+\varepsilon_{mj}\right\rangle$. Therefore, given Equation (3.1), expected maximum utility, *E(U)*, is

$$E(U)=\int_{\varepsilon_{11}=-\infty}^{+\infty}\int_{\varepsilon_{12}=-\infty}^{+\infty}\cdots\int_{\varepsilon_{mj}=-\infty}^{+\infty}\cdots\int_{\varepsilon_{MJ}=-\infty}^{+\infty}\max\left(V_{11}+\varepsilon_{11},V_{12}+\varepsilon_{12},\ldots,V_{mj}+\varepsilon_{mj},\ldots,V_{MJ}+\varepsilon_{MJ}\right)$$
$$f\left(\varepsilon_{11},\varepsilon_{12},\ldots,\varepsilon_{mj},\ldots,\varepsilon_{MJ}\right)d\varepsilon_{MJ}\cdots d\varepsilon_{mj}\cdots d\varepsilon_{12}d\varepsilon_{11}. \tag{3.31}$$

Equation (3.31) is the equation for the expected value of the function $\max\left(\left\langle V_{mj}+\varepsilon_{mj}\right\rangle\right)$. Recall that the individual knows his or her maximum utility; $E(U)$ is our expectation of it. Equation (3.31) can be written more simply by dividing the density into *C* regions such that in region *ni* alternative *ni* is chosen (i.e., in region *ni*, alternative *ni* has maximum utility). Dividing into these *ni* regions, one obtains

$$E(U)=\sum_{n=1}^{M}\sum_{i=1}^{J_n}\int_{\varepsilon_{ni}=-\infty}^{+\infty}\left(V_{ni}+\varepsilon_{ni}\right)F_{ni}\left(\left\langle V_{ni}+\varepsilon_{ni}-V_{mj}\right\rangle\right)d\varepsilon_{ni}\,, \tag{3.32}$$

where, as noted in Equation (3.7) $\int_{\varepsilon_{ni}=-\infty}^{+\infty}F_{ni}\left(\left\langle V_{ni}+\varepsilon_{ni}-V_{mj}\right\rangle\right)d\varepsilon_{ni}=Prob(ni)$.

Equation (3.32) identifies expected maximum utility for **any** discrete choice model that is consistent with Equation (3.1). In this sense Equation (3.32) is quite general, and one could, in theory, plug any specific CDF, $F(\langle \varepsilon_{mj} \rangle)$, into Equation (3.32) to derive the expected maximum utility associated with that CDF. A critical issue, as with the derivation of the *Prob(ni)*, is when Equation (3.32) will have a closed-form solution. It has a closed-form solution if one assumes the generalized extreme value distribution denoted in Equation (3.8), as is now demonstrated.

To obtain expected maximum utility for the two-level NL model, substitute Equation (3.10) into Equation (3.32) to obtain

$$E(U) = \sum_{n=1}^{M} \sum_{i=1}^{J_n} \int_{\varepsilon_{ni}=-\infty}^{+\infty} (V_{ni} + \varepsilon_{ni}) \exp\left\{ -\sum_{m=1}^{M} a_m \left[\sum_{j=1}^{J_m} \exp\left(-s_m\left(V_{ni} + \varepsilon_{ni} - V_{mj}\right)\right) \right]^{1/s_m} \right\}$$
$$\times a_n \left[\sum_{j=1}^{J_n} \exp\left(-s_n\left(V_{ni} + \varepsilon_{ni} - V_{nj}\right)\right) \right]^{(1/s_n)-1} \exp(-s_n \varepsilon_{ni}) d\varepsilon_{ni}. \tag{3.33}$$

Simplify by making the change of variables $w = V_{ni} + \varepsilon_{ni}$ ($\Rightarrow d\varepsilon = dw$ because V_{ni} is a constant, and $\varepsilon_{ni} = w - V_{ni}$) to obtain

$$E(U) = \sum_{n=1}^{M} \sum_{i=1}^{J_n} \int_{w=-\infty}^{+\infty} w \exp\left\{ -\sum_{m=1}^{M} a_m \left[\sum_{j=1}^{J_m} \exp\left(-s_m\left(w - V_{mj}\right)\right) \right]^{1/s_m} \right\}$$
$$\times a_n \left[\sum_{j=1}^{J_n} \exp\left(-s_n\left(w - V_{nj}\right)\right) \right]^{(1/s_n)-1} \exp\left[-s_n\left(w - V_{ni}\right)\right] dw. \tag{3.34}$$

Note that the term in Equation (3.34),

$$\exp\left\{ -\sum_{m=1}^{M} a_m \left[\sum_{j=1}^{J_m} \exp\left(-s_m\left(w - V_{mj}\right)\right) \right]^{1/s_m} \right\} = \exp\left[-D \exp(-w)\right]$$

where

$$D = \sum_{m=1}^{M} a_m \left[\sum_{j=1}^{J_m} \exp\left(s_m V_{mj}\right) \right]^{1/s_m}, \tag{3.35}$$

and that the term in Equation (3.34),

$$\left[\sum_{j=1}^{J_n}\exp(-s_n(w-V_{ni}))\right]^{(1/s_n)-1} = \exp(-w)\exp(s_n w)\left[\sum_{j=1}^{J_n}\exp(s_n V_{nj})\right]^{(1/s_n)-1}.$$

Substituting these two simplifications into Equation (3.34) and moving all of the terms that do not contain w, with the exception of D, to the left of the integral sign, one obtains

$$E(U)$$

$$=\sum_{n=1}^{M}\sum_{i=1}^{J_n} a_n \exp(s_n V_{ni})\left[\sum_{j=1}^{J_n}\exp(s_n V_{nj})\right]^{(1/s_n)-1}\int_{w=-\infty}^{+\infty} w\exp(-w)\exp[-D\exp(-w)]dw. \tag{3.36}$$

Now examine the first term in Equation (3.36). It equals D. This follows from Euler's Theorem, as is now demonstrated. D, Equation (3.35), is homogenous of degree one in $\langle \exp(V_{mj})\rangle$, and

$$\frac{\partial D}{\partial \exp(V_{ni})} = \exp(-V_{ni})a_n \exp(s_n V_{ni})\left[\sum_{j=1}^{J_n}\exp(s_n V_{nj})\right]^{(1/s_n)-1}. \tag{3.37}$$

Therefore, by Euler's Theorem,[31]

$$\sum_{n=1}^{M}\sum_{i=1}^{J_n}\exp(V_{ni})\frac{\partial D}{\partial \exp(V_{ni})}$$

$$=\sum_{n=1}^{M}\sum_{i=1}^{J_n}\exp(V_{ni})\left\{\exp(-V_{ni})a_n\exp(s_n V_{ni})\left[\sum_{j=1}^{J_n}\exp(s_n V_{nj})\right]^{(1/s_n)-1}\right\}$$

$$=\sum_{n=1}^{M}\sum_{i=1}^{J_n}a_n\exp(s_n V_{ni})\left\{\left[\sum_{j=1}^{J_n}\exp(s_n V_{nj})\right]^{(1/s_n)-1}\right\}$$

$$= D. \tag{3.38}$$

---

[31] Euler's Theorem states $D=\sum_{n=1}^{M}\sum_{i=1}^{J_n}\gamma_{ni}\frac{\partial D}{\partial \alpha_{ni}}$ if D is homogenous of degree one in the $\langle \gamma_{mj}\rangle$. In our case, $\gamma_{ni}=\exp(V_{ni})$.

Since the first term in Equation (3.36) equals D, Equation (3.36) implies

$$E(U) = \int_{w=-\infty}^{+\infty} wD\exp(-w)\exp[-D\exp(-w)]dw . \tag{3.39}$$

This is where things get exciting. Note that the density function for an extreme value distribution with mode = ln(D) is[32]

$$f(w) = D\exp(-w)\exp[-D\exp(-w)]. \tag{3.40}$$

Therefore, since $E(w) = \int_{w=-\infty}^{+\infty} wf(w)dw,$ Equation (3.39) is the expected value (mean) of an extreme value distribution with a scale parameter of 1. It is well known that this expected value is ln$D$ + 0.57721, where 0.57721 is Euler's Constant. Therefore, expected maximum utility is

$$E(U) = \ln D + 0.57721 . \tag{3.41}$$

E(U) can be interpreted as the expected maximum utility for a representative individual. Equation (3.41) is used in Section 3.7 to derive a compensating variation and an equivalent variation from the NL model. Remember that *E(U)* is the expected maximum utility per choice occasion and that there will be a different *E(U)* for each type of individual.

For example: In the **model of participation and site choice**, the season is divided into a finite number of periods (choice occasions) so *E(U)* is expected maximum utility per choice occasion. Expected maximum utility for the season is the sum of the per-period expected utilities. If attributes vary from period to period, expected utility will vary across the periods.

In the **model of site choice with saltwater sites, lakes and rivers**, each trip is a choice occasion so *E(U)* is the expected maximum utility **per-trip**. Per-trip expected maximum utility does not easily translate into seasonal expected maximum utility.

continued

---

[32] For more details on the extreme value distribution see Equation (3.25), *Diversion* 3 and Johnson *et al.* (1994).

As we will see in the derivation of compensating variation, the distinction between per-period and per-trip expected maximum utility is quite important.

As an aside, note that it can be shown that

$$\frac{\partial E(U)}{\partial V_{ni}} = Prob(ni)\,. \tag{3.42}$$

Said loosely, Equation (3.42) is the discrete-choice random-utility analog of Roy's Identity where V_{ni} is interpreted as the negative of the *normalized price* of alternative *ni*.

3.6 THE FUNCTIONAL FORMS OF THE CONDITIONAL INDIRECT UTILITY FUNCTIONS, $\langle V_{mj} \rangle$, AND BUDGET EXHAUSTION

Let *I* denote the budget for the choice occasion, p_{mj} the price (cost) of alternative *mj*, β^{mj} the vector of other observed attributes of alternative *mj*, and *G* the vector of characteristics of the individual, excluding budget, that influence the choice of alternative. The choice set consists of *C* mutually exclusive alternatives and a numeraire composite good. During each choice occasion, the individual is constrained to consume one, and only one, of the *C* alternatives, and then spends the rest of his or her budget on the numeraire good. For example, if alternative *ni* is chosen, $(I - p_{ni})$ is spent on the numeraire good and budget exhaustion requires that V_{mj} is restricted to functions of the form[33]

$$V_{mj} = V_{mj}\left(\left(I - p_{mj}\right), \beta^{mj}, G\right) \;\forall\; mj\,. \tag{3.43}$$

---

[33] More generally, $V_{mj}((I - p_{mj}), p_{num}, \beta^{mj}, G)$ where p_{num} is the price of the numeraire. Since this function is an indirect utility function, it must possess all the required properties of such functions. These properties are continuity, homogeneity of degree zero in $\left(I, p_{num}, p_{mj}\right)$, nondecreasing in $\left(I - p_{mj}\right)$, and nonincreasing and quasiconvex in p_{nun}. Assuming all individuals in the population face the same price for the numeraire, p_{num} is set equal to one without loss of generality, and all $V_{mj} = V_{mj}\left(\left(I - p_{mj}\right), \beta^{mj}, G\right)$ are consistent with $V_{mj} = V_{mj}\left(\left(I - p_{mj}\right), p_{num}, \beta^{mj}, G\right)$ being homogeneous of degree zero in $\left(I, p_{num}, p_{mj}\right)$, and nonincreasing and quasiconvex in p_{num}. Regularity then requires only that $V_{mj} = V_{mj}\left(\left(I - p_{mj}\right), \beta^{mj}, G\right)$ be continuous in $((I - p_{mj}, \beta^{mj})$ and nondecreasing in $(I - p_{mj})$.

Denote $\partial V_{mj} / \partial(I - p_{mj}) = \mu((I - p_{mj}), \beta^{mj}, G)$, where $\mu(.)$ is the marginal utility of money, that is, the utility that the individual gets from the marginal unit of the numeraire. Regularity requires that $\mu(.)$ is nonnegative.

Consider first cases where $\mu(.)$ is not a function of $(I - p_{mj})$ or β^{mj}. Such models will be referred to as models with *zero income effects,* that is, models where, for a given individual, the marginal utility of money is a constant, independent of which alternative is chosen. For example,

$$V_{mj} = \mu(G)(I - p_{mj}) + h_{mj}(\beta^{mj}, G) \;\forall mj \,. \tag{3.43a}$$

Note that Equation (3.43a) allows the marginal utility of money to be different for different individuals; e.g., it could vary as a function of age, race, gender, or fishing ability.[34] Models consistent with Equation (3.43a) are called *zero income effects* models because the budget, I, does not influence the choice probabilities. Choosing a model with *zero income effects* means that data on the budget per choice occasion need not be collected, but also means that compensating variations are constrained to not vary by income level.

The reason that the budget drops out of the choice probabilities is that any attribute (budget, price or other attribute) that adds the same constant to each of the C conditional indirect utility functions will not influence the choice of alternative [$\mu(G)I$ is one such constant].

Looking ahead, when there are *zero income effects*, the compensating and equivalent variations for any proposed change are equal and easy to estimate. Because of this, in the applied literature it is very common to assume that

$$V_{mj} = \mu_0(I - p_{mj}) + h_{mj}(\beta^{mj}, G) \;\forall mj \,, \tag{3.43a$'$}$$

where μ_0 is the same constant for all individuals. However, the more general Equation (3.43a) is often preferable because it allows for more variation in choices, and allows willingness to pay to vary across individuals as a function of their characteristics.

Things get more complicated when there are income effects. Models where $\mu(\cdot)$ is a function $(I - p_{mj})$ or β^{mj} are deemed models with *income effects.* These are models where the marginal utility of money varies as I varies or because the utility from the numeraire depends on which of the discrete alternatives is chosen. I will consider just a few simple examples. Consider first a

---

[34] Some of these individual characteristics might be correlated with the budget. Buchanan *et al.* (1998), in a model to explain the choice of mountain bike sites, find μ to be a function of the individual's characteristics, so does Morey *et al.* (1997), in a study valuing the preservation of monuments, where gender is a significant determinant of μ.

model where the marginal utility of money depends on which alternative is chosen but not on the budget.[35]

$$V_{mj} = \mu_{mj}(I - p_{mj}) + h_{mj}(\beta^{mj}, G) \ \ \forall mj . \qquad (3.43b)$$

Diversion 5: Consider the system of conditional indirect utility functions.

$$V_{mj} = \mu_{m}(I - p_{mj}) + h_{mj}(\beta^{mj}, G) \ \forall mj . \qquad (3.43b\text{-}1)$$

The budget, I, will influence whether the alternative chosen is of type m, but will not influence which alternative of type m will be chosen.

More generally, consider some attribute of the individual, g_k that enters all of the conditional indirect utility functions as "$+ \alpha g_k$ ". It will not influence the probabilities. Alternatively, if g_k interacts with one or more of the site characteristics, it will affect choice.

A rationale for Equation (3.43b) is the marginal enjoyment the individual gets from units of the numeraire, although independent of the number of units consumed, is dependent on which alternative was chosen. This would result if some of the alternatives were more or less complementary with the numeraire.

Now consider models where the marginal utility an individual gets from consuming the numeraire does not depend on which alternative was chosen but depends on the amount of the numeraire consumed. For example,

$$V_{mj} = \mu\left(G, \left(I - p_{mj}\right)\right)\left(I - p_{mj}\right) + h_{mj}\left(\beta^{mj}, G\right) \ \forall \, mj . \qquad (3.43c)$$

Consider two cases of Equation (3.43c): models where $\partial\mu(.) / \partial(I - p_{mj}) \neq 0 \ \forall mj$ (denote these as models with *continuous income effects* and models where $\mu(G,(I - p_{mj}))$ is a step function in $(I - p_{mj})$ (denote these as models with *step income effects)*. The distinction is important for data collection, estimation, and the calculation of the compensating variation. An example of a *continuous income effects* model is

$$V_{mj} = \mu_0(I - p_{mj}) + \mu_1(I - p_{mj})^2 + h_{mj}(\beta^{mj}, G) \ \ \forall \, mj . \qquad (3.43c\text{-}1)$$

---

[35] Note that Equation (3.43b) is a special case of $V_{mj} = \mu(\beta^{mj}, G)(I - p_{mj}) + h_{mj}(\beta^{mj}, G) \ \forall \, mj$.

Estimation of continuous income effects models requires data on the budget per choice occasion.[36]

An example of a *step income effects* model is

$$V_{mj} = g(I - p_{mj}) + h_{mj}(\beta^{mj}, G) \; \forall \, mj \qquad (3.43c\text{-}2)$$

where

$$g(I - p_{mj}) = \mu_0 (I - p_{mj}) \text{ if } (I - p_{mj}) \le I^0,$$
$$g(I - p_{mj}) = \mu_0 (I^0) + \mu_1 (I^1 - p_{mj} - I^0) \text{ if } I^1 \ge (I - p_{mj}) > I^0,$$
$$g(I - p_{mj}) = \mu_0 (I^0) + \mu_1 (I^1 - I^0) + \mu_2 (I - p_{mj} - I^1) \text{ if } (I - p_{mj}) > I^1.$$

Denote this function, $g(I - p_{mj})$, a step function of $(I - p_{mj})$, where μ_0 is the marginal utility of the first I^0 units of the numeraire, μ_1 is the marginal utility of the next $I^1 - I^0$ units of the numeraire, etc. There is no presumption that the sequence μ_0, μ_1, μ_2 is either monotonically increasing or decreasing. Assuming *step income effects* is a simple and often realistic way to incorporate income effects. For example, if one believes that willingness to pay for a policy scenario remains constant over broad income ranges but does depend on whether one is poor, a two-step function would be appropriate. In addition, incorporating income effects in this manner does not require detailed budget data, just the appropriate budget category.

Returning to the general issue of how site attributes affect site choice, any site characteristic that enters all the conditional indirect utility functions as a linear term with a common parameter, and that varies in magnitude across alternatives but does not vary in magnitude across the alternatives in *m*, will influence whether an alternative of type *m* is chosen, but not which alternative in *m*. For example, if size is an attribute, all alternatives of type *m* are size 10, and the coefficient on size is the same in all of the conditional indirect utility functions for alternatives of type *m*, conditional on choosing an alternative of type *m*, size will not influence which of the alternatives of type *m* you will choose.

---

[36] Models with *continuous income effects* include Morey *et al.* (1993), Buchanan (1998) and Herriges and Kling (1997). Morey *et al.* (1993) include all alternatives in the choice set and assume the budget per choice-occasion is yearly income divided by the specified number of choice occasions. Buchanan *et al.* (1998) estimate a model where the choice set includes only mountain bike sites, and they assume the daily budget available for mountain biking is 1/30 of monthly discretionary income.

For example, in the **model of site choice with saltwater sites, lakes and rivers**, expected catch rate is likely to be an important attribute of all of the sites. Assume there is some variation in catch but that all lake sites have the same catch rate and the coefficient on catch is the same constant in all of the conditional indirect utility functions for lake sites. In this case, catch rate will influence whether one chooses a lake site, but, conditional on a lake trip being chosen, will not influence which specific lake is visited.

3.7 COMPENSATING VARIATION AND EQUIVALENT VARIATION

Let $P \equiv \langle p_{mj} \rangle$, $\beta \equiv \langle \beta^{mj} \rangle$, and consider a change from the initial state $\{I^0, P^0, \beta^0\}$ to some proposed state $\{I^1, P^1, \beta^1\}$. For the choice occasion, maximum utility in the initial state is

$$U^0 = \max\left(\left\langle U^0_{mj} \right\rangle\right) = \max\left(\left\langle V^0_{mj} + \varepsilon_{mj} \right\rangle\right) \equiv U\left(I^0, P^0, \beta^0, G, \left\langle \varepsilon_{mj} \right\rangle\right), \quad (3.44)$$

and maximum utility in the proposed state is[37]

$$U^1 = \max\left(\left\langle U^1_{mj} \right\rangle\right) = \max\left(\left\langle V^1_{mj} + \varepsilon_{mj} \right\rangle\right) \equiv U\left(I^1, P^1, \beta^1, G, \left\langle \varepsilon_{mj} \right\rangle\right). \quad (3.45)$$

Denote maximum utility in the proposed state with compensation, c, subtracted from the budget

$$\begin{aligned} U^1(c) &= \max\left(\left\langle U^1_{mj}(c) \right\rangle\right) \\ &= \max\left(\left\langle V^1_{mj}(c) + \varepsilon_{mj} \right\rangle\right) \\ &\equiv U\left(I^1 - c, P^1, \beta^1, G, \left\langle \varepsilon_{mj} \right\rangle\right), \end{aligned} \quad (3.46)$$

where

$$V^1_{mj}(c) \equiv V_{mj}\left(\left(I^1 - p^1_{mj} - c\right), \beta^{mj1}, G\right). \quad (3.47)$$

---

[37] Note that $\left\langle \varepsilon_{mj} \right\rangle$ is assumed not state specific; that is, $\left\langle \varepsilon^0_{mj} \right\rangle = \left\langle \varepsilon^1_{mj} \right\rangle$, a questionable but universal assumption.

Note that $U^1(c=0)=U^1$. For the choice occasion, the compensating variation, *CV*, that the individual associates with a change from $\{I^0,P^0,\beta^0\}$ to $\{I^1,P^1,\beta^1\}$ is that *c* which equates U^0 and $U^1(c)$; that is,

$$U^0\left(I^0,P^0,\beta^0,G,\langle\varepsilon_{mj}\rangle\right)\equiv U\left(I^1-CV,P^1,\beta^1,G,\langle\varepsilon_{mj}\rangle\right). \qquad (3.48)$$

The *CV* is known to the individual but is a random variable from the researcher's perspective; to know *CV* one must know $\langle\varepsilon_{mj}\rangle$. For an improvement, the *CV* is nonnegative and often zero. For a deterioration, the *CV* is nonpositive and often zero. For example, if the change is a deterioration in alternative *lk* and an individual was not choosing *lk*, the individual's *CV* is zero. For this deterioration, the *CV* is negative for only those individuals that were choosing *lk*.

The equivalent variation, *EV*, is defined in an analogous manner. Denote maximum utility in the initial state with compensation, *cc*, added to the budget:

$$\begin{aligned}U^0(cc)&=\max\left(\langle U^0_{mj}(cc)\rangle\right)\\&=\max\left(\langle V^0_{mj}(cc)+\varepsilon_{mj}\rangle\right)\\&\equiv U\left(I^0+cc,P^0,\beta^0,G,\langle\varepsilon_{mj}\rangle\right),\end{aligned} \qquad (3.49)$$

where

$$V^0_{mj}(cc)\equiv V_{mj}\left(\left(I^0-p^0_{mj}+cc\right),\beta^{mj0},G\right). \qquad (3.50)$$

Note that $U^0(cc=0)=U^0$. For the choice occasion, the equivalent variation, *EV*, that the individual associates with a change from $\{I^0,P^0,\beta^0\}$ to $\{I^1,P^1,\beta^1\}$ is that *cc* which equates $U^0(cc)$ and U^1; that is,

$$U\left(I^0+EV,P^0,\beta^0,G,\langle\varepsilon_{mj}\rangle\right)\equiv U\left(I^1,P^1,\beta^1,G,\langle\varepsilon_{mj}\rangle\right). \qquad (3.51)$$

Like the *CV*, the *EV* is known to the individual but is a random variable from the researcher's perspective.

The *CV* and *EV* are always of the same sign. For an improvement, the *CV* is how much the individual would be willing to pay, per choice occasion, for the improvement, and the *EV* is how much the individual would have to be paid to voluntarily forego the improvement. For a deterioration, the *CV* is how much the individual would have to be paid to voluntarily accept the deterioration, and the *EV* is how much the individual would be willing to pay to stop the deterioration.

The *CV* will vary across individuals for two reasons: the $\langle V_{mj} \rangle$ can vary across individuals, and for individuals with the same $\langle V_{mj} \rangle$, $\langle \varepsilon_{mj} \rangle$ will vary across individuals. The *CV* for a given individual will also vary across choice occasions because the $\langle \varepsilon_{mj} \rangle$ vary across choice occasions. The $\langle V_{mj} \rangle$ will vary across individuals for many reasons: differences in income, different costs for alternatives, and differences in other individual characteristics that affect the $\langle V_{mj} \rangle$. Denote all individuals who have the same $\langle V_{mj} \rangle$ as individuals of the same *type*.

Each individual has a specific *CV*, but from the researcher's perspective the *CV* for individuals of a given *type* is a random variable with some density function, *f*(*CV*). Note that although the *CV* for a given change can be positive for some individuals and negative for others, it will either be nonnegative or nonpositive, but not both, for all individual of the same type. The only exception would be a zero *CV* for all individuals of the same type. f(*CV*) will have a finite range, and one end of the range will be zero. For example, for an improvement in alternative *mj*, all other alternatives remain unchanged, the *CV* will be zero for all those individuals of this type that do not choose alternative *mj* in the new state, and the maximum *CV* will be the *CV* for those who chose alternative *mj* before it was improved.[38] More generally, denote the *CV* for an individual that chooses *mj* both before and after a change *CV*(*mj*|*mj*). *CV*(*mj*|*mj*) is the *c* that equates $\left(V^{1}_{mj}(c) + \varepsilon_{mj}\right)$ and $\left(V^{0}_{mj} + \varepsilon_{mj}\right)$, so it does not depend on $\langle \varepsilon_{mj} \rangle$ and can be easily calculated.[39]

The median *CV* for individuals of a given *type*, CV^{med}, can be zero. For example, if alternative *mj* is improved, all other alternatives unchanged, and the probability of choosing alternative *mj* is less than 0.5 in the improved state ($Prob^{1}(mj) < 0.5$), CV^{med} =0 because the majority of individuals of this type are not choosing *mj* in the new state. In contrast, if alternative *mj* is improved, all other alternatives unchanged, and $Prob^{0}(mj) > 0.5$, CV^{med} =*CV*(*mj*|*mj*). For a deterioration in alternative *mj*, all other alternatives unchanged, CV^{med} =0 if $Prob^{0}(mj) < 0.5$ and CV^{med} =*CV*(*mj*|*mj*) if $Prob^{1}(mj) > 0.5$. Approximation of CV^{med} for probabilities not in these ranges is discussed below.

Denote the expected value of the *CV* for individuals of a given type, *E*(*CV*). In general, it is not possible to directly calculate *E*(*CV*) from Equation (3.48);

---

[38] If the individual chooses alternative *mj* and then alternative *mj* is improved with no changes in the other alternatives, the individual will also choose *mj* after the change because *mj* maximizes utility in both states.

[39] In contrast, consider the *CV* for an individual that initially choose alternative *ni* and then switches to alternative *mj*, *CV*(*ni*|*mj*). It depends on both ε_{ni} and ε_{mj}.

the primary exception is when there are *zero income effects* or *step income effects*.[40] However, it is possible to approximate E(*CV*). Note that the range of the *CV* provides upper and lower bounds on E(*CV*), and, as the above example indicates, these can sometimes be calculated. Denote the *CV* for the *representative* individual of a given type CV^R, where CV^R is the monetary compensation (or payment) in the proposed state that would make the expected maximum utility in the proposed state equal to the expected maximum utility in the initial state; that is,

$$E(U^0) \equiv E[U(I^0, P^0, \beta^0, G, \langle \varepsilon_{mj} \rangle)]$$
$$= E[U(I^1 - CV^R, P^1, \beta^1, G, \langle \varepsilon_{mj} \rangle)], \qquad (3.52)$$

where expected maximum utility, *E(U)*, is defined by Equations (3.41) and (3.35). *E(U)* is the utility of a representative individual in that it is maximum utility if $\varepsilon_{mj} = 0 \ \forall mj$. CV^R is the random-utility analog of the standard definition of the compensating variation in terms of a continuous utility function.[41] The distinctions between E(*CV*), CV^R and CV^{med} were first considered by Hanemann (1985). A revised version of that paper appears in this book as Chapter 2.

Define the EV^R, per choice occasion, as

---

[40] It is possible to create examples where it is possible to solve for *E*(*CV*) even when there are income effects, but the problem quickly becomes analytically intractable and is intractable for most estimated models. Consider a simple example with only two alternatives, where alternative 1 is improved and alternative 2 remains the same. In this case, there are only three possible behavior types: those who choose 1 both before and after the change, those that initially chose 2 but switch to 1, and those that choose 2 in both states. No one will switch from 1 to 2. One can easily calculate *CV*(1|1), and *CV*(2|2)=0. One can also calculate the proportion of individuals that will choose each behavior type. The proportion of individuals that choose 1 in both states is $Prob^0(1)$, and the proportion that choose 2 in both states is $Prob^1(2)$, so the proportion that switches from 2 to 1 is $1 - Prob^0(1) - Prob^1(2)$. Therefore, $E(CV) = Prob^0(1)CV(1|1) + \theta$, where θ is $f(\varepsilon_1, \varepsilon_2)CV(2|1)$ integrated over that part of the density function where individuals of this type switch from 2 to 1. Even in this simple case, this might be a difficult integral to solve analytically, but there are examples where it can be solved.

[41] To avoid confusion, note that the term *representative consumer* has two possible meaning in the ML and NL literature: the above meaning, and as a *consumer* whose utility function over continuous amounts of each alternative represents the aggregate behavior of a group individuals who are individually constrained to choose only one alternatively, but collectively choose some of each alternative. For details on this latter meaning see, Anderson *et al.* (1987 and 1992), Verboven (1996), and Smith and Von Haefen (1997).

$$E(U^1) \equiv E\left[U\left(I^1, P^1, \beta^1, G, \langle \varepsilon_{mj} \rangle\right)\right]$$
$$= E\left[U\left(I^0 + EV^R, P^0, \beta^0, G, \langle \varepsilon_{mj} \rangle\right)\right], \qquad (3.53)$$

that is, the monetary compensation (or payment) in the initial state that would make expected maximum utility in the initial state equal to expected maximum utility in the proposed state.

If one imposes *zero income effects* [Equation (3.43a)], Equation (3.45) can be solved for CV^R, and $CV^R = EV^R$. Specifically,

$$CV^R = EV^R$$
$$= (1/\mu)\left\{E\left[U\left(I^0, P^1, \beta^1, G, \langle \varepsilon_{mj} \rangle\right)\right]\right.$$
$$\left. - E\left[U\left(I^0, P^0, \beta^0, G, \langle \varepsilon_{mj} \rangle\right)\right]\right\} + (I^1 - I^0) \qquad (3.54)$$
$$= (1/\mu)[\ln D^1 - \ln D^0],$$

where D is defined in Equation (3.35), D^1 is D evaluated at $\{I^1, P^1, \beta^1\}$ and D^0 is D evaluated at $\{I^0, P^0, \beta^0\}$. Intuitively, in the case of *zero income effects*, CV^R is just the change in expected maximum utility converted into a money metric by multiplying by the inverse of the constant marginal utility of money, $(1/\mu)$.[42]

In addition, if there are zero income effects, $CV^R = E(CV) = CV^{med} = E(EV) = EV^R = EV^{med}$. For details see Hanemann (1985) or McFadden(1996).[43] When there are zero income effects, the easiest way to calculate $E(CV)$ is to calculate CV^R using Equation (3.54).

When there are *step income effects*, and the policies that are under consideration have welfare effects small enough so that the marginal utility of money at $(I - p_{mj} - c)$ is the same as at $(I - p_{mj})$, Equation (3.54) still applies. With broad steps in the marginal utility of money function, the researcher can estimate compensating variations that vary by income category without subjecting herself to the complication described next.[44]

---

[42] Note that when there are *zero income effects*, if one incorrectly multiples the prices of all the alternatives by $\lambda > 0$ and re-estimates the model, the value of the likelihood function with not change and expected maximum utility will not change, but the estimated marginal utility of money will be wrong, and using Equation (3.4), one will estimate λCV^R rather than CV^R. That is, making alternative prices twice (half) as large as they should be will incorrectly double (halve) the *CV* estimates.

[43] It follows that when there are zero income effect, CV^{med} cannot be the largest or smallest *CV*, unless all *CV* are equal.

When there are *continuous income effects*, $CV^R \neq EV^R$, Equation (3.45) cannot be solved to obtain a closed-form solution for the CV^R and Equation (3.46) cannot be solved to obtain a closed-form solution for the EV^R. However, it is still easy to numerically calculate an individual's CV^R, or EV^R, for any proposed change. For example, given the estimated parameter values, an individual's CV^R for any proposed change can be calculated by using any numerical minimization algorithm to find the CV^R that minimizes

$$\left\{E\left[U\left(I^0, P^0, \beta^0, G, \langle \varepsilon_{mj} \rangle\right)\right] - E\left[U\left(I^1 - CV^R, P^1, \beta^1, G, \langle \varepsilon_{mj} \rangle\right)\right]\right\}^2$$

where $E(U)$ is defined by Equation (3.41).[45] The CV^R that minimizes this expression will be the individual's CV^R for the change.

Hanemann (1985) and McFadden (1996) demonstrate that when there are continuous income effects $CV^R \neq E(CV)$, and Hanemann demonstrates that CV^R can be greater than or less than $E(CV)$.

If one wants to approximate $E(CV)$ and there are continuous income effects, there is the issue of how best to approximate it. One approximation is CV^R.

With effort, one can more accurately approximate $E(CV)$. It is possible to randomly draw an $\langle \varepsilon_{mj} \rangle$ vector from the GEV distribution (Equation (3.8)) and then calculate the individual's CV conditional on the drawn $\langle \varepsilon_{mj} \rangle$ being the individual's true epsilons. That is, for the drawn $\langle \varepsilon_{mj} \rangle$, find the c that solves Equation (3.48).[46] An approximation to the $E(CV)$ can be obtained by calculating CV for each of t random draws from the GEV distribution and taking the average. Denote this approximation, $\hat{E}(CV)$. As $T \to \infty, \hat{E}(CV) \to E(CV)$. An approximation to CV^{med} ($\hat{CV}^{med}$) is the median of these t CV estimates.

The steps in calculating $\hat{E}(CV)$ are the same for both the NL model and its special case the ML model, but are much easier to implement for the ML model. This is because the ML model requires only that one make independent draws from the univariate extreme value distribution, but the NL model requires that one draw C dimensional vectors from a GEV distribution. The latter is much more difficult.

---

[44] For example, Morey *et al.* (1997) found a *step income effects* model more appropriate than either a *zero* or *continuous income effects* model, and from it derive estimates of willingness-to-pay for monument preservation that are significantly lower for the poor. Work by Morey *et. al* (1998b) on the choice of health care providers in Nepal indicates that the choice of provider depends on whether one is poor, but does not vary continuously with income.

[45] For example one can use the *optimization* routine in the statistical package *Gauss* or the *FindMinimum* command in the mathematical software *Mathematica*.

[46] In general, there will not be a closed-form solution for c. However, given $\langle \varepsilon_{\cdot} \rangle$, c can be estimated by using the optimization procedure in *Gauss* (*Optmum*) to search for the c that minimizes $M = \left[U'(c) - U^o\right]^2$.

Consider first a C alternative ML model with continuous income effects. Let $\langle \varepsilon_{mj}^{\tau} \rangle \equiv (\varepsilon_{11}^{\tau},\ldots,\varepsilon_{C}^{\tau})$, $\tau = 1,2,\ldots, t$, where each ε_{mj}^{τ} is a separate draw from the univariate extreme value distribution [Equation (3.25)]. The vector $\langle \varepsilon_{mj}^{\tau} \rangle$ is constructed by taking C such draws. Given $\langle \varepsilon_{mj}^{\tau} \rangle$, calculate CV^{τ} for draw τ. CV^{τ} is the individual's exact compensating variation if $\langle \varepsilon_{mj}^{\tau} \rangle$ is the epsilon vector that the individual actually experiences during that choice occasion. Calculate CV^{τ} for each of the $\langle \varepsilon_{mj}^{\tau} \rangle$, and approximate $E(CV)$ with

$$\hat{E}(CV) = (1/T)\sum_{\tau=1}^{T} CV^{\tau}.$$

Practically speaking, the number of draws, t, should be sufficiently large so that

$$(1/T)\sum_{\tau=1}^{T} CV^{\tau}$$

does not significantly change if t is increased. This can be a large number.

For the ML model with continuous income effects, implementing this procedure requires a method for taking random draws from the univariate extreme value distribution. It is well known that $y = F(x) \sim u(0,1)$, where $F(x)$ is the cumulative density function for any scalar random variable x, and $u(0,1)$ is the uniform distribution on the unit interval. That is, the distribution of any univariate CDF is uniform on the 0–1 interval. Consider the inverse function, $x = F^{-1}(y)$. If ξ is a random draw from $u(0,1)$, $\varepsilon = F^{-1}(\xi)$ is a random draw from $F(\varepsilon)$. Since *Gauss*, *Mathematica,* and other math/stat packages have built-in commands for taking random draws from the univariate distribution, one can use $\varepsilon = F^{-1}(\xi)$ to generate a random draw from any univariate CDF. Given the extreme value CDF [Equation (3.25)], $\varepsilon = F^{-1}(\xi) = -\ln(-\ln(\xi))$ and $-\ln(-\ln(\xi))$ is a random draw from the extreme value distribution if ξ is a random draw from the unit interval uniform distribution.

In contrast, for a NL model, to calculate $\hat{E}(CV)$ one must draw C dimensional epsilon vectors from the GEV distribution [Equation (3.8)]. McFadden (1996) has developed a technique to do this, but implementation is not for the faint of heart. The technique is complicated and computer intensive because it must account for the correlations across the alternatives implied by the nesting structure.

Herriges and Kling (1997) consider whether calculating $\hat{E}(CV)$, rather than CV^{R}, is worth the extra effort when one's intent is to estimate $E(CV)$. To investigate this issue, they calculate $\hat{E}(CV)$ for three different policy scenarios for nine different estimated models. For each model, $T = 1000$. The models vary in terms of the nesting structure and in the form income enters the $\langle V_{mj} \rangle$. The application is sport fishing and seems to be the first calculation of $\hat{E}(CV)$ for an estimated NL model with continuous income effects. They compare $\hat{E}(CV)$ and CV^{R} for an increase in catch rates for two different models; both models have continuous income effects; one is ML and the other NL. These comparisons are made at the averages over the sample and by income quartiles. For the NL model, the average of the sample CV^R is \$16.15 and the $\hat{E}(CV)$ is \$16.95, whereas for the ML model they are both \$17.41. The estimated CV^R and $\hat{E}(CV)$, which vary by income, also match closely by income quartiles. None of the differences are statistically significant. Although one should be hesitant to draw general conclusions from specific examples, the results from Herriges and Kling demonstrate that CV^R can closely approximate $\hat{E}(CV)$. Hanemann (1985) also has a numerical example where the CV^R closely approximates $E(CV)$.

In contrast, McFadden (1996) has demonstrated that the bias in CV^R as an estimate of $E(CV)$ can be larger than in the above examples if the policy causes very large changes in utility. He constructs a simple two-alternative example where it is possible to calculate, for a simple change, both the $E(CV)$ and the CV^R. The example has no prices and one site characteristic, where the level of the characteristic at the second site is held at zero. The model is ML and the budget, I, enters the two conditional indirect utility functions as $\sqrt{I}$, where $I =$ 1. For an increase in the site characteristic at site one from zero to 0.1, the bias in CV^R is 2.5%, for an increase from zero to 0.4, the bias in CV^R is 10.4%, and for an increase from zero to 1.0, the bias in CV^R is 29.9%.

McFadden (1996) also calculates $\hat{E}(CV)$ for three, three-alternative NL models, all with zero income effects. He chose models with zero income effects so $E(CV)$ could be calculated exactly and compared to the $\hat{E}(CV)$. The three models differ in terms of the assumed value for s. For $s = 1$ (a ML model), 755 draws were needed to reduce the error in $\hat{E}(CV)$ to less than 5%; for $s = 2$, 3206 draws were required; and for $s = 10$, 18,820 draws were required. These results indicate that fewer draws will be needed to accurately approximate $E(CV)$ with $\hat{E}(CV)$ when the model with income effects is ML rather than NL.

Given the difficulties associated with calculating $\hat{E}(CV)$, McFadden (1996) has developed bounds on $E(CV)$ that can be estimated without taking draws from a GEV distributions. For details see, McFadden (1996), Herriges and Kling (1997) and the comments above on calculating the range of the CV.

In summary, CV^R, $E(CV)$, and CV^{med} are measures of central tendency for $f(CV)$; $E(CV)$ is the mean of the distribution and CV^{med} is the median. Remember that generally there will be a different $f(CV)$ for each type of individual. The three measures of central tendency are equal when there are zero income effects and often equal when there are step income effects. When there are continuous income effects, CV^R and $\hat{E}(CV)$ both approximate $E(CV)$, and $\hat{E}(CV)$ can be made as accurate as needed by basing it on a large enough number of draws. $\hat{CV}^{med}$ can be calculated when calculating $\hat{E}(CV)$.

Note that in a just produced discussion paper, Karlstrom (1998) uses duality theory to characterize $E(CV)$ in the presence of income effects as an integral that can be numerically calculated as accurately as required. This characterization has the potential to avoid both the computational intensity associated with stimulating $E\left(\hat{CV}\right)$ and the potential for approximation error associated with CV^R.

Since these measures of central tendency are functions of the estimated parameters values and the parameter estimates are random variables with a variance-covariance matrix, these three measures of central tendency are also random variables from the researcher's perspective, so it is often important to estimate, for each type of individual, a confidence interval on the desired measure. Details on how to do this are provided in *Diversion 6*.

Diversion 6: Estimating the confidence interval on CV^R (or $\hat{E}(CV)$ or $\hat{CV}^{med}$). One, for example, typically estimates CV^R at the estimated parameter values (the mean values of the estimated variance-covariance matrix). A 95% confidence interval for CV^R is obtained by taking a large number of random draws from the estimated variance-covariance matrix, calculating CV^R for each of these draws to form a distribution of the CV^R estimates, and then forming the 95% confidence interval by deleting the top and bottom 2.5% of the distribution. Note that even if the number of draws is very large, the mean of the CV^R estimates will not, in general, equal the CV^R calculated at the estimated parameters. This is due to the nonlinearity of the *CV* function—typically they are very similar.

One randomly draws a parameter vector as follows: Let $\hat{b}$ be the $p \times 1$ estimated parameter vector, where *cov* is its $p \times p$ estimated variance-covariance matrix. A randomly drawn parameter vector is $\hat{b}_r = \hat{b} + srcov' rndn(p,1)$, where *rndn*(p,1) is a $p \times 1$ random draw from a standard normal and *srcov* is the Cholesky decomposition of *cov*. The number of draws should be sufficiently large so that increasing the number of draws does not change the confidence interval.

Recall that *CV* is not the per year (or per season) compensating variation, but rather the compensating variation per choice occasion. If the year is divided into a fixed number of choice occasions (e.g. weeks), the choice set includes all possible alternatives, $\langle V^0_{mj} \rangle$ does not vary across choice occasions, and $\langle V^1_{mj} \rangle$ do not vary across choice occasions, the compensating variation for the year (season) is easily obtained by multiplying the per-period *CV* by the number of periods in the year (season).[47] Factors that might cause variation in $\langle V_{mj} \rangle$ across choice occasions include weather, temperature, and catch rates. If the $\langle V^0_{mj} \rangle$ and $\langle V^1_{mj} \rangle$ vary across choice occasions, one has to estimate *CV* for each choice occasion, and then sum across choice occasions.

Alternatively, if the choice set is restricted (does not include all alternatives), things are more complicated and one cannot get the compensating variation for the year by simply multiplying the compensating variation per choice occasion by the number of choice occasions in the year. Models of site choice have restricted choice sets. The problem is that when the choice set is restricted, the number of choice occasions in the year becomes a function of the attributes of the alternatives in the restricted choice set. Multiplying the *CV* by the number of choice occasions in the initial state , $\{I^0, P^0, ß^0\}$, provides only a lower bound on the compensating variation for the year. Multiplying the *CV* by the number of choice occasions in the proposed state, $\{I^1, P^1, ß^1\}$, provides only an upper bound on the compensating variation for the year. Neither is necessarily a close approximation. Details are provided in Morey (1994). See also Herriges *et al.* (1997).

For example: In the **model of participation and site choice**, the year is divided into a finite number of periods and each period includes all alternatives, so *CV* is the per-period compensating variation and the compensating variation for the year is easily obtained by multiplying the *CV* by the number of periods.

In the **model of site choice with saltwater sites, lakes, and rivers**, choice occasions are trips and on each trip the individual fishes (staying home is not an option). In this case, *CV* is the compensating variation per trip. Define $trips^0$ as the predicted number of trips in the initial state and $trips^1$ as the predicted number of trips in the proposed state. *CV* multiplied by $trips^0$ is a lower bound on the yearly *CV*. *CV* multiplied by $trips^1$ is an upper bound.

---

[47] Note that alternatives can be grouped. For example, the complete set of alternatives facing the individual could be lumped in two categories, fishing trips and nonfishing trips, where nonfishing trips include staying at home or going bowling. For example, Morey *et al.* (1993) have a 50 choice occasion, nine alternative model where eight of the alternatives are salmon fishing sites and the ninth alternative is not taking a salmon fishing trip. Morey *et al.* (1995 and 1997) have a 60 choice occasion model where in each period the angler chooses among 32 alternatives: 26 river segments, five regions, and not river fishing in Montana. There is a common presumption that the more aggregated the treatment of other alternatives, the larger, in absolute value, will be the estimated *CV* for a change in the disaggregated group of interest (see, for example, Montgomery and Needelman (1997). There is no theoretical foundation for this conjecture; aggregating alternatives is different from excluding alternatives from the choice set. Plantinga *et al.* (1997) demonstrate the conjecture to be false with some empirical counterexamples.

3.8 EXPANDING THE NEST

The NL model can be expanded into as many levels as one desires. For a three-level nest, Equation (3.1) expands to

$$U_{lmj} = V_{lmj} + \varepsilon_{lmj} \qquad \forall (lmj) \in C \qquad \text{(3.1-3 level)}$$

where the l dimension of the choice set is characterized in term of L distinction types. As before, the m dimension has M distinct types and the j dimension has J distinct types. To generate a simple three-level NL model where $s_m = s \ \forall m$ and $a_m = 1 \ \forall m$ assume[48]

$$F(\langle \varepsilon_{lmj} \rangle) = \exp\left\{ -\sum_{l=1}^{L} \left[\sum_{m=1}^{M_l} \left[\sum_{j=1}^{J_{lm}} \exp(-s\varepsilon_{lmj}) \right]^{(t/s)} \right]^{1/t} \right\}. \qquad \text{(3.8-3 level-1)}$$

If $t = s$, this collapses to a two-level nest. The derivation of the *Prob(gni)* and expected maximum utility follow the same logic as in the two-level case; the notation is just messier. If one bashes through the derivations, one obtains

$$Prob(gni) = \frac{\exp(sV_{gni}) \left[\sum_{m=1}^{M_g} \left[\sum_{j=1}^{J_{gm}} \exp(sV_{lmj}) \right]^{(t/s)} \right]^{(1/t)-1} \left[\sum_{j=1}^{J_{gn}} \exp(sV_{gnj}) \right]^{((t/s)-1)}}{\sum_{l=1}^{L} \left[\sum_{m=1}^{M_l} \left[\sum_{j=1}^{J_{lm}} \exp(sV_{gmj}) \right]^{(t/s)} \right]^{1/t}}$$

and per-choice occasion expected maximum utility is

$$\mathrm{U} = \ln \mathrm{D} + 0.57721, \qquad (3.41)$$

where

$$\mathrm{D} = \sum_{l=1}^{L} \left[\sum_{m=1}^{M_l} \left[\sum_{j=1}^{J_{lm}} \exp(sV_{lmj}) \right]^{(t/s)} \right]^{1/t}. \qquad \text{(3.35-3 level 1)}$$

---

[48] A necessary and sufficient condition for this function to be globally well-behaved is $s \geq t \geq 1$.

One example of a three-level nest: A model of participation and site choice for Atlantic Salmon fishing (Morey *et al.*, 1993) with $C = 9$ alternatives (staying at home and visiting one of eight salmon rivers). Assume L has two elements: 1= going salmon fishing and 0 = not going salmon fishing. M_1 has two elements: 1= fishing a river in Maine and 2 = fishing a river in Canada. J_1 includes five rivers in Maine and J_2 includes three rivers in Canada.

A three-level nest seems appropriate because one would expect the random components in the conditional indirect utility functions for the Maine rivers to be more correlated with each other than they are with the random components in the conditional indirect utility functions for the Canadian rivers. One would also expect the random components in the conditional indirect utility functions for the rivers to be more correlated with each other than they are with the random component in the conditional indirect utility functions for nonparticipation.

Equation (3.8-3 level) takes the form

$$F(\langle \varepsilon_{lmj} \rangle) = \exp\Big(-\exp(-\varepsilon_0) - \Big\{ \big[\exp(-s\varepsilon_{11}) + \ldots + \exp(-s\varepsilon_{15})\big]^{(t/s)} + \big[\exp(-s\varepsilon_{21}) + \ldots + \exp(-s\varepsilon_{23})\big]^{(t/s)} \Big\}^{1/t} \Big) \quad (3.16\text{-}3 \text{ level-1})$$

and the probability of choosing the first river in Canada is

$$Prob(121) = \exp(sV_{121}) \Big\{ \big[\exp(sV_{111}) + \ldots + \exp(sV_{115})\big]^{(t/s)} + \big[\exp(sV_{121}) + \ldots + \exp(sV_{123})\big]^{(t/s)} \Big\}^{(1/t)-1} \Big) A_1 / B$$

where

$$A_1 \equiv \big[\exp(sV_{121}) + \ldots + \exp(sV_{123})\big]^{(t/s)-1}$$

and

$$B = \Big(\exp(V_0) + \Big\{ \big[\exp(sV_{111}) + \ldots + \exp(sV_{115})\big]^{(t/s)} + \big[\exp(sV_{121}) + \ldots + \exp(sV_{123})\big]^{(t/s)} \Big\}^{1/t} \Big).$$

In conclusion, consider a more general three-level NL model, where[49]

$$F(\langle \varepsilon_{lmj} \rangle) = \exp\left(-\sum_{l=1}^{L} x_l \left\{ \sum_{m=1}^{M_l} a_m^{t_l} \left[\sum_{j=1}^{J_{ml}} \exp(-s_m \varepsilon_{lmj}) \right]^{(t_l/s_m)} \right\}^{1/t_l} \right)$$

$$= \exp\left(-\sum_{l=1}^{L} \left\{ \sum_{m=1}^{M_l} \left[\sum_{j=1}^{J_{ml}} \exp(-s_m[\varepsilon_{lmj} - \alpha_m - \chi_l]) \right]^{(t_l/s_m)} \right\}^{1/t_l} \right)$$

(3.8-3 level-2)

where $a_m = \exp(\alpha_m)$, and $x_l = \exp(\chi_l)$. In which case,

Prob(gni)

$$= \frac{\exp(s_n V_{gni}) x_g a_n^{t_g} \left\{ \sum_{m=1}^{M_g} a_m^{t_g} \left[\sum_{j=1}^{J_{gm}} \exp(s_m V_{gmj}) \right]^{(t_g/s_m)} \right\}^{(1/t_g)-1} \left[\sum_{j=1}^{J_{gn}} \exp(s_n V_{gnj}) \right]^{(t_g/s_n)-1}}{\sum_{l=1}^{L} x_l \left\{ \sum_{m=1}^{M_l} a_m^{t_l} \left[\sum_{j=1}^{J_{lm}} \exp(s_m V_{lmj}) \right]^{(t_l/s_m)} \right\}^{1/t_l}}$$

$$= \exp(s_n[\chi_g + \alpha_n + V_{gni}]) \left\{ \sum_{m=1}^{M_g} \left[\sum_{j=1}^{J_{gm}} \exp(s_m[\chi_g + \alpha_m + V_{gmj}]) \right]^{(t_g/s_m)} \right\}^{(1/t_g)-1}$$

$$\times \frac{\left[\sum_{j=1}^{J_{gn}} \exp(s_n[\chi_g + \alpha_n + V_{gnj}]) \right]^{(t_g/s_n)-1}}{\sum_{l=1}^{L} \left\{ \sum_{m=1}^{M_l} \left[\sum_{j=1}^{J_{lm}} \exp(s_m[\chi_l + \alpha_m + V_{lmj}]) \right]^{(t_l/s_m)} \right\}^{1/t_l}}.$$

(3.16-3 level-2)

The $\langle \chi_l \rangle$ add a group-specific constant term to each of the $\langle V_{lmj} \rangle$ for each of the L groups, and the $\langle \alpha_m \rangle$ add a group-specific constant term to each of the V_{lmj} for each of the M groups,

---

[49] Given $a_m > 0\ \forall m$, $x_l > 0\ \forall l$, the necessary and sufficient conditions for this density function to be globally well behaved are $\{s_m \geq t_l \geq 1\ \forall m \in M_l\}$, $l = 1,2,\ldots,L$.

$$D = \sum_{l=1}^{L} x_l \left\{ \sum_{m=1}^{M_l} a_m^{t_l} \left[\sum_{j=1}^{J_{lm}} \exp\left(s_m V_{lmj}\right) \right]^{(t_l/s_m)} \right\}^{1/t_l} . \quad (3.35\text{-}3 \text{ level-2})$$

3.9 EXAMPLE GAUSS CODE

```
@ nstl-3lv.cmd June 30, 92 @
@this is the gauss program that was used to estimate the three level NL model
of Atlantic Salmon Fishing that was described in the last example box. For
more details see Morey et al. (1993) @

library maxlik; @ These three commands load the maximum likelihood mod-
ule in Gauss @
#include maxlik.ext;
maxset;

dataset = "mst4lgt"; @ the data is stored in the Gauss data set "mst4lgt" @
output file = nstl-3lv.out on;

proc li(b,x); @ "li" is the procedure that generates the ln of the lik function. "li"
is called below by the maximum liklihood module, "maxlik" @

local ppy, evp, evd, evm, evk, evs, evns, evnb, evq, evn, vp, vm, vd, vk, vs, vns,
vnb, vq, vn, inclusm, inclusc, inclusp, inclus, linclus, lsump, lmsum, lcsum, x;

ppy = x[.,4]/50; @ x[.,4] is income @

@ the following are the exp of the conditional indirects with the
conditional indirects for the site alternatives multiplied by s;i.e b[11]. Note that
the conditional indirect for nonparticipation, n, is not multiplied by s because it
cancels out. @

@ In the following b[4] is a constant term, b[11]=s, b[12] = t, x[.,1] = years
salmon fishing. x[.,2] = 1 if member of a fishing club and zero otherwise, x[.,3]
= individual's age, x[.,5] = number of periods individual did not salmon fish,
x[.,6]- x[.,13] are the expected catch rates at the eight sites, x[.,14] -x[.,21]are
trip costs for the eight sites, and x[.,22]- x[.,29] are the number of trips each
individual took to each of the eight sites, @
```

```
evp = exp(b[11]*(b[1]*(ppy-x[.,14])+b[2]*x[.,6]+b[3]*x[.,6]^.5
 +b[10]*((1728.4720+ppy-x[.,14])^.5)));
evm = exp(b[11]*(b[1]*(ppy-x[.,15])+b[2]*x[.,7]+b[3]*x[.,7]^.5
 +b[10]*((1728.4720+ppy-x[.,15])^.5)));
evd = exp(b[11]*(b[1]*(ppy-x[.,16])+b[2]*x[.,8]+b[3]*x[.,8]^.5
          +b[10]*((1728.4720+ppy-x[.,16])^.5)));
evk = exp(b[11]*(b[1]*(ppy-x[.,17])+b[2]*x[.,9]+b[3]*x[.,9]^.5
          +b[10]*((1728.4720+ppy-x[.,17])^.5)));
evs = exp(b[11]*(b[1]*(ppy-x[.,18])+b[2]*x[.,10]+b[3]*x[.,10]^.5
          +b[10]*((1728.4720+ppy-x[.,18])^.5)));

evns= exp(b[11]*(b[1]*(ppy-x[.,19])+b[2]*x[.,11]+b[3]*x[.,11]^.5
 +b[10]*((1728.4720+ppy-x[.,19])^.5)));
evnb= exp(b[11]*(b[1]*(ppy-x[.,20])+b[2]*x[.,12]+b[3]*x[.,12]^.5
 +b[10]*((1728.4720+ppy-x[.,20])^.5)));
evq = exp(b[11]*(b[1]*(ppy-x[.,21])+b[2]*x[.,13]+b[3]*x[.,13]^.5
 +b[10]*((1728.4720+ppy-x[.,21])^.5)));

@the next line is the exp of the condit indirect for nonpartic @

evn = exp(b[1]*ppy+b[4]+b[5]*x[.,1]+b[6]*x[.,2]+b[7]*x[.,3]
 +b[8]*x[.,1]^.5+b[9]*x[.,3]^.5+b[10]*((1728.4720+ppy)^.5));

vp=ln(evp); vm=ln(evm); vd=ln(evd); vk=ln(evk); vs=ln(evs);vns=ln(evns);
vnb=ln(evnb); vq=ln(evq); vn=ln(evn);

@ Note b[12] is t @

inclusm = (evp+evm+evd+evk+evs)^(b[12]/b[11]);
inclusc = (evns+evnb+evq)^(b[12]/b[11]);
inclusp = (inclusm + inclusc)^(1/b[12]);

@ inclus is the denomin in all the prob @

inclus = evn + inclusp;
linclus=ln(inclus);
lsump = ((1/b[12])-1)*ln(inclusm+inclusc);
lmsum = ((b[12]/b[11])-1) * ln(evp+evm+evd+evk+evs);
lcsum = ((b[12]/b[11])-1) * ln(evns+evnb+evq);

@ the next command calculates the contribution to the log of the lik function
for each indiv in the sample @
```

```
retp(x[.,22].*(vp + lsump + lmsum - linclus)
 + x[.,23].*(vm + lsump + lmsum - linclus)
 + x[.,24].*(vd + lsump + lmsum - linclus)
 + x[.,25].*(vk + lsump + lmsum - linclus)
 + x[.,26].*(vs + lsump + lmsum - linclus)
 + x[.,27].*(vns+ lsump + lcsum - linclus)
 + x[.,28].*(vnb+ lsump + lcsum - linclus)
 + x[.,29].*(vq + lsump + lcsum - linclus)
 + x[.,5].*(vn - linclus));
endp;

@ the following are the converged values from the 6/30/92 run - the AJAE
estimates @

startv = {.002190, -1.729160, 5.912200, 8.850202, .095329, -.805250,.170146,
-1.227537, -1.856089, 1.088725, 1.307125, .611724};

_title = "NSTL-3LEV INCOME EFFECTS ";
_mlmiter = 2000;
_mlgtol = .0001;
{bbb,f0,g,h,retcode}=maxprt(maxlik("mst4lgt",0,&li,startv));

bmm94 = bbb; save bmm94; output off;
```

REFERENCES

Adamowicz, W.J., Swait, J., Boxall, P., Louviere, J., and Williams, M. (1996), "Perceptions versus Objective Measures of Environmental Quality in Combined Revealed and Stated Preference Models of Environmental Valuation," paper presented at the 1996 AERE workshop, Combining Stated and Revealed Preference Data to Estimate the Demand for and Benefits from Environmental Amenities, Boulder CO.

Adamowicz, W.J., Louviere, J., and Williams, M. (1994), "Combining Stated and Revealed Preference Method for Valuing Environmental Amenities," *Journal of Environmental Economics and Management*, 26, 271–92.

Amemiya, T. (1978), "On a Two-Step Estimation of a Multivariate Logit Model," *Journal of Econometrics*, 8, 12–21.

Anderson, S.P., De Palma, A., and Thisse, J. (1987), "The CES is a Discrete Choice Model," *Economic Letters*, 23, 139–40.

________ (1992), *Discrete Choice Theory of Product Differentiation,* MIT Press, Cambridge Massachusetts.

Bockstael, N.E., Hanemann, W.M., and Kling, C.L. (1987), "Modeling Recreational Demand in a Multiple Site Framework," *Water Resources Research,* 23, 951–60.

Bockstael, N.E., Hanemann, W.M., and Strand, I.E. (1986), "Measuring the Benefits of Water Quality Improvements Using Recreation Demand Models," report prepared for the Environmental Protection Agency under Cooperative Agreement CR-811043-01-0, Washington D.C.

Bockstael, N.E., McConnell, K.E., and Strand, I.E. (1989), "A Random Utility Model of Sport Fishing: Some Preliminary Results for Florida," *Marine Resource Economics*, 6,245–60.

_________ (1991), "Recreation", in *Measuring the Demand for Environmental Quality*, (John B. Braden and Charles Kolstad, eds.), New York, North Holland.

Börsch-Supan, A. (1990), "On the Compatibility of Nested Logit Models with Utility Maximization," *Journal of Econometrics*, 43, 373–88.

Brownstone, D. and Small, K.A. (1989), "Efficient Estimation of Nested Logit Models," *Journal of Business and Economic Statistics*, 7, 67–74.

Buchanan, T., Morey, E.R., and Waldman, D.M. (1998), "Happy Trails to You: The Impact of Trail Characteristics and Access Fees on a Mountain Biker's Trail Selection and Consumer's Surplus," discussion paper, Department of Economics, University of Colorado-Boulder.

Cameron, T.A. (1982), Qualitative Choice Modeling of Energy Conservation Decisions, unpublished Ph.D. Dissertation, Princeton University, Department of Economics.

__________ (1985), "A Nested Logit Model of Energy Conservation Activity by Owners of Existing Single Family Dwellings," *The Review of Economics and Statistics*, 55, 205–11.

Carson, R., Hanemann, W.M., and Wegge, T. (1987), "Southcentral Alaska Sport Fishing Study," report prepared by Jones and Stokes Associates for Alaska Department of Fish and Game, Anchorage, AK.

Caulkins, P., Bishop, R., and Bouwes, N. (1986), "The Travel Cost Model for Lake Recreation: A Comparison of Two Methods for Incorporating Site Quality and Substitution Effects," *American Journal of Agricultural Economics*, 68, 291–97.

Chen, H.Z. (1996), "Angler's Perceptions of Environmental Quality and Benefit Estimation in Multinomial Probit Model: A Simulation Approach", paper presented at the 1996 AERE workshop, Combining Stated and Revealed Preference Data to Estimate the Demand for and Benefits from Environmental Amenities, Boulder CO.

Chen, H.Z., Lupi, F., and Hoehn, J. (1997), "An Empirical Assessment of Multinomial Probit and Logit Models of Recreation Demand," forthcoming as Chapter 5 in *Valuing Recreation and the Environment: Revealed Preference Methods in Theory and Practice,* (J.A. Herriges and C.L. Kling, eds.), Edward Elgar Publishing Ltd..

Creel, M. and Loomis, J. (1992), "Recreation Value of Water to Wetlands in the San Joaquin Valley: Linked Multinomial Logit and Count Data Trip Frequency Models," *Water Resources Research*, 28, 2597–606.

Feenburg, D. and Mills, E. (1980), *Measuring the Benefits of Water Pollution Abatement*, Academic Press, New York.

Hanemann, W.M. (1978), A Methodological and Empirical Study of the Recreation Benefits from Water Quality Improvements, PhD dissertation, Department of Economics, Harvard University.

_________ (1985), "Welfare Analysis with Discrete Choice Models," working paper, Department of Resource and Agricultural Economics, University of California, Berkeley, March.

Hauber, A.B. and Parsons, G.R. (1996), "Nesting Structure Choice in a Random Utility Model of Recreation Demand," discussion paper, Department of Economics, University of Delaware, October.

Hausman, J.A., Leonard, G.K., and McFadden, D. (1995), "A Utility-Consistent, Combined Discrete Choice and Count Data Model: Assessing Recreational Use Losses Due to Natural Resource Damage," *Journal of Public Economics*, 56, 1–30.

Hausman, J.A. and Wise, D. (1978), "A Conditional Probit Model of Qualitative Choice: Discrete Decisions Recognizing Interdependence and Heterogenous Preferences," *Econometrica* 46, 403–26.

Hensher, D.A. (1986), "Sequential and Full Information Maximum Likelihood Estimation of a Nested Logit Model," *The Review of Economics and Statistics*, 56, 657–67.

Herriges, J.A. and Kling, C.L. (1997), "Nonlinear Income Effects in Random Utility Models," discussion paper, Department of Economics, Iowa State University, June 4.

_________ (1996), "Testing the Consistency of Nested Logit Models with Utility Maximization," *Economic Letters*, 50, 33–39.

Herriges, J.A., Kling, C.L., and Phaneuf, D.J. (1997), "Corner Solution Models of Recreation Demand: A Comparison of Competing Frameworks," forthcoming as Chapter 6 in *Valuing Recreation and the Environment: Revealed Preference Methods in Theory and Practice,* (J.A. Herriges and C.L. Kling, eds.) Edward Elgar Publishing Ltd.

Hoehn, J.P., Tomasi, T., Lupi, F., and Chen, H.Z. (1996), "An Economic Model for Valuing Recreational Angling Resources in Michigan," report submitted to the Environmental Response Division, Michigan Department of Environmental Quality, December.

Johnson, N.L., Kotz, S., and Balakrishnan, N. (1994), *Continuous Univariate Distributions* - second edition, Vols. 1 and 2, Wiley, New York.

Jones, C.A. and Sung, Y.D. (1992), "Models for Censored Duration Data, Competing Risks, and Time-Varying Covariates: with an Application to Recreational Trip Demand," discussion paper, NOAA, US Department of Commerce.

Karlstrom, A. (1998), "Hidesian Welfare Measures in a Nonlinear Randm Utility Framework," discussion paper, Department of Infrastructure and Planning, Royal Institute of Technology, Stockholm.

Kling, C.L. and Herriges, J.A. (1995), "An Empirical Investigation of the Consistency of Nested Logit Models with Utility Maximization," *American Journal of Agricultural Economics*, 77, 875–84.

Kling, C.L. and Thomson, C.J. (1996), "The Implications of Model Specification for Welfare Estimation in Nested Logit Models," *American Journal of Agricultural Economics*, 78 103–14.

Layton, D.F. (1996), "Rank Ordered, Random Coefficients Multinomial Probit Models for Stated Preference Surveys: An Investigation of Preference Heterogeneity, IIA and Contingent Ranking Data," paper presented at the 1996 AERE workshop, Combining Stated and Revealed Preference Data to Estimate the Demand for and Benefits from Environmental Amenities, Boulder CO.

Manski, C.F. and Lerman, S.R. (1977), "The Estimation of Choice Probabilities from Choice-Based Samples," *Econometrica*, 45, 1977–1988.

McFadden, D. (1978), Modeling the Choice of Residential Location, Chapter 3 in *Spatial Interaction Theory and Planning Models* (A. Karlqvist, L, Lundqvist, F. Snickars and J Weibull, eds.) North-Holland, Amsterdam.

________ (1981), Econometric Models of Probabilistic Choice, Chapter 5 in *Structural Analysis of Discrete Data with Econometric Applications*, (C. Manski and D. McFadden eds.), MIT Press, Cambridge, MA.

________ (1989), "A Method of Simulated Moments For Estimation: Discrete Response Models Without Numerical Integration," *Econometrica*, 57, 995–1026.

________ (1996), "Computing Willingness-to-Pay in Random Utility Models," discussion paper, Department of Economics, University of California, Berkeley.

Milon, J.W. (1988), "A Nested Demand Shares Model of Artificial Marine Habitat Choice by Sport Anglers," *Marine Resources Research*, 5, 191–213.

Montgomery, M. and Needelman, M. (1997), "The Welfare Effects of Toxic Contamination in Freshwater Fish," *Land Economics*, 73, 211–23.

Morey, E.R. (1981), "The Demand for Site-Specific Recreational Activities: A Characteristics Approach," *Journal of Environmental Economics and Management*, 8, 245–71.

________ (1994), "What is Consumer's Surplus Per Day of Use, When is it a Constant Independent of the Number of Days of Use, and What Does It Tell Us About Consumer's Surplus?" *Journal of Environmental Economics and Management, 26*, 257–70.

Morey, E.R., Breffle, W.S., Rowe, R.D., and Waldman, D.M. (1995), "Revised Report and Rebuttal: Assessment of Damages to Anglers and Other Recreators from Injuries to the Upper Clark Fork River Basin," report prepared by Hagler Bailly Consulting for the State of Montana, Natural Resource Damage Litigation Program, October 18.

________ (1998a), "Estimating the Damages for Injuries to Trout in Montana's Clark Fork River: Participation, Site Choice, and Endogenous Expected Catch Rates," discussion paper, Department of Economics, University of Colorado, Boulder.

Morey, E.R. and Rossmann, K. (1998), "Estimating the Willingness to Pay for Reducing Acid Deposition, Injuries to Cultural Resources: Choice Experiments and Individual-Specific Parameters," research paper, Department of Economics, University of Colorado, Boulder.

Morey, E.R., Rossmann, K., Chestnut, L., and Ragland, S. (1997), "Valuing Acid Deposition Injuries to Cultural Resources," a report prepared for the National Acid Precipitation Assessment Program by the University of Colorado and Hagler Bailly Consulting, May 14.

Morey, E.R., Rowe, R.D., and Watson, M. (1993), "A Repeated Nested-Logit Model of Atlantic Salmon Fishing," *American Journal of Agricultural Economics*, 75, 578–92.

Morey, E.R., Sharma, V.R., and Mills, A. (1998b), "Estimating Malaria Patient's Household Compensating Variations for Health Care Proposal in Nepal," discussion paper, Department of Economics, University of Colorado, Boulder.

Morey, E.R., Shaw, W.D. and Rowe, R.D. (1991), "A Discrete Choice Model of Recreational Participation, Site Choice, and Activity Valuation When Complete Trip Data Are Not Available," *Journal of Environmental Economics and Management*, 20,181–201.

Pakes, A. and Pollard, D. (1989), "Simulation And the Asymptotics of Optimization Estimators," *Econometrica*, 57, 1027–57.

Parsons, G.R. and Kealy, M.J. (1992), "Randomly Drawn Opportunity Sets in a Random Utility Model of Lake Recreation," *Land Economics*, 68, 93–106.

________ (1995), "A Demand Theory for Number of Trips in a Random Utility Model of Recreation," *Journal of Environmental Economics and Management*, 29, 357–67.

Parsons, G.R. and Needleman, M.S. (1992), "Site Aggregation in a Random Utility Model of Recreation," *Land Economics*, 68, 418–33.

Plantinga, A.J., Parsons, G.R., and Boyle, K.J. (1997), "Focused Choice Sets and Targeted Aggregation in Random Utility Model," discussion paper, Department of Economics, University of Maine.

Smith, V.K. and Von Haefen, R. (1997), "Welfare Measurement and Representative Consumer Theory," discussion paper, Department of Economics, Duke University.

Swait, J. and Adamowicz, W. (1996), "The Effect of Choice Environment and Task Demand on Consumer Behavior: Discriminating Between Contribution and Confusion," paper presented at the 1996 Canadian Resource and Environmental Economics Study Group, Montreal.

Train, K.E. (1998), "Recreation Demand Models with Taste Differences Over People," *Land Economics*, 74, 262–76.

Verboven, F. (1996), "The Nested Logit Model and Representative Consumer Theory," *Economic Letters*, 50, 57–63.

4. Mixed Logit Models for Recreation Demand

Kenneth E. Train

4.1 INTRODUCTION

Recreation demand analysis has relied heavily on logit models as a means of representing recreators' choices (Caulkins *et al.*, 1986; Bockstael *et al.*, 1987 and 1989; Parsons and Needelman, 1992; Parsons and Kealy, 1992; Morey *et al.*, 1993; Hausman *et al.*, 1995.) Logit has many desirable properties, one of which is that the choice probabilities are easy to calculate. However, logit models place restrictions, described in Section 4.2 below, which can be unrealistic in many settings. While this limitation has been recognized for many years (McFadden, 1975), logits have continued to be used extensively because of the difficulty of estimating more flexible models.

Mixed logits are a generalization of logit that do not exhibit the restrictive patterns of logit and can accurately represent a much wider variety of choice situations. While computationally more demanding than logit, mixed logits are becoming increasingly feasible to utilize. The purpose of this paper is to describe mixed logit models, their properties and estimation, and to provide an illustration of their application.

Consider a recreator who makes a choice among a set of alternatives. (For example, an angler chooses a fishing site from the many sites that are available for a given trip.) The set of alternatives that are available to the recreator is denoted as set J. A choice model gives the probability that the recreator chooses a particular alternative among those in J. Choice models differ in the formula for this probability. With a logit model, the probability that the recreator chooses alternative i from set J is given by the formula:

$$L_i = \frac{\exp(bx_i)}{\sum_{j \in J} \exp(bx_j)}$$

where x_i is a (column-) vector of observed variables relating to alternative i and b is a (row-) vector of fixed coefficients. A mixed logit generalizes this formula by allowing the vector of coefficients, b, to be random rather than fixed. In particular, a mixed logit takes the form:

$$P_i = \int L_i(\beta) f(\beta) d\beta$$

where P_i is the probability that the recreator chooses alternative i from set J, $L_i(\beta)$ is the logit function evaluated at parameters β:

$$L_i(\beta) = \frac{\exp(\beta x_i)}{\sum_{j \in J} \exp(\beta x_j)}$$

and $f(\beta)$ is a density function on the coefficient vector. Essentially, a mixed logit is a weighted average of standard logits evaluated at different points. The density $f(\beta)$ determines the weights and is called the "mixing distribution".[1]

The earliest applications of mixed logits seem to have been Boyd and Mellman (1980) and Cardell and Dunbar's (1980) analyses of automobile demand. These early models were estimated on market share data rather than customer-specific choice data, such that the integration, which is computationally difficult, needed to be performed only once rather than for each sampled decision-maker. Advances in computer speed, as well as in our understanding of numerical methods for integration and the structure of mixed logits, have prompted renewed interest. In the sections below, we describe properties of mixed logits, their relation to utility theory, their estimation, and their use with panel data. We conclude with an example of a mixed logit model of anglers' choice of fishing site among Montana rivers.

4.2 SUBSTITUTION PATTERNS

Logit exhibits a property called "independence from irrelevant alternatives" which restricts the substitution patterns that the model can represent. In particular, for a logit model, the ratio of probabilities for any two alternatives, i and k, is given by

---

[1] Of course, when the mixing distribution is degenerate at b (i.e., when $f(b) = 1$ and $f(\beta) = 0$ for all β not equal to b), the mixed logit probability becomes the standard logit probability.

$$\frac{L_i}{L_k} = \frac{\exp(bx_i)}{\exp(bx_k)}$$

since the denominators of L_i and L_k cancel. Importantly, this ratio does not depend on "irrelevant"—that is, other—alternatives. Because of this property, a change in the attributes of one alternative changes the probabilities of the other alternatives proportionately, such that the ratio of these probabilities remains the same. To be explicit, the percent change in the probability for alternative *i* that results from a change in the *m*th attribute of alternative $j \neq i$, is

$$\frac{d \ln L_i}{dx_j^m} = -b^m L_j .$$

Since this formula is the same for all $j \neq i$, the logit model implies that a change in attributes of alternative *j* brings about the same percent change in the probabilities for all other alternatives. For example, if an improvement in one fishing site induces 5% of the anglers at other sites to switch to the improved site, then the logit model implies that exactly 5% at *each* other site switch. This substitution pattern can be unrealistic in many settings. For example, if 7% of the anglers from a nearby or similar site switch, while only 3% from a further or less similar site switch to the improved site, then logit will misrepresent the substitution pattern by requiring that the same percent switching occurs at all sites.

Mixed logit does not exhibit "independence from irrelevant alternatives" or the restrictive substitution patterns of logit. The ratio of mixed logit probabilities P_i / P_k depends on all the data, including attributes of alternatives other than *i* and *k*. (The denominators are inside the integral and therefore do not cancel.) The percent change in the probability for one alternative given a change in an attribute of another alternative is:

$$\frac{d \ln P_i}{dx_j^m} = -\frac{1}{P_i} \int \beta^m L_i(\beta) L_j(\beta) f(\beta) d\beta$$

$$= -\int \beta^m L_j(\beta) \left[\frac{L_i(\beta)}{P_i} \right] f(\beta) d\beta,$$

which is different for each alternative. A 5% reduction for one alternative need not imply (as with logit) a 5% reduction in each other alternative. Rather, the substitution pattern depends on the specification of the variables and mixing distribution, which can be determined empirically. In particular, the percent change in probability varies with the correlation between $L_i(\beta)$ and $L_j(\beta)$ over different values of β, which is determined by the analyst's choice of variables and mixing distribution. For example, to represent a situation where an improvement in alternative j draws more proportionately from alternative i than alternative k, the analyst can specify an element of x that is positively correlated between i and j but negatively correlated between j and k, with a mixing distribution that allows the coefficient of this variable to vary.

McFadden and Train (1997) show that any random utility model can be approximated arbitrarily closely by a mixed logit with appropriate choice of variables and mixing distribution. This result, which is discussed in detail below, implies than any substitution pattern can be represented by a mixed logit. The true substitution pattern in any situation is inferred through specification tests on the data rather than imposed *a priori* by the form of the model.

A comparison with nested logit is useful here. A nested logit with non-overlapping[2] nests exhibits the restrictive "independence from irrelevant alternatives" property within each nest but not across nests (McFadden, 1978; Ben-Akiva and Lerman, 1985; Train, 1986.) While not as restrictive as logit, it nevertheless imposes a particular substitution pattern on the data. For a change in an attribute of alternative j, the percent change in probability is the same for all alternatives that are in the same nest as j. The percent change is also the same for all alternatives that are in another nest, though this percent is different than for those in the same nest as j. If overlapping nests are specified, nested logit can represent a wide range of substitution patterns. However, estimation of nested logits with overlapping nests is computationally difficult, perhaps more-so than a mixed logit. As we discuss below, a mixed logit can approximate a nested logit with either overlapping or non-overlapping nests.

---

[2]If the set of alternatives is partitioned into subsets, called "nests," such that each alternative falls into only one subset, then the nests are called "non-overlapping." For example, fishing sites can be partitioned into river and lake sites, which are non-overlapping nests. If subsets of alternatives are defined such that an alternative can be a member of more than one subset, then the subsets are called "overlapping nests." An example is to define the subset of fishing sites that have a particular species of fish, with one subset for each relevant species: a site that has more than one species falls into more than one nest.

4.3 RELATION TO UTILITY-MAXIMIZING BEHAVIOR

4.3.1 Random-Parameters, or Random-Coefficients, Logit

The mixed logit formula can be derived from utility-maximizing behavior in several ways that are formally equivalent but provide different interpretations. The most straightforward derivation, and most widely used in recent applications, is based on random coefficients. The decision-maker faces a choice among the alternatives in set *J*. The utility of alternative *i* is specified as

$$U_i = \beta x_i + \varepsilon_i$$

where x_i are observed variables that relate to the alternative and the decision-maker, β are coefficients of these variables that vary over decision-makers with density $f(\beta)$, and ε_i is a random term that is iid extreme value. (The subscript *n*, denoting the decision-maker, is suppressed for convenience at this stage; it enters below when describing the likelihood function.) This specification is the same as for standard logit except that β varies over decision-makers rather than being fixed.

The decision-maker knows the value of his/her own β and ε 's for all $i \in J$ and chooses alternative *i* if and only if $U_i > U_j$ for all $j \neq i$. The analyst observes the *x*'s but does not observe β or the ε 's. If the analyst observed β, then the choice probability would be standard logit, since the ε 's are iid extreme value. That is, the probability conditional on β is

$$L_i(\beta) = \frac{\exp(\beta x_i)}{\sum \exp(\beta x_j)}.$$

However, the analyst does not know β. The choice probability is therefore the integral of $L_i(\beta)$ over all possible values of β.

$$P_i = \int L_i(\beta) f(\beta) d\beta .$$

The distribution of β depends on underlying parameters, such as the mean and covariance of β. The goal of model estimation is to estimate these parameters of the distribution of β. In a standard logit, the distribution of β is degenerate at its mean, such that estimating the fixed coefficients is equivalent to estimating the mean β, with higher-order moments assumed to be zero. With mixed logit, the distribution is in general non-degenerate, and non-zero higher-order moments are estimated along with the mean.

In most applications (Revelt and Train, 1996, Mehndiratta, 1996, Ben-Akiva and Bolduc, 1996), $f(\beta)$ has been specified as independent of the attributes of the decision-maker. Examples include $\beta \sim N(b,W)$ or $\ln(\beta) \sim N(b,W)$ with b and W consisting of fixed parameters that are estimated. The lognormal distribution is useful when the coefficient is known to have the same sign for every decision-maker, such as a price coefficient that is known to be negative for everyone. Variation in tastes that are related to observed attributes of the decision-maker are captured through specification of the explanatory variables x. For example, cost might be divided by the decision-maker's income to allow the value or relative importance of cost to decline as income rises. The random coefficient of this variable then represents the variation over people with the same income in the value that they place on cost. The mean valuation of cost declines with income while the variance around the mean is fixed.

Observed attributes of the decision-maker can also enter $f(\beta)$ so that higher-order moments of taste variation can also depend on attributes of the decision-maker. Bhat (1996a and b) specifies, in a mode-choice situation, the coefficients of cost and time to be log-normally distributed with the mean of the log of the coefficients depending on attributes of the person; e.g., $\ln(\beta_c) \sim N(\alpha z,\omega)$ where β_c is the cost coefficient and z are observed attributes of the person and α and β are fixed parameters that are estimated. In this set-up, both the mean and variance of β_c depend on observed attributes of the person: the mean of β_c is $\exp(\alpha z)\exp(\omega^2/2)$ and the variance is $\exp(2\alpha z)(\exp(\omega^2)-1)$. Stated succinctly, entering attributes of the decision-maker into x allows the mean tastes to vary with these attributes, while entering them into $f(\beta)$ can, depending on the specification of $f(\beta)$, allow the higher-order moments to vary with these attributes. In either case, variation in tastes that are not related to observed attributes of the decision-maker are necessarily captured in the specification of $f(\beta)$.

4.3.2 Error-Components Interpretation

A mixed logit model can be used without a random-coefficients interpretation, rather as representing error components that create correlations among the utilities for different alternatives. Utility is specified:

$$U_i = \theta x_i + \mu z_i + \varepsilon_i$$

where x_i and z_i are vectors of observed variables relating to alternative i, θ is a vector of fixed coefficients, μ is a vector of random terms with zero mean, and ε_i is distributed iid extreme value. The terms in μz_i are error components that, along with ε_i, define the stochastic portion of utility. For the standard logit model, μ is identically zero, such that there is no correlation in utility over alternatives. This lack of correlation gives rise to the "independence from irrelevant alternatives" property and its restrictive substitution patterns. With non-zero error components μz_i, utility is correlated over alternatives: $Cov(U_i, U_j) = z_i' \operatorname{var}(\mu) z_j$. Various correlation patterns, and hence substitution patterns, can be obtained by appropriate choice of variables to enter as error components. For example, an analog to nested logit is obtained by specifying a dummy variable for each nest, which equals 1 for each alternative in the nest and zero for alternatives outside the nest. The random term that is multiplied by the dummy (i.e., the corresponding element of μ) therefore enters the utility of each alternative in the nest, inducing correlation among these alternatives, and does not enter any of the other alternatives, thereby not inducing correlation between alternatives in the nest with those outside the nest. The variance of the random term captures the magnitude of the correlation; it is analogous to the "inclusive value coefficient" of nested logit models (or, more precisely, to one minus the inclusive value coefficient.) Allowing different variances for the random terms for different nests is analogous to allowing the inclusive value coefficient to differ across nests in a nested logit. An analog to overlapping nests is captured with dummies that identify overlapping sets of alternatives.

Other types of variables can be used to define error components. Brownstone and Train (1996) use a continuous variable, an ordered discrete variable, and two dummy variables that identify overlapping nests of alternatives. They find that the mixed logit with these error components provides substantially more realistic substitution patterns than a standard logit. Importantly, the greater realism is obtained by adding only four extra parameters to a model that had 26 parameters in its standard logit form.

Of course, error-components and random-coefficients specifications are equivalent. Under the random-coefficient motivation, utility is specified as $U_i = \beta x_i + \varepsilon_i$ with random β. The coefficients β can be decomposed into their mean θ and deviations μ, such that $U_i = \theta x_i + \mu x_i + \varepsilon_i$, which has error components defined by $z_i = x_i$. Conversely, under an errors-components motivation, utility is $U_i = \theta x_i + \mu z_i + \varepsilon_i$, which is equivalent to a random-parameters model with fixed coefficients for variables x_i and random coefficients with zero means for variables z_i. If x and z overlap (in the sense that the same variables enter x and z), the coefficients of these variables can be considered to vary randomly with mean θ and the same distribution as μ around their mean.

Though formally equivalent, the way an analyst thinks about his/her model affects the specification of the mixed logit. For example, when thinking in terms of random parameters, it is natural to allow each variable's coefficient to vary and perhaps even to allow correlations among the coefficients. This is the approach pursued by Revelt and Train (1996). However, when the primary goal is to represent substitution patterns appropriately through the use of error components, the emphasis is placed on specifying variables that can induce correlations over alternatives in a parsimonious fashion so as to provide sufficiently realistic substitution patterns. This is the approach taken by Brownstone and Train (1996). The goals differed in these studies, with Revelt and Train being interested in the pattern of tastes, while Brownstone and Train were more concerned with prediction. The number of explanatory variables also differed, with Revelt and Train examining six variables, such that estimating the joint distribution of their coefficients was a reasonable goal, while Brownstone and Train included 26 variables. Expecting to estimate the distribution of 26 coefficients might be unreasonable, and yet thinking in terms of random parameters instead of error components can lead the analyst to such unreasonable expectations. It is important to remember that the mixing distribution, whether motivated by random parameters or error components, captures correlations among unobserved factors. There is a natural limit on how much one can learn about things that are not seen.

4.3.3 Approximation to any Choice Model

McFadden and Train (1997) show than any random utility model can be approximated to any degree of accuracy by a mixed logit with appropriate choice of variables and mixing distribution. An intuitive basis for this proof can easily be provided. Suppose the true model is $U_i = \alpha z_i + \eta_i$ where z_i are variables relating to alternative *i*, α is fixed and η_i follows any distribution. Any random utility model can be expressed in this form. The model can be transformed to be more compatible to our purposes. In particular, utility can be rewritten, without loss of generality, as $U_i = \beta x_i$ where x_i are variables relating to alternative *i* and β are are random with any distribution.[3] Conditional on β, the person's choice is fully determined since U_i is known for each *i*. The conditional probability is therefore:

$$q_i(\beta) = I\left(\beta x_i > \beta x_j \; \forall j \neq i\right)$$

where $I(\cdot)$ is a 1–0 indicator of whether the event in parentheses occurs. (This conditional probability is deterministic in the sense that the probability is either zero or one: conditional on all the unknown random terms, the decision-

---

[3] Define $d_{ij} = 1$ if *i*=*j* and zero otherwise. Let $d_i' = \{d_{i1},\ldots,d_{iJ}\}$ and $\eta = \{\eta_1,\ldots,\eta_J\}$. Then $x_i' = \{z_i, d_i\}$ and $\beta = \{\alpha, \eta\}$. Then $U_i = \beta x_i$.

makers' choice is completely determined.) The unconditional choice probability is the integral of $q_i(\beta)$ and over β:

$$Q_i = \int I(\beta x_i > \beta x_j \; \forall j \neq i) f(\beta) d\beta \, .$$

We can approximate this probability with a mixed logit. Scale utility by λ: $U_i = (\beta / \lambda) x_i$. This scaling does not affect the model since utility maximization is unaffected by scaling. Then add an iid extreme value term: $U_i^* = (\beta / \lambda) x_i + \varepsilon_i$. The addition of the extreme value term does change the model, since it changes the utility of each alternative. However, we need to add it in order to obtain a mixed logit. And, as we will show (this is the purpose of the proof), adding the extreme value term is innocuous.

The mixed logit probability based on this utility is:

$$P_i = \int L_i(\beta / \lambda) f(\beta) d\beta$$

where

$$L_i(\beta / \lambda) = \frac{\exp[(\beta / \lambda) x_i]}{\sum_{j \in J} \exp[(\beta / \lambda) x_j]} .$$

As λ approaches zero, the coefficients β / λ in the logit formula grow large and $L_i(\beta / \lambda)$ approaches a 1–0 indicator for the alternative with the highest utility. That is, $L_i(\beta / \lambda)$ approaches $I(\beta x_i > \beta x_j \; \forall j \neq i)$ as λ approaches zero. For a sufficiently small value of λ, $L_i(\beta / \lambda)$ is sufficiently close to $I(\beta x_i > \beta x_j \; \forall j \neq i)$ for P_i to approximate Q_i arbitrarily closely. Essentially, by scaling the coefficients upwards sufficiently, the mixed logit based on these scaled coefficients is arbitrarily close to the true model. Stated equivalently, adding an extreme value term to true utility, which makes the model into a mixed logit, does not change utility in any meaningful way when the scale of utility is sufficiently large. We return to this issue when discussing estimation below.

This demonstration is not intended to suggest that raising the scale of utility is how the analyst would actually proceed in specifying a mixed logit as an approximation to the true model. Rather, the demonstration simply indicates that if no other means for specifying a mixed logit to approximate the true model can be found, then this re-scaling procedure can be used to attain the approximation. Usually, a mixed logit can be specified that adequately reflects the true model without needing to resort to an upward scaling of utility. For example, the true model will usually contain some iid term that is added to the utility of each alternative. Assuming an extreme value distribution for this term is perhaps close enough to reality to be empirically indistinguishable from other distributional assumptions for the iid term. In this case, the scale of utility is determined naturally by the variance of this iid term. The analyst's task is simply to find variables and mixing distribution that capture the other parts of utility. The re-scaling of utility is only needed if the true model does not contain an iid term whose distribution is adequately close to an extreme value. In these cases, the proof indicates that an iid extreme value term can be added anyway without violence to the model, by raising the scale of utility sufficiently that its addition does not change the identity of the alternative with the highest utility.

The demonstration that a mixed logit can approximate any random utility model is different and more powerful than the "mother logit" theorem which states that any choice probabilities can be approximated by the standard logit formula (McFadden, 1975; Train, 1986.) For the mother logit theorem, attributes of one alternative are allowed to enter the "utility" function of other alternatives. This use of cross-alternative variables allows the logit function to approximate any choice probability; however, since true utility does not depend on attributes of other alternatives (at least under standard economic concepts), a logit formula based on cross-alternative variables is not consistent with utility-maximizing behavior. The resulting model cannot be used for welfare analysis, such as calculation of compensating variations. This limitation is important for recreation demand, since the goal is often to measure the impact of environmental and other changes. In contrast, a mixed logit can approximate any utility specification as well as the resulting choice probabilities. Mixed logit provides an approximation that does not leave the realm of utility theory and consequently can be used for welfare analysis.

4.4 ESTIMATION

A mixed logit is well suited to simulation methods for estimation. We now add notation for decision-makers. A sample of N decision-makers is observed in one choice situation apiece (generalization to repeated choices follows). Decision-maker n faces a choice among set J_n alternatives with utility $U_{jn} = \beta_n x_{jn} + \varepsilon_{jn} \; \forall j \in J_n$, and is observed to choose alternative $i(n)$. (We label the alternative that decision-maker n chooses as $i(n)$ rather than i_n because the latter would entail double-level subscripts when P or x is subscripted by i_n . Labeling the chosen alternative as i without denoting the decision-maker is inappropriate since different decision-makers choose different alternatives such that i for one decision-maker is not the same as i for another decision-maker.) The researcher observes $x_{jn}\ \forall j \in J_n$ but does not observe β_n or ε_{jn}. Each $\varepsilon_{jn}, j \in J_n$, is iid extreme value. The coefficients β_n are distributed in the population with density $f(\beta|\theta^*)$ where θ^* refers collectively to the true parameters of this distribution (such as the mean and covariance of β). The researcher knows the functional form $f(\cdot)$ and wants to estimate the parameters β.

The log-likelihood function is:

$$LL(\theta) = \sum_n \ln P_{i(n)n}(\theta)$$

where

$$P_{i(n)n}(\theta) = \int L_{i(n)n}(\beta) f(\beta|\theta) d\beta$$

$$L_{i(n)n}(\beta) = \frac{\exp(\beta x_{i(n)n})}{\sum_{j \in J_n} \exp(\beta x_{j(n)n})}.$$

The probabilities are approximated through simulation for any given value of θ. (1) Draw a value of β from $f(\beta|\theta)$ and label it β^1 with the superscript referring to the first draw. (2) Calculate the logit formula $L_{i(n)n}(\beta^1)$ with this draw. (3) Repeat steps 1 and 2 many times, and average the results. This average is the simulated probability:

$$SP_{i(n)n}(\theta) = \frac{1}{D} \sum_d L_{i(n)n}(\beta^d)$$

where D is the number of draws. (4) Conduct steps 1–3 for each sampled decision-maker, using a different set of draws for each.[4]

SP is an unbiased estimator of *P* by construction. Its variance decreases as *D* increases. *SP* is strictly positive, such that ln(*SP*) is defined, which is useful for

[4] See Lee (1992) for an estimator that uses the same draws for all observations.

approximating the log-likelihood function below. *SP* is smooth (continuous and twice differentiable) in the parameters θ and the data, which facilitates the numerical search for the maximum of the likelihood function and the calculation of elasticities. And *SP* sums to one over alternatives, which is useful in forecasting.

The simulated likelihood function is constructed with the simulated probabilities:

$$SLL(\theta) = \sum_n \ln SP_{i(n)n}(\theta).$$

The maximum simulated likelihood estimator (MSLE) is the value of θ that maximizes *SLL*.[5] Lee (1992), Hajivassiliou and Ruud (1994), and McFadden and Train (1997) derive properties of this estimator. Note that even though *SP* is unbiased for *P*, *SLL* is not unbiased for *LL* because of the log transformation. The bias decreases as *D* rises. When *D* rises at any rate with *N*, MSLE is consistent. When *D* rises faster than $\sqrt{N}$, MSLE is asymptotically equivalent to the maximum likelihood estimator (MLE). The asymptotic covariance of the estimator is $H^{-1}GH^{-1}$, where *G* is the outer product of the gradient and *H* is the hessian.[6] For a correctly specified model and with *D* rising faster than $\sqrt{N}$, *G* approaches *H* asymptotically, as for MLE, such that G^{-1} is an easy-to-compute estimator of the asymptotic covariance matrix. However, McFadden and Train (1997) point out that, for small samples, simulation noise reduces G^{-1}, even though simulation noise necessarily increases the true variance of MSLE; standard errors based on G^{-1} therefore have the perverse tendency to rise when the number of draws rises. $H^{-1}GH^{-1}$ does not exhibit this unfortunate small sample property.

The simulated mixed logit probability can be related to accept/reject methods of simulation. For any random utility model, an accept/reject simulator is constructed as follows. (1) A draw of the random terms is taken. (2) The utility of each alternative is calculated based on this draw, and the alternative with the highest utility is identified. (3) Steps 1 and 2 are repeated many times; the simulated probability for an alternative is the proportion of draws for which the alternative is identified as having the highest utility. This simulator is unbiased

---

[5] GAUSS code to estimate mixed logits has been written in fairly user-friendly fashion by Train, Revelt, and Ruud. It is available for downloading, along with a manual and sample runs. Go to Train's home page at http://elsa.berkeley.edu/~train and scroll down to the section on free software.

[6] Denote the dimension of θ as *K*. Define the $K \times N$ vector $g = \dfrac{d \ln SP_{i(n)n}(\theta)}{d\theta}$.

Then $G = gg'$. *H* is the $K \times K$ vector of second derivatives of $SLL(\theta)$ with respect to θ.

by construction. However, it is not strictly positive for any finite number of draws. It is also not smooth but rather a step-function: constant within ranges of parameters for which the identity of the alternative with the highest utility does not change for any draws, and with jumps where changes in the parameters change the identity of the alternative with the highest utility. Numerical methods for MSLE based on the accept/reject simulator are hampered by these characteristics.

Accept/reject methods were proposed by Lerman and Manski (1981) for probit models but found to require an infeasibly large number of draws for the resulting estimator to be reasonably accurate. Advances in computer speed make the taking of many draws more feasible now than then. However, the lack of smoothness and the chance of a zero simulated probability are intrinsic limitations. Ben-Akiva and Bolduc (1996) and McFadden (1989) have proposed using a logit kernel within an accept/reject simulator as a way of smoothing the simulator and guaranteeing that it be strictly positive. That is, instead of using the 1–0 indicator for the alternative with the highest utility in each draw, use the logit formula based on the utility that is calculated for each alternative with that draw:

$$L_i = \frac{\exp\left(V_i^d / \lambda\right)}{\sum_j \exp\left(V_j^d / \lambda\right)}$$

where V_i^d is the utility of alternative i calculated from draw d of the random terms, and λ is a scaling parameter that determines the "tightness" of the kernel. As λ approaches zero, this "smoothed accept/reject" simulator approaches the traditional accept/reject simulator.

The mixed logit simulator is simply this logit-kernel-smoothed accept/reject simulator. The theorem that a mixed logit can approximate any random utility model can be viewed from this perspective. The true model is simulated with accept/reject methods (that is, for each draw of the random terms, calculate the utility of each alternative). The mixed logit replaces the 1–0 indicator with the logit formula. The scale of the utility entering the logit formula can be set arbitrarily high such that the simulated probabilities based on the logit kernel are arbitrarily close to the 1-0 indicator and yet are still smooth and strictly positive.

4.5 PANEL DATA

The specification is easily generalized to allow for repeated choices by each sampled decision-maker. The simplest specification treats the coefficients that enter utility as varying over people but being constant over choice situations for each person. Utility from alternative i in choice situation t by person n is $U_{int} = \beta_n x_{int} + \varepsilon_{int}$ with ε_{int} being iid extreme value over time, people, and alternatives. Person n's chosen alternative in period t is denoted $i(n,t)$. Conditional on β, the probability for the person's sequence of T choices is the product of logit formulas:

$$Y_n(\beta) = \prod_{t=1}^{T} L_{i(n,t)nt}(\beta)$$

where

$$L_{i(n,t)nt}(\beta) = \frac{\exp\left(\beta x_{i(n,t)nt}\right)}{\sum_j \exp\left(\beta x_{j(n,t)nt}\right)}.$$

The unconditional probability is the integral of this product over all values of β:

$$Z_n(\theta) = \int Y_n(\beta) f(\beta|\theta) d\beta.$$

The log-likelihood function is then:

$$LL(\theta) = \sum_n \ln Z_n(\theta).$$

The probability Z is simulated similarly to the probability for one choice period. A draw of β is taken from its distribution; the logit formula is calculated for each period; and the product of these logits is taken. This process is repeated for many draws, and the results are averaged. The simulated probability replaces Z in the likelihood function, and the estimated parameters are the value of θ that maximizes the simulated likelihood function.[7]

The coefficients associated with each person can be specified to vary over time in a variety of ways. For example, each person's tastes might be serially correlated over choice situations, such that utility is

---

[7] GAUSS software to estimate mixed logits on panel data is also provided at Train's website. See footnote 5.

$$U_{int} = \beta_{nt} x_{int} + \varepsilon_{int}$$

$$\beta_{nt} = \rho \beta_{nt-1} + \mu_{nt}$$

where μ_{nt} has zero mean and is iid over n and t. Simulation of the probability for the sequence of choices proceeds by (1) drawing μ for the initial period and calculating the logit formula for this period using β equal to this value of μ, (2) drawing μ for the second period, calculating β as ρ times the β from the first period plus the new μ, and calculating the logit formula based on this β, (3) and so on for all the T periods, (4) taking the product of the T logits, and (5) repeating steps 1–4 for numerous sequences of draws of μ and averaging the results. The burden placed on simulation is greater than with coefficients being constant over time for each person, requiring T times as many draws.

State-dependence, whereby a person's choice in one period affects his/her choice in later periods, can be introduced by allowing the utility from an alternative to depend on previous choices—either through lagged dependent variables or by specifying each person's coefficients to depend on previous choices. However, if choices and data are not observed from the start of the process (i.e., from the first choice situation that the person faces), as is usually the case with recreation demand models, the issue of initial conditions must be confronted (Heckman, 1981). That is, the analyst must somehow represent the probability of the first observed choice, which depends on the previous, unobserved choices. This issue is no different for mixed logits than in general whenever state-dependence and customer-heterogeneity (i.e., unobserved factors that are correlated over choice situations—in our case, the β's) are both present.

4.6 APPLICATION

As an illustration, we present a mixed logit of anglers' choice of river fishing site in Montana, estimated on data developed and described by Desvousges, Waters, and Train (1995, 1996). The specification, from Train (1998), takes a random-coefficients form. Angler n faces a choice among J_{nt} sites for trip t among T_n trips. Utility is $U_{int} = \beta_n x_{int} + \varepsilon_{int}$, with coefficients β_n varying over anglers but not over trips for each angler. The probability of the sequence of sites chosen by each angler is given by Z_n above.

A total of 59 possible river sites were defined based on geographical and other relevant factors. Each site contains one or more of the stream segments used in the Montana River Information System. The following variables enter as elements of x for each site:

1. Fish stock, measured in 100 fish per 1000 feet of river.
2. Aesthetics rating, measured on a scale of 0 to 3, with 3 being the highest.
3. Trip cost: cost of traveling from the angler's home to the site, including the variable cost of driving (gas, maintenance, tires, oil) and the value of time spent driving (with time valued at one-third the angler's wage.)
4. Indicator that the Angler's Guide to Montana lists the site as a major fishing site.
5. Number of campgrounds per US Geological Survey (USGS) block in the site.
6. Number of state recreation access areas per USGS block in the site.
7. Number of restricted species at the site.
8. Log of the size of the site, in USGS blocks.

The coefficients of variables 4–7 can logically take either sign; for example, some anglers might like having campgrounds while other anglers prefer the privacy that comes from not having nearby campgrounds. Each of these coefficients is given an independent normal distribution with mean and standard deviation that are estimated. The coefficients for trip cost, fish stock, and aesthetics ratings of the site are expected to have the same sign for all anglers with only their magnitudes differing over anglers. These coefficients are given independent lognormal distributions.[8] The mean and standard deviation of the log of the coefficient is estimated, and the mean and standard deviation of the coefficient itself are calculated from these estimates. Since the lognormal distribution is defined over the positive range and trip cost is expected to have a negative coefficient for all anglers, the negative of trip cost enters the model. The coefficient for the log of size is assumed to be fixed. This variable accounts for the fact that the probability of visiting a larger site is higher than that for a smaller site, all else equal. Having the coefficient of this variable vary over people, while possible, would not be particularly meaningful.

The sample consists of 962 river trips taken by 258 anglers during the period July 1992 through August 1993. Simulation was performed using one thousand draws for each sampled angler. The results are given in Table 4.1. The standard deviation of each random coefficient is highly significant, indicating that these coefficients do indeed vary in the population.

[8] Train (1998) and Revelt and Train (1996) estimate mixed logits with coefficients that are correlated.

Table 4.1 Mixed Logit Model of River Fishing Site Choice

		Parameter	Std error
Fish Stock	Mean of ln(coefficient)	-2.876	0.6066
	Std. Dev. of ln(coefficient)	1.016	0.2469
Aesthetics	Mean of ln(coefficient)	-0.7942	0.2287
	Std. Dev. of ln(coefficient)	0.8493	0.1382
Trip cost (neg.)	Mean of ln(coefficient)	-2.402	0.0631
	Std. Dev. of ln(coefficient)	0.8012	0.0781
Guide lists major	Mean of coefficient	1.018	0.2887
	Std. Dev. of coefficient	2.195	0.3518
Campgrounds	Mean coefficient	0.1158	0.3233
	Std. Dev. of coefficient	1.655	0.4350
Access areas	Mean coefficient	-0.9499	0.3610
	Std. Dev. of coefficient	1.888	0.3511
Restricted Species	Mean coefficient	-0.4989	0.1310
	Std. Dev. of coefficient	0.8989	0.1640
Log(size)	Coefficient	0.9835	0.1077
Likelihood ratio index		0.5018	
Log-likelihood at convergence		-1932.33	

Consider first the normally distributed coefficients. The estimated means and standard deviations of these coefficients provide information on the share of the population that places a positive value on the site attribute and the share that places a negative value. The distribution of the coefficient of the indicator that the Angler's Guide to Montana lists the site as a major site obtains an estimated mean of 1.018 and estimated standard deviation of 2.195, such that 68% of the distribution is above zero and 32% below. This implies that being listed as a major site in the Angler's Guide to Montana is a positive inducement for about two-thirds of anglers and a negative factor for the other third who apparently prefer more solitude. Campgrounds are preferred by about half (53%) of anglers and avoided by the other half. And about one-third of anglers (31%) are estimated to prefer having numerous access areas, while the other two-thirds prefer there being fewer access areas.

The point estimates for the log-normal distributions imply that the coefficients of fish stock, aesthetics, and trip cost have the following median, mean, and standard deviations.[9]

	Median	Mean	Std.Dev.
Fish Stock	0.0563	0.0944	0.1270
Aesthetics	0.4519	0.6482	0.6665
Trip cost	0.0906	0.1249	0.1185

The ratio of an angler's fish stock coefficient to his/her trip cost coefficient is a measure of the amount that the angler is willing to pay to have additional fish in the river. Recalling that the ratio of two independent log-normally distributed terms is also log-normally distributed, we can calculate moments for the distribution of willingness to pay. The log of the ratio of the fish stock coefficient to the trip cost coefficient has estimated mean -0.474 and standard deviation 1.29. The ratio itself therefore has median 0.62, mean 1.44, and standard deviation 2.96. That is, the average willingness to pay to have the fish stock raised by 100 fish per 1000 feet of river is estimated to be $1.44, and there is very wide variation in anglers' willingness to pay for additional fish stock. Similarly, $9.87 is the estimated average willingness to pay for a site that has an aesthetics rating that is higher by 1, and again the variation is fairly large.

As this application illustrates, the mixed logit provides more information than a standard logit since the mixed logit estimates the extent to which anglers differ in their preferences for site attributes. As stated above, the standard deviations of the coefficients enter significantly, indicating that a mixed logit provides a significantly better representation of the choice situation than standard logit, which assumes that coefficients are the same for all anglers.[10] The mixed logit also accounts for the fact that several trips are observed for each sampled angler and that each angler's preferences apply to each of his/her trips. These advantages come at a cost of greater computation time. In our

---

[9] If coefficient α is lognormally distributed such that $\ln\alpha \sim N(m,s^2)$, then α has median $\exp(m)$, mean $\exp(m+s^2/2)$, and variance $\exp(2m+s^2)[\exp(s^2)-1]$.

[10] Similarly, Bhat (1996a,b), Revelt and Train (1996), Brownstone and Train (1996), and Train (1998) compare logits with mixed logits and find that mixed logits fit the data better, with the standard deviations of random coefficients entering significantly. In some studies (Bhat, 1996a; Train, 1998; and for some of the attributes in Revelt and Train, 1996), the ratios of coefficients and welfare measures are fairly similar between the logit and mixed logit models, while other studies (Bhat, 1996b, and for other attributes in Revelt and Train, 1996) found fairly different values. There is probably no general answer on whether ratios of coefficients and other welfare measures obtain similar values in logits and mixed logits: the answer is necessarily situation- and model-specific.

application, the mixed logit required several hours to run, while the standard logit took less than one minute.

REFERENCES

Ben-Akiva, M., and Bolduc, D. (1996), "Multinomial Probit with a Logit Kernel and a General Parametric Specification of the Covariance Structure," working paper, Department d'economique, Universite laval, Quebec, Canada.

Ben-Akiva, M. and Lerman, S. (1985), *Discrete Choice Analysis*, MIT Press.

Bhat, C. (1996a), "Accommodating Variations in Responsiveness to Level-of-Service Measures in Travel Mode Choice Modeling," working paper, Department of Civil Engineering, University of Massachusetts at Amherst.

Bhat, C. (1996b), "Incorporating Observed and Unobserved Heterogeneity in Urban Work Travel Choice Modeling," working paper, Department of Civil Engineering, University of Massachusetts at Amherst.

Bockstael, N., W. Hanemann, and C. Kling, 1987, "Estimating the Value of Water Quality Improvements in a Recreational Demand Framework," *Water Resources Research,* 23, 951–60.

Bockstael, N., McConnell, K., and Strand, L. (1989), "A Random Utility Model for Sportsfishing: Some Preliminary Results for Florida," *Marine Resources Economics,* 6, 245–60.

Boyd, J. and Mellman, R. (1980), "The Effect of Fuel Economy Standards on the U.S. Automotive Market: An Hedonic Demand Analysis," *Transportation Research,* 14A, No. 5-6, 367–78.

Brownstone, D., and Train, K. (1996), "Forecasting New Product Penetration with Flexible Substitution Patterns," forthcoming, *Journal of Econometrics.*

Cardell, N. and Dunbar, F. (1980), "Measuring the Societal Impacts of Automobile Downsizing," *Transportation Research*, 14A, No. 5-6, 423–34.

Caulkins, P. R. Bishop, and Bouwes, N. (1986), "The Travel Cost Model for Lake Recreation: A Comparison of Two Methods for Incorporating Site Quality and Substitution Effects," *American Journal of Agricultural Economics*, 68, 291–97.

Desvousges, W., and Waters, S. (1995), "Report on Potential Economic Losses Associated with Recreational Services in the Upper Clark Fork River Basin," Vol. III and Appendices, Triangle Economic Research, 1000 Park Forty Plaza, Suite 200, Durham, NC 27713.

Desvousges, W., Waters, S., and Train, K. (1996), "Supplemental Report on Potential Economic Losses Associated with Recreational Services in the Upper Clark Fork River Basin," Triangle Economic Research, 1000 Park Forty Plaza, Suite 200, Durham, NC 27713.

Hajivassiliou, V. and Ruud, P. (1994), "Classical Estimation Methods for LDV Models using Simulation," *Handbook of Econometrics*, Vol. IV, R. Engle and D. McFadden, eds., Elsevier Science B.V.

Hausmann, J., Leonard, G., and McFadden, D. (1995), "A Utility-Consistent, Combined Discrete Choice and Count Data Model: Assessing Recreational Use Losses Due to Natural Resource Damage," *Journal of Public Economics*, 56, 1–30.

Heckman, J. (1981), "The Incidental Parameters Problem and the Problem of Initial Conditions in Estimating a Discrete Time-Discrete Data Stochastic Process," in C. Manski and D. McFadden, eds., *Structural Analysis of Discrete Data with Econometric Applications,* MIT Press.

Lee, L. (1992), "On Efficiency of Methods of Simulated Moments and Maximum Simulated Maximum Estimation of Discrete Response Models," *Econometrica*, 8, 518–52.

Lerman, S. and Manski, C. (1981), "On the Use of Simulated Frequencies to Approximate Choice Probabilities," in C. Manski and D. McFadden, eds., *Structural Analysis of Discrete Data with Econometric Applications*, MIT Press.

McFadden, D. (1975), "On Independence Structure and Simultaneity in Transportation Demand Analysis," working paper No. 7511, Urban Travel Demand Forecasting Project, Department of Economics, University of California, Berkeley.

McFadden, D. (1978), "Modelling the Choice of Residential Location," in A. Karquist et al., eds., *Spatial Interaction Theory and Planning Models*, North-Holland.

McFadden, D. (1989), "A Method of Simulated Moments for Estimation of Discrete Choice Models without Numerical Integration," *Econometrica*, 57, 995–1026.

McFadden, D. and Train, K. (1997), "Mixed MNL Models for Discrete Response," working paper, Department of Economics, University of California, Berkeley.

Mehndiratta, S. (1996), "Time-of-Day Effects in Inter-City Business Travel," Ph.D. thesis, Department of Civil Engineering, University of California, Berkeley.

Morey, E., Rowe, R., and Watson, M. (1993), "A Repeated Nested-Logit Model of Atlantic Salmon Fishing, " *American Journal of Agricultural Economics*, 75, 578–92.

Parsons, G. and Kealy, M. (1992), "Randomly Drawn Opportunity Sets in a Random Utility Model of Lake Recreation," *Land Economics*, 68, 93–106.

Parsons, G., and Needleman, M. (1992), "Site Aggregation in a Random Utility Model of Recreation," *Land Economics*, 68, 418–33.

Revelt, D., and Train, K. (1996), "Mixed Logit with Repeated Choices: Households' Choices of Appliance Efficiency Level," forthcoming, *Review of Economics and Statistics.*

Train, K. (1986), *Qualitative Choice Analvsis*, MIT Press.

Train, K. (1998), "Recreation Demand Models with Taste Differences over People," *Land Economics*, 74, No. 2, 230–39.

5. An Empirical Assessment of Multinomial Probit and Logit Models for Recreation Demand

Heng Z. Chen, Frank Lupi, and John P. Hoehn[1]

5.1 INTRODUCTION

The random utility model is widely used in contemporary travel cost studies of recreation demand. Almost all random utility models in the recreation literature are specified as multinomial logit or as nested logit. One reason for this is the ability of these models to incorporate a large number of substitutes without sacrificing ease of estimation. Another strength of these models is that measuring the welfare effects of changes in site characteristics is straightforward (Bishop and Heberlein, 1979; Small and Rosen, 1981; Hanemann, 1982; among others).

The independence of irrelevant alternatives (IIA) property of multinomial logit is a well known and often cited drawback of the multinomial logit formulation of random utility models (see for example Chapter 3 by Morey). With nested logit models, IIA is partially relaxed.[2] In many empirical studies, the generalization embodied in the nested logit has been shown to be important (Morey, Rowe, and Watson 1993; Herriges and Kling 1997; Hausman, Leonard, and McFadden 1995). As an alternative to the logit model, the multinomial probit model can be used to provide a general correlation pattern across choices without exhibiting the IIA property. This model has seen little application in recreation demand because the probit model with more than four choices was difficult to estimate prior to recent advances in econometric theory and computing power.

---

[1] The corresponding author, Heng Z. Chen, is at American Express Travel Related Services, 10400 North 25th Avenue, Phoenix, AZ 85021. Frank Lupi and John Hoehn are, respectively, Visiting Assistant Professor and Professor in the Department of Agricultural Economics, Michigan State University, East Lansing, MI 48824.

[2] Specifications such as the random parameter logit or random parameter probit can also relax IIA, see Chapter 4 by Train or Chen and Cosslett (1998).

This chapter empirically investigates the implications of error distributions that relax IIA. The application is to Great Lake fishing site choices made by Michigan trout and salmon anglers. The underlying theoretical framework is the repeated random utility model. The following repeated random utility models were estimated: (i) a simple multinomial logit, (ii) a nested logit, (iii) a simple multinomial probit with independent errors, and (iv) two multinomial probits with correlated errors. The probit models were estimated using simulated maximum likelihood methods. The results demonstrate the feasibility of estimating multinomial probits for the large choice sets encountered in recreation demand analysis.

In the remaining sections of this chapter, the logit and probit models are specified and the estimation and identification of multinomial probit are also reviewed for recreation demand. Next, by using a recreation fishing demand data set, the parameter estimates are presented for each of the models. Predictions of fishing trips under baseline site quality characteristics and under a range of changes in site quality characteristics are compared across the models. Examining a range of changes in site quality allows the changes in trip demand to be compared across model specifications at the site level. Trip predictions are also calculated for sites where quality was not changed so that the implications of IIA can be illustrated. In addition, welfare measures for the various changes in site quality characteristics are calculated for each of the estimated models.

5.2 MULTINOMIAL LOGIT AND PROBIT MODELS

Let the random utility of choosing alternative j be written as $U_j = x_j\beta + u_j$ where x_j are the explanatory variables for the utilities of alternatives $j = 1,\ldots,J$. u_j is the random taste term, unobservable to the researcher. By the hypothesis of random utility maximization, if j is chosen, it implies $U_j \geq U_l$ for $l = 1,\ldots, J$. These inequalities are used to specify the probability that each of the alternatives is chosen. The model for the choice probabilities will follow from the distribution of the error terms u.

5.2.1 Multinomial Logit Models

If the u_j are assumed to be i.i.d. with a type I extreme value (EV) distribution, then the joint distribution of the errors is

$$F(u) = \exp\left(-\sum_{j=1}^{J} \exp(-u_j)\right),$$

and the choice probabilities are given by

$$\Pr(j) = \frac{\exp(x_j\beta)}{\Sigma_l \exp(x_l\beta)}. \tag{5.1}$$

From (5.1), it is clear that the probability ratio between choices j and k is independent of the utility functions other than that of alternatives j and k

$$\frac{\Pr(j)}{\Pr(k)} = \frac{\exp(x_j\beta)}{\exp(x_k\beta)}.$$

This is often referred to as the IIA property of the multinomial logit model (5.1).

To partially relax IIA by deriving a two-level nested logit, we can partition the set of alternatives into G groups. Assume that the vector of errors u has the following form of Generalized Extreme Value (GEV) distribution function,

$$F(u) = \exp\left\{-\sum_{g=1}^{G}\left(\sum_{j\in B_g}\exp(-u_{j_g}/\lambda_g)\right)^{\lambda_g}\right\}$$

where B_g is the set of alternatives of group g for g = 1,…,G, and λ_g is the distribution parameter. It can be shown that the corresponding choice probabilities are

$$\Pr(j) = \Pr(j|B_g)\times\Pr(g)$$

$$= \frac{\exp(x_j\beta/\lambda_g)}{\Sigma_{j\in B_g}\exp(x_j\beta/\lambda_g)}\times\frac{\exp(\lambda_g IV_g)}{\Sigma_{g=1}^{G}\exp(\lambda_g IV_g)}$$

$$= \frac{\exp(x_j\beta/\lambda_g)}{\exp((1-\lambda_g)IV_g)}\times\frac{1}{\Sigma_{g=1}^{G}\exp(\lambda_g IV_g)}, \tag{5.2}$$

where $IV_g = \ln(\Sigma_{j\in B_g}\exp(x_j\beta/\lambda_g))$ is the inclusive value of group g. Similar to the multinomial logit model, it is easy to see that the probability ratio of any two alternatives that are within the same group g is still independent of the utility functions of the other alternatives. That is, IIA holds within groups. What is different now is that the probability ratio between alternatives j and k that are not within the same group, say group g and group s, depends not only on the utility functions of alternatives j and k, but also on the group inclusive values IV_g and IV_s. That is

$$\frac{\Pr(j)}{\Pr(k)} = \frac{\exp(x_j\beta)}{\exp(x_k\beta)} \times \frac{\exp((1-\lambda_s)IV_s)}{\exp((1-\lambda_g)IV_g)}.$$

The probability ratio remains independent of all alternatives in groups other than g and s. Thus, the nested logit exhibits a property similar to IIA, which we will call independence of irrelevant groups (IIG).

5.2.2 Multinomial Probit Models

One way to avoid the restricted substitution patterns embodied in models with IIA and IIG is to employ the normal distribution for the random terms, i.e., assume $u \sim N(0, \Sigma_u)$ with the density function

$$f(u) = \frac{1}{\sqrt{2\pi|\Sigma_u|}} \exp(-\frac{1}{2}u'\Sigma_u^{-1}u)$$

where Σ_u is the covariance matrix. The resulting choice probability *Pr(j)* is

$$\Pr(j) = \int_{-\infty}^{\infty} du_j \int_{-\infty}^{(x_j-x_1)\beta+u_j} du_1 \cdots \int_{-\infty}^{(x_j-x_J)\beta+u_j} du_J \cdot f(u_1,\ldots,u_J|\Sigma_u)$$

$$= \int_{-\infty}^{\infty} F_j((x_j - x_l)\beta + u_j, \forall l \neq j) du_j. \tag{5.3}$$

Unlike the logit models, the probability ratio between any two alternatives *Pr(j)/Pr(k)* depends on utility functions of all alternatives regardless of the covariance structure in Σ_u. Thus, the IIA assumption is not maintained for the multinomial probit model. This generalization comes at the cost of having to evaluate the high dimension integrals in (5.3).

Several simulators have been introduced recently to approximate multinomial probit choice probabilities through Monte Carlo simulations. We demonstrate the feasibility of multinomial probit estimation using the smooth recursive simulator, often called the GHK simulator, independently introduced by Geweke (1991), Hajivassiliou and McFadden (1990), and Keane (1990). We use the GHK simulator because it is continuous in the parameter space $\beta \otimes \Sigma_u$. Based on the root mean squared error criterion, Hajivassiliou, McFadden, and Ruud (1992) show that the GHK simulator is unambiguously the most reliable method for simulating normal probabilities, compared to the twelve other simulators they considered.

To estimate the probit models using simulated maximum likelihood estimation, the choice probabilities in the likelihood function are replaced by the simulated probabilities from (5.3). The resulting likelihood function is then maximized so that estimation can be achieved by using conventional optimization packages. As the sample size and the number of replications in the simulation of the choice probabilities increase, maximization of the simulated likelihood function yields parameter estimates that possess the asymptotic properties of conventional maximum likelihood estimates (Gourieroux and Monfort, 1993). Consequently, statistical inference based on these asymptotic properties can be implemented with simulated maximum likelihood estimates.

5.2.3 The Empirical Comparisons and The Probit Model Identification

In this chapter, we take an empirical approach to compare the probit and logit models. This is motivated in part by the fact that there is not much literature regarding the probit model for recreation demand when there are many site choices. One would like to investigate the similarity and differences between the widely used logit model and the probit model in terms of IIA properties, welfare measurement and trip predictions. However, the comparisons between the logit and probit models are hindered due to the difficulty of directly comparing the error distributions. For example, consider a logit model with $J = 3$. We can nest the first two alternatives into one group and the third alternative into another group. A generalized extreme value distribution with this nesting structure is

$$F(u) = \exp\left\{-(\exp(-u_1 / \lambda) + \exp(-u_2 / \lambda))^{\lambda} - \exp(-u_3)\right\}$$

provided $0 < \lambda \leq 1$. It is not clear which normal distribution matches this generalized extreme value distribution.

Furthermore, in specifying the covariance matrix for the probit model when there are many site choices, it is almost impossible to estimate all elements in the covariance matrix. Assumptions to simplify the matrix are necessary for empirical applications. How to normalize and to rescale the simplified covariance matrix may be important due to the interdependence between β's and Σ_u (Dansie, 1985 or Bunch, 1991). To see this point, let the covariance matrix of the three alternative probit model be

$$\Sigma_u = \begin{pmatrix} \sigma_1^2 & \sigma_{12} & \sigma_{13} \\ & \sigma_2^2 & \sigma_{23} \\ & & \sigma_3^2 \end{pmatrix}.$$

The normalization of the utility function $U_j = x_j\beta + u_j$ based on, say, choice 3 yields $U_j^* = x_j^*\beta + u_j^*$ with $x_j^* = x_j - x_3$ and $u_j^* = u_j - u_3$ for $j = 1$ and 2. The covariance matrix for u^* is

$$\Sigma_{u^*} = \begin{pmatrix} \sigma_1^{*2} & \sigma_{12}^* \\ & \sigma_2^{*2} \end{pmatrix}$$

with $\sigma_1^{*2} = \sigma_1^2 + \sigma_3^2 - 2\sigma_{13}$, $\sigma_2^{*2} = \sigma_2^2 + \sigma_3^2 - 2\sigma_{23}$, and $\sigma_{12}^* = \sigma_1^2 - \sigma_{13} - \sigma_{23} + \sigma_{12}$. The probit model can only be identified if either one of the β's or one of the σ^*'s is preset to a constant. If we fix σ_{12}^*, there are only two identifiable parameters out of the six in Σ_u with

$$\Sigma_u = \begin{pmatrix} \sigma_1^2 & \overline{\sigma}_{12} & \overline{\sigma}_{13} \\ & \sigma_2^2 & \overline{\sigma}_{23} \\ & & \overline{\sigma}_{33}^2 \end{pmatrix} \tag{5.4}$$

where σ_1^2 and σ_2^2 are to be estimated, $\overline{\sigma}_{12}, \overline{\sigma}_{13}, \overline{\sigma}_{23}$, and $\overline{\sigma}_{33}^2$ are some fixed constants required by the identification conditions. Thus, $\overline{\sigma}_{ij}$'s and σ_{ij}'s are inter-dependent, and the estimates of β's also depend on $\overline{\sigma}_{ij}$'s.

5.3 THE MODELS, DATA, AND ESTIMATION RESULTS

We model the fishing choices of Michigan anglers for trips targeting Great Lakes trout and salmon. The fishing sites are defined by the stretch of Great Lakes shoreline within each of Michigan's coastal counties. In all, there are 41 counties that support salmon and trout fishing on the Great Lakes. When the stay-home alternative is included, the choice set can be as large as 42 alternatives per choice occasion. Before we discuss the data set and the model estimation results, we will first specify the covariance matrices of the probit models for recreation fishing demand in Michigan.

5.3.1 Covariance Matrices of the Probit Model for Recreation Demand

While the dimension of the covariance matrix for our empirical examples can be as large as 42, computational and data limitations mean that we cannot recover every element in the matrix even after imposing the normalization and rescaling conditions. One approach is to impose restrictions on the covariance matrix based on researchers' judgments about the relative similarity and difference between alternatives. For example, in a random utility model of recreation demand, one might believe that the variance of the random term for the stay-home alternative is different from the variance of the random terms for the fishing sites. In this case, one can adopt the following block structure for the covariance matrix to mimic the nested logit model in which the stay-home alternative is grouped into a different nest from the fishing sites.

$$\Sigma_u = \begin{pmatrix} \sigma_d^2 & \sigma_0 & \cdots & \sigma_0 & \sigma_{dh} \\ & \sigma_d^2 & \cdots & \sigma_0 & \sigma_{dh} \\ & & \ddots & \vdots & \vdots \\ & & & \sigma_d^2 & \sigma_{dh} \\ & & & & \sigma_h^2 \end{pmatrix}.$$

There are only four different parameters $\sigma_d^2, \sigma_h^2, \sigma_0$, and σ_{dh} in this matrix to allow for the flexibility in the error terms. If we normalize against the stay-home choice h, the resulting J-dimensional matrix for $u^* = u - u_h$ is

$$\Sigma_{u^*} = \begin{pmatrix} \sigma_d^{*2} & \sigma_0^* & \cdots & \sigma_0^* \\ & \sigma_d^{*2} & \cdots & \sigma_0^* \\ & & \ddots & \vdots \\ & & & \sigma_d^{*2} \end{pmatrix}.$$

If we pre-fix σ_0^* in Σ_{u^*} to a constant due to the rescaling condition, there is only one parameter to be estimated in Σ_u. One of $\{\sigma_d^2, \sigma_h^2, \sigma_0, \sigma_{dh}\}$ can be estimated by pre-fixing the rest. For example, we can elect to estimate σ_d^2 by prefixing $\sigma_h^2 = c_{hh}, \sigma_0 = c_0$, and $\sigma_{dh} = c_{dh}$

$$\Sigma_u = \begin{pmatrix} \sigma_d^2 & c_0 & \cdots & c_0 & c_{dh} \\ & \sigma_d^2 & \cdots & c_0 & c_{dh} \\ & & \ddots & \vdots & \vdots \\ & & & \sigma_d^2 & c_{dh} \\ & & & & c_{hh} \end{pmatrix}. \tag{5.5}$$

Alternatively, we can elect to estimate σ_h^2 by pre-fixing $\sigma_d^2 = c_d, \sigma_0 = c_0$ and $\sigma_{dh} = c_{dh}$

$$\Sigma_u = \begin{pmatrix} c_d & c_0 & \cdots & c_0 & c_{dh} \\ & c_d & \cdots & c_0 & c_{dh} \\ & & \ddots & \vdots & \vdots \\ & & & c_d & c_{dh} \\ & & & & \sigma_h^2 \end{pmatrix}. \tag{5.6}$$

In the empirical application, we will estimate two correlated probit models using (5.5) and (5.6), and consider different constants for c_d, c_0, c_{dh}, and c_{hh} to illustrate how the parameter estimates change with the covariance matrix specification.[3]

5.3.2 Data Sets

The behavioral data comes from a 1994 survey of recreational fishing in Michigan that was conducted at Michigan State University. See the report by Hoehn, Tomasi, Lupi, and Chen (1996) for details. From the Michigan data, we selected individuals with at least one single-day trip targeting Great Lakes trout and salmon during the 1994 open water season (April 1 to October 31). There are of 325 of these trips from 90 individuals. Summary statistics for the data are presented in Table 5.1.

---

[3] The probit models based on specification (5.5) and (5.6) will be the same if there is one and only one identifiable parameter in the block covariance matrix Σ_u. However, if there were more than one identifiable parameter, the two correlated probit models would likely be different due to different constants c_d, c_0, c_{dh}, and c_{hh}.

Table 5.1 Summary Statistics of the Data Set

Variables	Mean	Std	Min	Max
tripcost	145.763	49.634	70.620	256.900
chinook	0.036	0.029	0	0.110
coho	0.013	0.021	0	0.107
lake	0.039	0.056	0	0.210
rainbow	0.007	0.010	0	0.044
age	45.405	16.459	19	81
edu	13.281	2.454	6	18
gender	0.865	0.344	0	1
$region_1$	0.025	0.155	0	1
$region_2$	0.228	0.420	0	1

The first row of Table 5.1 presents the trip cost variable for the 325 observations on the sites that were visited by the individuals. The second to the fifth rows report the catch rate variables for the 41 sites. The last five rows present summaries of the characteristics of the 90 individuals. The definitions of the explanatory variables are as follows: *tripcost*: the trip cost is defined as the sum of the estimated time cost and driving cost of the trip in dollars. Individual specific driving costs were estimated using fuel cost and vehicle data reported in the survey. Environmental site quality variables are *chinook, coho, lake,* and *rainbow*: the seasonal average catch-per-hour of chinook salmon, coho salmon, lake trout, and rainbow trout, respectively. The catch rates were derived from creel surveys and were previously employed by Jones and Sung (1992). Individual characteristics variables include *age*: respondent's age in years. *edu*: respondent's years in education. *gender*: a dummy variable, 1 for male, 0 for female. $region_1$: a dummy variable, 1 if respondent's home county is in Detroit tri-county region, 0 otherwise. $region_2$: a dummy variable, 1 if respondent's home county is in Mid-Michigan region, 0 otherwise.

Since about 97% of the observed single-day trips in the survey were within 150 miles one-way driving distance, we used this distance to define the feasible fishing sites for each of individual. Thus, on each choice occasion, an individual's feasible choice set consists of the stay-home alternative and all Great Lake sites (counties) that are within 150 miles from their residence. The average sample member has about 13 sites in their feasible choice set per occasion. Since we permit at most one trip in each choice occasion, we partitioned the fishing season into 45 choice occasions, the maximum observed number of trips taken by any individual in the sample.[4]

5.3.3 Estimation Results

Five models are estimated in this chapter: one independent multinomial logit model (I-Logit); one nested logit model (N-Logit); one independent multinomial probit model (I-Probit); and two correlated probit models with (5.5) and (5.6) as covariance matrices—C-Probit(5) and C-Probit(6), respectively. The detailed estimation results are presented in the appendix.

As described above, when the error terms u_j are i.i.d. and follow a type I EV distribution, the choice probabilities have the independent logit form. The log likelihood value for the I-Logit model is -1521.38. To estimate a nested logit model (N-Logit), a natural approach is to separate the stay-home alternative from the various fishing sites using a two-level nest, which might reflect the correlation patterns in Σ_u for the probit model. The top level is the choice of whether to participate on each occasion, the second level is which site to go fishing at, given the participation. This nesting structure yields a log likelihood value of -1420.97, significantly higher than the I-Logit model.

When the error terms u_j are distributed i.i.d. normal, an independent probit (I-Probit) results where the identity matrix is used as the covariance matrix. All of the probit models are estimated using 400 replications. The log likelihood value for the I-Probit is -1504.54. The independent probit model fits the data better than the independent logit model.

C-Probit(5) is specified by using (5.5), and σ_d^2 is identified by fixing $c_0 = 0.1$, $c_{dh} \doteq 0$, and $c_{hh} = 1$. Alternatively, estimation of C-Probit(6) is based on (5.6), and σ_h^2 is identified by fixing $c_{dd} = 3$, $c_0 = 2$ and $c_{dh} = 0$. As expected, the log likelihood values for the both correlated probit models are the same, -1443.95, and provide significantly better fits than the I-Probit model.

The coefficient estimates of the two probit models are different due to the arbitrary selection of the values for the constants for the identification conditions. However, if the coefficients are divided by the trip cost coefficient, they are virtually the same. This verifies that there is one and only one parameter in the block covariance matrix Σ_u that can be identified and estimated. For each

---

[4] We also experimented with different number of choice occasions using the independent multinomial logit model (see the following section). As one might expect, the parameters and the likelihood value change with the number of choice occasions because the probability of taking a trip in a given occasion will increase as the length of the choice occasion decreases. However, the results such as the trip prediction and welfare measurement appear to be insensitive to the number of choice occasions based on the estimated independent logit model.

of the models, Table 5.2 presents the standardized coefficients of site quality, the site quality coefficient divided by the negative of the trip cost coefficient. The sum in the final column is the sum of the standardized site quality coefficients for each model.

Table 5.2 Catch Rate Coefficients/Trip Cost Coefficient

Models	Chinook salmon	Coho salmon	Lake trout	Rainbow trout	Sum
C-Probit(5)	6.769	2.533	0.831	16.132	26.265
C-Probit(6)	6.769	2.533	0.831	16.132	26.265
I-Probit	3.809	3.151	1.389	10.126	18.475
N-Logit	6.434	2.903	0.098	14.600	24.035
I-Logit	1.976	2.963	0.965	8.463	14.365

From the last column of the table, we see that the two correlated probit models are identical to each other. The nested logit model is also similar to the correlated models. The independent models appear to be different. However, one should keep it in mind that the welfare measurements are function of both the error structure (the probabilities) and the standardized coefficients (Small and Rosen, 1981). In the next section, we will empirically assess the welfare measurements for these models using some policies.

5.4 THE MODEL ASSESSMENT USING POLICIES

This section addresses the empirical importance of the distributional assumptions on each model's trip predictions and benefit estimates. In order to illustrate the performance of each model, we examine policy scenarios ranging from site closure to drastic improvements in site quality. Specifically, we change site quality at Muskegon county (site i, which is centrally located on Lake Michigan) by multiplying the catch rates at the site by $\{0.5, 1, 1.5, 2, 2.5, 3\}$. In addition, we also close site i. We examine the IIA/IIG properties by estimating the choice probabilities to Oceana county (site j) and Ottawa county (site k), the two counties that are adjacent to site i. The predicted trips to each of these sites and the total trip participation will be compared. Welfare measurements are also compared across the models for both the site quality change policy and the site closure policy.

To examine the IIA/IIG restriction, the probability ratios of site *j* and site *k* are calculated. We only calculated these ratios for individuals with all three sites (*i, j,* and *k*) in their feasible choice set, about one third (n^*=33) of the individuals. This was done since IIA for these sites is only relevant if all three sites are in the choice set. In Table 5.3, the ratios are presented for each of the models and for each of the policies. For the independent logit model, the ratio remains constant for each individual with a mean of 10.96 for all policies due to the IIA assumption. For the nested logit model, the mean ratio is 30.52 since IIA is maintained within the group of fishing sites. The site closure policy and the site quality change policy yield the identical ratios for the logit models. On the other hand, the probit models don't exhibit the algebraic property of IIA/IIG. For the probit models, we do not have closed form solutions for the choice probabilities so the ratios are simulated using 1000 replications.

As expected, the ratios of the C-Probit models are much larger than those of the other models. The ratios also change as the quality at site *i* changes from the modest to the drastic, including the site closure. A possible explanation for the large ratios is that for the C-Probit models, there are substantial variations in the predicted probabilities to sites *j* and *k*, as compared to the other models. As an example, suppose that the predicted probability of one model to site *j, k* is 0.00001, 0.1, respectively, for individual A, and 0.1, 0.00001, respectively, for individual B. The mean ratio is (0.00001/0.1 + 0.1/0.00001)/2 = 500.00005. This appears to be the case of the correlated probit models. The sum of the predicted probabilities to both sites is the same, 0.10001 for each individual. On the other hand, suppose there is another model that predicts two similar probabilities to both sites *j* and *k*. Thus the ratios will be small even though the sum of the two probabilities can also equal 0.10001 for either individual A or B. This appears to be the case of the I-Probit, I-Logit, and N-Logit models. This suggests that the C-Probit models are more flexible than the other models in terms of differentiating the sites with high probability from the sites with low probability, rather than predicting that all sites have similar probabilities.

The predicted trips to all sites, as well as a subset of the sites, are presented in Table 5.4. At the participation level, the baseline predicted total trips per individual are basically the same for the five models (the first five rows of column q_i in Table 5.4). At the site level, the correlated probit models and the nested logit model are similar to each other, though different from the independent probit and logit models (the q_i column and the remaining rows). When the policy change moves away from the baseline, the differences between models become more pronounced. As the quality at site *i* increases, the independent probit model predicts the largest total trip increase, which is due to (1) the large increase of trips to site *i* and (2) the sluggish decrease of trips to other sites, such as sites *j* and *k*. The pattern of sluggish decreases is even more evidenced in the independent logit model in that it has both the least amount of trip

Table 5.3 Mean Probability Ratios $\frac{1}{n^*}\Sigma_{t=1}^{n^*}(\Pr_j^t / \Pr_k^t)$

Models	close i	$0.5q_i$	q_i	$1.5q_i$	$2q_i$	$2.5q_i$	$3q_i$
C-Probit(5)	1184.47	1214.42	1262.38	1501.90	2251.86	4204.71	9272.98
C-Probit(6)	1184.87	1214.83	1262.81	1502.41	2252.67	4206.34	9276.94
I-Probit	53.24	56.31	56.55	57.14	58.36	60.60	64.27
N-Logit	30.52	30.52	30.52	30.52	30.52	30.52	30.52
I-Logit	10.96	10.96	10.96	10.96	10.96	10.96	10.96

Table 5.4 The Estimated Trips per Individual

	Models	close q_i	$0.5q_i$	q_i	$1.5q_i$	$2q_i$	$2.5q_i$	$3q_i$
Total trips	C-Probit(5)	3.57	3.58	3.60	3.66	3.80	4.03	4.34
	C-Probit(6)	3.57	3.58	3.60	3.66	3.80	4.03	4.34
	I-Probit	3.45	3.52	3.61	3.79	4.11	4.62	5.40
	N-Logit	3.60	3.60	3.61	3.64	3.69	3.78	3.89
	I-Logit	3.43	3.54	3.61	3.74	3.94	4.26	4.73
Trips to site *i*	C-Probit(5)	0	0.06	0.21	0.55	1.08	1.71	2.30
	C-Probit(6)	0	0.06	0.21	0.55	1.08	1.70	2.29
	I-Probit	0	0.11	0.23	0.46	0.86	1.51	2.41
	N-Logit	0	0.05	0.20	0.50	0.95	1.44	1.84
	I-Logit	0	0.11	0.20	0.34	0.56	0.91	1.43
Trips to site *j*	C-Probit(5)	0.14	0.13	0.10	0.05	0.02	0	0
	C-Probit(6)	0.14	0.13	0.10	0.05	0.02	0	0
	I-Probit	0.17	0.16	0.15	0.14	0.13	0.11	0.08
	N-Logit	0.14	0.12	0.09	0.04	0.01	0	0
	I-Logit	0.15	0.15	0.15	0.14	0.14	0.13	0.12
Trips to site *k*	C-Probit(5)	0.12	0.11	0.09	0.07	0.04	0.01	0
	C-Probit(6)	0.12	0.11	0.09	0.07	0.04	0.01	0
	I-Probit	0.16	0.16	0.15	0.15	0.14	0.12	0.10
	N-Logit	0.10	0.09	0.07	0.05	0.03	0.01	0
	I-Logit	0.16	0.16	0.15	0.15	0.15	0.14	0.14

Table 5.5 The Welfare Measurements per Individual

Models	close q_I	$0.5q_i$	q_i	$1.5q_i$	$2q_i$	$2.5q_i$	$3q_i$
C-Probit(5)	-1.65	-0.132	0	3.92	12.65	27.91	49.81
C-Probit(6)	-1.60	-1.29	0	3.96	12.71	27.89	49.67
I-Probit	-1.83	-1.06	0	2.23	6.51	14.31	27.46
N-Logit	-1.47	-1.16	0	3.37	10.59	22.69	39.37
I-Logit	-1.55	-0.66	0	1.13	3.04	6.19	11.22

NOTE: The welfare measures for the probit models were simulated using 1000 replications and following the procedure described in Chen and Cosslett (1998).

increase to site i and the least amount of trip decrease to sites j and k. Thus, from the site substitution perspective, the independent logit model is least flexible due to IIA.

Furthermore, the nested logit model has the smallest increase in the total trips, in part because the estimated inclusive value coefficient is very small ($\lambda = 0.04$). If we look at the site level, it also becomes clear that as the quality at site i increases, both the correlated probit models and the nested logit model yield basically the same level of trip reduction to the substitute sites j and k. But the correlated probit models yield a much larger trip increase to site i than the nested logit model. (This pattern is similar to the independent probit vs. independent logit.) For example, for the $3q_i$ policy when the trips to sites j and k are about zero, the difference in total trips between the correlated probit and the nested logit (4.34−3.89) is almost entirely due to the trip difference at site i between the two models (2.30−1.84) or (2.29−1.84 due to the rounding). Thus, the correlated probit models are more sensitive to the policy change with a larger net trip increase than the nested logit model.

There are also some interesting differences across the models in terms of welfare measurements. Although the correlated probit models are ranked third in total trip change, the welfare gains are the largest as the quality at site i increases, followed by the nested logit model, the independent probit model, and the independent logit model with roughly 82%, 54%, 25%, respectively, of the values of the correlated probit models. While the independent logit model yields the largest trip change, the welfare gain appears to be the smallest for the site quality improvement due to, again, the IIA restriction and the small standardized site quality coefficients for the I-Logit (Table 5.2).

For the policies involving changes in site quality, the differences in the welfare measures mirror the differences in the estimated standardized site quality coefficients (c.f., the last column of Table 5.2) with substantial variability across the models. However, of all the policies considered, the welfare measures for the site closure policy exhibit the least variability across models. This may be because the site closure policy can be viewed as raising the trip cost of site i to ∞, which dominates the other terms associated with the site quality coefficients in the utility function. As a result, the welfare measures for the site closure policy depend more on the probabilities and less on the standardized site quality coefficients, as compared with the site quality policies.

5.5 SOME REMARKS

As illustrated in the preceding tables, the two correlated probit models with different covariance matrices yield different coefficient estimates for β's and

Σ. But, if the coefficient estimates of β are divided by the trip cost coefficient, they are virtually the same. Furthermore, the trip predictions, welfare measurements, and the log likelihood values are the same as well (with some minor variation due to the simulations). This illustrates that the estimates of β's and Σ are interdependent. Since there is only parameter that can be identified for the block covariance matrix Σ_u, C-Probit(5) and C-Probit(6) should yield the same underlying preference. It is noticed that if there are k identifiable parameters in a covariance matrix, and we only estimate a subset of all the identifiable parameters, then which parameters we estimate can change the model results.

In terms of the IIA property, the results showed that the correlated probit exhibited site substitution patterns that were dramatically different from the patterns of the other models. Although the probability ratios for the I-Probit model also change with site quality, they don't change as much as with the correlated probit models.

The baseline predictions of the total trips per individual are basically the same for the five models, regardless of whether one model fits the data set better than the others. The model differences are revealed as the policy scenarios move away from the baseline. At the site level, the independent probit model shows more interactions across sites than the independent logit model, which is least flexible. The nested logit model shows a more rapid change in trips to sites $i, j,$ and k than the independent logit model due to the two-level nest. The correlated probit models appear to be the most sensitive to the site quality improvement, showing a rapid trip increase at the policy site and a rapid trip decrease at the other sites. If we measure the model's flexibility of site substitution using two components (1) the trip increase at the policy site and (2) the trip decrease at the other sites, the correlated probit models can be ranked as the most flexible, followed by the independent probit model or the nested logit model. The independent logit model is clearly the least flexible.

Even though the nested logit suffers from IIA/IIG, it fits the data set better than the other models considered in this chapter, especially the independent models. This reinforces the importance of distinguishing between diverse alternatives (stay-home versus fishing sites) when selecting an error structure for a model. Of course, the results presented here are only based on models with relatively simple nesting and covariance structures. More complicated nesting structures could be compared to probits with more complicated covariance structures. With the nested logits one needs to be concerned about whether or not the estimated λ lies within the unit interval for the consistency with the hypothesis of random utility maximization (McFadden, 1981). These concerns are only expected to be heightened as the nesting structure increases in complexity. On the other hand, with multinomial probits of comparable complexity, consistency with random utility maximization is maintained since the covariance matrix needs to be positive definite for the probit model to be estimated.[5]

Although we try to reflect the covariance matrix Σ_u by constructing the two-level nest structure, the nested logit model and the correlated probit model are different due to different error distributions. These differences result in significant impacts on the model's coefficient estimates and policy analysis. For a given policy, the welfare measurement of one model could be 25% of the other, and the trip prediction of one model could be 72% of the other. Thus, the parametric distribution assumption deserves further research.

APPENDIX

Independent Logit Model

Parameters	Estimates	t-statistics	Estimates/- β_1
β_1 *cost*/100	-3.600	-20.354	-1.000
β_2 *chinook*	7.114	2.670	1.976
β_3 *coho*	10.667	2.772	2.963
β_4 *lake*	3.474	2.159	0.965
β_5 *rainbow*	30.468	4.089	8.463
β_6 *tpdy*	25.862	17.519	7.184
β_7 $region_1$	0.284	0.715	0.079
β_8 $region_2$	0.357	2.323	0.099
β_{10} ln(*age*)	-2.920	-14.117	-0.811
β_{11} ln(*edu*)	-5.508	-12.684	-1.530
β_{12} *gender*	-1.904	-8.642	-0.529

Log likelihood value is -1521.38.
tpdy = 1 if a trip was taken during the choice occasion, 0 otherwise.

[5] During the iterations, the positive definite covariance matrix can be guaranteed by specifying and estimating the upper (or lower) triangular matrix through the decomposition of Σ_u .

Nested Logit Model:

Parameters	Estimates	t-statistics	Estimates/- β_1
β_1 *cost*/100	-5.292	-17.466	-1.000
β_2 *chinook*	34.047	6.814	6.434
β_3 *coho*	15.362	2.255	2.903
β_4 *lake*	0.517	0.093	0.098
β_5 *rainbow*	77.253	6.520	14.600
β_6 *tpdy*	4.225	2.470	0.798
β_7 $region_1$	1.306	3.437	0.248
β_8 $region_2$	0.744	5.211	0.141
β_9 ln(*age*)	-0.002	-0.009	-0.000
β_{10} ln(*edu*)	-0.502	-1.386	-0.112
β_{11} *gender*	-0.812	-3.684	-0.153
λ	0.041	0.957	0.008

Log likelihood value is -1420.97

Independent Probit Model

Parameters	Estimates	t-statistics	Estimates/- β_1
β_1 *cost*/100	-1.749	-20.181	-1.000
β_2 *chinook*	6.660	4.632	3.809
β_3 *coho*	5.510	4.632	3.151
β_4 *lake*	2.429	2.393	1.389
β_5 *rainbow*	17.708	4.427	10.126
β_6 *tpdy*	13.978	17.136	7.993
β_7 $region_1$	0.172	0.819	0.098
β_8 $region_2$	0.190	2.069	0.109
β_9 ln(*age*)	-1.522	-12.717	-0.870
β_{10} ln(*edu*)	-2.662	-11.601	-1.522
β_{11} *gender*	-1.006	-7.863	-0.575

Log likelihood value is -1504.54 using 400 replications.

Correlated Probit Model(5)			
Parameters	Estimates	t-statistics	Estimates/ - β_1
β_1 *cost*/100	-0.237	-2.003	-1.000
β_2 *chinook*	1.602	1.978	6.769
β_3 *coho*	0.600	1.378	2.533
β_4 *lake*	0.197	0.748	0.831
β_5 *rainbow*	3.819	2.037	16.132
β_6 *tpdy*	3.386	3.347	14.304
β_7 $region_1$	0.628	3.740	2.655
β_8 $region_2$	0.366	4.852	1.545
β_9 ln(*age*)	-0.148	-1.129	-0.627
β_{10} ln(*edu*)	-0.485	-1.987	-2.048
β_{11} *gender*	-0.485	-4.098	-2.051
σ_d	0.327	31.298	1.379

Log likelihood : -1443.95 using 400 replications.
Covariance matrix (5) with $c_0 = 0.1$, $c_{dh} = 0$, and $c_{hh} = 1$.

Correlated Probit Model(6)			
Parameters	Estimates	t-statistics	Estiamtes/ - β_1
β_1 *cost*/100	-2.903	-18.055	-1.000
β_2 *chinook*	19.648	7.528	6.769
β_3 *coho*	7.352	1.861	2.533
β_4 *lake*	2.412	0.873	0.831
β_5 *rainbow*	46.829	6.622	16.132
β_6 *tpdy*	41.518	3.289	14.303
β_7 $region_1$	7.705	1.584	2.654
β_8 $region_2$	4.483	1.619	1.544
β_9 ln(*age*)	-1.820	-1.723	-0.627
β_{10} ln(*edu*)	-5.946	-2.947	-2.048
β_{11} *gender*	-5.952	-2.317	-2.050
σ_h	12.780	1.929	4.403

Log likelihood : 1443.95 using 400 replications.
Covariance matrix (5) with with $c_{dd} = 3$, $c_0 = 2$, and $c_{dh} = 0$.

REFERENCES

Bishop, R. and Heberlein, T. (1979), "Measuring Values of Extra Market Goods: Are Indirect Measures Biased?" *American Journal of Agricultural Economics*, 61(5):926–30.

Bunch, D.S. (1991) "Estimatibility in the Multinomial Probit Model." *Transportation Research - B*, 25B(1):1–12.

Chen, H.Z. and Cosslett, S.R. (1998), "Environmental Quality Preference and Benefit Estimation in Multinomial Probit Models: A Simulation Approach." *American Journal of Agricultural Economics*, 78, No. 3.

Dansie, B. R. (1985), "Parameter Estimability in the Multinomial Probit Model." *Transportation Research - B*, 19B(6):526–28.

Geweke, J.F. (1991), "Efficient Simulation From the Multivariate Normal and Student-t Distributions Subject to Linear Constraints." Computer Science and Statistics: *Proceedings of the Twenty-Third Symposium on the Interface*. Alexandria, VA: American Statistical Association.

Gourieroux, C. and Monfort, A. (1993), "Simulation-Based Inference, A Survey With Special Reference to Panel Data Models." *Journal of Econometrics*, 59: 5–33.

Hajivassiliou, V., and McFadden, D. (1990) "The Method of Simulated Scores for the Estimation of LDV Models with an Application to External Debt Crises." Cowles Foundation Discussion Paper No. 967.

Hajivassiliou, V., McFadden, D., and Ruud, P. (1992), "Simulation of Multivariate Normal Orthant Probabilities: Theoretical and Computational Results." Cowles Foundation Discussion paper No. 1021.

Hanemann, W.M. (1982), "Applied Welfare Analysis with Qualitative Response Models." Working Paper No. 241. California Agricultural Experiment Station, Giannini Foundation of Agricultural Economics, University of California, Berkeley.

Hausman, J.A., Leonard, G.K., and McFadden, D. (1995), "A Utility-Consistent, Combined Discrete Choice and Count Data Model: Assessing Recreational Use Losses Due to Natural Resource Damage." *Journal of Public Economics*, Vol. 56:1–30.

Herriges, J.A. and Kling, C.L. (1997), "Performance of Nested Logit Models When Welfare Estimation is the Goal," *American Journal of Agricultural Economics* 79, 792–802.

Hoehn, P.J., Tomasi, T., Lupi, F., and Chen. H.Z. (December 1996), "An Economic for Valuing Recreational Angling Resources in Michigan." Project report, Department of Agricultural Economics, Michigan State University.

Jones, C.A. and Sung, Y.D. (1993), "Valuation of Environmental Quality at Michigan Recreational Fishing Sites: Methodological Issues and Policy Applications." Project report, EPA Contract No. 816247-01-2, September.

Keane, M.P. (1990), "Four Essays in Empirical Macro and Labor Economics." Ph.D. Dissertation. Brown University.

McFadden, D. (1981), "Econometric Models of Probabilistic Choice," in *Structural Analysis of Discrete Choice Data with Econometric Applications*, edited by C.F. Manski and D. McFadden. MIT Press.

Morey, E.R., Rowe, R.D., and Watson, M. (1993), "A Repeated Nested-Logit Model of Atlantic Salmon Fishing." *American Journal of Agricultural Economics*, 75(3): 578–92.

Small, K.A. and Rosen, H. (1981), "Applied Welfare Economics With Discrete Choice Models." *Econometrica*, 49(1):105–30.

6. Corner Solution Models of Recreation Demand: A Comparison of Competing Frameworks

Joseph A. Herriges, Catherine L. Kling, and Daniel J. Phaneuf[1]

6.1 INTRODUCTION

There is a rich history of recreation demand models estimated using household level data on the number of visits to multiple recreation sites and the travel costs associated with each visit. Over the last 40 years, the state of the art in these models has evolved from fairly simple systems of demand equations to econometrically and theoretically sophisticated variants of the discrete choice models pioneered by McFadden. While the applications themselves have varied greatly, they have shared the common challenge of how to deal with the prevalent occurrence of corner solutions; i.e., the fact that while many recreationists use more than one site, they typically choose not to visit some sites while making multiple visits to others. The presence of these corners has provided a challenge to analysts in terms of specifying both the underlying behavioral model used to explain recreationists' choices and the econometrics of recreation demand.

In this paper, we compare and contrast two state-of-the-art approaches to modeling multiple site recreation demand: the linked site selection and participation model and the Kuhn–Tucker model.[2] The linked model was originally developed by Bockstael, Hanemann, and Strand (1986) and

---

[1] The authors would like to thank Kerry Smith for helpful comments on an earlier draft of this chapter.

[2] A third approach for dealing corner solutions is the repeated nested logit model developed by Morey *et al.* (1993). We provide a brief discussion of this model in Section 6.2, contrasting it with the linked site selection/participation and Kuhn–Tucker frameworks. However, due to space constraints, we do not provide an empirical example. See Morey *et al.* (1995) for a more extensive discussion of the repeated nested logit model as well as the general corner solutions problem.

Bockstael, Hanemann, and Kling (1987) (hereafter BHK), but has received considerable attention in recent years, with modifications by Hausman, Leonard, and McFadden (1995) (HLM), Feather, Hellerstein, and Tomasi (1995) (FHT), and Parsons and Kealy (1995) (PK), as well as several contributions in this volume (Train; Chen, Lupi, and Hoehn). The Kuhn–Tucker model, on the other hand, is a relative newcomer to the recreation demand arena. We provide a brief description of each approach and assess their relative strengths and weaknesses. Variants of each model are then estimated using a data set on angling in the Wisconsin Great Lakes region.

The purpose of this exercise is not to identify one approach as the best, but rather to discuss the relative theoretical and conceptual merits of the alternative approaches and to compare and assess how each model performs on a common data set. In this sense, we are interested in how well the models fit the underlying data and what welfare estimates they generate for common changes in site prices and/or quality characteristics. If the welfare estimates resulting from these models are similar, we can be more confident that decisions about model choice will not generate widely divergent welfare estimates. On the other hand, if the models generate significantly different point estimates of welfare change, the analyst's model choice takes on greater significance.

6.2 THE COMPETING FRAMEWORKS

This section provides a brief overview of both the linked and Kuhn–Tucker models, as well as the repeated nested logit model developed by Morey *et al.* (1993). In the final subsection, we briefly mention alternative models that can handle corner solutions.

6.2.1 The Linked Model

Models of this genre have their roots in discrete choice analysis of consumer selection of a single good from among a finite set of alternatives, such as the choice of transportation mode or housing type. In these single choice settings, researchers have generally relied upon the familiar multinomial logit (MNL) or nested logit (NL) specifications. Beyond yielding convenient likelihood functions for estimation, logit models are often justified on the basis of their consistency with McFadden's (1981) hypothesis of random utility maximization (RUM). The RUM hypothesis conjectures that individual agents choose from among the available alternatives in order to maximize their utility and that the distribution of choices made in the population is a reflection, in part, of the distribution of individual preferences. Given certain assumptions regarding this distribution of preferences, the MNL or NL specifications result.[3]

The strong utility theoretic foundation of RUM models has made them a natural choice in modeling site selection in the recreation demand literature. However, site selection models alone capture only one aspect of the recreation demand problem and an important addition to RUM models has been necessary to make them applicable to most recreation demand data sets. In particular, rather than choosing a single alternative from among a set of alternatives, recreationists face a number of choice occasions over which they may be observed to choose different sites. Thus, there is both a discrete component to the recreationist's decision (which site to visit on a given choice occasion) and a continuous choice (how many trips to take in a season). Recreation demand analysts have therefore adapted the discrete choice models by identifying and linking together these two distinct components of the consumer's recreation decision. In one component, an aggregate demand for the total number of trips recreationists take in a season is modeled (BHK refer to this as the macro-allocation decision, while HLM refer to this as the first stage in their model). A second component entails the estimation of a site selection model. In this component, the recreationist's choice among the available sites on each choice occasion is modeled (BHK term this the micro-allocation decisions, while HLM consider this the second stage in a two-stage budgeting process). This second component is simply an implementation of a standard discrete choice model.

One of the first analysts to see the value of RUM models in recreation demand applications was Hanemann (1978). Other early applications included Feenburg and Mills (1980) and Caulkins, Bishop, and Bouwes (1986). However, it was not until the work of Bockstael, Hanemann, and Kling (1987) that the first component of the model was added to the site selection model to provide a more complete picture of recreationist's behavior. Creel and Loomis (1992), Bockstael, McConnell, and Strand (1989), Hausman, Leonard, and McFadden (1995), and Feather, Hellerstein, and Tomasi (1995), among others, have all followed in this tradition, although there have been important differences in how they link the two components of the models and how they compute welfare estimates from the model parameter estimates. These differences are discussed in detail following the development of the standard linked model structure, beginning with the site selection component.

---

[3] Consistency with the RUM hypothesis holds globally for the MNL specification, but requires additional restrictions in the case of NL. See McFadden (1981), Börsch-Supan (1990), and Herriges and Kling (1996) for additional discussion. The multinomial probit (MNP) provides an alternative RUM model, but has received relatively little attention until recently due to the difficulties associated with its estimation.

As noted earlier, the site selection component of the linked model generally begins with the specification of a discrete choice RUM model. The utility that an individual receives from choosing to visit site j ($j = 1, \ldots, J$) on a given choice occasion is assumed to take the form of the conditional indirect utility function[4]

$$U_j = V_j + \varepsilon_j \tag{6.1}$$

where

$$V_j = V_j(y - p_j, \mathbf{q}_j) \tag{6.2}$$

denotes the nonstochastic portion of consumer's utility, y is the per-choice occasion income, p_j is the cost of visiting site j, and $\mathbf{q}_j = (q_{j1}, \ldots, q_{jK})'$ is vector of K site attributes (e.g., fishing catch rates). The error term ε_j captures the variation in preferences among individuals in the population. On any given choice occasion, the consumer is assumed to visit the recreation site that yields the greatest utility, so that the probability that site j is chosen is given by

$$\pi_j = \text{Prob}\left(V_j + \varepsilon_j > V_k + \varepsilon_k \quad \forall k \neq j\right). \tag{6.3}$$

By specifying the distribution of the error vector $\varepsilon \equiv (\varepsilon_1, \ldots, \varepsilon_J)'$, different standard site selection models result. For example, if the ε_j's are i.i.d. extreme value variates, the MNL model results, whereas with ε drawn from a generalized extreme value (GEV) distribution the NL model results. Alternatively, if the ε's are drawn from a multivariate normal distribution, the MNP results. In what follows, we adopt a nested logit formulation since it and the multinomial logit have accounted for the vast majority of applications and the nested formulation provides a means for relaxation of the independence of irrelevant alternatives assumption.

The nested logit model of site selection requires that the analyst group the available set of alternatives into *nests* of similar sites. Thus, alternatives within the same nest are assumed to be better substitutes for each other than alternatives in different nests. The site selection probability in equation (6.3) can then be expressed as (McFadden, 1981; Maddala, 1983; Morey, 1999)

---

[4] The indirect utility function is *conditional* on the alternative chosen. In general, the J alternatives facing an individual on a given choice occasion may include not only which site to visit, but also what type of activity to undertake at that site (e.g., shore fishing versus boat fishing). For simplicity, in this discussion, we treat sites and alternatives as synonymous.

$$\pi_j = \frac{e^{V_j/\theta_{n(j)}}\left[\sum_{i \ni n(i)=n(j)} e^{V_i/\theta_{n(j)}}\right]^{(\theta_{n(j)}-1)}}{\sum_{m=1}^{N}\left[\sum_{k \ni n(k)=m} e^{V_k/\theta_m}\right]^{\theta_m}}, \tag{6.4}$$

where $n(j)$ is an index function that equals m (m=1,..., N) if site j has been assigned to nest m by the analyst, N denotes the total number of nests, and θ_m (m=1,..., N) is a parameter (known as the dissimilarity coefficient for nest m) that measures the degree of similarity of sites within the nest.[5] Once a specific functional form for the utility function is specified, simultaneous estimation of the coefficients can be accomplished by maximizing the log of the likelihood function, defined as the sum over the sample of the log of the probabilities from (6.4).

A useful construct from the site selection model is the inclusive value, defined as

$$I = I(y,\mathbf{p},\mathbf{q}) = \ln\left(\sum_{m=1}^{N}\left[\sum_{k \ni n(k)=m} e^{V_k(y-p_k,\mathbf{q}_k)/\theta_m}\right]^{\theta_m}\right), \tag{6.5}$$

where $\mathbf{p} \equiv (p_1,\dots,p_J)'$ and $\mathbf{q} \equiv (\mathbf{q}_1',\dots,\mathbf{q}_J')'$. The inclusive value has been interpreted as a measure of the expected maximum utility from the site characteristics. Indeed, if the utility function in (6.2) is specified as linear in income, the compensating variation *per choice occasion* associated with a change in prices or environmental quality can be expressed analytically as[6]

$$C = \frac{1}{\beta_y}\left[I(y,\mathbf{p}^0,\mathbf{q}^0) - I(y,\mathbf{p}^1,\mathbf{q}^1)\right], \tag{6.6}$$

---

[5] The parameter θ_m is known as the *dissimilarity* coefficient since the smaller it gets, the more similar are the alternatives within the nest when compared to alternatives outside of the nest. Global consistency with the RUM hypothesis requires that θ_m lie in the unit interval, with $\theta_m = 1 \; \forall \; m = 1,\dots,N$ yielding the MNL specification.

[6] See, for example, Small and Rosen (1981), Hanemann (1982,1999).

where the superscripts on the price and quality attributes are used to distinguish the new (superscript 1) and original (superscript 0) levels and β_y is the marginal utility of income.[7] If the total number of trips taken by an individual (T) is unaffected by the these changes to the site prices and quality attributes, then the total compensating variation is simply $C \cdot T$. However, since T is unlikely to remain fixed, the second component is added to the linked model to capture possible changes in the participation decision. It is in the specification of the participation equation that the two components of the model are explicitly linked.

A generic form for the participation equation is given by

$$T = h(\mathbf{L}, \mathbf{c}, Y) + \mu, \tag{6.7}$$

where **L** is a vector of variables that link the participation equation to the site selection model, **c** denotes a vector of other variables thought to explain total number of trips, Y denotes annual income and μ is a random error term. Three basic versions of the participation model in equation (6.7) have emerged in the literature, differing both in terms of the variables used to link the components of recreation demand and the methods used to extract welfare estimates.[8]

In the first variant, BHK suggest using the inclusive value (6.5) computed from the site selection model as an explanatory variable in the participation equation, noting that the inclusive value represents "the value of different alternatives weighted by their probabilities of being chosen." Thus the participation demand equation becomes

$$T = h_1(I, \mathbf{c}, Y) + \mu, \tag{6.8}$$

where "I" is the inclusive value defined in (6.5). To compute overall welfare measures, BHK suggest using equation (6.6) to estimate the per choice occasion welfare effect of a policy change and to multiply this by the number of trips predicted by (6.8), computed at the new level of prices and/or qualities. Thus, the estimated total welfare change becomes:

---

[7] If the utility function is nonlinear in income, there is no closed-form solution for the compensating or equivalent variation and numerical methods must be used (see McFadden (1995) and Herriges and Kling (1997)).

[8] Applications of the linked model have also differed in terms of the econometric techniques and functional forms used to estimate parameters for the participation equation, including tobit or Heckman models to account for the censoring of the data and various count data models that reflect the count nature of trip data.

$$W_1 = \frac{1}{\hat{\beta}_y}\left[\hat{I}\left(y,\mathbf{p}^0,\mathbf{q}^0\right) - \hat{I}\left(y,\mathbf{p}^1,\mathbf{q}^1\right)\right]\hat{h}_1\left[\hat{I}\left(y,\mathbf{p}^1,\mathbf{q}^1\right),\mathbf{c},Y\right], \qquad (6.9)$$

where the carats are used to denote fitted parameters or models. Although this approach has intuitive appeal, the authors acknowledge that it is not fully utility theoretic. A variation on W_1 calculates total welfare (before and after a policy change) as the product of the predicted number of trips (h_1) and the monetized welfare per trip $\left(I/\beta_y\right)$.[9] The corresponding welfare measure naturally becomes:

$$W_1^* = \frac{\hat{I}^0\hat{h}_1^0}{\hat{\beta}_y} - \frac{\hat{I}^1\hat{h}_1^1}{\hat{\beta}_y}. \qquad (6.9')$$

Parsons and Kealy (1995) and Feather, Hellerstein, and Tomasi (1995) offer similar alternative representations of the linked model. Like the BHK variant, their models begin with estimation of a site selection model, followed by a participation equation. However, they do not use the inclusive value to link the models. Instead, they use the estimated probabilities associated with the alternatives from the site selection model to compute the "expected price" of a trip and the "expected quality" of a trip (PK refer to the latter as the expected utility of the trip). The expected price for each individual is computed as the sum of that individual's travel costs to the various sites weighted by the estimated probabilities of visiting each site. A similar weighting scheme is used for each site quality attribute. These variables are then used in the estimation of the participation model as

$$T = h_2(\overline{p}, \overline{\mathbf{q}}, Y) + \mu, \qquad (6.10)$$

where

$$\overline{p} = \sum_{j=1}^{J} \hat{\pi}_j p_j , \qquad (6.11)$$

$$\overline{\mathbf{q}} = (\overline{q}_1, \ldots, \overline{q}_K)' , \qquad (6.12)$$

[9] See, for example, Creel and Loomis (1992).

$$\overline{q}_k = \sum_{j=1}^{J} \hat{\pi}_j q_{jk} \qquad (6.13)$$

and the $\hat{\pi}_j$'s are the predicted probabilities from equation (6.4).

In evaluating changing site price and/or quality attributes, FHT use a welfare measure analogous to equation (6.9), multiplying the per choice occasion compensating variation in (6.6) by the expected number of trips under the new attributes as predicted by the participation model in (6.10). PK, on the other hand, interpret the participation equation in (6.10) as the relevant demand equation and integrate under it with respect to price to yield consumer surplus measures of quality and/or price changes. Thus, the welfare change associated with the improvement in a single site attribute would be computed as

$$W_2 = \int_{\overline{p}^0}^{\overline{p}^1} \hat{h}_2(p, \overline{q}^0, Y)\,dp + \int_{\overline{q}^0}^{\overline{q}^1} \hat{h}_2(\overline{p}^1, q, Y)\,dq, \qquad (6.14)$$

where the superscripts indicate the level at which the expected prices and qualities are evaluated.

The final variant on the linked model was developed by Hausman, Leonard and McFadden (1995) and represents a blending of the first two approaches. Like BHK, HLM use a variant of the inclusive value to link the site selection and participation models, but they construct welfare measures using a consumer surplus argument similar to that employed by PK. The other major difference between the HLM approach and other variants on the linked model is that the authors claim their model is utility theoretic, consistent with a two-stage budgeting process. Authors of the other variants generally acknowledge that they are not "...derived from a single overall utility maximization problem," (Parsons and Kealy, 1995, p. 360) but instead represent a reasonable approximation to such a problem.

The site selection stage in HLM is identical to those in other linked models. The differences emerge at the participation stage, with[10]

$$T = h_3(\tilde{p}, Z, Y) + \mu, \qquad (6.15)$$

where Z is a vector of individual characteristic assumed to affect participation and

---

[10] HLM model the number of trips as a count random variable.

$$\tilde{p} \equiv \frac{-I(y,\mathbf{p},\mathbf{q})}{\beta_y}, \tag{6.16}$$

is the negative of the per trip consumer surplus arising from recreation, which HLM interpret as a price index in a two-stage budgeting process. Equation (6.15) is then interpreted as the first stage in the budget allocation process, with the consumer deciding how much to spend on recreation. The site selection model represents the second stage in which the recreation budget is allocated among sites.

The ability to interpret the linked model of HLM as utility-consistent would provide a strong basis for choosing it from among the variants in the literature. Unfortunately, as recently noted by Smith (1997), the authors' proof of consistency relies upon an assumption that does not hold in general.[11] Specifically, HLM assume that:

$$T = \frac{y_F}{\tilde{p}} \tag{6.17}$$

where

$$y_F \equiv \sum_{j=1}^{J} p_j x_j, \tag{6.18}$$

denotes the total level of expenditures allocated to recreation in the first stage, with x_j denoting the number of trips taken to site j. To see that equation (6.17) will not hold in general, consider the case in which the site selection model is MNL and the nonstochastic portion of the indirect utility function in equation (6.2) is given by the simplest of specifications; i.e.,

$$V_j = -\beta_y p_j, \; j = 1, \ldots, J. \tag{6.19}$$

Under these circumstances, the price index in equation (6.16) becomes:

---

[11] Shonkwiler and Shaw (1997) also demonstrate that a two-stage budgeting model, using total trips as the aggregator function for the participation stage and an MNL model for the site selection stage, cannot be derived from a utility theoretic framework. They suggest an alternative to the linked model, using total distance traveled as the aggregator function for the participation stage, and demonstrate that their model can be derived from a utility theoretic framework.

$$\tilde{p} = \frac{-1}{\beta_y} \ln\left(\sum_{j=1}^{J} e^{-\beta_y p_j}\right), \tag{6.20}$$

and the assumption in equation (6.17) corresponds to requiring that:

$$\sum_{j=1}^{J} x_j = \frac{\sum_{j=1}^{J} p_j x_j}{\frac{-1}{\beta_y} \ln\left(\sum_{j=1}^{J} e^{-\beta_y p_j}\right)}. \tag{6.21}$$

Clearly, this need not hold in general. Even for this simple specification, equation (6.21) will typically hold only if either (a) the prices for all of the sites are the same (in which case all of the sites are equivalent from the individual's perspective) or (b) $p_j < \infty$ for one site j and $p_k \to \infty \ \forall k \neq j$ (in which case only site j is visited). If the indirect utility V_j is allowed to be a more general function, including income and site quality attributes, even these conditions will not insure the desired equality in equation (6.17).

Thus, analysts employing linked models of recreation demand are left with the task of choosing from among three variants linking the site selection and participation stage, none of which derive from a unified utility theoretic framework, but each of which has at least some intuitive appeal as an approximation to the consumer's underlying problem. In our empirical section below, we employ the HLM participation model. The linking variable, $\tilde{p}$, has the attractive interpretation as the monetized utility per trip and, when the marginal utility of income is constant across individuals, the HLM model is equivalent (except for a scaling factor) to the more traditional BHK variant.

A second decision in applying the linked model of recreation demand is the choice of welfare measures. HLM, for example, treat their participation model as providing a demand equation for trips and estimate welfare changes using standard consumer surplus measures. Thus, the welfare change associated with a quality site improvement would be computed as

$$W_3 = \int_{\tilde{p}^1}^{\tilde{p}^0} \hat{h}_3(p, Z, Y)\,dp. \tag{6.22}$$

This approach, however, is predicated on the consistency of their model with utility theory. Without this consistency, the interpretation of the participation model as a demand equation becomes questionable and it is no longer clear that areas under the participation curve correspond to consumer surplus. In the empirical section below, we compute welfare measures for the HLM model using the welfare measure advocated by Creel and Loomis (1992), W_1^* of equation (6.9′). We also present the per choice occasion estimates from the site selection model alone.

Finally, despite the difficulties associated with the various linked models, they remain the dominant approach to integrating the site selection and participation decisions associated with recreation demand. This is due, in large part, to the ability of these models to handle a large number of recreation sites without having to resort to site aggregation. Furthermore, with recent improvements in computing power, analysts are now able to capture potentially complex substitution possibilities among sites in the site selection stage of the model using multinomial probit (see Chen, Lupi, and Hoehn, 1998), multi-level nested logit and random coefficient specifications (see Train, 1998).

6.2.2 The Kuhn–Tucker Model

The Kuhn–Tucker model, in contrast to linked models, relies upon a single structural framework to simultaneously model the site selection and participation decisions and to control for possible corner solutions. Initially developed by Wales and Woodland (1983) and Hanemann (1978) and refined by Bockstael, Hanemann, and Strand (1986), the Kuhn–Tucker model begins by assuming that individual preferences are randomly distributed in the population. By specifying a parametric form for the consumer's direct utility function, standard Kuhn–Tucker conditions can be used to identify the participation and site selection probabilities needed to estimate preferences and construct welfare measures.[12] Despite its appeal as a structural model, the Kuhn–Tucker model has received little attention in the applied literature, with only one application to the modeling of recreation demand (Phaneuf, Kling, and Herriges (1997), hereafter PKH). However, with recent advances in computing power, the burden of estimating this highly nonlinear model have eased and additional applications may be forthcoming.

Formally, the Kuhn–Tucker model begins with the assumption that consumer preferences over the J alternative sites can be represented by a random utility function, which they maximize subject to a budget constraint and a set of non-negativity constraints. In particular, the consumer's problem is to

[12] The Kuhn–Tucker approach can also begin with the specification of the indirect utility function, as outlined by Lee and Pitt (1986) and Bockstael, Hanemann, and Strand (1986).

$$\underset{\mathbf{x},z}{Max}\ U(\mathbf{x},z,\mathbf{q},\gamma,\varepsilon) \tag{6.23}$$

s.t.

$$\mathbf{p}'\mathbf{x} + z = Y, \text{ and} \tag{6.24}$$

$$z \geq 0, x_j \geq 0, \ j = 1,\ldots,J \tag{6.25}$$

where $U(\cdot)$ is assumed to be a quasiconcave, increasing, and continuously differentiable function of $(\mathbf{x},z)$, $\mathbf{x} \equiv (x_1,\ldots,x_J)'$ is the vector of site-specific trips, z is the numeraire good which is assumed to be necessary, $\mathbf{p} \equiv (p_1,\ldots,p_J)'$ is a vector of site prices, $\mathbf{q} \equiv (\mathbf{q}'_1,\ldots,\mathbf{q}'_J)'$ is a vector of site attributes, γ is a vector of parameters, and $\varepsilon \equiv (\varepsilon_1,\ldots,\varepsilon_J)'$ is a vector of random disturbances capturing the variation of preferences in the population.

The first-order necessary and sufficient Kuhn–Tucker conditions for the utility maximization problem can be written[13]

$$\begin{gathered} U_j(\mathbf{x},Y-\mathbf{p}'\mathbf{x};\mathbf{q},\gamma,\varepsilon) \leq U_z(\mathbf{x},Y-\mathbf{p}'\mathbf{x};\mathbf{q},\gamma,\varepsilon)p_j, \\ x_j \geq 0, \\ x_j\left[U_j - U_z p_j\right] = 0, \end{gathered} \tag{6.26}$$

for $j = 1,\ldots,J$, where $U_j \equiv \partial U/\partial x_j$ and $U_z \equiv \partial U/\partial z$. By invoking some simplifying assumptions (i.e., $\partial U_j/\partial \varepsilon_k = 0\ \forall k \neq j\ \ \partial U_j/\partial \varepsilon_j > 0\ \forall j = 1,\ldots,J$, and $U_{z\varepsilon} = 0$), these first-order conditions can be rewritten as

$$\begin{gathered} \varepsilon_j \leq g_j(\mathbf{x},Y,\mathbf{p};\mathbf{q},\varepsilon), \\ x_j \geq 0, \\ x_j\left[\varepsilon_j - g_j(\mathbf{x},Y,\mathbf{p};\mathbf{q},\varepsilon)\right] = 0 \end{gathered} \tag{6.27}$$

for $j = 1,\ldots,J$. Equation (6.27), along with the specification of the joint density function $f_\varepsilon(\cdot)$ for ε, provides the necessary information to construct the likelihood function. For example, an individual who chooses to visit only

---

[13] Additional details of the model specification can be found in Phaneuf, Kling, and Herriges (1997).

the first k sites (i.e., $x_j > 0$ $j = 1,\ldots,k$ and $x_j = 0$ for $j = k+1,\ldots,J$) contributes the following term to the likelihood function:

$$\int_{-\infty}^{g_{k+1}} \cdots \int_{-\infty}^{g_M} f_\varepsilon(g_1,\ldots,g_k,\varepsilon_{k+1},\ldots,\varepsilon_M)\, abs|J_k|\, d\varepsilon_{k+1}\cdots d\varepsilon_M \tag{6.28}$$

where J_k denotes the Jacobian for the transformation from ε to $(x_1,\ldots,x_k,\varepsilon_{k+1},\ldots,\varepsilon_J)'$. There are 2^J possible combinations of sites visited and the similar contribution to the likelihood function can be constructed for each.

Conceptually, this Kuhn–Tucker model of recreation demand is appealing, providing a unified and utility theoretic framework for modeling both the participation and site selection decisions. Furthermore, unlike the linked model, it is unified econometrically, with a single error structure driving both participation and site selection. These features of the model, however, come at a cost. The associated likelihood function is highly nonlinear, increasing in complexity as the number of available sites increases, with the number of possible Jacobian terms doubling with each additional site. This has led those applying the Kuhn–Tucker model to date to rely upon relatively simply specifications for the direct utility function and error structures that yield closed-form choice probability expressions.[14]

In the empirical section below, we follow PKH by using the direct utility function originally suggested by Bockstael, Hanemann, and Strand (1986), with

$$U(\mathbf{x},z,\mathbf{q},\gamma,\varepsilon) = \sum_{j=1}^{J} \psi_j(q_j,\varepsilon_j)\ln(x_j+\theta) + \ln(z) \tag{2.29}$$

where

$$\psi_j(q_j,\varepsilon_j) = \exp\left(\sum_s^S \delta_s q_{js} + \varepsilon_j\right) \quad j = 1,\ldots,J, \tag{2.30}$$

$\gamma = (\delta,\theta)$ and q_{js} denotes the sth quality characteristics associated with site j. In this model, weak complementarity holds if $\theta = 1$. The functional form for

---

[14] To be fair to the Kuhn–Tucker model, these same type of assumptions have dominated the site selection stage of the linked models appearing in the literature. Only recently have analysts departed significantly from the traditional MNL or NL error specifications and linear functional forms for the nonstochastic portion of site utility (i.e., V_j in equation (6.2)).

the g_j in equation (6.27) becomes

$$g_j(\mathbf{x}, y, \mathbf{p}; \mathbf{q}, \gamma) = \ln\left[\frac{p_j(x_j + \theta)}{Y - \sum_{k=1}^{J} p_k x_k}\right] - \sum_{s=1}^{S} \delta_s \quad j = 1, \ldots, M. \tag{6.31}$$

In addition, we assume that the ε_j's are independent and identically distributed negative extreme value variates with parameters $\eta = 0$ and λ. Given these assumptions, the likelihood terms in equation (6.28) become:[15]

$$\exp\left(-\sum_{j=1}^{k} \frac{g_j}{\lambda}\right) abs\left|J_k\right| \exp\left[-\sum_{j=1}^{J} \exp\left(\frac{-g_j}{\lambda}\right)\right]. \tag{6.32}$$

We now turn to welfare measurement using the Kuhn–Tucker model. If $V(\mathbf{p}, Y; \mathbf{q}, \gamma, \varepsilon)$ denotes the solution to the utility maximization defined in equations (6.23) through (6.25) above, then the compensating variation (C) associated with a change in the price and attribute vectors from $(\mathbf{p}^0, \mathbf{q}^0)$ to $(\mathbf{p}^1, \mathbf{q}^1)$ can be implicitly defined by

$$V(\mathbf{p}^0, Y; \mathbf{q}^0, \gamma, \varepsilon) = V(\mathbf{p}^1, Y + C(\mathbf{p}^0, \mathbf{q}^0, \mathbf{p}^1, \mathbf{q}^1, Y; \gamma, \varepsilon); \mathbf{q}^1, \gamma, \varepsilon). \tag{6.33}$$

Note that $C(\mathbf{p}^0, \mathbf{q}^0, \mathbf{p}^1, \mathbf{q}^1, Y; \gamma, \varepsilon)$ is a random variable and that the nonlinearity of the functions will generally make numerical techniques necessary for its solution. PHK describe in detail a numerical algorithm for computing the expected compensating variation associated with a price or quality change. We briefly summarize the procedure here. Given an estimator of γ, say $\hat{\gamma} \sim g_{\hat{\gamma}}$, a large number of parameter vectors ($\gamma^{(i)}, i = 1, \ldots, N_\gamma$) are drawn from $g_{\hat{\gamma}}$.

For each $\gamma^{(i)}$, Monte Carlo integration is used to construct $\hat{C}^{(i)} \equiv E_\varepsilon\left[C(\mathbf{p}^0, \mathbf{q}^0, \mathbf{p}^1, \mathbf{q}^1, Y; \gamma^{(i)}, \varepsilon)\right]$ by drawing a series of disturbance vectors ε from f_ε and using numerical bisection to solve for C in equation (6.33) for each draw of ε. Averaging over the C's generated in this manner yields a consistent estimate of $\hat{C}^{(i)}$ given $\gamma^{(i)}$. The empirical distribution of the $\hat{C}^{(i)}$'s can in turn be used to construct confidence intervals on the average compensating variation. The complexity of the welfare calculations in the Kuhn–Tucker

[15] General expressions for the likelihood function's terms and the associated Jacobians can be found in PKH.

model represent another drawback to their use, but one which should diminish as computing power improves.

6.2.3 The Repeated Nested Logit Model

A third framework used in the literature to combine the recreational site selection and participation decisions is the repeated nested logit (or RNL) model developed by Morey, Rowe, and Watson (1993) (hereafter MRW). Here, we provide a brief overview of this approach, but, due to space constraints, do not estimate the RNL model in our empirical section. A detailed discussion of this model can be found in MRW and Morey *et al.* (1995).

At the heart of the RNL model are two assumptions. First, the recreation season is assumed to consist of a fixed number of choice occasions (S), during which each recreationist is assumed to make at most one trip. For example, in MRW, the authors assume that S=50, dividing the year into roughly one week intervals. Second, the choice occasion decisions are assumed to be independent not only across individuals, but also across choice occasions for the same individual. Thus, where and whether an individual chooses to participate during a given occasion is assumed to be independent of previous recreation choices. These two assumptions enable MRW to jointly model the participation and site selection decisions as an extension of the basic site selection model.

Formally, during a given choice occasion, the individual faces $J+1$ alternatives, the possibility of visiting one of J sites or choosing not to recreate at all, with the utility of alternative j on choice occasion s given by:

$$U_{js} = V_{js} + \varepsilon_{js},\ j = 0, 1, \ldots, J. \tag{6.34}$$

Choosing alternative $j = 0$ corresponds to not traveling during that choice occasion. The error vectors $\varepsilon_s \equiv (\varepsilon_{0s}, \ldots, \varepsilon_{Js})'$ are assumed to be distributed independently across both choice occasions and individuals. For a given choice occasion and individual, MRW assume that the error terms (i.e., the ε_s's) are drawn from a generalized extreme value distribution yielding nested logit choice probabilities. In the first level of the nest, the individual chooses whether or not to recreate, with subsequent nesting levels used to distinguish which sites are visited if they choose to recreate.

The primary advantage of the RNL framework is that, given the two assumptions outlined above, the model yields a utility theoretic approach to combining the site selection and participation decisions that is relatively easy to estimate and construct welfare measures for. Unfortunately, as Morey *et al.* (1995) note, the two assumptions required to make the model utility theoretic are nontrivial. The number of choice occasions is assumed to be exogenously determined and the same for all recreationists. Furthermore, it must be chosen by the analyst. To our knowledge, there is no research available regarding the impact that choice of S has on the welfare measures computed using the RNL model. The second assumption (i.e., that participation and site selection decisions are independent across choice occasions and individuals) is also questionable, precluding habit formation or learning from past experiences. It should be noted, however, that a similar assumption underlies the site selection stage of most linked models. While some studies estimate their site selection model using data on an individual's most recent trip (e.g., Kling and Thompson (1996)), most employ a complete enumeration of individual's trips during a season (e.g., Creel and Loomis (1992) and BHK). Each trip is then treated as an independent observation on site selection, assuming away any correlation among trips made by the same individual. While recent advances in computing power may soon allow for a panel data approach to the analyzing site selection data, the current state of the art for both the RNL and site selection is to treat trips as independent across choice occasions.

6.2.4 Other Noteworthy Approaches

There are a handful of alternative models that can also handle corner solutions. Although space is too limited here to provide a thorough presentation and analysis, we wish to mention the models for completeness and because in some cases, these models may provide attractive alternatives to the linked, Kuhn–Tucker, or repeated nested logit models. The first category of alternative models falls under the rubric of systems of demand equations. One of the first such models in recreation is a study of the value of introducing an additional set of lakes in southern Missouri by Burt and Brewer (1971). In addition to estimating a system of demands, they also tested for and imposed symmetry of the cross-price effects to assure the path independence of their consumer surplus measures. Cichetti, Fisher, and Smith (1976) also provide an early application of systems of demands. A recent application of demand systems by Ozuna and Gomez (1994) estimates count models using seemingly unrelated regression techniques. The varying parameter models of Vaughan and Russell (1982), Smith, Desvousges, and McGivney (1983) and Smith and Desvousges (1985)), among others provide additional examples of systems of demand equations with a specific focus on environmental quality. To deal with corner solutions, these models would need to be modified to account for the effect of corners on the structure of demand equations. Most notably, when an individual does not visit (consume) one of the sites, the prices and qualities of that site drop out of the demand equation (see Phaneuf, Kling, and Herriges (1997)).

A final approach worth mentioning is the innovative model developed by Provencher and Bishop (1997) which explicitly accounts for the intraseasonal dynamic nature of the problem. Such an approach holds promise to better understand the continuous decision of how many trips recreationists take in a season.

6.3 THE DATA

The data set used below to estimate and compare the linked and Kuhn–Tucker models of multiple site recreation demand concerns angling behavior in the Wisconsin Great Lakes region. The usage data come from two mail surveys of angling behavior conducted in 1990 by Richard Bishop and Audrey Lyke at the University of Wisconsin-Madison.[16] The surveys provide detailed information on the 1989 angling behavior of Wisconsin fishing license holders, including the number and destination of fishing trips to Wisconsin Great Lakes region, the distances to each destination, the type of angling preferred, and the socio-demographic characteristics of the survey respondents. A total of 487 completed surveys were available for analysis, including 240 individuals who had visited one or more of the 22 destinations identified for the Wisconsin Great Lakes region and 247 who fished only inland waterways (i.e., non-users from the perspective of the Great Lakes region).[17] We have aggregated the destinations of Great Lakes anglers into four sites: Lake Superior, South Lake Michigan, North Lake Michigan, and Green Bay. Kaoru, Smith, and Liu (1995) and Parsons and Needelman (1992) discuss the implications of site aggregation decisions in recreation demand, specifically for the case of RUM models. At issue is the fact that the analyst must define what constitutes a choice alternative and which alternatives the recreationist considers. Misspecification of the choice set can lead to biased parameter estimates, and benefit estimates tend to be sensitive to aggregation decisions. Although Parsons and Kealy (1992) have demonstrated a method for avoiding aggregation in RUM models by randomly drawing each individual's choice set from a large universe of sites, most authors have relied on characteristics of the available data and common sense to make aggregation decisions.

The aggregation strategy for this study divides the Wisconsin portion of the Great Lakes into distinct geographical zones consistent with the Wisconsin Department of Natural Resources classification of the lake region. The degree of aggregation in this study is less an issue than in those cited above, since the

---

[16] Details of the sampling procedures and survey design are provided in Lyke (1993). We are grateful to Richard Bishop and Audrey Lyke for providing us with this data. Any errors in using the analysis of their data are, of course, our own.

[17] These sample figures do not include the 22 recreationists excluded from our analysis who reported more than fifty recreation trips during 1989.

variation in the physical characteristics of the destinations in each site is small compared to the large geographical differences in the four sites. Table 6.1 summarizes both the average number of trips to and percentage of the sample visiting each of the aggregate sites.

Table 6.1 Data Summary of Average Site Characteristics

	Lake Superior	North Lake Michigan	South Lake Michigan	Green Bay
Fishing Trips	2.75 (13.33)	1.56 (6.32)	2.35 (8.92)	0.65 (3.07)
Percentage Visiting Site	13.1 (33.8)	20.5 (40.4)	23.2 (42.3)	9.9 (29.8)
Price	177.84 (172.59)	123.70 (172.92)	85.88 (139.62)	129.11 173.54)
Lake Trout	4.66 (6.00)	2.19 (3.08)	2.90 (4.59)	0.08 (0.16)
Chinook Salmon	1.05 (1.40)	4.81 (3.06)	2.72 (2.39)	3.63 (3.21)
Coho Salmon	2.71 (2.09)	0.49 (0.55)	4.00 (5.39)	0.51 (0.78)
Rainbow Trout	0.11 (0.14)	1.81 (2.61)	1.20 (1.28)	0.12 (0.21)
Catch Rate Index	6.81 (7.91)	5.78 (5.15)	2.92 (2.90)	2.00 (2.17)
Effective Toxins	0.60 (0.49)	2.27 (1.87)	3.46 (2.85)	2.27 (1.87)

Note: Catch rates are measured here in terms of fish caught per person per 100 hours of effort. Standard deviations are reported below the averages. In the analysis below, the catch rates were rescaled to reflect catch rates per person per hour of effort.

The price of a trip to each of the four fishing sites consists of both the direct cost of getting to the site and the opportunity cost of the travel time. Round trip direct travel costs were computed for each destination and each individual by multiplying the number of round trip miles for a given individual–destination combination by the cost per mile for the vehicle class driven, as provided by the American Automobile Association. The cost of the travel time was constructed using one-third of the individual's wage rate as a measure of the hourly opportunity cost of recreation time and assuming an average travel speed of forty-five miles per hour to compute travel time.[18] The price of visiting a destination (i.e., p_j) is then the sum of these two components.[19] As indicated in Table 6.1, the cost of visiting the Great Lakes sites averaged between $86 per trip for South Lake Michigan to $178 per trip for the more remote Lake Superior region.

Two household characteristics are included in the estimated linked and Kuhn–Tucker models, annual income and a dummy variable indicating boat ownership. For the sample as a whole, income averaged just under $44,000 per year, with almost 22 percent owning their own boat.

Two types of quality attributes (i.e., q_{jk}'s) are used to characterize the four recreation sites: fishing catch rates and toxin levels. In constructing the catch rate variables, we focus our attention on the catch rates for the four aggressively managed salmonoid species: lake trout, rainbow trout, coho salmon, and chinook salmon. Creel surveys by the Wisconsin Department of Natural Resources provide catch rates for each of these species that are broken down by angling method, including private boat, charter fishing, and pier/shore angling. Catch rates for the four species were formed for each individual–destination pair. Catch rates for each of the four aggregate zones were then formed as the catch rates of the most frequently visited destination within that zone if it was visited, or the average of the catch rates within that zone if it was not. Data from the Wisconsin angling survey were used to match the mode-specific catch rates to each individual angler based upon their most frequent mode of fishing.

The second site characteristic used in our empirical analysis is toxin levels. De Vault *et al.*(1989) provide average toxin levels in lake trout (ng/kg-fish) for locations throughout the Great Lakes region. These were matched on the basis of proximity to our four aggregate sites to form a basic toxin measure for each site, T_j j=1, ...,4.[20] However, since toxin levels are likely to influence visitation decisions only if the consumer perceives a safety issue, we use information from the Wisconsin angling survey to form an "effective toxin level" variable $E_j \equiv T_j D$ for j=1,...,4, where D=1 indicates that the respondent was concerned about the toxin levels in fish and D=0 otherwise. As one might expect, the

---

[18] Data on trip lengths were not available, so that it was necessary to assume that on site time was constant for all trips.

[19] Prices are calculated for each individual for each destination. The price of the site is the price of the most frequently visited destination if the site was visited, or the average of the destinations if it was not. The site attribute variables described below are similarly computed. See Phaneuf (1997) for further details on variable descriptions.

[20] While there are a variety of toxins reported in the De Vault *et al.*(1989) study, we use the levels of toxins 2-,3-,7-, and 8-TCDD, which are generally responsible for the fish consumption advisories issued by states in the region.

effective toxin levels, summarized in Table 6.1, are highest at the South Lake Michigan site, surrounded by the densely populated and industrial communities of Chicago, Milwaukee and Gary, Indiana.

6.4 RESULTS

In this section we provide details of the empirical specification and resulting parameter estimates, followed by a series of welfare measures based upon the competing linked and Kuhn–Tucker models.

6.4.1 Model Specification and Parameter Estimates

The Linked Model. As in any empirical exercise, in addition to selecting the variables to include in the estimation, it is also necessary to select functional forms and error structures for the estimating equations. In the case of the linked model, there are two components or stages and thus two estimating equations that must be specified. Ideally, the error terms and functional forms of these equations would be specified so that they were wholly consistent with one another and derivable from a unified structural model of consumer preferences. However, as noted in Section 6.2.1, the linked model is not utility theoretic and, hence, requires the use of separate reduced-form equations for each stage.

The site selection model in equation (6.1) requires the specification of both the nonstochastic (V_j) and stochastic (ε_j) elements of the model. We have chosen to estimate two distinct functional forms for V_j: a linear form and a Generalized Leontief (GL). It was our intention to choose a form that has been commonly estimated (the linear specification) as well as one that can be viewed as a second order approximation (the Generalized Leontief). The stochastic elements are assumed to be drawn from a generalized extreme value distribution, yielding the nested logit site selection probabilities in equation (6.4), with an underlying nesting structure that groups the North and South Lake Michigan sites (see Figure 6.1). The two Lake Michigan sites are the most similar in terms of both their physical characteristics and fishing stocks.

Table 6.2 provides parameter estimates for three variants of the site selection model. The first variant (S1) employs an indirect utility function that is linear in $(y-p)$, the effective toxins level E and each of the four catch rate variables (R_i, i = lake trout, chinook salmon, coho salmon, and rainbow trout).[21] The coefficients on $(y-p)$ and toxins are of the expected signs and

[21] In the estimation, $(y-p)$ is measured in terms of units of \$10,000, with the per-choice-occasion income (y) defined as monthly income. The choice of units used in measuring income is important only when there are nonlinear income effects in the site selection model, as is the case in the GL site selection model (S3).

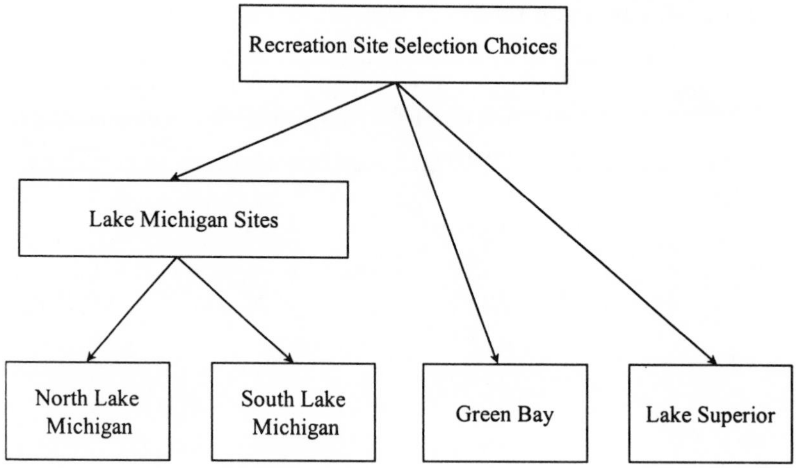

Figure 6.1 Nested Logit Model Structure

statistically significant at the 1 percent level, but the signs on the four catch rate variables do not conform well to our expectations. Although coho and rainbow both exhibit significantly positive effects, both lake trout and chinook exhibit significantly negative effects. The dissimilarity coefficient, θ , is estimated to be 1.47 and is significantly greater than 1.00, suggesting that the nested structure provides a better fit of the data than a straight multinomial logit model. However, an inclusive value coefficient that is greater than 1.00 also suggests that the model is inconsistent with the random utility maximization hypothesis.[22]

We view the large inclusive value coefficient and the unintuitive signs on the catch rate variables to indicate that this first variant of the site selection model may be mis-specified. Thus, we investigate an alternative formulation. In particular, rather than enter each catch rate variable alone, we use the following catch rate index:

$$R_I \equiv \sum_i R_i \overline{F_i} \tag{6.35}$$

where $\overline{F_i}$ denotes the percentage of anglers indicating that they were fishing for the ith fish species (i = lake trout, etc.). Summary statistics for R_I are provided by site in Table 6.1.

---

[22] The requirement that the inclusive value lie in the unit interval for consistency with utility maximization can be relaxed if the analyst is concerned only with consistency locally (see Börsch-Supan (1990) and Herriges and Kling (1996)).

Table 6.2 Site Selection Models

Variables	Linear-Indiv. Catch Rates (S1)	Linear-Catch Rate Index (S2)	Generalized Leontief- Catch Rate Index (S3)
$y-p$	227.25	277.03	-112.18
	(2.36)	(2.08)	(10.58)
E	-0.17	-0.11	0.61
	(0.98E-2)	(0.78E-2)	(0.08)
$R_{\text{lake trout}}$	-11.82		
	(0.53)		
$R_{\text{chinook salmon}}$	-20.58		
	(0.97)		
$R_{\text{coho salmon}}$	2.00		
	(0.54)		
$R_{\text{rainbow trout}}$	14.79		
	(1.47)		
R_I		8.12	-3.94
		(0.21)	(0.69)
$\sqrt{y-p}$			337.25
			(13.38)
$\sqrt{E}$			-3.76
			(0.37)
$\sqrt{R_I}$			7.69
			(0.73)
$\sqrt{(y-p)E}$			1.85
			(0.33)
$\sqrt{(y-p)R_I}$			-2.91
			(1.09)
$\sqrt{E \cdot R_I}$			-0.23
			(0.12)
θ	1.47	1.00	0.84
	(0.03)	(0.02)	(0.02)
log likelihood	-1822.71	-1766.33	-1639.84

Notes: Standard errors are in parentheses below the point estimates.

Using this catch rate index (R_I) in a linear functional form yields our second variant on the site selection model (S2), with parameter estimates reported in column 2 of Table 6.2. In this model, all variables exhibit the anticipated signs and the standard error estimates support statistical significance of the variables. Furthermore, the dissimilarity coefficient is no longer significantly different from 1.00, yielding consistency with the RUM hypothesis.

Our third variant on the site selection model (S3) uses the nonlinear Generalized Leontief form for the indirect utility function. For this specification, we used the catch rate index just discussed rather than the four separate catch rate variables. This choice was made partly for expedience (the Generalized Leontief places large demands on the data) and partly based on the results from the two linear specifications. The resulting coefficient estimates are reported in the third column of Table 6.2. While the parameters in this nonlinear model are more difficult to interpret than their linear counterparts, they are all statistically significant at a 95 percent confidence level. Furthermore, the parameters can be used to determine for each individual and site combination the marginal utilities of income, toxins, and catch rate. As one would hope, the marginal utility of income is positive and declining with income.[23] Similarly, the marginal utility of fish catch rates is positive and diminishing. Finally, toxins have the expected negative impact on utility, with a marginal utility of -0.17 on average over the sample. Turning to the dissimilarity coefficient, we find that θ is estimated to lie within the unit interval and is significantly different from 1.00 at the 99 percent confidence level. This suggests both consistency of the model with utility maximization and the superiority of the nested structure to a straight multinomial logit model. Finally, we note that the nonlinear Generalized Leontief specification yields a significant reduction in the log likelihood function, with a likelihood ratio test of the restriction of GL model to the linear model rejected at 1 percent significance level.

The site selection model provides the first stage in the linked model's representation of recreation demand. The second component of the linked model requires the specification of the participation equation. Based on the discussion of the alternative approaches in section 6.2.1, we have adopted the HLM strategy for linking the two components. Thus, we use the index $\tilde{p}$ from equation (6.16) (i.e., the negative of the per trip consumer surplus) as the linking variable. Since there are three different site selection models estimated, we estimate a separate participation equation for each of these indices. The computation of $\tilde{p}$ for the two linear site selection models is straightforward; it is simply the inclusive value defined in equation (6.5) divided by the estimated marginal utility of income (the coefficient on $(y-p)$). However, in the Generalized Leontief model, there is no simple analog. By construction, the marginal utility of income is not constant so a single parameter does not represent its value.

[23] On average, the marginal utility of income is 0.02, ranging from 0.008 to 0.05 over the sample.

However, it is still straightforward to compute the inclusive value following equation (6.5). In order to monetize this value, we have computed the estimated marginal utility of income for each individual at their current consumption levels and use this in place of β_y in equation (6.16). Although each individual's marginal utility of income will change with deviations from that point, this value provides a first order approximation and, for want of a better alternative, seems to be a reasonable way to implement the HLM version of the linked model when the site selection model is nonlinear in income.

Two functional forms are used in estimating the participation equation: linear and Generalized Leontief. Since there are three site selection models that can be used to form $\tilde{p}$, a total of six participation models result. In addition to the index, $\tilde{p}$, each equation contains a constant term, annual income (y) and a dummy variable taking on the value of "1" if the respondent owns a boat and fishes by boat, and "0" otherwise (B). Finally, since our data is censored (about half of the sample take no angling trips to the Wisconsin Great Lakes fisheries), we use a Tobit estimator.

The first three columns in Table 6.3 present the estimated coefficients for linear participation equations (labeled models L1 through L3). In all three of these models, the ownership of a boat has the expected positive impact on participation, increasing the number of trips per year by roughly 12 under all three specifications. However, the coefficients on $\tilde{p}$ and y are both less consistent with our expectations and among the various specifications. For example, HLM interpret $\tilde{p}$ as a price index and anticipate a corresponding negative coefficient. Given that the model is not consistent with utility theory, we avoid this interpretation of $\tilde{p}$. Nonetheless, one would still expect that, as the consumer surplus per trip decreases (and $\tilde{p}$ increases), the total number of trips would decline. Unfortunately, in model (L1) the coefficient on the index $\tilde{p}$ is not of the anticipated sign. In the other two linear models, the price coefficient is of the correct sign, but is statistically significant at the 5% level only in model (L2). The income term is also only significant in model (L2) and suggests, in that case, that angling in this region is an inferior good.

Columns 4–6 of Table 6.3 contain the results from using a Generalized Leontief functional form for the participation stage (with the models labeled G1 through G3). The choice of the first stage site selection model (used in constructing $\tilde{p}$) has much greater influence on the parameter estimates of these specifications than in the linear case. Many of the parameters change sign and/or size moving among the three nonlinear specifications. Furthermore, the importance of using a nonlinear participation model appears to depend on the site selection model to which it is linked. It is only in the case of model G2 that the generalization to the nonlinear specification yields a significantly improved fit, based on a likelihood ratio test of linear models as restrictions on the corresponding GL model. Interestingly, the estimates of σ are quite stable across all six of the models.

Table 6.3 Tobit Participation Models

Functional Form:	Linear			Generalized Leontief		
Site Selection Model Used to form the Index $\tilde{p}$:	Linear 4 Catch Rates (L1)	Linear Catch Rate Index (L2)	GL Catch Rate Index (L3)	Linear 4 Catch Rates (G1)	Linear Catch Rate Index (G2)	GL Catch Rate Index (G3)
Constant	-3.67* (1.46)	-5.38* (1.50)	-2.04 (2.11)	4.46 (7.85)	-11.00 (8.16)	7.48 (15.37)
y	0.33E-03 (0.42E-03)	-0.17E-02* (0.54E-03)	-0.22E-03 (0.18E-03)	0.16E-((0.02)	0.06* (0.01)	0.02* (0.99E-02)
$\tilde{p}$	0.38E-03 (0.49E-03)	-0.02* (0.66E-02)	-0.65E-03 (0.54E-03)	-0.65E-02 (0.03)	-0.79* (0.20)	-0.05* (0.03)
B	12.74* (1.40)	12.49* (1.38)	12.63* (1.39)	17.60* (6.04)	24.61* (5.94)	34.09* (11.11)
$\sqrt{y}$				1.54* (0.77)	-0.75 (0.83)	-1.60* (0.95)

Table 6.3 continued

Functional Form:	Linear			Generalized Leontief		
Site Selection Model Used to form the Index $\tilde{p}$:	Linear 4 Catch Rates (L1)	Linear Catch Rate Index (L2)	GL Catch Rate Index (L3)	Linear 4 Catch Rates (G1)	Linear Catch Rate Index (G2)	GL Catch Rate Index (G3)
$\sqrt{-\tilde{p}}$				-1.74* (0.86)	2.66 (2.98)	3.12* (1.70)
$\sqrt{y}\sqrt{-\tilde{p}}$				-0.61E-02 (0.05)	-0.44* (0.11)	-0.07* (0.03)
$\sqrt{y}\sqrt{B}$				-1.00* (0.51)	0.79 (0.52)	-0.37 (0.24)
$\sqrt{-\tilde{p}}\ \sqrt{B}$				1.04* (0.55)	-2.92 (1.84)	0.52 (0.38)
σ	11.80* (0.58)	11.70* (0.57)	11.77* (0.57)	11.73* (0.58)	11.45* (0.55)	11.56* (0.56)
log likelihood	-1093.58	-1087.63	-1093.16	-1089.72	-1075.30	-1088.57

Notes

a. Standard errors are reported in parentheses below the coefficient estimates.

b. Significance at the 5% level is indicated by an asterisk next to the coefficient estimate.

The Kuhn–Tucker Model. To provide the most apt comparison possible with the linked models, we have estimated two versions of the Kuhn–Tucker model outlined in Section 6.2.2, equations (6.29) through (6.31). In the first version (K1), we use four separate catch rate variables, while in the second version (K2) we use only the catch rate index.[24] Both versions also include a constant, the "effective" toxins variable E described in the previous section, and the dummy variable (B) indicating the ownership of a boat, as well as site prices and income.

Table 6.4 contains the coefficient estimates from the two specifications of the Kuhn–Tucker model. In general, the coefficients have the expected signs and, with the exception of the coefficient on lake trout catch rates, are statistically different from zero at a 5 percent critical level or better. Furthermore, unlike the linked model, the parameter estimates obtained using the Kuhn–Tucker framework are remarkably consistent across the two specifications of the catch rate variables. In both models, higher toxin levels significantly reduce the perceived quality of a site, whereas the ownership of a boat increases the utility obtained from site visitation. Higher catch rates also enhance site quality, with marginal improvements in the catch rates of Chinook salmon and rainbow trout having the largest impact. Even the negative and statistically insignificant impact of lack trout catch rates on perceived site quality is not unexpected since, among anglers, lake trout are typically considered to be a less desirable species. The coefficient on aggregate catch rate (R) is also positive, lying roughly at the average level of the individual catch rate coefficients, and is statistically different from zero using a 1 percent critical level.

The other coefficient of interest is θ. As noted in PKH, the Kuhn–Tucker model in equations (6.29) through (6.31) does not impose weak complementarity, an assumption used throughout the recreation demand literature. Weak complementarity implies that all value associated with a recreational site consists of use value alone, precluding non-use value. In our Kuhn-Tucker model, weak complementarity holds only if $\theta = 1$. The models presented in Table 6.4 suggest that weak complementarity is rejected in the current application, with θ being significantly different from 1 at a 5 percent critical level under both

---

[24] We began this analysis assuming that we would only use the four separate catch rate variables as we had previously estimated the K–T model on this data using individual catch rates with good results (see Phaneuf, Kling, and Herriges (1997)). However, as noted above, the results were less than appealing when these same variables were used in the linked model. Thus, we felt an alternate specification was warranted to provide comparisons among the models and to put the linked model in the best possible light. Note also that the results reported in Phaneuf, Kling, and Herriges (1997) omit the "Boat" variable and use slightly more observations than the results reported here.

Table 6.4 Kuhn–Tucker Model

Variables	Four Catch Rates (K1)	Aggregate Catch Rate (K2)
Constant	-9.38**	-9.14**
	(0.23)	(0.23)
$R_{\text{lake trout}}$	-0.70	
	(1.85)	
$R_{\text{chinook salmon}}$	13.53**	
	(2.31)	
$R_{\text{coho salmon}}$	5.65**	
	(1.57)	
$R_{\text{rainbow trout}}$	16.86**	
	(4.68)	
R_I		8.61**
		(1.02)
E	-0.06*	-0.07**
	(0.03)	(0.02)
B	1.17**	1.20**
	(0.14)	(0.16)
θ	1.45**	1.39**
	(0.20)	(0.19)
γ	1.32**	1.37**
	(0.05)	(0.06)
log likelihood	-1629.07	-1651.31

Notes
a. Standard errors are reported in parentheses below the coefficient estimates.
b. Significance at the 1% level is indicated by two asterisks next to the coefficient estimate and significance at the 5% level is indicated by a single asterisk.

specifications and suggesting that there is non-use value associated with the Great Lakes region.[25]

[25] The rejection of weak complementarity in the current model is, of course, not a general test of the weak complementarity assumption, but conditional upon the specific functional form being employed here. One might extend the current model, for example, by allowing the θ_j's to vary by site and test for weak complementarity with respect to a subset of sites.

6.4.2 Welfare Estimates

Because the linked and the Kuhn–Tucker models are distinct approaches with different underlying structures, functional forms, and error assumptions, the results of estimation are not directly comparable. Caution must also be exercised in concluding from these results that one approach is uniformly superior to the other, since the performance of the models depends not only on the framework chosen but also on assumptions made within the framework. Nonetheless both approaches provide the means to arrive at the same ends. Both models can be used to estimate the welfare changes associated with changing the price and quality attributes of sites within the Great Lakes region. In this section, the modeling frameworks are used to evaluate the welfare implications of three policy scenarios:

- *Scenario 1: Reduced Toxin Levels.* Under this first policy scenario, we consider the welfare implications of a twenty percent reduction in the effective toxin levels at all four sites (i.e., $E_j,\ j = 1,\ 2,\ 3,\ 4$).

- *Scenario 2: Loss of Lake Michigan Coho Salmon.* Under this policy scenario, state and local efforts to artificially stock Coho salmon in Lake Michigan and Green Bay would be suspended. It is assumed that the corresponding Coho catch rates (i.e., $R_{coho\ salmon}$) would be driven to zero for all but the Lake Superior site. The aggregate catch rate variable (i.e., R) would be affected through changes to the individual catch rate components in equation (6.35).

- *Scenario 3: Loss of the South Lake Michigan Site.* Under this final policy scenario, use of the South Lake Michigan portion of the Great Lakes region would be suspended. This change is represented conceptually in the recreation demand models by sending the price of visiting South Lake Michigan to infinity.

For each policy scenario, we compute the total welfare reduction associated with the policy for each of the six linked models and for the two variations on the Kuhn–Tucker model. The welfare measure used for the linked models is W_1^* defined in equation (6.9′), whereas the compensating variation of the policy shift, implicitly defined by equation (6.33), is used for the Kuhn–Tucker models. Finally, since some studies in the literature focus only on estimating welfare changes per choice occasion, abstracting from changes in the total number of trips, we provide per choice occasion welfare estimates for each policy scenario using the three site selection models in Table 6.2. The complete set of welfare measures are provided in Table 6.5.

Table 6.5 Point Estimates of Welfare Reduction

			Policy Scenario		
Model	Variant	Units	Toxin Reduction	Coho Extinction	Loss of South Lake Michigan
Linked	L1	$/year	146.05	-116.95	-2404.14
	L2	$/year	-122.24	401.76	1515.30
	L3	$/year	0.74	42.23	235.16
	G1	$/year	-314.10	172.68	3148.33
	G2	$/year	-238.83	1011.86	2483.52
	G3	$/year	11.17	149.51	729.87
Site Selection	S1	$/choice	-70.75	38.24	724.06
	S2	$/choice	-3.05	8.20	37.12
	S3	$/choice	-0.47	37.12	27.55
Kuhn–Tucker	K1	$/year	-59.79	372.59	533.77
	K2	$/year	-73.82	400.55	583.03

Examination of the welfare estimates yields a number of conclusions. First, the linked model's welfare measures are quite sensitive to model specification (e.g., whether individual catch rates are used, as in models L1 and G1, or an aggregate catch rate is used, as in models L2 and G2). For example, since the toxin reduction under policy scenario 1 represents an improvement in environmental conditions, one would expect the welfare loss to be negative. This is the case for only half of the linked models, with the welfare loss estimated to range from $146 to $314 per year. Second, the difficulties associated with the linked model's welfare measures emerge at both the site selection and participation stages. Thus, while the site selection models (S1 through S3) all yield negative *per choice occasion* welfare losses due to the toxin reduction, the point estimates differ by orders of magnitude across the three model specifications. Despite the consistency in sign on these per choice occasion welfare losses, the participation stage of the linked model often converts these to a positive welfare loss *per year*, due in large part to the fact that the coefficient on the index $\tilde{p}$ is of the wrong sign, predicting that the number of trips decreases with an increase in per choice occasion welfare.[26] In contrast, the Kuhn–Tucker model's welfare measures both have the expected negative signs and fall within a relatively narrow range (-$60 to -$74).

The welfare measures for policy scenarios two and three follow a similar pattern. The extinction of Coho salmon is estimated to yield a welfare loss per choice occasion of only $8 when the linear aggregate catch rate site selection model is used (S2). This loss in increased five-fold if either individual catch rates are used (S1) or a nonlinear specification is employed (S3). While the corresponding annual welfare loss are more consistent in sign, they continue to range widely. In the case of loosing the South Lake Michigan site, the welfare loss ranges from -$2404 to $3148. In contrast, the Kuhn–Tucker model's welfare predictions are relatively insensitive to the model specification.

6.5 FINAL COMMENTS

In this chapter, we have discussed the linked and Kuhn–Tucker frameworks for modeling recreation demand from both conceptual and empirical perspectives. Although the models are conceptually quite different, both approaches can be used to estimate the welfare effects of changes in site attributes, which can then be compared. The primary strength of the Kuhn–Tucker approach lies in the unified and utility theoretic framework it provides for modeling both the site selection and participation decisions and which can be used to derive utility theoretic welfare measures based on compensating or equivalent variation. In contrast, despite the intuitive appeal of its components, the linked model cannot be derived from a common underlying specification of preferences. Furthermore, it is not clear which of the competing welfare measures identified in the literature is preferred, since there is not a utility theoretic model from which they can be derived.

The strength of the linked model lies in the ease with which it can be estimated and used to compute welfare measures. The traditional nested logit model of site selection can be employed even when there are a large number of sites/alternatives available to recreationists. Furthermore, if the analyst is willing to assume a constant marginal utility of income, closed form expressions exist for the per choice occasion welfare effect of a policy change. In contrast, the complexity of the Kuhn–Tucker model has limited its use to date to problems involving relatively few alternatives, with both the stochastic and nonstochastic components of consumer preferences restricted to relatively simple functional

---

[26] HLM experienced similar problems with their application of the linked model to Alaskan recreation, obtaining a positive coefficient on their price index variable in two of their four participation models.

forms. Furthermore, the welfare measures, while utility theoretic, require numerical methods to construct. It should be noted, however, that these advantages of the linked model have diminished over time for several reasons. First, efforts to relax the restrictive nature of the nested logit site selection models (e.g., Train, 1999, Chen *et al.,* 1999, and Herriges and Kling, 1997), have increased the computational burden associated with both their estimation and welfare predictions, restricting in turn the number of choice alternatives they can be used to model. Second, recent increases in computing power have significantly diminished the burden of computing welfare measures for Kuhn–Tucker models and open the door to relaxing the functional forms used within this framework.

In the application of the Kuhn–Tucker and linked models to the specific case of Great Lakes angling, it appears that the Kuhn–Tucker model performs better. The welfare measures resulting from the various specifications of the linked model are sensitive to specification for both the seasonal and per choice occasion measures. Welfare effects also vary by magnitude and sign across the specifications, with no clear basis for choosing among the competing measures. In contrast, the Kuhn–Tucker model yields welfare measures that have the expected signs, are reasonable in magnitude, and which are stable across the two specifications for the model.

The fact that the Kuhn–Tucker model appears to outperforms the linked models in this specific case should not be interpreted to mean it is always the preferred model. As noted in Section 6.2 the use of the Kuhn–Tucker model requires aggregation of possible recreation destinations into a small number of sites. In the case of the Great Lakes study, it was possible to aggregate in a geographically consistent manner such that the sites themselves exhibited distinct characteristics, while the destinations within the sites did not vary greatly. For other applications the aggregation strategy may not be so straightforward, and relevant information may be lost in the aggregation. In these types of applications, the linked model may be preferred based on its ability to handle a large number of available sites, with the information lost in using two reduced forms for estimation justified based on the information gained in site variability.

Analysts modeling multiple site recreation demand problems with data sets exhibiting a prevalence of corner solutions in the future will need to choose the modeling framework based on the number of sites being modeled, the aggregation options, and the availability of computer resources. If the number of sites is small or a natural aggregation strategy exists, the Kuhn–Tucker model is likely the best choice. If there are many alternatives, for which the sites within a geographical proximity are quite different from each other, the loss of utility consistency may be offset by the information gained in keeping the unique sites separate.

REFERENCES

Bockstael, N.E., Hanemann, W.M., and Kling, C.L. (1987), 'Estimating the Value of Water Quality Improvements in a Recreation Demand Framework,' *Water Resources Research* 23, 951–60.

Bockstael, N.E., Hanemann, W.M., and Strand, I.E. (1986), *Measuring the Benefits of Water Quality Improvements Using Recreation Demand Models*, Vol. 2, Washington D.C.: U.S. Environmental Protection Agency, Office of Policy Analysis.

Bockstael, N.E., McConnell, K.E., and Strand, I.E. (1989), 'A Random Utility Model for Sportfishing: Some Preliminary Results for Florida,' *Marine Resource Economics* 6, 245–60.

Börsch-Supan, A. (1990), 'On the Compatibility of Nested Logit Models with Utility Maximization,' *Journal of Econometrics* 43(2), 373–88.

Brownstone, D. and Small, K.A. (1989), 'Efficient Estimation of Nested Logit Models,' *Journal of Business and Economic Statistics* 7, 67–74.

Burt, O.R. and Brewer, D. (1971), 'Estimation of Net Social Benefits from Outdoor Recreation,' *Econometrica* 39, 813–231.

Caulkins, P., Bishop, R., and Bouwes, N. (1986), 'The Travel Cost Model for Lake Recreation: A Comparison of Two Methods for Incorporating Site Quality and Substitution Effects,' *American Journal of Agricultural Economics* 68(2), 291–97.

Chen, H.Z., Lupi, F., and Hoehn, J. (1999), 'An Empirical Assessment of Multinomial Probit and Logit Models for Recreation Demand,' in J.A. Herriges and C.L. Kling (eds.), *Valuing Recreation and the Environment*, Aldershot: Edward Elgar, pp. 141–62.

Cichetti, C., Fisher, A., and Smith, V. (1976), 'An Econometric Evaluation of a Generalized Consumer Surplus Measure: The Mineral King Controversy,' *Econometrica* 44, 1259–76.

Creel, M. and Loomis, J.B. (1992), 'Recreation value of wetlands in the San Joaquin Valley: Linked Multinomial Logit and Count Data Trip Frequency Models,' *Water Resources Research* 28, 2597–2606.

De Vault, D.S., Hesselberg, R., Rodgers, P.W., and Feist, T.J. (1989), 'Contaminant Trends in Lake Trout and Walleye from the Laurentian Great Lakes,' *Journal of Great Lakes Research* 22, 884–95.

Feenberg, D. and Mills, E. (1980), *Measuring the Benefits of Water Pollution Abatement*, New York: Academic Press.

Feather, P., Hellerstein, D., and Tomasi, T. (1995), 'A Discrete-Count Model of Recreation Demand,' *Journal of Environmental Economics and Management* 29 (2), 316–22.

Hanemann, W.M. (1978), *A Methodological and Empirical Study of the Recreation Benefits from Water Quality Improvement*, Ph.D. dissertation, Department of Economics, Harvard University.

Hanemann, W.M. (1982), 'Applied Welfare Analysis with Qualitative Response Models,' California Agricultural Experiment Station, October.

Hanemann, W.M. (1999), 'Applied Welfare Analysis with Discrete Choice Models,' in J.A. Herriges and C.L. Kling (eds), *Valuing Recreation and the Environment*. Aldershot: Edward Elgar, pp. 33–64.

Hausman, J.A., Leonard, G.K. and McFadden, D. (1995), 'A Utility-Consistent, Combined Discrete Choice and Count Data Model: Assessing Recreational Use Losses Due to Natural Resource Damage,' *Journal of Public Economics* 56, 1–30.

Herriges, J.A. and Kling, C.L. (1996), 'Testing the Consistency of Nested Logit Models with Utility Maximization,' *Economics Letters* 50(1), 33–40.

Herriges, J.A. and Kling, C.L. (1999), 'Nonlinear Income Effects in Random Utility Models,' *Review of Economics and Statistics*, forthcoming.

Kaoru, Y., Smith, V.K., and Liu, J.L. (1995), 'Using Random Utility Models to Estimate the Recreational Value of Estuarine Resources,' *American Journal of Agricultural Economics* 77(1), 141–51.

Kling, C.L. and Thomson, C.J. (1996), 'The Implications of Model Specification for Welfare Estimation in Nested Logit Models.' *American Journal of Agricultural Economics* 78(1), 103–14.

Lee, L.F. and Pitt, M.M. (1986), 'Microeconometric Demand Systems with Binding Nonnegativity Constraints: The Dual Approach,' *Econometrica* 54(6), 1237–42.

Lyke, A.J. (1993), *Discrete Choice Model to Value Changes in Environmental Quality: A Great Lakes Case Study*, Ph.D. dissertation, Department of Agricultural Economics, University of Wisconsin-Madison.

Maddala, G.S. (1983), *Limited-Dependent and Qualitative Variables in Econometrics*, Cambridge: Cambridge University Press.

McFadden, D.L. (1981), 'Econometric Models of Probabilistic Choice,' in C.F. Manski and D.L. McFadden (eds), *Structural Analysis of Discrete Data*, Cambridge, MA: MIT Press, pp. 198–272.

McFadden, D.L. (1995), 'Computing Willingness-to-Pay in Random Utility Models,' draft manuscript, Department of Economics, University of California, Berkeley.

Morey, E. (1981), 'The Demand for Site-Specific Recreational Activities: A Characteristics Approach,' *Journal of Environmental Economics and Management* 8, 345–71.

Morey, E. (1984), 'The Choice of Ski Areas: Estimation of a Generalized CES Preference Ordering with Characteristics, Quadratic Expenditure Functions and Non-additivity,' *Review of Economics and Statistics* 66, 584–90.

Morey, E. (1985), 'Characteristic, Consumer's Surplus and New Activities: A Proposed Ski Area,' *Journal of Public Economics* 26, 221–36.

Morey, E. (1999), 'TWO RUMs UnCLOAKED: Nested-Logit Models of Site Choice and Nested-Logit Models of Participation and Site Choice,' in J.A. Herriges and C.L. Kling (eds), *Valuing Recreation and the Environment*. Aldershot: Edward Elgar, pp. 65–120.

Morey, E.R., Rowe, R.D. and Watson, M. (1993), 'A Repeated Nested-Logit Model of Atlantic Salmon Fishing,' *American Journal of Agricultural Economics* 75(3), 578–92.

Morey, E.R., Waldman, D., Assane, D., and Shaw, D. (1995), 'Searching for a Model of Multiple-Site Recreation Demand that Admits Interior and Boundary Solutions,' *American Journal of Agricultural Economics* 77(1), 129–40.

Ozuna, T. and Gomez, I. (1994), 'Estimating a System of Recreation Demand Functions Using a Seemingly Unrelated Poisson Regression Approach,' *Review of Economics and Statistics* 76, 356–60.

Parsons, G.R. and Kealy, M.J. (1992), 'Randomly Drawn Opportunity Sets in a Random Utility Model of Lake Recreation,' *Land Economics* 68(1), 93–106.

Parsons, G.R. and Needelman, M.S. (1992), 'Site Aggregation in a Random Utility Model of Recreation,' *Land Economics* 68(4), 418–33.

Parsons, G.R. and Kealy, M.J. (1995), 'A Demand Theory for Number of Trips in a Random Utility Model of Recreation,' *Journal of Environmental Economics and Management* 29(3), 418–33.

Phaneuf, D.J. (1997), *Generalized Corner Solution Models in Recreation Demand*, Ph.D. dissertation, Department of Economics, Iowa State University.

Phaneuf, D.J., Kling, C.L., and Herriges, J.A. (1997), 'Estimation and Welfare Calculations in a Generalized Corner Solution Model with an Application to Recreation Demand,' draft manuscript, Iowa State University.

Provencher, B. and Bishop, R. (1997), 'An Estimable Dynamic Model of Recreation Behavior with an Application to Great Lakes Angling,' *Journal of Environmental Economics and Management* 33, 107–27.

Shonkwiler, J.S. and Shaw, W.D. (1997), 'The Aggregation of Conditional Demand Systems,' working paper, presented at W-133 Regional Project Annual Meetings, July.

Small, K.A. and Rosen, H.S. (1981), 'Applied Welfare Economics with Discrete Choice Models,' *Econometrica* 49, 105–30.

Smith, V. Kerry (1997), 'Combining Discrete Choice and Count Data Models: A Comment,' mimeograph.

Smith, V.K. and DesVousges, W.H. (1985), 'The Generalized Travel Cost Model and Water Quality Benefits: A Reconsideration,' *Southern Economics Journal* 51, 371–81.

Smith, V.K., Desvousges, W.H., and McGiveney, M.P. (1983), 'Estimating Water Quality Benefits: An Econometric Analysis,' *Southern Economic Journal*, 50, 422–37.

Train, K.E. (1999), "Mixed Logit Models for Recreation Demand," in J.A. Herriges and C.L. Kling (eds), *Valuing Recreation and the Environment*, Aldershot: Edward Elgar, pp.121–40.

Vaughan, W.J. and Russell, C.S. (1982), *Fresh Water Recreational Fishing: The National Benefits of Water Pollution Control*, Washington D.C. Resources for the Future.

Wales, T.J. and Woodland, A.D. (1983), 'Estimation of Consumer Demand Systems with Binding Nonnegativity Constraints,' *Journal of Econometrics* 21, 263–85.

7. Joint Estimation of Contingent Valuation and Truncated Recreational Demands[1]

Kenneth E. McConnell, Quinn Weninger, and Ivar E. Strand

7.1 INTRODUCTION

Two approaches for valuing recreational and environmental amenities, the travel cost model (TCM) and contingent valuation (CV), are often viewed as substitutes. Revealed preference (RP) methods, such as the TCM, have the cogent evidence that comes from people actually paying money for non-marketed goods. The recovery of stated preferences (SP) facilitates greater variation in the goods that may be valued and the attributes associated with the various environmental amenities. The seminal contribution by Cameron (1992) combines information about preferences from CV and actual travel cost information in a single valuation model that utilizes the more attractive features of each method. Cameron exploits the supposition that different portions of the same preference function are revealed by the TCM and CV. The modeling approach provides a promising new tool that may be superior to the sum of its parts and enhances the understanding of the correspondence between revealed and stated preferences.

Since Cameron's early paper, extensions and refinements that combine RP and SP have emerged. Adamowicz *et al.* (1994) estimate preferences for recreational sites with multiple attributes using SP and a random utility model. They characterize the purpose of their research as using the CV results to help estimate the behavioral model. Implicit in this use is a test of the consistency of behavioral methods and CV methods.[2] In related work, Larson *et al.* (1994)

---

[1] An earlier version of this paper was presented at the 1993 Allied Social Science meetings in Anaheim, CA.

[2] The outcome of this test is ambiguous, because the test for equality of coefficient form the two different models cannot be rejected (p. 287) but the estimates of net benefits from access to sites though not tested statistically, seem quite different (Table V).

use observations on trips and the results of a CV survey to estimate jointly the parameters of well defined cost functions for whale watching. In a paper that combines aspects of both Adamowicz *et al.* (1994) and Larson *et al.* (1994), Eom and Smith (1994) estimate joint and separate models of behavior and SP to estimate the demand for produce.

The recent Association of Environmental and Resource Economists conference on combining stated and revealed preferences underscores the importance and promise of these developments. The conference and the papers presented there presage a new era in non-market valuation that combines stated and revealed preferences to value environmental resources. The adjectives "calibrated" and "cooperative" capture the spirit of this research. Research in combining RP and SP information seems a promising setting for developing methods to calibrate SP valuation models. Using RP and SP information cooperatively in empirical estimation can improve efficiency.

This chapter focuses on developments in combining RP and SP information since this work and illustrates a novel approach. The model developed here is intuitively simple and circumvents two problems encountered by Cameron in combining RP and SP information that are yet unsolved in the literature. Cameron (1992) and more recently Adamowicz *et al.* (1994) specify a recreation site demand function and an indirect utility difference function to model the RP and SP for individual recreators. The two elements, an inter-temporal choice and a contemporaneous choice, are combined in a single estimation procedure. The consistency of the model requires that the site demand function and utility difference function derive from the same underlying direct utility function. This requirement limits the choice of functional forms that may be used in the model. In the model developed here, a recreational site demand function is not considered. This freedom considerably increases the range of acceptable functional specifications (compared with Cameron, 1992, p. 309). In fact, all utility difference and willingness to pay functions that conform to consumer demand theory are permissible.[3]

Second, the model explicitly allows for differences in the underlying structures that govern RP and SP decisions. These differences may result from the hypothetical nature of CV and its effect on SP decisions. For example, if SP alters the decision process of individuals, its manifestation may be as discrepancies in underlying preference structures for the RP and SP components of the model. The model of this chapter provides a simple and appealing framework for combining the RP and SP information in a way that enhances the model's

[3] Obviously, if one wished to estimate parameters for both the inter-temporal and contemporaneous decisions, our model would have to be extended. However, obtaining "values" from one choice occasion may be sufficient for the situation at hand. Situations for which our specification might hold include trips that occur once a season or year.

intuitive appeal. The structure of the model is as follows. We use indirect utility differences to model two decisions. The first is a choice between money income incurred to travel to a recreation site and the utility derived from access; this is the RP component of the model. The second decision is between a hypothetical increase in the travel costs to the site and utility from access; this is the SP component of the model. The model is made stochastic for empirical estimation with the random utility hypothesis. We deal explicitly with the discrepancies in underlying preference structures by allowing them to be completely independent of one another in the limiting case. In other words, the preference structure that governs the RP decision may be completely independent from the preference structure that governs the SP decision. If so, the information gleaned from SP methods is arbitrary and can lead to unreliable estimates of trip value. On the other hand, when the underlying preference structure is identical, both the RP and SP decisions provide useful information for valuing environmental amenities.

An especial advantage of the approach is its applicability for on-site studies. Frequently the only cost-effective way of sampling users of certain recreational resources is to sample on-site. There are numerous occasions when CV studies of resource users are relevant. For example, studies of congestion or other highly variable measures of environmental quality require a close correspondence between the application of a CV question and measurement of the quality variable. This can best be accomplished with an on-site CV survey. Once on-site, however, users have already demonstrated a willingness to pay for access by overcoming the hurdle of travel costs to get to the site. Since users are located at varying distances from the site, their decision to take a trip contains valuable information about preferences. We use this information along with a CV response in a model similar to the double-bounded dichotomous choice model that has recently emerged in the CV literature.

Hanemann, Loomis, and Kanninen (1991) (HLK) developed an improvement on the one question discrete choice model by asking an additional question, also yes or no, depending on the response to the first question. The double-bounded dichotomous choice CV requires only a minor additional contribution of effort by both researcher and respondent but improves the statistical efficiency of the single question dichotomous choice CV. We briefly describe the double-bounded model to aid development of the on-site CV model presented here.

The double-bounded CV adaptation of the referendum model involves a series of questions. For concreteness, suppose that we are interested in obtaining a daily value of access to a recreational site. A stylized double-bounded CV model might be as follows:

(A) Would you pay $\$X$ for access to this site?

Then, based on the answer to A:

(B) Would you pay \$ $(X + \Delta X)$ for access to this site?

If the answer to A is yes, ΔX is positive and then the respondent is asked a higher number. If the answer to A is no, ΔX is negative and the respondent is asked a lower number. There are four possible responses: yes and no to A and yes and no to B. In all cases, the second question gives more information. In two cases, A = yes and B = no as well as A = no and B = yes, the second question actually bounds willingness to pay between \$$X$ and \$$(X + \Delta X)$. In the other two cases, yes to A and B and no to A and B, the distribution is truncated at a higher or lower level than a single question, giving more information than in the single question technique. HLK demonstrate the increase in efficiency from exploiting the extra bound from the second question.

The purpose of both single and double CV questioning approaches is to narrow the estimate of willingness to pay while avoiding the complications that arise from direct elicitation of willingness to pay. This idea forms the basis for the two decisions that are implicit in the on-site CV survey. In our model, the decision to take the trip is the analogue to question (A) in the double-bounded CV model. The distinct difference is that the first bound to willingness to pay is the threshold of the travel costs instead of a randomly selected CV bid. Thus, it is the result of actual behavior, RP, as opposed to strictly SP information.

When introducing behavior into the model, care must be taken to assure that the preference structure associated with the actual and contingent behavior is not necessarily equated. One problem is that an on-site CV question is made *ex post*, whereas the individual made the decision to take the trip (incurred the costs), *ex ante*. The information set available to the individual may be different for the two decisions and thus could cause differences in structure of unobserved preferences. These differences can be partially accommodated by allowing the preference structures to differ in the CV and behavioral settings. The following section explores this possibility and provides a way to efficiently utilize on-site samples for both their contingent and behavioral information.

7.2 THE MODEL

In studies of the demand for recreation, there is a close correspondence between the type of survey and econometric structure. To understand the context of our model, it is helpful to know something of the data on which the models are to be developed. Our data on recreational fishing link an intercept survey and a follow-up phone survey. During 1987 and 1988, a subset of anglers, who were intercepted at east coast recreational fishing sites by interviewers for the National Marine Fisheries Service's Marine Recreational Fisheries

Statistics Survey, were given a follow-up telephone survey. During the phone interview, anglers who had taken at least one overnight trip were asked a simple referendum-type CV question. The trip frequently was a multiple-day trip such as a three-day business trip or a week's vacation. On this phone survey, anglers were interviewed about the costs they incurred on their trip.[4] The respondent is then asked the question:

> If your costs for fishing on this day had increased by [*randomly selected* $5, 15, 30, 50, 75, 100, 150, 200], would you still have gone fishing?

This question induces a yes or no response, as in the typical referendum model, but the response is hypothetical behavior. It is perhaps more appropriate to call this a contingent response question. Whatever the name, it yields estimates of willingness to pay when a discrete choice model is fitted to the yes-no responses. The usual procedures would call for the estimation of logit or probit. While the straightforward application of the referendum model provides estimates of willingness to pay, it does not exploit the fact that respondents to the CV question had already demonstrated a willingness to pay by taking a trip.

There is more information because we know that the angler took a trip based on an *ex ante* assessment of the utility to be derived from the trip. If all respondents have uniform preferences, then, holding other things constant, such as *ex ante/ex post* differences, individuals who have come from longer distances (spent more money) should be less likely to respond positively to the CV question regarding an increase in costs. The additional travel costs detracts from the available surplus leaving a smaller residual once on site. We attempt to exploit this information.

One way to exploit this data is to specify the probability or likelihood of observing the data. A specific parametric functional form may then be used to represent the probability and econometric techniques employed to search for specific parameters that maximize the likelihood. In our sample of on-site recreators, we have two possible outcomes:[5]

(A) trip is taken; the referendum CV answer is no;

(B) trip is taken; the referendum CV answer is yes.

Consequently, the likelihood function, L, of observing the sample takes the following form

$$L = \prod_{i \in A} \frac{\text{P(trip, no to CV)}}{\text{P(trip)}} \prod_{i \in B} \frac{\text{P(trip, yes to CV)}}{\text{P(trip)}} \qquad (7.1)$$

---

[4] For a detailed explanation of this data set, see McConnell *et al.* (1992).

[5] If the entire population were sampled, the likelihood function would be where C denotes no trip. However, there are no data for people who fall into the no trip cell.

This likelihood function provides the basic structure for combining CV responses and behavioral data. Different assumptions about the structure of preferences result in different models. Exact stochastic specifications are required for estimation.

The responses of the sample of recreators can be modeled in a referendum framework. Here we choose to structure the responses as utility-differences, but as long as the marginal utility of income is constant across alternatives and independent of income for a given individual, it does not matter whether we use the indirect utility function or the expenditure function.

We assume that individual utility is deterministic but that some components of utility are unobservable from the perspective of the researcher. The unobservable components are treated as a random variable. Let $V_1(y-c;s)$ be the deterministic utility from taking a trip, where y is income, c is the cost of the trip and s is a vector of other explanatory variables. If the individual does not take the trip, deterministic utility is given by $V_0(y;s)$. Let ε_i, i=0,1, be the unobserved component of preferences. Define utility as the sum of random and deterministic elements: $U_i \equiv V_i + \varepsilon_i$. The individual takes the trip if $U_1 > U_0$ or if

$$V_1(y-c;s) - V_0(y;s) > \varepsilon_0 - \varepsilon_1. \tag{7.2}$$

We observe only people for whom (7.2) holds. It is the sample selection criterion.

Let Δc denote the cost increase that is proposed to the individual on the CV question. The deterministic part of the utility function is the same as in (7.2). In modeling the CV response, we allow the unobserved component of preferences resulting from the hypothetical CV to differ from the unobserved component that influenced the trip decision. As revealed by the CV question, utility implied by a ‘yes’ response is

$$U_1 = V_1(y-c-\Delta c;s) + \theta_1,$$

where θ_1 is again a mean zero random variable which represents unobserved preferences. The utility of not taking the trip is

$$U_0 = V_0(y;s) + \theta_0.$$

The individual will respond yes to the CV question if $U_1 > U_0$ or if

$$V_1(y-c-\Delta c;s) - V_0(y;s) > \theta_0 - \theta_1. \tag{7.3}$$

The difference between (7.2) and (7.3) is that the random term differs and (7.3) has the additional costs imposed by CV. The random elements , $\varepsilon \equiv \varepsilon_0 - \varepsilon_1$ in (7.2) and $\theta \equiv \theta_0 - \theta_1$ in (7.3) are subject to competing interpretations. In all applications, we will be using the utility difference $V_1(y-c;s)-V_0(y;s)$ or $V_1(y-c-\Delta c;s)-V_0(y;s)$. Call the deterministic utility differences $\Delta v(y;c)$ or $\Delta v(y,c+\Delta c)$ and the random utility differences $\Delta u(y;c)$ or $\Delta u(y,c+\Delta c)$ where $\Delta v(y,c) \equiv V_1(y-c;s)-V_0(y;s)$ so that

$$\frac{\partial v_1}{\partial c} = -\frac{\partial v_1}{\partial y} < 0.$$

(In these expressions the vector *s* is suppressed.) These random differences are possibly correlated. The extent that they are correlated will lead to different models.

The following three cases show different interpretations for the structure of preferences and the corresponding random elements , ϵ and θ, as well as their statistical implications.

7.2.1 Case 1: Transitory Preference Structure

Suppose that revealed and stated preference structures are unrelated to one another. The possibility may seem remote but cannot be excluded a priori. In fact, the absence of a meaningful relationship between RP and SP is the basis of the criticism of the CV method. In the current model, a zero relationship between revealed and stated preferences leads to what we term a transitory error structure in the stochastic specification of the model. The motivation for the transitory error is as follows: when the individual is considering the trip, he examines a host of factors such as whether it will rain, whether he will get seasick, whether the fish "are biting", etc. In the random utility framework, these factors are unobserved by the investigator and their influence is captured by ε . Once the trip is complete, however, perhaps all of the randomness associated with the trip decision utility difference, ε , has been resolved. The trip decision and the CV response represent different choice events. From this the simplest discrete choice model emerges. The likelihood of the joint decisions becomes

$$\begin{aligned} P(\text{trip, yes to CV}|\text{trip}) &= P(\Delta v(y,\ c) > \varepsilon, \Delta v(y,\ c+\Delta c)\ >\ \theta | \Delta v(y,\ c) > \varepsilon) \\ &= \frac{F_\varepsilon(\Delta v(y,\ c))\ F_\theta(\Delta v(y,\ c+\Delta c)),}{F_\varepsilon(\Delta v(y,\ c))} \end{aligned} \tag{7.4}$$

where $F_\varepsilon(.)$ and $F_\theta(.)$ are the cumulative distribution function for ε and θ respectively. (Note that $\Delta v(y,c) > \Delta v(y,c+\Delta c)$ as long as Dc > 0, because $\Delta v = V_1(y-c) - V_0(y)$.) Since the random components ε and θ are assumed independent, the trip decision does not influence the CV response. The probability of a trip, $F_\varepsilon(\Delta v(y,c))$ may be cancelled and (7.4) re-written as

$$P(\text{yes to CV}) = P(\Delta v(y,c+\Delta c) > \theta). \tag{7.5}$$

Of course, P(no to CV) = 1 - P(yes). Equation (7.5) follows from assuming that the random component influencing behavior disappeared after the choice, and that a separate uncorrelated random component of tastes influences the CV response.

7.2.2 Case 2: Permanent Preference Structure

Now suppose that underlying preferences that guide the RP and SP decisions are identical. This possibility leads to an unobservable component of utility that remains constant in the trip decision and the CV response. The unobserved component of utility is a permanent part of preferences. In effect, this assumes that the errors, ε and θ, are identical and the unobserved component of preferences is unchanged throughout the decision process. The likelihood function then becomes similar to the HLK function. The probability of taking a trip and answering yes to the CV question is

$$\begin{aligned} P(\text{trip, yes to CV}|\ \text{trip}) &= P(\Delta v(y,c) > \varepsilon, \Delta v(y,c+\Delta c) > \varepsilon | \Delta v(y,c) > \varepsilon) \\ &= \frac{F_\varepsilon(\Delta v(y,c+\Delta c)).}{F_\varepsilon(\Delta v(y,c))} \end{aligned} \tag{7.6}$$

The conditional probability that ε is jointly less than the two numbers is simply the conditional probability that ε is less than the smaller. Since $\Delta v(y,c)$ is decreasing in c, $\Delta v(y,c+\Delta c) < \Delta v(y,c)$ and $P(\Delta v(y,c) > \varepsilon), \Delta v(y,c+\Delta c))$. The probability of taking a trip but saying no to the CV question is

$$\begin{aligned} P(\text{trip, no to CV}|\text{trip}) &= P(\Delta v(y,c+\Delta c) < \varepsilon < \Delta v(y,c) | \Delta v(y,c) > \varepsilon) \\ &= \frac{F_\varepsilon(\Delta v(y,c)) - F_\varepsilon(\Delta v(y,c+\Delta c))}{F_\varepsilon(\Delta v(y,c))}. \end{aligned} \tag{7.7}$$

Equations (7.6) and (7.7) make up part of the likelihood function for the HLK model. The HLK likelihood function includes two additional terms (the equivalent of no to trip, yes and no to CV questions) that are naturally excluded from trip—CV data extracted from a sample selected from people who have taken the trip. We do not sample 'no to the trip' people.

7.2.3 Case 3: Correlated Preference Structure

The third model is the most general. We assume that the underlying preference structures used in the decision to take a trip (the RP decision) and the CV response (the SP decision) are related in a meaningful and informative way. The unobserved random component of utility from the trip decision is neither independent of nor identical to the random component that arises in the CV response. The two special cases are nested within this more general model. Jointness allows a random component from the response to the trip decision to influence the CV response. In the present application, the existence of correlated disturbances implies that an unexpected high utility from the trip will induce an unexpected (high or low depending on the correlation) utility in the CV question. Ignoring the correlation means misspecifying the model, biasing the coefficients. This bias is shown in the Monte Carlo analysis below. The probability of a trip and a yes response to the CV question is

$$P(\text{trip, yes to CV}|\text{trip}) = P(\Delta v(y,c) > \varepsilon, \Delta v(y,c+\Delta c) > \theta | \Delta v(y,c) > \varepsilon) = \frac{F(\Delta v(y,c), \Delta v(y,c+\Delta c); \rho),}{F_\varepsilon(\Delta v(y,c))} \quad (7.8)$$

where $F(\cdot,\cdot;\rho)$ is the bivariate cumulative distribution function for the random variables ε and θ and ρ is the correlation coefficient. The (trip, no to CV) probability is given by

$$\text{P(trip, no to CV}|\text{trip}) = P(\Delta v(y,c) > \varepsilon, \Delta v(y,c+\Delta c) < \theta | \Delta v(y,\ c) > \varepsilon) = \frac{F(\Delta v(y,c)) - F(\Delta v(y,c), \Delta v(y,c+\Delta c); \rho).}{F(\Delta v(y,c))} \quad (7.9)$$

This model is the most general of the three. Note that when $\Delta = 0$, (7.8) becomes

$$P(\text{trip, yes to CV}|\text{trip}) = \frac{F_\varepsilon(\Delta v(y,c)) F_\theta(\Delta v(y,c+\Delta c))}{F_\varepsilon(v(y,c))},$$

which is the same as expression (7.4) or (7.5). When $\varepsilon \equiv \theta$, then naturally $\rho = 1$ and the second model is the correct specification.

These models are similar to the truncated versions of linear models that result from only observing the positive parts of the model. In a computational sense, these models are sometimes difficult to estimate (see Maddala 1983, p. 281). We test these models with Monte Carlo experiments and then estimate them on a sample of recreational anglers that spawned the idea. The third model, in the untruncated case, is the stochastic structure form estimated by Cameron and Quiggin (1992) for strictly CV responses. Indeed, Altaf and DeShazo (1994) argue that the double-bounded referendum model induces correlation between the errors.

7.3 MONTE CARLO SIMULATION

To demonstrate the workings of this model, we perform several simple Monte Carlo experiments. These experiments show the value of combining observations from different responses. They also show the importance of understanding the correlation between the structure of preferences or, in the random utility model context, the random component of preferences.

For this experiment, one thousand synthetic agents are assigned a linear utility difference function. This utility difference determines whether to take a trip and then specifies a yes or no response to a contingent valuation scenario. For the ith individual, the trip utility difference is

$$\Delta U^{trip} = \gamma_0 + \gamma_1 cost_i + \gamma_2 X_{2i} + \gamma_3 X_{3i} + e_i^{trip}, \tag{7.10}$$

where $cost_i$ is the travel costs required to reach the site, X_{2i} and X_{3i} are respectively continuous and discrete (zero/one) explanatory variables that represent exogenous attributes of the trip, and γ_j ($j = 0, 1, 2, 3$) is a vector of parameters. A standard normal error term, e_i^{trip}, is added to represent the unobserved component of preferences. The parameter vector is chosen so that approximately 65% of the 1000 recreators have a positive trip utility difference in (7.10), and so choose to participate. For these individuals, the trip takers, a second utility difference is specified as

$$\Delta U_i^{cv} = \gamma_0 + \gamma_1(cost_i + \Delta cost_i) + \gamma_2 X_{1i} + \gamma_3 X_{2i} + e_i^{cv}. \tag{7.11}$$

Here $\Delta cost_i$ is a randomly chosen cost increment designed to represent an on-site CV process. The error term in (7.11), e_i^{cv}, is also a standard normal random variable. It is the unobserved component of preferences that emerge from the CV scenario. The relationship between e_i^{trip} and e_i^{cv} is manipulated to simulate the three models explained in the previous section. The experiment was repeated 200 times for each error structure. Each experiment has drawn 1000 observations, equivalent to the general population. Approximately 650 observations become on-site recreation users and these provided the data for the maximum likelihood estimators. The true parameters are set to $\gamma_0 = 0.15$,

$\gamma_1 = -0.11$, $\gamma_2 = 0.1$, and $\gamma_3 = 0.2$. The parameters are selected to approximate a demand curve, i.e., γ_1 would be the price parameter and the other parameters shifters. The numeric values could be manipulated without changing the conclusions materially.

The mean estimates, mean squared error and bias for these parameters are reported in Tables 7.1 through 7.3 for the three error structures. In experiment 1, data on cost, $\Delta cost$, X_1 and X_2, and e_i^{trip} and e_i^{cv} are independent of one another. This error structure is consistent with models 1 and 3 ($\rho = 0$) but not with model 2. The incorrectly specified model 2 could not be estimated even with the simulated data. The results from models 1 and 3 are as expected. The mean square error in both models is similar and the bias in the parameter estimates tends to zero.

For experiment 2, e_i^{trip} is set equal to e_i^{cv}. This is the case of identical, permanent preferences. The bivariate model is not defined when $\rho = 1$ and consequently only models 1 and 2 can be estimated for this error structure. Model 2 is the correctly specified model and the bias in the estimated parameters tends to zero, as expected. The estimates produced by the model 1 specification are strongly biased. For example, the model 1 mean estimate of γ_0 was 1.006, over 600% greater than the true value of 0.15. In experiment 3 the correlation coefficient was set to 0.836. All three models can be estimated with this error structure. Model 3 is correct for this error specification and is the only one that produces unbiased parameter estimates.

Table 7.1 Monte Carlo Results: Simulation of CV Question, Conditional on Taking a Trip—Experiment 1 (Error structure: e^{trip}, e^{cv} independent)

Model	*Coefficients*			
	γ_0	γ_1	γ_2	γ_3
Model 1				
Mean of coefficient estimate		-0.110	0.097	0.199
Mean-squared error		0.0	0.003	0.020
Bias		0.0	-0.003	-0.001
Model 2		Did not converge		
Model 3				
Mean of coefficient estimate	-0.146	-0.100	0.092	0.184
Mean-squared error	0.490	0.0	0.005	0.023
Bias	-0.004	0.0	-0.008	-0.016

Table 7.2 *Monte Carlo Results: Simulation of CV Question, Conditional on Taking a Trip—Experiment 2 (Error structure: $e^{trip} = e^{cv}$)*

Model	Coefficients			
Model 1	γ_0	γ_1	γ_2	γ_3
Mean of coefficient estimate	1.156	-0.141	0.064	0.158
Mean-squared error	1.170	0.001	0.005	0.024
Bias	1.006	-0.031	-0.036	-0.042
Model 2				
Mean of coefficient estimate	0.136	-0.111	0.101	0.201
Mean-squared error	0.429	0.000	0.007	0.045
Bias	-0.014	-0.001	0.001	0.001
Model 3	–	–	–	–

Table 7.3 *Monte Carlo Results: Simulation of CV Question, Conditional on Taking a Trip—Experiment 3 (Error structure: $e^{trip} = e^{cv}$ jointly normal)*

Model	Coefficients			
	γ_0	γ_1	γ_2	γ_3
Model 1				
Mean of coefficient estimate	0.928	-0.131	0.074	0.149
Mean-squared error	0.738	0.001	0.008	0.022
Bias	0.778	-0.021	-0.026	-0.051
Model 2				
Mean of coefficient estimate	-0.487	-0.095	0.181	0.230
Mean-squared error	1.099	0.001	0.009	0.052
Bias	-0.637	0.015	0.031	0.030
Model 3				
Mean of coefficient estimate	0.147	-0.111	0.105	0.197
Mean-squared error	0.608	0.000	0.006	0.037
Bias	-0.003	-0.001	0.005	-0.003

Table 7.4 Recreational Anglers: Descriptive Statistics for Behavioral/ Contingent Valuation Model

Range of Total Cost	Number of Responses	% Responding Yes	Mean Total Cost $
0–75	67	82.1	54.63
75–100	68	69.1	88.60
100–150	141	54.6	121.53
150–200	69	43.5	174.07
200–250	82	47.7	220.72
250+	24	16.7	288.05

7.4 ESTIMATING THE MODEL ON A SAMPLE OF RECREATIONAL ANGLERS

The purpose of this section is to estimate the model with actual on-site recreation data. The analysis of this section is part of a larger study of marine recreational fishing. In this study intercepted anglers were questioned by phone for a two-month period of recreational fishing days. After two months, the details of a specific trip for a single day, as part of a larger visit, may be vague. The multiple purpose nature of long visits, especially vacations and business trips, compound the simple economics. As we discuss further below, the lag between the planning of the trip and the CV question puts a potential *ex ante/ex post* wedge in the analysis. Nevertheless, this approach illustrates an easy way of integrating CV observations with actual behavior.

We estimate the models on 451 observations of CV-trip behavior visits between New York and South Carolina. These overnight fishing trips were taken in 1988–89. Table 7.4 shows the number of responses, percent responding yes and the mean total costs for six trip-cost categories.[6] There appears to be a correlation in trip costs and the percentage of "Yes" responses to the CV question, suggesting the third model specification may be appropriate. To estimate the model, we need to specify the deterministic portion of the indirect utility function. The utility difference is

[6] Trip costs were based on the variable expenses associated with the day's trip and no opportunity cost of time was included. Travel expenses were calculated at $.22 per mile from the previous night's lodging to the fishing site.

$$\Delta v(y,c) = V_1(y-c) - V_0(y) \tag{7.12}$$

where V_1 is the utility from fishing and V_0 is the utility from not fishing. Obviously some aspects of fishing matter, so that ΔV should be specified as a function of some fishing characteristics. Utility from the fishing day has the following specification:

$$V_1(y-c) = \alpha^* + \alpha_2(y-c) + \alpha_3 BIG, \tag{7.13}$$

where y is income, c is the trip costs and *BIG* is a zero one indication equal to one if the angler was seeking big game fish and 0 otherwise. The marginal utility of income, α_2, is positive. There were 77 big game trips taken (17% of the total). It is reasonable that the trip should yield greater utility if the angler sought big game. Hence α_3 is expected to be positive. With no fishing, deterministic utility is given by

$$V_0(y) = \alpha^0 + \alpha_2 y. \tag{7.14}$$

Combining (7.13) and (7.14) gives

$$\Delta v_1(y,c) = \alpha_1 - \alpha_2 c + \alpha_3 BIG, \tag{7.15}$$

where $\alpha_1 \equiv \alpha^* - \alpha^0$. This is the deterministic portion of utility. Only relative values for α_i's, that is, α_i / σ, are estimated. Further, the relative values are all that are needed for purposes of valuation. That is, when it comes to monetary valuation, no scaling issue is present because scale does not matter. We assume that the random component of preferences from the RP and SP decisions are distributed bivariate normal.

7.5 EMPIRICAL RESULTS

The results from the estimation are given in Table 7.5. Two of the three cases discussed were estimated with maximum likelihood methods using functions written in Gauss; the maximum likelihood estimation would not converge under the assumption of Model 2. This is not unexpected when we recall the results of the Monte Carlo simulation in Section 7.3. Even with the well-behaved synthetic data, an incorrectly specified model would not converge. Evidence suggests that the unobserved preferences were not identical throughout the actual trip decision and the subsequent contingent valuation question.

Table 7.5 presents parameter estimates standard errors, likelihood function values and chi-squared statistics for the first and third model. The parameters all have correct sign and are of plausible magnitude. However, the constant term for model 3 is not significantly different from zero, leading to large confidence intervals for estimates of willingness to pay.

Aside from the standard reward of looking at parameter estimates for yet another CV study of recreational fishing, there are two ideas with empirical implications. First, the results provide a way of testing whether behavior is consistent with CV responses. Second, if the models are consistent, this approach can help give CV-generated estimates greater efficiency by providing bounds on errors. This was proved by HLK. However, if the models are not consistent, then obviously no efficiency gains are available. We provide some further empirical evidence.

There are several ways to assess the influence of the behavioral information on the estimates of the CV model. First, do the parameter estimates change when we introduce the behavioral evidence? This can be tested by testing for equality of parameters in model 1 versus model 3. Pairwise tests of the null hypothesis

$$\alpha_i(\text{Model 1}) = \alpha_i(\text{Model 3}),\ i = 1,3$$

yield t-statistics of 0.49, 0.26 and 0.53. On a pairwise basis, we cannot reject the hypothesis that the parameters are equal. If behavioral responses were quite different from responses to CV (as critics of CV maintain) then this hypothesis would be rejected. In terms of the consistency of stated versus revealed preferences, we can say that introducing evidence from RP does not change the parameter estimation model based on SP. The absence of support for the idea that SP is consistent with RP stems from the larger standard errors for model 3. This in turn comes from the correlation between the two errors, and the consequently more complicated likelihood function.

A second test can be done on the vectors of estimated willingness to pay. The willingness to pay estimates are given by the expected value of

$$WTP = \frac{\alpha_1 + \alpha_3 BIG}{\alpha_2} + \frac{\theta}{\alpha_2},$$

where θ is the error. The expected WTP is given for both models by:

$$EWTP = \frac{\alpha_1 + \alpha_3 BIG}{\alpha_2}. \tag{7.16}$$

The coefficients in Table 7.5, along with the fact that mean $BIG = 0.17$, provide the estimates of *EWTP* in Table 7.6. The 90% confidence interval are calculated by drawing 1000 normal vectors with the mean and covariance matrix of the estimated parameters, calculating *EWTP* as in (7.16) and discarding the lowest and highest 5%. These estimates along with 90% confidence intervals are reported in Table 7.6.

Two big differences are apparent in Table 7.6. First, *EWTP* for the correlated case (model 3) is approximately one-half of the uncorrelated case. Second, the confidence intervals for the correlated case are much wider, including a large negative segment. Of course, the large confidence interval for model 3 stems from the large standard errors. The model is much more complicated to estimate with nonzero correlation, but if there were perfect harmony between RP and SP responses, the errors would be the same. Then model 1 would hold. However, the more complicated likelihood function that is necessitated by model 3 may be too great a penalty. It makes model estimation much more difficult even if the errors are almost the same.

Table 7.5 Model Estimation Results for Day Trips

Coefficient	Model 1: Transitory Preference Structure ($\rho = 0$)	Model 3: Correlated Preference Structure
α_1	0.9539 (0.1648)[a]	0.3963 (0.7357)
α_2	-0.6053[c] (0.0983)	-0.5554[c] (0.1629)
α_3	0.3553 (0.1670)	0.5238[b] (0.2722)
ρ	≡0	0.6989 (0.3662)
log likelihood	-286.08	-285.58
model chi-square	46.81	47.81
Number of observations	451	451

[a] Standard errors are in parentheses.
[b] Because ρ is restricted to the [-1,1] interval, the information matrix does not provide consistent estimates of the standard errors. Bootstrap standard errors are reported for Model 3.
[c] The original cost data were divided by 100 for more accurate numerical estimation. Consequently in the calculation of the mean WTP, the estimate of α_2 should be divided by 100.

Table 7.6 Estimated Mean Willingness to Pay by Recreational Anglers

Model	*EWTP* at *BIG* = 0.17	90% Confidence Intervals
Model 1	\$168	\$141 to \$202
Model 3	\$87	-\$187 to \$216

7.6 CONCLUSIONS

This chapter presents a model to value a recreation site using information from RP and SP sources. The model is similar and representative of recent developments in combining RP and SP information to value non-market environmental amenities. We exploit the underlying premise of the travel cost model, that gaining access to a recreation sites incurs a travel cost burden. Once on-site, an individual has demonstrated a willingness to pay to gain access. More specifically, the utility derived from taking a trip must exceed the utility derived from the foregone travel cost income. On-site surveys that ask the individual to make the same decision in the presence of higher (hypothetical) travel costs, provides valuable additional information that can be used to estimate willingness to pay. We show how to combine the RP and SP information in a single stochastic model to estimate the underlying preference structure. The corresponding willingness to pay for access to the recreation site is then readily obtained.

The model has several attractive features. First, the model specification is intuitively simple. Second, it exploits potential discrepancies between the underlying preference structures used to take the trip (the RP component) and the underlying preference structure used to answer the contingent response scenario (the SP component). Finally, the model facilitates on-site recreation surveys which themselves have advantages over other survey methods. On-site surveys target the segment of the population that includes the recreation site of interest in their choice set. In contrast, a randomly administered survey of an entire population may results in low interception of users of the study recreation site.

We think the most promising part of the model presented here is its ability to incorporate decisions about behavior with responses to discrete choice CV models. Using only on-site data, one cannot test behavior versus CV. But it is possible to investigate the influence of the behavioral information on the CV responses and to formulate hypotheses that allow one to reject the idea that CV is consistent with behavior.

REFERENCES

Adamowicz, W., Louviere, J., and Williams, M. (1994). "Combining Revealed and Stated Preference Methods for Valuing Environmental Amenities." *Journal of Environmental Economics and Management* 26, 271–92.

Altaf, M. and DeShazo, J. (1994). "Bid Elicitation in the Contingent Valuation Method: the Double Referendum Format and Induced Strategic Behavior."

Cameron, T.A. (1992). "Combining Contingent Valuation and Travel Cost Data for the Valuation of Nonmarket Goods." *Land Economics* 68, 302–17.

Cameron, T.A. and Quiggin, J., (1992). "Estimation Using Contingent Valuation Data From a 'Dichotomous Choice With Follow-Up Questionnaire." University of California, LosAngeles Working Paper.

Eom, Y.S. and Smith, V.K. (1994). "Calibrated Nonmarket Valuation."

Hanemann, M.W., Loomis, J., and Kannenin, B. (1991). "Statistical Efficiency of Double-Bounded Dichotomous Choice Contingent Valuation." *American Journal of Agriculture Economics* 73. No. 4, 1255–63.

Larson, D.M., Loomis, J., and Chien, Y.-L. (1994). "Combining Behavioral and Conversational Approaches to Value Amenities." Contributed paper at the American Agricultural Economics Association, August.

Maddala, G.S. (1983). *Limited Dependent and Qualitative Variables in Econometrics*, Cambridge University Press, New York.

McConnell, K.E., Strand, I.E., Valdes, S., and Weninger, Q. (1992). "The Economic Value of Mid and South Atlantic Sportfishing." University of Maryland, Report #CR-811043-01-0.

8. Nonresponse Bias in Mail Survey Data: Salience vs. Endogenous Survey Complexity*

Trudy Ann Cameron, W. Douglass Shaw, and Shannon R. Ragland

8.1 INTRODUCTION

The purpose of this chapter is to demonstrate the opportunities for, and utility of, explicit modeling of survey response/nonresponse. A good understanding of the relationship between survey response propensities and observable behavioral relationships within just the subsample of respondents can help inform researchers and policy makers about the likely nature of nonresponse biases.

All types of survey research are plagued by the nonresponse problem to a varying degree. And there are always tradeoffs to be considered in deciding upon what type of survey method to use. The main alternatives are in-person surveys, mail surveys, and telephone surveys. Each has advantages and disadvantages. In-person surveys can be extremely costly, but they allow for interviewer/respondent interaction and permit the use of pictures or other visual aids in order to convey complex information. Telephone surveys allow the same give-and-take, but all information must be conveyed verbally, so the survey cannot involve much complexity. Mail surveys preclude interaction between the respondent and an interviewer, but they are relatively cheap and allow supporting information in the form of pictures or data summaries.

For each of these survey methods, the researcher must also consider whether to pursue a sample from the general population, or to target particular groups. Presumably, for many applications, the research goal is to characterize the distribution of preferences (or demands, or opinions or behaviors) in the general population. At best, however, a survey can only describe the characteristics of that group of individuals who were eligible to respond because they were

---

* This data set employed in this chapter was collected as part of a study managed by Hagler Bailly Consulting, Inc., under contract with the U.S. Army Corps of Engineers (contract #TCN93357).

contacted as part of an "intended sample" which has ideally been drawn at random from the population it is intended to represent. Any systematic nonresponse to a survey means that the resulting estimating sample will NOT be a random sample from the targeted population. Biases in the sample, if substantial, can mean significant biases in the implications of any analysis based on these nonrandom responses.

Mail surveys, the topic of this chapter, have long been a popular method for gathering research information. They continue to be employed in a wide variety of disciplines where household decisions, preferences, or behaviors need to be quantified. As with all survey methods, a perennial concern with the design of mail surveys has been the maximization of response rates (Dillman, 1978). However, even with aggressive campaigns of follow-up reminder postcards, nominal payments to respondents, and replacement mailings, there almost always remains a persistent nonresponse group.

The issues discussed in this chapter are relevant to a very broad community of investigators who rely on data gathered from mail surveys, but the discussion here will be cast in terms of an example where a mail survey has been used to collect demand information concerning non-market environmental goods. Economic models used with these types of data have included travel cost models, random utility models, and contingent valuation or behavior models.

Section 8.2 of this chapter reviews a selection of findings concerning survey response/nonresponse that have appeared in the broader marketing and social science literature, as well as a small number of studies focussing on this issue within the boundaries of environmental economics. Section 8.3 covers the manner in which these earlier insights are reflected in the modeling of nonresponse in our specific illustrative environmental valuation context. Section 8.4 outlines a rudimentary model of water-based recreational trip taking, to be estimated using the sample of respondents to a mail survey—with and without corrections for selectivity.

Section 8.5 provides a discussion of the empirical findings in our specific application. First, we present an overall model of survey response/nonresponse decisions. Then, for four different but related surveys, we compare uncorrected respondent-only models for reported trips with the results from joint models of both the response/nonresponse decision and reported trips. Section 8.6 concludes with comments on the apparent implications of our simple illustration for mail survey estimates of demand and welfare in a broader context.

8.2 REVIEW OF THE RELEVANT LITERATURE ON RESPONSE/NONRESPONSE

Much of the general survey research literature on nonresponse has been devoted to studies of the relative effectiveness of different choices that might be made regarding survey design and administration in order to maximize response rates. Fox et al. (1988) describe a meta-analysis of some of these design issues and strategies as they apply to mail surveys. The classes of factors they consider are all under the control of the researcher and include several related to the content of the cover letter, the amount and type of incentives offered, the form of respondent contact and follow-ups, the type of postage used for outgoing and return mail, and the topic, length, color, complexity and format of the questionnaire itself.

Among environmental economists, Dillman (1978) has been the standard handbook on design methods to maximize response for mail and telephone surveys.[1] Maximizing response rates remains extremely important, but we are concerned here with the task of correcting demand and welfare models for any nonresponse that remains. To do this, we must acknowledge that nonresponse results from the decision-making process of survey recipients. Heterogeneity across the intended sample in socio-demographic characteristics and in behavior patterns related to the survey topic may account for a significant portion of the systematic differences in response rates.

McDaniel *et al.* (1987) provide an excellent summary of survey research that focuses on the demographic characteristics of nonrespondents. They also cite research that investigates psychographic or behavioral differences between respondents and nonrespondents. Paraphrasing their summary, nonrespondents to surveys tend to be less educated, of lower socioeconomic class, white, of foreign-born parentage, older, married, residents in urban areas, and living in the Northeast U.S. Psychologically and behaviorally, nonrespondents also tend to be less emotionally stable, less effective as employees, less gregarious, lower in sense-of-leadership, less widely read, less proficient in writing ability, low on order and dependency but high on aggression, dominance, autonomy and intraception, and less responsible, less tolerant, and less intellectual in personality characteristics.

McDaniel *et al.* (1987) make the point that this assortment of apparent tendencies from individual studies of nonresponse may not be generalizable to other studies. Their results do, however, strongly support the common contention that the "salience" of the survey topic to the survey recipient can have a substantial bearing on the probability that the survey will be completed and returned. This conforms to an earlier meta-analysis by Heberlein and Baumgartner (1978).

Regional differences in populations may also have an effect on response rates. (See, for example, Jobber and Saunders (1988), Jobber *et al.* (1991),

---

[1] Some subsequent research concerning the prescriptions in Dillman (1978) is described in Dillman *et al.* (1984). Twenty-nine different elements of the "total design method" were either adhered-to or not for samples taken from eleven different states in the U.S. and the consequences for response-rates evaluated.

Ayal and Hornick (1986), and evidence of Canadian–U.S. differences in Goyder (1985).)

Another determinant of response propensity that seems not to have been addressed elsewhere in the literature is the potential for endogeneity in the actual complexity of the survey completion task for different individuals. The amount of time or intellectual effort required for someone to provide the information requested on the survey instrument may be directly related to the level of activity in the behaviors that the survey is attempting to measure. If time constraints are binding, more-active individuals will tend to be under-represented in the respondent sample. Both endogenous survey complexity and survey topic salience will be greater for active individuals. Which one of these two competing effects ultimately dominates will depend upon the applications.

8.2.1 Previous Strategies

In 1989, Mitchell and Carson (pp. 267–82) reviewed the problem of nonresponse as it affected contingent valuation surveys up to that time. They described econometric methods for sample selection bias correction but concluded that "Unfortunately, these methods may be of limited use in contingent valuation studies when little or no information is available on factors affecting the probability of responding to the survey. ... We know of no CV study that has attempted to use these techniques to correct for sample selection bias."

The most common strategy for addressing nonresponse in environmental valuation surveys has been to provide marginal means for a limited set of sociodemographic variables (e.g. income, age), calculated for the respondent sample and for the population it is intended to represent. If these means are similar, little more is said. The problem is that even though respondents and nonrespondents may appear similar on a selection of *observable* sociodemographic attributes, there may be important *unobservable* forms of heterogeneity that affect both response propensities and demand for the environmental good. For example, respondents to a recreational fishing survey may tend to be more-avid anglers than nonrespondents, and avidity may not be measured.

Most researchers have treated survey nonresponse as a problem that has no easy solution. Whitehead (1991) asserts that correction for self-selection bias requires information about nonrespondents, obtained either through screener surveys or follow-up surveys. Edwards and Anderson (1987) emphasize that "from a practical standpoint the test for selection bias resulting from nonrespondents' self-censorship" requires that one "interview a high percentage of nonrespondents." They note that "This need presents a substantial, technical challenge for contingent valuation studies." In contrast, the present chapter offers a tractable general strategy for modeling and correcting for nonresponse to mail surveys.

There are only a very few cases in the existing literature on environmental valuation via survey-based methods where researchers have attempted to control for nonresponse bias. Edwards and Anderson (1987) limit their empirical analysis to cases of questionnaire *item nonresponse*, rather than complete *unit nonresponse*. In particular, they find that omission of observations due to protest bids or zero willingness-to-pay does not appear to produce any additional selectivity bias. Aggressive nonresponse conversion efforts allowed them to achieve an eventually very high response rate, but no data were available on the persistent nonrespondents who remained.

In two other cases, the task of nonresponse evaluation has been facilitated because the researchers have access to supplementary databases where other *individual-specific* information can be linked to each targeted potential respondent. (See Whitehead *et al.* 1993; Englin *et al.* 1996; and Fisher 1996.)

This chapter differs from previous and concurrent efforts to explore nonresponse bias in the environmental economics literature in that it illustrates a technique that can be applied with any mail survey conducted in the United States.[2]

8.3 MODELING PROPENSITY TO RESPOND TO OUR SPECIFIC MAIL SURVEY

The mail survey data we will use for our illustration comes from a four-version survey of water-based recreational participation (at lakes, reservoirs, and rivers) within the Columbia River system in the U.S. states of Washington, Oregon, Idaho and western Montana, plus the southern portions of the Canadian provinces of British Columbia and Alberta. The "intended" sample in this case was designed to span most of the groups that might potentially be users of water recreation sites along the Columbia River system. The so-called "extent of the market" is always an issue (and sometimes a controversial one) when trying to quantify demand for nonmarket goods. Here, the extent of the market was deemed to coincide roughly with the geographical watershed for the Columbia River system. It is generally advisable to sample a geographical area wider than the distribution of individuals likely to have positive demands for a recreational site. If distance is a significant determinant of demand, one would prefer to be able to observe demands falling to zero *within* the geographic scope of the sample, rather than to have to try to guess at what distance *beyond* the

[2] For a number of other countries, analogous methods are potentially feasible, depending on the availability of similar types of Census and distance data.

geographical boundaries of the sampled population the market might end.

The larger study is discussed in detail in Callaway *et al.* (1995) and portions are also summarized in Cameron *et al.* (1996). In the latter paper, we employed some crude sample selection correction methods. In that paper, however, we combined the revealed preference recreational trip data used in the present paper with stated preference (contingent behavior) data on respondents' probable choices under counterfactual water level conditions at different sites. The fact that we had to combine real and hypothetical choice data at different levels of time-aggregation presented some complex modeling problems that precluded anything more than a rudimentary two-stage correction method for survey nonresponse. In the course of that endeavor we came to the realization that the determinants and consequences of survey nonresponse in nonmarket resource valuation applications are potentially extremely important. In the present analysis, we have thus pruned away all the hypothetical choice data in order to illustrate more cleanly the nonresponse problem. Relying solely on the actual choice data means that the simple travel-cost type models presented here cannot explore the effects of water levels on demand (since there was minimal independent variation in water levels in the actual data). Nevertheless, these simplified models afford an excellent opportunity to contrast the implied demand functions, with and without nonresponse correction, for four different (but closely related) surveys.

One of the four different versions of our survey instrument was randomly chosen and sent to each of 7034 addresses.[3] We are interested, first of all, in modeling the propensity for each copy of the survey instrument to be returned. Of these targeted households, 2513 returned surveys that were sufficiently complete for their data to be included in our demand analyses, for an overall raw response rate of 35.73%. Wiseman and Billington (1984) address the issue of standardizing the definition of "response rate" in applied statistics. In the present study, the response rate is defined as the number of questionnaires used in the estimation process divided by the total number of questionnaires mailed out. No prior adjustments are made to the denominator (for example, for "returned undeliverable" or other exclusions that are frequently allowed before making this computation).

One task we face is to control for the fundamentally different expected response rates in different sampling strata. It is not always feasible to rely upon a strictly representative sample from the general population in modeling the demand for environmental amenities. In many cases, it is expedient to combine a basic general population sample with other convenient samples. In our illustration, for example, a little over 40% of the estimating sample is from a general

[3] However, there were several strata in our intended sample. Completely random assignment of versions occurred in our general population stratum. Random assignment of relevant versions within some of our other strata is discussed below.

population survey. In addition, there were four other subsamples. (The four different survey versions were assigned completely randomly within and across these different sampling strata, with some minor exceptions noted below.) We intentionally over-sample people who live in close proximity to the environmental good to be valued (i.e. in "Adjacent Counties"), and these respondents make up about 44% of the estimating sample.[4]

We include an initial small convenience sample (called the "Phase 1" sample), accounting for about 6% of our observations. We also include people who are known to be users of the resources in question, by intercepting and recruiting them on site (the "Known User" sample, accounting for about 8% of surveys).[5] Finally, we also have a subsample of potential foreign users, drawn from major urban areas of the nearest cross-border regions (the "Canadian" sample—about 2%). Dummy variables identifying our four auxiliary strata groups are included in our overall response/nonresponse model.

For this survey, Dillman's prescriptions were followed as closely as possible in order to maximize overall response rates. Among other things, we used a booklet format and a follow-up postcard reminder (although we did not call people who did not respond, nor did we use incentives such as payment or a chance to win a prize).

There are some special features of the survey design, however, that must be highlighted. First, each of the four different versions focuses on a separate geographic region. The visual aids (photographs, both actual and computer-modified) that accompanied each questionnaire were different. While effort was devoted to making the written portions of the survey as comparable as possible, their different regional emphases may have resulted in differing appeal or salience to different types of respondents. In our model, survey response/nonresponse decisions are allowed to vary systematically according to survey version.

The zip code information is the key to generating variables that may go part way towards capturing the salience of the survey topic and unobserved tendency to engage in water-based recreation via the demographic or socioeconomic characteristics of the potential respondent's neighborhood. In designing our response/nonresponse model, we need to keep in mind that for a mail survey in the US, often nothing is likely to be known about each member of the intended sample beyond their mailing address (including zip code) and what version of the survey they were sent. Even if a survey research firm protects respondent

---

[4] For households in the intended sample in counties adjacent to a particular water, one survey version was randomly selected from the subset of versions that included that water as a focal water.

[5] As for the Adjacent Counties sample, visitors to a particular water were randomly assigned a survey version from the subset of survey versions that included that water as a focal water.

confidentiality by redacting the name and street address of each respondent, it is possible that zip codes can be retained, since they rarely would allow unique identification of any respondent.

We thus attempt to capture both salience of the survey topic to each respondent and his or her likely recreational activity level using an array of proxy variables. Even from the cover of the survey—the first thing a respondent would see—our survey topic is easily construed to be water-based recreation. Both a recipient's actual and potential experience with water-based recreation could be expected to influence response propensity. One way to attempt to capture this potential experience is by using distances between the recipient's home and each of the bodies of water featured in their particular version of the questionnaire. First, we employ the individual distances between the recipient's origin zip code and each of the three or four specific Federal Projects along the Columbia River system which are singled out for emphasis on his or her particular version of the questionnaire. (We call these the "focal waters.") These waters are either reservoirs behind hydroelectric dams or run-of-river stretches below these dams. The identities of these waters differ by survey version, so when we pool all of the data for use in one model, we interact each of these distances with dummy variables for each version. We have also calculated the distances from each respondent's zip code to each of five "other" fresh waters. These five alternative waters are not federal projects and thus were not specifically mentioned on the survey questionnaire. The average of these five distances is used to represent the accessibility of other nearby water recreation opportunities. This average is also interacted with survey version dummy variables, since the set from which these "other" waters is drawn differs across survey versions.[6]

Our distance data were calculated using the ZIPFIP computer program (Hellerstein *et al.* 1993). Given origin and destination zip codes, this software allows the user to generate approximate road distances between the centers of these zip codes. These distances are constructed from "great circle" distances, modified by a factor (unique to each state) that converts these distances into average road distances in a manner that controls for differing densities of roadways in each state. We identified the zip codes containing (or nearest to) each of the water bodies in our study region. In combination with the zip code for each potential respondent's address, we merge these distances with the response/nonresponse data.

The zip codes for the intended sample are also the key that allows us to merge the data set with a wide array of variables from the 1990 Census (available

[6] Saltwater recreation opportunities may be viewed by some households as substitutes for the freshwater recreation opportunities they are being asked to consider. Saltwater resources were not considered in this survey.

from the STF3 data tapes). All variables are descriptors of the zip code area, rather than the individual, but to the extent that the geographical areas covered by zip codes are relatively homogeneous, some portion of the heterogeneity in these characteristics across survey recipients can be captured by these aggregate data. The Census data provide zip code populations as well as counts of persons in each of a variety of categories. Appendix Table 8.A-1 gives the Census-based variables we have considered, with details concerning how these were calculated from the constituent variables (using the variable names from the Census tapes). Census variables other than these ones may be important predictors of response/nonresponse in other applications.

A portion of our intended sample also consisted of Canadians. The general nonresponse research cited in the previous section certainly suggests that response rates should be allowed to vary systematically by country. We use a dummy variable to shift the response index for Canadian survey recipients. Within the U.S., however, rather than using regional jurisdictional dummy variables such as states or counties, we elect to rely directly upon sociodemographic variations. These are the factors that such dummy variables would presumably be capturing.

It is also potentially important to control for any variations in survey format across the sample. Many environmental valuation surveys rely upon contingent scenarios (either contingent valuation or contingent behavior). These scenarios differ across versions of the survey instrument and these differences could conceivably influence response rates. In the wake of the debate about "embedding," for example, some environmental valuation surveys have been designed to assess the effectiveness of different amounts of context for the valuation exercise. The level of descriptive detail for each scenario involved may differ a little or a lot across the individuals who make up the intended sample. Alternately, the nature or scope of the good to be valued may differ across survey versions. These variations in the survey instrument may themselves lead to differential response rates, and this possibility seems not to have been pursued.

8.4 MODELING SURVEY RESPONSE PROPENSITIES AND RECREATIONAL TRIPS

The first question is whether there are systematic differences across people in their propensities to respond to the version of the questionnaire that they receive. We address this question using pooled data for all 7034 questionnaires that were distributed in the course of this study.

The second question is whether failure to consider the consequences of systematic nonresponse can lead to any appreciable distortion in the implications of demand models estimated using only respondent data. We demonstrate the empirical importance of controlling for nonresponse in a model of the individual's total demand for trips to *any* water in the region featured on the questionnaire, regardless of specific destination. Since the set of relevant waters varies across versions, we estimate these demand models separately for each version. We construct a rough proxy for "accessibility" of water recreation opportunities by calculating the average distance from the respondent's home zip code to the nearest five waters (be they focal federal projects or "other" waters) in the target region for the survey. Ex ante, one would expect that the less accessible these recreation opportunities—i.e. the greater this average distance—the fewer total trips an individual will take. This variable plays the usual role that would be played by a comprehensive travel cost variable in a more-formal recreational demand specification.

Of course, it would be possible to use our simple demand specifications heroically to derive the associated welfare implications of failing to correct for nonresponse biases. Welfare measures are typically the goal of most recreational demand modeling exercises. However, substantial distortions to the estimated demand functions will typically imply corresponding distortions in the welfare results calculated from these estimated functions. We elect to focus attention here on the demand models as the root source of these welfare estimate distortions.

Overall, 1347 of our 2513 respondents took positive numbers of trips and these trip-takers averaged 12.4 trips apiece, with a standard deviation of 16.4 trips. A continuous distribution is assumed to be an adequate approximation to the conditional distribution of trip-taking propensities, suggesting a Tobit-type model for trips in order to accommodate the sizeable observed frequency of zero trips.

Let $y_i^* = x_i'\beta + \varepsilon_i$ be the latent propensity to return a completed response to the questionnaire that was mailed to household i. Since y_i^* is unobservable, the response/nonresponse outcome associated with each mailing is evaluated in terms of the associated observable variable $y_i = 1$ if the questionnaire is returned completed and $y_i = 0$ if the questionnaire is either not returned, or is returned insufficiently complete to be included in the analysis.[7] The vector of variables x_i includes Census zip code characteristics, variables that capture the differences among survey versions, the different sample strata, and the distance variables that partially proxy for the probable salience of the survey topic to targeted households.

---

[7] In a more-elaborate model, the specification could distinguish between complete nonresponse and unusable responses. However, this would require a trivariate joint density for FIML estimation.

Let $q_i^* = z_i'\gamma + v_i$ be each respondent's propensity to take water-based recreation trips to water bodies in the geographical area stipulated in each version of the questionnaire. If $q_i^* > 0$, then observed water recreation trips $q_i = q_i^*$. If we have $q_i^* \leq 0$, then observed trips will be $q_i = 0$. The vector z_i includes a rudimentary set of individual attributes intended to explain systematic variations in numbers of trips, including the accessibility of the sites, income, age, and holdings of activity-specific permits or capital equipment (specifically, fishing licenses and boats).

We assume y_i^* is distributed N(0,1), with variance normalized to unity because the binary nature of y_i will not allow us to discern the scale of y_i^*. Let q_i^* be distributed $N(z_i'\gamma, \sigma^2)$, since the observable portion of q_i^* does allow the scale to be identified. We wish to jointly model both the individual's decision about whether to respond to the questionnaire and, conditional on response, the number of trips taken. This is a Tobit model with a sample selection correction, ideally estimated by Full Information Maximum Likelihood (FIML). For a textbook description, see Greene (1995, p. 624).

A little intuition will help with the development of the appropriate log-likelihood function. The domain of the joint density function can be partitioned into three distinct regions. The first region is characterized by $y_i^* > 0$ and $q_i > 0$ (respondents with nonzero observed trips). The second region has $y_i^* > 0$ and $q_i = 0$ (respondents with zero trips). The third region has $y_i^* < 0$ and thus q_i unknown (the nonrespondents).

For observations in the first region, the joint density can be conveniently expressed as the marginal density of q_i (observed) times the conditional density of y_i^* given the value of q_i. The random variable q_i is $N(z_i'\gamma, \sigma^2)$ and $f(y_i^* | q_i)$ is also normal with mean $x_i'\beta + \rho[(q_i - z_i'\gamma)/\sigma]$ and variance $(1-\rho^2)$, since the variance of y_i^* is normalized to unity. The term for the marginal distribution of q_i will look like the ordinary maximum likelihood regression formula. The term for the conditional distribution will look like the term for a conventional MLE probit model for the positive domain of the latent variable. For this region, then, the contribution of one observation to the log-likelihood function is:

$$\log \mathcal{L}_{1i} = \left\{ -0.5\log(2\pi) - \log(\sigma) - 0.5\left[\frac{(q_i - z_i'\gamma)^2}{\sigma^2}\right]\right\} + \log[1 - \Phi(R_i)]$$

where $R_i = -\{x_i'\beta + \rho[(q_i - z_i'\gamma)/\sigma]\}/(1-\rho^2)^{0.5}$.

For the second region, we assume that all values of $q_i^* < 0$ are manifested in the observed data as $q_i = 0$. Here, we must use the appropriate cumulative density associated with the bivariate normal distribution. If $\Phi(a,b,\rho)$ denotes the cumulative standard bivariate normal density function evaluated up to limits a and b, the log-likelihood terms for observations in this second region are given by:

$$\log \mathcal{L}_{2i} = \log\left[\Phi\left(x_i'\beta, -z_i'\gamma / \sigma, -\rho\right)\right].$$

For the third region of the domain of the joint density, all that is known is that $y_i^* < 0$, so we use the simple marginal distribution of y_i^*, employing a term like the one that applies to the negative domain of a conventional probit log-likelihood:

$$\log \mathcal{L}_{3i} = \log \Phi\left[-x_i'\beta\right].$$

Putting all three of these terms together, the full log-likelihood objective function can be expressed as:

$$\underset{\beta,\gamma,\sigma,\rho}{Max} \log \mathcal{L} = \sum\nolimits_{y_i=1,q_i>0} \log \mathcal{L}_{1i} + \sum\nolimits_{y_i=1,q_i=0} \log \mathcal{L}_{2i} + \sum\nolimits_{y_i=0} \log \mathcal{L}_{3i} \,.$$

A full-information maximum likelihood (FIML) Tobit model with sample selection is available in the LIMDEP econometric software package.

8.5 RESULTS

8.5.1 A Pooled Data Response/Nonresponse Model

Table 8.1 provides descriptive statistics for the entire intended sample of 7034 addresses. This is the universe of addresses to which questionnaires were mailed. The variables (described briefly in the body or footnotes to the table) either describe the type of subsample or are obtained by utilizing zip codes to calculate distances or to merge with the available Census data. Appendix Table A-1 provides an inventory of all of the Census variables that were examined in preliminary models. Only those variables that were robustly significant determinants of response rates across a variety of exploratory specifications are included in the models to follow. (In other applications, different Census variables may prove important.)

Table 8.2 gives the results for a pooled-data probit model that uses all 7034 addresses in the intended sample and attempts to explain provision of a usable response as a function of everything known about the zip code of the target

Table 8.1 Descriptive Statistics[a], Response/Nonresponse Sample (n = 7034) (means; standard deviations for non-binary variables in parentheses)

VERSION	1 (n = 1428)	2 (n = 1433)	3 (n = 2095)	4 (n = 2078)
OVERALL RESPONSE RATE	0.357	=1 if response sufficiently complete (0 otherwise)		
VERSION RESPONSE RATE	0.348	0.352	0.352	0.373
HAVE_FOCAL_DIST_DATA	0.941	= 1 if distance data available for all specified waters		
HAVE_OTHER_DIST_DATA	0.966	= 1 if distance data available, five nearest "other" waters		
HAVE_CENSUS_DATA	0.956	= 1 if 1990 Census data available for zip code		
ADJACENT_COUNTIES	0.436	= 1 if "Adjacent Counties" sample (0 otherwise)		
PHASE_1	0.0553	= 1 if "Phase 1" sample (0 otherwise)		

Notes

[a] Identity of the specific waters to which distances are measured differs across survey versions:

Version 1: WATER_1 = Hungry Horse Reservoir, WATER_2 = Lake Pend Oreille, WATER_3 = Lake Koocanusa, WATER_4 = Kootenai River, 5_OTHER_WATERS = nearest 5 other waters in the Version 1 region;

Version 2: WATER_1 = Dworshak Lake, WATER_2 = Clearwater River, WATER_3 = Lower Granite Lake, WATER_4 = Lake Pend Oreille, 5 OTHER WATERS = nearest 5 other waters in the Version 2 region;

Version 3: WATER_1 = Lake Roosevelt, WATER_2 = Lake Umatilla, WATER_3 = Lower Granite Lake, 5_OTHER_WATERS = nearest 5 other waters in the Version 3 region;

Version 4: WATER_1 = Lake Roosevelt, WATER_2 = Dworshak Lake, WATER_3 = Lower Granite Lake, WATER_4 = Lake Pend Oreille, 5_OTHER_WATERS = nearest 5 other waters in he Version 4 region.

Table 8.1 continued

VERSION	1 (n = 1428)	2 (n = 1433)	3 (n = 2095)	4 (n = 2078)
KNOWN_USER	0.0819	= 1 if "Known User" sample (0 otherwise)		
CANADIAN	0.0213	= 1 if Canadian sample (0 otherwise)		
VERSION DUMMIES	-	0.204	0.298	0.295
DISTANCE_WATER_1	0.239 (1.06)	0.362 (0.955)	0.813 (1.48)	0.506 (0.935)
DISTANCE_WATER_2	0.347 (1.20)	0.333 (0.920)	0.466 (0.880)	0.798 (1.44)
DISTANCE_WATER_3	0.270 (1.09)	0.289 (0.804)	0.784 (1.39)	0.668 (1.23)
DISTANCE_WATER_4	0.258 (1.06)	0.430 (1.21)	-[b]	0.730 (1.34)
AVG_DIST_5_OTHER_WATERS	0.209 (1.05)	0.198 (0.664)	0.304 (0.668)	0.388 (0.771)

[b] Survey Version 3 had only three “focal waters,” so there is no WATER_4 for Version 3 in any of these tables.

PROP_LANGUAGE_ISOLATED	0.00484 (0.00696)	= Proportion of zip code population language-isolated
PROP_PUBLIC_INCOME	0.0246 (0.0149)	= Proportion of zip code population on public assistance income
PROP_URBAN_AREAS	0.504 (0.398)	= Proportion of zip code population in urban area
PROP_RESOURCE_OCCUP	0.0269 (0.0327)	= Proportion of zip code population in agric., fishing, or forestry-related occupations
PROP_SS_INCOME	0.102 (0.0451)	= Proportion of zip code population on social security income

*Table 8.2 Pooled Data: Probit Model for Survey Response/Nonresponse (n = 7034) (point estimates; asymptotic t-ratios in parentheses; ** = 5%, * = 10% level)*

VARIABLE	VERSION 1[a]	VERSION 2	VERSION 3	VERSION 4
CONSTANT	-5.41	-	-	-
	(-0.10)			
HAVE_FOCAL_DIST_DATA	-0.944	-	-	-
	(-8.04)**			
HAVE_OTHER_DIST_DATA	5.83	-	-	-
	(0.11)			
HAVE_CENSUS_DATA	-0.0414	-	-	-
	(-0.26)			
ADJACENT_COUNTIES	0.0516	-	-	-
	(0.94)			
PHASE_1	0.198	-	-	-
	(2.77)**			
KNOWN_USER	0.452	-	-	-
	(5.79)**			
CANADIAN	0.0560	-	-	-
	(0.00)			
VERSION DUMMIES	-	-0.0120	0.338	0.106
		(-0.13)	(2.07)**	(0.96)

DISTANCE_WATER_1	0.0300 (0.25)	-0.0127 (-0.06)	-0.103 (-1.24)	-0.138 (-1.62)
DISTANCE_WATER_2	0.000649 (0.01)	-1.43 (-2.68)**	-0.150 (-1.46)	0.339 (1.35)
DISTANCE_WATER_3	0.244 (0.90)	1.52 (3.02)**	-0.0171 (-0.30)	-0.314 (-1.16)
DISTANCE_WATER_4	-0.229 (-1.19)	0.153 (3.29)**	-[b]	0.169 (1.33)
AVG_DIST_5_OTHER_WATERS	-0.0893 (-2.33)**	-0.110 (-1.28)	0.309 (1.73)*	-0.279 (-1.52)
PROP_LANGUAGE_ISOLATED	-5.91 (-2.06)**	-	-	-
PROP_PUBLIC_INCOME	-4.25 (-3.40)**	-	-	-
PROP_URBAN_AREAS	0.149 (2.45)**	-	-	-
PROP_RESOURCE_OCCUP	0.736 (1.04)	-	-	-
PROP_SS_INCOME	1.04 (2.39)**	-	-	-
log $\mathcal{L}$	-4341.5			

Notes:
[a] All parameters estimated in a single model. Version dummy variables are interacted with all distance variables because waters corresponding to each "numbered distance" differ across versions.
[b] Version 3 had only three "focal waters." See footnotes to Table 8.1 for identities of numbered waters for each Version.

household, the type of subsample it belonged to, and the version of the survey it received. In this model, we constrain to be identical across versions the effects of subsample membership and the Census zip code characteristics. The distance effects are allowed to differ across survey versions because these numbered distances are distances to different sets of waters on each different survey. We also include intercept-shifting dummy variables for each of Versions 2, 3, and 4.

We find that the "Phase 1" and "Known User" samples were statistically significantly more likely to respond. For known users, the subject matter of the questionnaire is undeniably salient, so this is not surprising. In contrast to expectations, the Canadian sample (population 5) does not appear to be statistically less likely to respond. However, this subsample is very small, and while comparable distance data were calculated by hand, no Census data were available for this sample, so the HAVE_CENSUS_DATA indicator variable is highly correlated with membership in the Canadian subsample. Thus our finding may not be conclusive.

Version 3 of the questionnaire appears to have produced systematically larger response rates. Distances to three of the specific waters described in the questionnaire significantly influenced response rates for recipients of version 2 of the questionnaire. The effect was negative for one water, and positive for two others.[8] Distances to the nearest "other" waters appears to matter only for versions 1 and 3 of the questionnaire.

Among the Census variables examined, the most robustly individually statistically significant variables were those intended to capture language isolation, proportion on public assistance income, proportion urban, and proportion on social security income. Language isolation decreases response probabilities, as does a greater neighborhood prevalence of public assistance income. Recipients in more urbanized areas are more likely to respond, as are those from areas with higher levels of employment in agriculture, fisheries or forestry, although the last is not statistically significant. Response propensity is also significantly higher, the greater the proportion of the neighborhood receiving social security income.[9]

---

[8] Since distances to waters may be negatively correlated with distances to major urban areas, which have not been controlled for in our models, these results may be open to different interpretations.

[9] Varying degrees of multicollinearity among some of the Census variables exist, but the purpose of the first-stage response/nonresponse model is to predict response probabilities, so this problem is not too troubling. The important result is that there is significant systematic variation in response probabilities.

8.5.2 Version-by-Version Total Trips Models

Here we consider ordinary Tobit models for total trips that ignore nonresponse problems and contrast their implications with those of FIML selectivity-corrected Tobit models that formally incorporate response propensities into the estimation process. In order to make the comparison most cleanly, we opt to limit our analyses by excluding all surveys that we sent to Canadian addresses or to addresses outside the main four-state region of the study. This means that the Canadian subsample is not used, and neither is a portion of the data from the Known User subsample. This avoids the problem of managing missing data for the Census variables (in the case of the Canadian data), and missing distance data (for the surveys sent outside the four-state region). With these adjustments, all FIML models converge easily. Without them, there are occasional problems because the coefficients on the dummies for availability of certain data types appear difficult to identify. This decision reduces the size of the pooled intended sample from 7034 to 6638 observations (a decrease of about 5.6%).

Table 8.3 gives descriptive statistics for the samples of usable responses from each of four versions of the survey. For these subsamples, we have actual respondent-specific individual sociodemographic information, which certainly involves less measurement error than the zip code proportions used for all observations in the first stage response/nonresponse model. However, the individual "home zip code to each water" distances are the same values that were computed for the entire intended sample of 7034, so they are also used to calculate the accessibility variables used here.

To a large extent, each of the survey versions was distributed randomly throughout the entire sampling area. If responses were entirely random, and survey distribution was entirely random, one would then expect that the means and variances in the income and age variables, as well as the proportions holding fishing licenses or owning boats, should be roughly identical. Some of these variables differ across versions by much more than one might expect. One reason might be that respondent concern for the sets of waters appearing in each version might vary. If avid boaters are more concerned about the waters featured in Version 1 than those featured in Version 3, for example, this could explain why the observed frequency of boat-ownership is 53% for Version 1 respondents but only 36% for Version 3 respondents.

Models for total trips ignoring nonresponse problems

Table 8.4 contains results obtained by using ordinary MLE Tobit regression models to explain total trips to any water in the region featured for each survey version.

Table 8.3 Descriptive Statistics (Respondents Only) for Total Trips Submodels[a]

VARIABLE	VERSION 1 (n = 474)	VERSION 2 (n = 498)	VERSION 3 (n = 730)	VERSION 4 (n = 768)
TOTAL TRIPS	10.1	9.15	3.56	5.76
(number)	(17.5)	(15.6)	(7.56)	(12.8)
ADJACENT_COUNTIES	0.555	0.492	0.355	0.369
(1=yes, 0=no)	(0.498)	(0.500)	(0.479)	(0.483)
PHASE_1	0.0401	0.0442	0.0836	0.0599
(1=yes, 0=no)	(0.196)	(0.206)	(0.277)	(0.237)
KNOWN_USER	0.198	0.155	0.0877	0.0807
(1=yes, 0=no)	(0.399)	(0.362)	(0.283)	(0.273)
AVG_DISTANCE	0.0848	0.0978	0.107	0.127
('000 miles)	(0.121)	(0.0962)	(0.111)	(0.0738)
HAVE_INCOME_DATA	0.831	0.845	0.853	0.850
(1=yes, 0=no)	(0.375)	(0.362)	(0.354)	(0.357)
INCOME	0.0284	0.0299	0.0319	0.0333
($'00,000)	(0.0266)	(0.0287)	(0.0285)	(0.0297)
HAVE_AGE_DATA	0.968	0.948	0.964	0.953
(1=yes, 0=no)	(0.175)	(0.223)	(0.186)	(0.2115)

AGE	5.14	5.00	5.09	4.94
(decades)	(1.74)	(1.86)	(1.83)	(1.87)
FISHING_LICENSE?	0.601	0.520	0.430	0.405
(1=yes, 0=no)	(0.490)	(0.500)	(0.495)	(0.491)
OWNS_BOAT?	0.530	0.450	0.363	0.385
(1=yes, 0=no)	(0.500)	(0.498)	(0.481)	(0.487)

Note: [a] Total number of responses analyzed is 2470, rather than 2513. Convergence could not be achieved for all versions with the parameterization necessary to accommodate all exceptional cases. We limit these analysis to the surveys distributed within the four U.S. Northwest states. By omitting the Canadian sample and those Known User observations outside this four-state region, we can avoid the use of dummy indicator variables for the availability or inavailability of distance and/or Census data. With this modification, the models converge readily.

Table 8.4 Total Trips without Nonresponse Correction

VARIABLE	VERSION 1	VERSION 2	VERSION 3	VERSION 4
CONSTANT	-22.1	-21.8	-11.9	-8.94
	(-3.01)**	(-3.60)**	(-3.80)**	(-1.81)*
ADJACENT_COUNTIES	6.81	9.77	8.21	5.97
(1=yes, 0=no)	(2.21)**	(3.49)**	(7.39)**	(2.45)**
PHASE_1	4.16	3.45	0.374	-0.131
(1=yes, 0=no)	(0.73)	(0.63)	(0.21)	(-0.04)
KNOWN_USER	24.1	22.0	10.0	19.1
(1=yes, 0=no)	(7.09)**	(6.88)**	(6.07)**	(6.04)**
AVG_DISTANCE	-44.7	-64.3	-12.1	-95.6
('000 miles)	(-4.29)**	(-4.25)**	(-2.74)**	(-5.60)**
HAVE_INCOME_DATA	-0.963	5.87	0.980	-1.03
(1=yes, 0=no)	(-0.31)	(1.88)*	(0.61)	(-0.45)
INCOME	48.2	22.3	17.3	69.0
($'00,000)	(1.18)	(0.61)	(0.93)	(2.60)**
HAVE_AGE_DATA	34.6	11.3	8.77	14.1
(1=yes, 0=no)	(4.50)**	(1.74)*	(2.64)**	(3.19)**
AGE	-4.00	-0.581	-1.35	-1.78
(decades)	(-5.82)**	(-0.85)	(-4.20)**	(-3.66)**

FISHING_LICENSE?	6.10	7.63	3.90	8.69
(1=yes, 0=no)	(2.69)**	(3.43)**	(3.72)**	(5.79)**
OWN_BOAT?	6.81	7.21	5.96	7.88
(1=yes, 0=no)	(3.15)**	(3.25)**	(5.57)**	(5.18)**
σ	19.3	19.1	10.8	15.7
	(24.70)**	(23.39)**	(24.80)**	(25.99)**
$\log \mathcal{L}$	-1475.281	-1395.142	-1493.579	-1649.096
Trips (fitted/actual)	11.6/10.1	10.1/9.15	6.38/3.56	6.65/5.76
Trips (fitted/actual)	3.84/3.02	3.46/2.50	2.84/1.48	2.28/1.18
general pop. sample	n = 98	n = 154	n = 346	n = 377

The base sampling category for these estimates is the general population sample. Intercept shift coefficients on the simple dummy variables for special subsamples imply that total trips are statistically significantly higher than in the general population subsample for the "Adjacent Counties" subsample and the "Known User" subsample, but not for the "Phase 1" preliminary sample. The AVG_DISTANCE variable measures average distances to the nearest five waters in the region featured on the questionnaire (be it a focus water for that version, or any other water). The coefficient on this distance index is negative and very strongly statistically significant across all versions. This supports its ex ante interpretation as a price-type variable.

The positive effect of income is statistically insignificant for all but Version 4. Age has a strongly statistically significant negative effect on trips for all versions except Version 2. Not surprisingly, the (potentially somewhat endogenous) variables indicating possession of a fishing license or a boat are strongly significantly correlated with the latent number of trips underlying this Tobit specification.[10]

The last row of Table 8.4 compares the sample averages of the fitted expected number of trips, according to these Tobit models. Note that these individual expected values are calculated as:

$$\Phi(z_i'\gamma / \sigma_\varepsilon)\left\{z_i'\gamma + \sigma_\varepsilon\left[\phi(z_i'\gamma / \sigma_\varepsilon) / \Phi(z_i'\gamma / \sigma_\varepsilon)\right]\right\},$$

where σ_ε is the estimated conditional error variance in the latent dependent variable of the Tobit model. The distributional assumptions of the Tobit model may be somewhat overly restrictive, since the fitted trips tend to overestimate the actual trips by a small amount in all four cases.

Models for total trips correcting for nonresponse problems

Table 8.5 gives results for total trips models analogous to those displayed in Table 8.4, but now these total trips models are estimated jointly with the parameters of a response/nonresponse model unique to that survey version. The response/nonresponse portions of each of these four models are distinct from the model presented in Table 8.2 in two ways. First, as noted above, the overall sample size has been slightly reduced and, second, there are no cross-version restrictions on the coefficients of the response/nonresponse models. Like the trips models, the response/nonresponse models are now estimated separately for each survey version.

---

[10] Keeping in mind that the aggregate total of all types of water-based recreation is being modelled in this illustrative application (sight-seeing, camping, picnicking, etc., not just fishing trips, for example), the fishing license and boat-ownership dummy variables are less likely to be completely jointly determined with the dependent TRIPS variable.

Table 8.5 FIML Joint Estimates of Response Submodel and Total Trips Submodels

VARIABLE	VERSION 1	VERSION 2	VERSION 3	VERSION 4
Probit Response Submodel				
CONSTANT	0.042	-0.141	-0.263	-0.386
	(0.19)	(-0.59)	-1.07)	(-1.84)*
ADJACENT_COUNTIES	-0.193	-0.281	0.0439	0.0142
(1=yes, 0=no)	(-1.98)	(-2.23)**	(0.39)	(0.12)
PHASE_1	0.321	0.00715	0.195	0.198
(1=yes, 0=no)	(1.43)	(0.04)	(1.75)*	(1.48)
KNOWN_USER	0.405	0.425	0.741	0.942
(1=yes, 0=no)	(2.68)**	(2.66)**	(5.10)**	(5.57)**
DIST_WATER_1	-0.548	-0.622	-0.117	-0.375
('000 miles)	(-2.68)**	(-2.47)**	(-1.24)	(-3.01)**
DIST_WATER_2	-0.0508	0.241	-0.183	0.0906
('000 miles)	(-0.19)	(0.37)	(-1.64)	(0.39)
DIST_WATER_3	1.19	0.0991	-0.0334	-0.110
('000 miles)	(3.51)**	(0.17)	(-0.58)	(-0.46)
DIST_WATER_4	-1.32	-0.0537	-[a]	0.259
('000 miles)	(-2.99)**	(-0.69)		(2.27)**
DIST_OTHER_WATER	0.618	0.384	0.374	-0.0856
('000 miles)	(3.51)**	(2.23)**	(1.79)*	(-0.33)
PROP_LANGUAGE_ISOLATED	6.95	-3.74	-5.05	-4.58
(in zip code)	(0.52)	(-0.39)	(-1.19)	(-1.15)

Note: [a] Version 3 contained only three "focal waters." See footnotes to Table 8.1 for the identities of numbered waters.

Table 8.5 continued

VARIABLE	VERSION 1	VERSION 2	VERSION 3	VERSION 4
PROP_PUBLIC_INCOME	-1.31	-0.758	-4.81	-6.24
(in zip code)	(-0.36)	(-0.24)	(-2.18)**	(-3.81)**
PROP_URBAN_AREAS	0.0890	0.180	0.255	0.208
(in zip code)	(0.50)	(1.29)	(2.42)**	(2.44)**
PROP_RESOURCE_OCCUP	0.911	-0.459	1.54	1.83
(in zip code)	(0.35)	(-0.26)	(1.36)	(1.76)*
PROP_SS_INCOME	-0.284	1.32	1.11	1.49
(in zip code)	(-0.26)	(1.27)	(1.37)	(2.45)**
Tobit Trips Submodel				
CONSTANT	-15.4	-7.83	-6.93	-21.6
	(-1.24)	(-0.87)	(-1.36)	(-4.16)**
ADJACENT_COUNTIES	9.43	11.6	8.04	4.40
(1=yes, 0=no)	(2.44)**	(3.10)**	(7.04)**	(1.66)*
PHASE_1	4.69	3.10	-0.241	3.35
(1=yes, 0=no)	(0.75)	(0.41)	(-0.10)	(0.80)
KNOWN_USER	23.8	16.1	7.74	22.6
(1=yes, 0=no)	(6.19)**	(3.35)**	(2.49)**	(6.98)**
AVG_DISTANCE	-46.7	-60.5	-12.9	-101.
('000 miles)	(-4.17)**	(-2.98)**	(-3.12)**	(-5.64)**
HAVE_INCOME_DATA	-1.45	6.14	1.07	-1.50
(1=yes, 0=no)	(-0.47)	(1.81)*	(0.66)	(-0.75)

INCOME	51.1	4.97	16.2	63.7
($'00,000)	(1.12)	(0.10)	(0.73)	(2.94)**
HAVE_AGE_DATA	35.4	11.3	8.61	13.0
(1=yes, 0=no)	(2.96)**	(1.50)	(3.15)**	(3.01)**
AGE	-3.94	-0.682	-1.36	-1.83
(decades)	(-5.62)**	(-0.97)	(-3.95)**	(-4.28)**
FISHING_LICENSE?	5.55	7.59	3.91	6.37
(1=yes, 0=no)	(2.05)**	(3.00)**	(3.13)**	(4.75)**
OWN_BOAT?	6.72	7.66	6.03	7.05
(1=yes, 0=no)	(3.12)**	(3.06)**	(4.61)**	(5.34)**
σ	20.5	22.3	11.4	20.8
	(14.47)**	(7.87)**	(9.08)**	(33.19)**
Error Correlation:				
ρ	-0.442	-0.619	-0.387	0.974
	(-2.23)**	(-3.55)**	(-1.22)	(59.9)**
$\log \mathcal{L}$	-2222.125	-2262.309	-2794.263	-2910.639
Trips (fitted/actual)	17.2/10.1	19.4/9.15	6.40/3.56	3.02/5.76
Trips (fitted/actual) general pop. sample	6.54/3.02 n = 98	9.84/2.50 n = 154	3.73/1.48 n = 346	0.88/1.18 n = 377

How do the response/nonresponse portions of these jointly estimated models vary across survey versions? Membership in the "Adjacent Counties" subsample matters for Versions 1 and 2, but not for the others. "Phase 1" subsample membership matters (marginally) only for Version 3. As expected, the "Known User" subsamples have strongly higher response rates for all four versions. Four of the five distance variables matter for Version 1, but only one or two of them matter for the other versions. None of the zip code Census variables matters for response/nonresponse for Versions 1 and 2, but some or most of them make a difference in Versions 3 and 4. So it appears that the cross-version parameter restrictions embodied in the results displayed in Table 8.2 may be excessive.

To cut directly to the chase, however, the key results for Table 8.5 are at the end of the table: the estimates of the error correlation, ρ, between the response submodel and the total trips submodel. If ρ is zero, there is no correlation between the error terms in the two parts of the model and there should be no distortion in any of the parameters of the total trips model due to survey nonresponse. What happens in these four examples? For Versions 1, 2, and 3, the estimate of ρ is negative, and it is strongly statistically different from zero for Versions 1 and 2. For Version 4, however, the estimate of ρ is very large and positive (0.974) and very significantly different from zero (with an asymptotic t-ratio of almost 60).

When the ρ parameter is negative, it means that failure to control for nonresponse will lead to *under*estimates of the number of trips. For Versions 1 and 2, our models suggest the presence of unobserved factors which make targeted households *less likely* to respond to our questionnaire than our response model predicts. These factors also make them *more likely* to take water-based recreational trips than our trips models would predict. In this case, the endogenous survey complexity effect appears to dominate: infrequent participants and non-users of these waters may have found it far easier to fill in our questionnaire. Rather than remembering numbers of trips to each site in different months, these people would simply have to fill in a lot of zeros. In contrast, people who engage in frequent trips for water recreation may have found the amount and detail of information required from them to be sufficiently great that they chose not to fill out and return the survey at all.[11]

It is worth emphasizing again that the finding of a negative error correlation is at odds with the common presumption (in the absence of any attempt to model nonresponse) that survey topic salience typically causes households with *higher* participation in an activity to be *more* likely to respond to surveys about that activity, biasing *upwards* the apparent aggregate activity level. But if higher participation also means the survey response task is markedly more difficult or time-consuming, this deterrent effect could easily outweigh the salience of the

[11] We owe this eminently sensible explanation to Michael Hanemann.

survey topic. Clearly, researchers must be cautious about assuming the net effects of nonresponse when the complexity of the survey completion task is endogenously determined.

How do the implications of the trip-taking portions of the models in Table 8.5 differ from the corresponding results in Table 8.4, without nonresponse correction? As expected given the strongly significant negative coefficients on this term for versions 1 and 2, the fitted expected numbers of trips controlling for systematic nonresponse are markedly different from the observed numbers of trips in the respondent sample. The models in Table 8.5 imply that samples without systematic nonresponse would have predicted much higher numbers of trips on average, and therefore greater aggregate utilization of the resource than implied by any demand model ignoring the selectivity problem. The differences are summarized in the last two rows of Table 8.5. Corrected average trips to the waters described in Version 1 are 17.2 (not 11.6), and trips to the waters of Version 2 average 19.4 (not 10.1). If we restrict our attention to the core general population subsample, corrected trips are 6.54 (not 3.84) for Version 1, and 9.84 (not 3.46) for Version 2.

What accounts for the different implications from Table 8.4 and Table 8.5 for Versions 1 and 2? First, the intercept parameters in the total trips models are markedly different between the uncorrected and corrected models. This amounts to a shift in the position of the implied demand curve. For version 2, the change in the coefficient on AVG_DISTANCE may also be important. To the extent that this variable serves as a proxy for price, we may also be seeing a change in the slope of the demand curve (and therefore in demand elasticity) when the nonresponse correction is undertaken. For Version 1, the point estimates suggest that the corrected demand is somewhat more price-responsive, while for Version 2, the corrected model suggests lesser price-responsiveness. Note that changes in the position and orientation of the estimated demand relationship will certainly translate into changes in the welfare calculations associated with the estimated model. In these two cases, welfare analyses for the waters featured in Versions 1 and 2 (with failure to correct for nonresponse bias) would result in potentially serious underestimates of the social value of these resources.

We have noted that for Version 4, the ρ estimate is large and positive and very significant. In this case, unobserved attributes that make respondents take *more* total trips than we would otherwise expect also lead them to be *more* likely to respond than we would anticipate based on their observed characteristics. For this group, we tentatively conclude that the survey topic salience effect outweighs the endogenous survey complexity effect. It seems plausible that this might be the case, relative to Versions 1 and 2, because of the smaller numbers of trips taken to the sites emphasized in Version 4. Of course, we have just argued that the observed numbers of trips to each site are biased by nonresponse. However, if most potential respondents to Version 4 have taken only a small number of trips to the sites featured on that version, the task of completing the questionnaire is not terribly daunting for any of them.

For Version 4, the nonresponse-corrected fitted number of trips is 3.02 (as opposed to 6.65 in the uncorrected model). For the core general population sample, corrected trips are only 0.88 (rather than 2.28). Systematically higher response rates for more-active users of these waters appear to have biased upward the apparent demand for those sites. Welfare analysis based on the uncorrected estimates would overstate (rather than understate) the social value of these less-visited waters.

8.6 CONCLUSIONS AND SUGGESTIONS FOR SUBSEQUENT MAIL-SURVEY-BASED RESEARCH

We have demonstrated that nonrandom nonresponse to a mail survey has the potential to cause substantial distortion in empirical estimates of subsequent econometric models. Researchers undertake surveys such as these in order to quantify the characteristics of demand for some nonmarket good for some target population. The goal might be merely to measure current demand and/or values (consumer's surplus) associated with a particular site. Or, the task may be more ambitious—perhaps to assess likely changes in use, or changes in values or consumer's surplus, when some attribute of the site(s) is changed. For any of these tasks, it is essential to be able to argue that the estimating sample is representative of the population from which it is drawn. Total use or value is obtained by scaling the results from the estimating sample up to the relevant population. With a biased sample, such a simple scaling will produce invalid results.

Our available illustrative sample of data is far from ideal for truly detailed utility-theoretic demand modeling of environmental values. Nevertheless, the persistent tendency for apparently nontrivial biases in key parameter estimates, even in a simplistic demand model, certainly leads one to suspect that analogous biases would be possible in more sophisticated demand and/or utility specifications implemented with richer data. This inference can readily be extended beyond the boundaries of environmental valuation to most other types of studies using mail survey data.

The main contribution of this chapter is its demonstration that differences across individuals in both survey topic salience and endogenous survey complexity can influence survey response propensities and lead to nonresponse bias in demand function estimation, and therefore also in welfare analysis. However, we have shown that reliance on little more than the zip code information available for each household in the target sample allows one to reconstruct a selection of variables that are potentially useful in response/nonresponse discrete choice models. Since our surveys ask respondents to consider environmental goods at specific identifiable geographical locations, distance is likely to be related to the salience of the good. Distance is also related to activity levels, since it is a primary determinant of access costs.

We also rely on the 1990 Census, aggregated to the level of zip codes, to provide crude measures of the socio-demographic characteristics of each potential respondent's neighborhood. We can also control for membership in different types of subsamples. In our example, many of these Census variables are shown to make a statistically significant contribution to explaining a potential respondent's propensity to complete and return our questionnaire. Similar geographic or socio-demographic considerations or convenience samples will be present in many other types of surveys and the implications of our example extend to any study using these data.

It would have been advantageous to have access to additional variables for this study. In some cases of environmental valuation, for example, it may be possible to solicit from each state information on the numbers of fishing licenses per zip code and/or the number of licensed boat trailers per zip code (for example).[12] One must assume that the direct mail advertising industry also knows a lot about the preferences of US residents by zip code. While such data are unlikely to be free, it may be possible to acquire data on the number of subscribers to certain publications by zip code, or membership in certain organizations. A selection of such zip code frequency variables could paint an even more informative picture of probable survey topic salience or relevant activity levels.

We recommend the use of full information maximum likelihood methods to estimate simultaneously both the response/nonresponse models and the activity level model for respondents. Further experimental survey research seems warranted in order to distinguish more clearly between factors that affect survey salience and others that determine endogenous survey complexity. Here, we can only infer that one or the other effect dominates based on the sign of the error correlation parameter. It is tempting to speculate on the feasibility of more-general models that might make the error correlation ρ across the response and activity equations vary systematically over different types of potential respondents.

Implementing a minimal model of response/nonresponse requires only that sufficient geographic information be retained for the entire intended sample.

---

[12] We use individual data on fishing licenses and boat ownership available for the respondent sample in the demand portion of our two-stage modelling exercise, but analogous zip code level variables could also contribute substantially to capturing the salience of water-recreation issues to the overall target population.

Researchers must also have access to recent Census data at a corresponding level of aggregation, as well as relevant distance-calculating software.

What is our recommendation? Any researcher using mail survey data should be strongly encouraged to *plan for*, and then to undertake, explicit modeling of response/nonresponse to his or her survey instrument in a manner analogous to that presented here. This is especially important if one expects considerable heterogeneity in the socio-demographic characteristics of potential respondents, or if geographical proximity to the place(s) or object(s) featured in the subject matter of the survey varies substantially across potential respondents. It is also important if there are different versions of the survey, or if portions of the working sample consist of nonrandom convenience samples appended to a base sample that is reasonably representative. The key insight is that *without* formal nonresponse modeling and correction, the default presumption must be that substantial nonresponse biases could easily be present in any statistical work conducted using only a sample of mail survey *respondents*. Furthermore, if survey complexity is endogenous, it is not even possible to sign these potential biases ex ante. These biases can distort not only estimates of the level or elasticity of demand in the population, but also estimates of the degree of substitutability among goods and overall welfare calculations.

APPENDIX: TABLE 8.6

Table 8.6 Candidate Census Variables for Response/Nonresponse Probit Submodel

ACRONYM	CONSTRUCTION FROM STANDARD CENSUS STF3 VARIABLES	INTERPRETATION
PERSONS	P1_1	Population of zip code area
PROP_URBAN_AREAS	P6_1/P1_1	Proportion residing in urban areas
PROP_WHITE	P8_1/P1_1	Proportion White ethnic
PROP_BLACK	P8_2/P1_1	Proportion Black ethnic
PROP_AMIN	P8_3/P1_1	Proportion Native American ethnic
PROP_ASIAN	P8_4/P1_1	Proportion Asian ethnic
PROP_OTHER	P8_5/P1_1	Proportion other ethnicity
PROP_LANGUAGE_ISOLATED	(P29_2+P29_4+P29_6)/P1_1	Proportion language-isolated
PROP_LONGTERM_RESIDENT	P43_1/P1_1	Proportion long-term resident (same dwelling in 1985)
PROP_COLLEGE_EDUC	(P60_6+P60_7)/P1_1	Proportion college-educated
PROP_RESOURCE_INDUST	P77_1/P1_1	Proportion in agriculture, fishing or forestry industries
PROP_RESOURCE_OCCUP	P78_9/P1_1	Proportion in agriculture, fishing or forestry occupations
PROP_SS_INCOME	P94_1/P1_1	Proportion on social security income
PROP_PUBINC_INCOME	P95_1/P1_1	Proportion on public assistance income
PROP_RETIRE_INCOME	P96_1/P1_1	Proportion with retirement income
MEDIAN_HHLD_INCOME	P80A_1/1000	Median household income ($'000)
MEDIAN_RENT	H43A_1/1000	Median rental rate ($'000)
MEDIAN_HOUSE_VALUE	H61A_1/1000	Median house value ($'000)

REFERENCES

Ayal, I. and Hornik, J. (1986) "Foreign Source Effects and Response Behavior in Cross-National Mail Surveys," *International Journal of Research in Marketing*, **3**, pp. 157–67.

Callaway, J.M., Ragland, S., Keefe, S., Cameron, T.A., Shaw, W.D. (1995) *Columbia River System Operation Review Recreation Impacts: Demand Model and Simulation Results*, report prepared for U.S. Army Corps of Engineers, Portland Oregon, by Hagler Bailly Consulting, Inc., Boulder, CO.

Cameron, T.A., Shaw, W.D., Ragland, S.R., Callaway, J.M., and Keefe, S. (1996) "Using Actual and Contingent Behavior Data with Differing Levels of Time Aggregation to Model Recreation Demand," *Journal of Agricultural and Resource Economics*, 21(1), 130–49.

Dillman, D.A. (1978) *Mail and Telephone Surveys: The Total Design Method*, New York: Wiley.

Dillman, D.A., Dillman, J.J., and Makela, C.J. (1984) "The Importance of Adhering to Details of the Total Design Method (TDM) for Mail Surveys," in D.C Lockhart (ed.) *Making Effective Use of Mailed Questionnaires. New Directions for Program Evaluation*, no. 21. San Francisco: Jossey-Bass.

Edwards, S.F. and Anderson, G.D. (1987) "Overlooked Biases in Contingent Valuation Surveys: Some Considerations," *Land Economics*, 63(2), 168–78.

Englin, J., Shonkwiler, J.S., and Shaw, W.D. (1996) "Count Models with Self-Selectivity Corrections: An Application to Recreational Demand Modeling," manuscript, Department of Applied Economics and Statistics, University of Nevada, Reno, NV 89557.

Fisher, Mark R. (1996) "Estimating the Effect of Nonresponse Bias on Angler Surveys," *Transactions of the American Fisheries Society*, 125, 118–26.

Fox, R.J., Crask, M.R., and Kim, J. (1988) "Mail Survey Response Rate: A Meta-Analysis of Selected Techniques for Inducing Response," *Public Opinion Quarterly*, 52, 467–91.

Goyder, J. (1985) "Nonresponse on Surveys: A Canada-United States Comparison," *Canadian Journal of Sociology*, 10(3), 231–51.

Greene, W.H. (1993) *Econometric Analysis*, New York: Macmillan.

Greene, W.H. (1995) *LIMDEP: User's Manual and Reference Guide*, Version 7.0. Bellport, NY: Econometric Software, Inc.

Heberlein, T. and Baumgartner, R. (1978) "Factors Affecting Response Rates to Mailed Questionnaires: A Quantitative Analysis of the Published Literature," *American Sociological Review*, 43, 447–62.

Hellerstein, D., Woo, D., McCollum, D., and Donnelly, D. (1993) *ZIPFIP: A ZIP and FIPS Database Users Manual*, Economic Research Service (ERA-NASS), 340 Victory Drive, Herndon, VA 22070 (1-800-999-6779).

Jobber, D., Mizra, H., and Wee, K.H. (1991) "Incentives and Response Rates to Cross-National Business Surveys: A Logit Model Analysis," *Journal of International Business Studies*, 711–21.

Jobber, D. and Saunders, J. (1988) "An Experimental Investigation into Cross-National Mail Survey Response Rates," *Journal of International Business Studies*, 483–89.

McDaniel, S.W., Madden, C.S., and Verille, P. (1987) "Do Topic Differences Affect Survey Nonresponse?" *Journal of the Market Research Society*, **29** (1), 55–66.

Mitchell, R.C. and Carson, R.T. (1989) *Using Surveys to Value Public Goods: The Contingent Valuation Method*. Washington, DC: Resources for the Future.

Whitehead, J.C. (1991) "Environmental Interest Group Behavior and Self-Selection Bias in Contingent Valuation Mail Surveys," *Growth and Change*, 22(1), 10–21.

Whitehead, J.C., Groothuis, P.A., and Blomquist, G.C. (1993) "Testing for Nonresponse and Sample Selection Bias in Contingent Valuation; Analysis of a Combination Phone/Mail Survey," *Economics Letters* 41, 215–20.

Wiseman, F. and Billington, M. (1984) "Comment on a Standard Definition of Response Rates," *Journal of Marketing Research*, 21, 336–38.

9. Recreation Demand Systems for Multiple Site Count Data Travel Cost Models

J.S. Shonkwiler[1]

9.1 INTRODUCTION

Recreation demand modeling is an important element of natural resource planning. Behavioral responses and valuations of recreationists are often used as components of benefit–cost analysis or environmental impact assessment. The travel cost model which defines a demand function for a recreation site has been employed by economists since the early 1960s (Smith, 1989). Yet a number of theoretical and empirical problems encompass the travel cost model. These include issues involving the count data structure of the dependent demand quantity and the treatment of multiple sites in the empirical specification. These two complications partly explain why typically analysts have relied on the random utility model (RUM) rather than the travel cost model to represent the individual's allocation of trips to a set of recreation sites.

Single site count data travel cost models have become increasingly more common (Hellerstein, 1991; Englin and Shonkwiler, 1995) as economists have recognized that travel cost studies permit demand to vary according to the traits of individual participants or participant groups. Further, recreation visitation data are subject to the fact that each respondent will report a discrete number of trips. The application of count data estimators (Johnson *et al.*, 1992) to the travel cost model thus is a logical extension to accommodate the particular properties of trip data. The study by Hellerstein and Mendelsohn (1993) provides theoretical foundations for linking the empirical count estimator to

---

[1] Professor, Applied Economics and Statistics Department, University of Nevada, Reno, Nevada 89557, (702) 784-1341. Comments by Daniel Hellerstein, Jeffrey Englin and Douglass Shaw are appreciated. Discussions with and research materials provided by Jeffrey LaFrance are gratefully acknowledged. Research supported by the Nevada Agricultural Experiment Station via Western Regional Research Project W-133. The U.S. Army Corps of Engineers, Bureau of Reclamation, and Bonneville Power Association provided funding for the collection of data.

the individual consumer's underlying optimization problem. Both Hellerstein and Mendelsohn (1993) and Haab and McConnell (1996) discuss methods for measuring consumer surplus under a variety of count data specifications so it is clear how to perform welfare analysis on the basis of a single equation count demand model for trips.

Yet a single, independent recreational site rarely exists. The proper evaluation of policy changes may require a systems approach if several sites are impacted simultaneously. Or if similar recreational experiences can be obtained at sources near a single recreation site of interest, there may be a high degree of substitutability among such sites. Although most travel cost studies to date have assumed independence in order to estimate demand, researchers recognize the probable important interdependencies of demands for sites due to the pioneering work of Burt and Brewer (1971). Subsequent studies by Cicchetti *et al.* (1976) and Sellar *et al.* (1985) have provided additional evidence to justify a systems approach. Unfortunately, travel cost analyses of household (or individual) demands for multiple recreational goods have not accounted for the discrete, non-negative integer characterization of trip data. The single published exception is the recent study by Ozuna and Gomez (1994). Ozuna and Gomez, however, adopt a highly restrictive econometric model that cannot accommodate overdispersion or negative covariances between equations, and they fail to recognize that welfare analysis in a systems context is altered when conditional expected demands have an exponential form.

This study attempts to synthesize the elements necessary to appropriately treat multiple site travel cost models of recreation demand when the decision variables are measured as trip counts. A flexible, multivariate count data probability model is adopted from the generalized linear modeling treatment of longitudinal data and modified to account for different levels of overdispersion in different equations. Because this model generates conditional demands with exponential form, a proper incomplete demand structure (LaFrance and Hanemann, 1989) will be imposed to insure that exact welfare analysis can be performed. The proposed techniques will then be applied to an empirical model of visits to four reservoirs on the Columbia River.

This chapter proceeds by first comparing and contrasting multiple site travel cost models to the RUM model. Next a utility theoretic foundation for the multiple site travel cost model with expected demand of exponential form is shown to exist in the form of a system of incomplete demands. Given the specifications implied by the incomplete demand system, the generalized estimating equations for multivariate count data are developed. Finally an empirical application is presented.

9.2 RUMS VS. MULTIPLE SITE TRAVEL COST MODELS

A conventional recreation site choice model is the multinomial logit model of McFadden (1974, 1998). McFadden's multinomial logit model possesses useful properties for analyzing the site allocation problem because visitation data are discrete and the model can be easily used to estimate exact per-trip welfare measures for site quality changes (we ignore the additional and tangential issue of allowance for income effects here). This model, while quite popular because of its attractive features in dealing with multiple sites, limits consideration of seasonal welfare changes due to the fact that the multinomial logit's site-specific demands are estimated conditional on total demand for all sites. Many recreation modelers have raised the point that consumer's surplus measures should come from some aggregate or unconditional demand function rather than from the site-specific conditional demands, because the former allows total seasonal consumption to change in response to site quality and price changes and the latter does not.

Intuitively, when one only has per-trip welfare measures, some assumption must be made about whether and how these can be added together to arrive at a welfare measure that can be interpreted as an annual (seasonal) maximum willingness to pay (WTP) to bring about some change. One line of research has sought to link the RUM with an aggregate demand quantity (Bockstael *et al.*, 1987, Feather *et al.*, 1995; Parsons and Kealy, 1995; Hausman *et al.*, 1995). Substantial attention has been devoted to determining the appropriate aggregate price to use in the aggregate demand equation when site-specific demands have been modeled using the multinomial logit specification. However, recent work by Shonkwiler and Shaw (1997), Smith (1997), and Smith and Von Haefen (1997) suggests the aggregate price indexes being proposed do not provide a utility theoretic link between the RUM and the aggregate demand equation.

The foregoing discussion leads to recognition of the fact that the data necessary to specify a random utility model are typically detailed enough to provide information on site-specific demands. In this situation the data are rich enough to allow calculation of a travel cost model to each individual recreation site, and it seems logical that this information should be exploited when developing models for multiple sites. The necessary techniques to accomplish such modeling consist of a demand system that allows calculation of unconditional welfare measures and a proper econometric technique to accommodate the discrete nature of the demand quantities.

9.3 INCOMPLETE DEMAND SYSTEMS

Specification of a system of demand equations naturally leads to the implications of consumer choice theory for assessing the structure imposed. As LaFrance (1990) has pointed out, three practical approaches can be considered for the demand system specification. First, broad aggregates of all goods available to the consumer can be used to reflect all choices in the consumption set. Second, separability can be imposed so that conditional demand equations involving a subset of commodities can be estimated. Third, an incomplete system of demand equations can be specified. Obviously, the first approach is unsatisfactory because interest is focused on individual commodities. The second approach suffers from (i) uncertainty as to the true nature of separability, (ii) not identifying the overall utility function but only a subutility function, and (iii) the interdependence between quantities demanded and group expenditure. This latter condition is exacerbated when many households have zero demands and consequently zero groupwise expenditure. Thus, substantial simultaneous equations bias would likely be encountered.

The incomplete demand system specification is an attractive alternative only if the preference structure it identifies is consistent with rational models of consumer behavior. Incomplete demand models can be related to an underlying utility maximization subject to a linear budget constraint and can be used to conduct proper welfare analysis (LaFrance and Hanemann, 1989). The incomplete demand structures that are consistent with such maximizing behavior were first catalogued in LaFrance and Hanemann (1984) for some common functional forms of demand equations. In the case of linear expected demands, the restrictions required for integrability are zero (or essentially zero) income effects and a symmetric negative definite cross price matrix. Burt and Brewer (1971) as well as Seller *et al.* (1985) imposed cross-equation symmetry of the price coefficients. Hence both studies imposed restrictions generally consistent with those suggested by a linear incomplete demand system. However, because both studies modeled discrete household demand data with linear models, their welfare calculations were compromised by their assumption that demands were continuously distributed.

Ozuna and Gomez specified a bivariate travel cost model using a discrete model proposed by Holgate. This model only admits positive or zero correlations between equations. They tested symmetric cross-equation price effects and stated that this is a necessary condition for path independence of the line integral used to compute the welfare effects of price changes. Clearly this is a requisite condition when expected demands have a linear form, but Ozuna and Gomez specified their expected Marshallian demands with an exponential form. That is they specified expected demand for the jth site ($j=1, 2, ..., k, ... J$) to have the form

$$E(q_j) = \exp\left(a_j + \sum_{k=1}^{J} \beta_{jk} p_k + \gamma_j I\right),$$

where the p_k denote the prices of the individual sites, I represents household income, and the observational subscript has been suppressed. They then imposed the restrictions that $\beta_{jk} = \beta_{kj}$. However the Slutsky symmetry conditions for this uncompensated model are $\beta_{jk} q_j + \gamma_j q_j q_k = \beta_{kj} q_k + \gamma_k q_j q_k$. So, irrespective of whether the γ_j are essentially zero, symmetry will generally not hold unless $\beta_{jk} = \beta_{kj} = 0$. Hence they should have tested for the absence of Marshallian cross-equation price effects—not their symmetry.

As mentioned, demand models which are based on an optimization hypothesis and which are applied to a subset of goods typically assume preferences are separable—thus allowing the analysis to focus on demand models for the goods of interest apart from other goods. The budget allocated to this group of separable goods is assumed known and the system yields only partial welfare measures. This can be contrasted with the key assumption of an incomplete demand system: prices outside the set of goods of interest do not vary. If this maintained hypothesis is reasonable, then unconditional welfare measures can be computed from a properly specified incomplete demand system. Given that prices of other goods are constant, the utility maximization problem under a linear budget constraint yields a system of incomplete demands which satisfy Slutsky symmetry and provide exact welfare measures for price changes of the goods of interest.

The functional form assumed for modeling the relationship between expected demands and conditioning variables will dictate the restrictions necessary to assure that the incomplete demand system satisfies proper integrability conditions. Fortunately, LaFrance and Hanemann (1984) have considered a number of functional forms and have detailed the restrictions consistent with integrability. In the empirical example which follows, their Log II specification is adopted. Consequently this particular functional form will be used to illustrate the incomplete demand system approach.

Assume that site-specific expected demands take the form

$$E(q_j) = \alpha_j \exp\left(\sum_{j=1}^{J} \beta_{jk} p_k\right) I^{\gamma_j} \tag{9.1}$$

where again I denotes household income and the observational index has been suppressed. One set of restrictions consistent with an incomplete demand system of this form is (LaFrance and Hanemann, 1984) $\alpha_j > 0, \beta_{jj} < 0, \beta_{jk} = 0 \; \forall j \neq k$ and $\gamma_j = \gamma \; \forall j$. These restrictions result in this Log II incomplete demand system having J free own-price parameters and one income coefficient. Therefore there are (J^2-1) price and income parameter restrictions implied by this functional form if it is to be consistent with the optimizing behavior underlying the incomplete demands. Although the restrictions imposed on this incomplete demand system appear severe, the requirement of zero Marshallian cross-price effects is largely unavoidable when adopting a model of expected demand that yields non-negative predicted demands. In contrast, linear specification of expected demand with symmetric cross-price coefficients and no income effects would result in a properly specified incomplete system—but at the cost of ignoring the discrete nature of the observed demand data and possibly predicting negative expected demand. Clearly this is a tradeoff that the analyst needs to consider.

Note that the Log II specification is much less restrictive than that of the standard conditional multinomial logit model which does not admit different own price coefficients, income, or other individual-specific shifters. Of course the logit model may be generalized to permit individual-specific characteristics when these are interacted with prices or site characteristics. On the other hand, allowing for differing price coefficients across sites can result in considerable complications (McFadden, 1998).

Individual-specific factors can enter the incomplete demand model and still satisfy the integrability restriction that $\alpha_j > 0$ by recognizing that we can specify $\alpha_j = \exp(a_j)$ where a_j is itself a function of conditioning variables which may correspond to an individual or household. Also since $I^\gamma = \exp(\gamma \ln I)$ we can rewrite the restricted model as $E(q_j) = \exp(a_j + \beta_j p_j + \gamma \ln I)$. The quasi-indirect utility function and expenditure function associated with this demand system are (LaFrance and Hanemann,1984)

$$u(p,I) = \frac{I^{1-\gamma}}{1-\gamma} - \sum_{j=1}^{J} \frac{\exp(a_j + \beta_j p_j)}{\beta_j} \tag{9.2}$$

and

$$e(p,u) = \left[(1-\gamma)\left(u + \sum_{j=1}^{J} \frac{\exp(a_j + \beta_j p_j)}{\beta_j}\right)\right]^{\frac{1}{1-\gamma}}. \tag{9.3}$$

It is apparent that the restricted specification explicitly rules out cross-price effects in the Marshallian site-specific demands. Note, however, that this does not imply a total lack of substitution between sites. The underlying Hicksian demands can be analyzed to determine the compensated cross-price effects. In fact it is likely that specific recreation sites are substitutes and the degree of substitution, s_{jk}, can be expressed by recognizing that the Slutsky equation for the Log II model has the form

$$s_{jk} = \frac{\gamma q_j q_k}{I}$$

which is non-negative if the coefficient on income is positive.

9.4 GENERALIZED LINEAR MODELS

We now focus on the statistical consequences of estimating a multivariate count data system with across equation parameter restrictions. Aitchison and Ho (1989) have pointed out that statistical analysis of multivariate counts has been largely ignored because of a lack of models which are flexible enough to accommodate both overdispersion (defined as the conditional variance being greater than the conditional mean) and the possibility of negative correlations between equations. They proposed compounding independent Poisson marginals with the multivariate log normal distribution. Aitchison and Ho called this the multivariate Poisson-log normal distribution because each equation's Poisson parameter was modeled as log normally distributed with unique mean, variance, and non-zero covariances with other location parameters. This approach was used by Shonkwiler (1995), but the estimation complexities encountered rule out its generalization to more than a small number of sites due to the presence of *J* integrals in the log likelihood function for a *J* equation system.

Instead we outline a modeling approach which had been widely embraced in the biometrics literature. Because most economists are unfamiliar with the generalized linear modeling methodology popularized by McCullagh and Nelder (1989), this discussion is aimed to be of a tutorial nature. We begin by considering the univariate case with a single response (dependent) variable y_i (i=1, 2, ..., N) which has expected value μ_i. This expected value is related to conditioning variables via a link function such that $\mu_i = f(X_i\beta)$, where X_i is the ith row of a $N\times k$ matrix and β is a k-element vector of unknown parameters. Each response is assumed to be independent. If the N-element vector of response variables, y, is characterized by a probability distribution that is a member of the linear exponential family (Gourieroux *et al.*, 1984), then a number of properties hold (McCullagh and Nelder, 1989). Primary among these properties is the result that if the conditional mean is properly specified, then maximum likelihood estimation of the β parameters yields consistent estimators even under distributional misspecification.

Consider the log likelihood, ℓ, of a univariate linear exponential model which could represent the normal regression model, the Poisson regression model, or the gamma regression model (Gourieroux *et al.*, 1994). The gradient of the log likelihood of a univariate linear exponential model when evaluated for the ith observation is given by the derivative $\partial \ell_i / \partial \beta = g_i = d_i' v_i^{-1}(y_i - \mu_i)$ where

$$v_i = Var(y_i) \text{ and } d_i = \partial \mu_i / \partial \beta' = [\partial \mu_i / \partial \beta_1 \vdots \partial \mu_i / \partial \beta_2 \vdots \cdots \vdots \partial \mu_i / \partial \beta_k].$$

It is assumed that v_i either depends upon known parameters or upon μ_i. Recognize that this gradient does not require knowledge of the underlying likelihood function. It is only necessary to know how the conditional mean depends on the parameter vector β and the form of the conditional variance. Maximum likelihood estimation of the vector β is accomplished by solving the k first order conditions

$$g = \sum_{i=1}^{N} g_i = 0.$$

The (negative) of the second derivative of the log likelihood is given by the expression $\partial^2 \ell_i / \partial \beta \partial \beta' = H_i = d_i' v_i^{-1} d_i$. Again note the simple form the hessian takes when the statistical model is a member of the linear exponential family. The outer product gradient matrix for the ith observation is defined by $M_i = d_i' v_i^{-1} (y_i - \mu_i)^2 v_i^{-1} d_i = g_i g_i'$. Variances of the estimated parameters which are robust to distributional misspecification may be constructed as (White, 1982; Gourieroux *et al.*, 1984) $V = H^{-1} M H^{-1}$ where $H = \sum H_i$ *and* $M = \sum M_i$. This robustness holds even if the form of v_i is misspecified.

To see how these results can be applied to the univariate Poisson regression model, we first adopt the traditional likelihood approach. Let λ_i take the place of μ_i, then write the log likelihood for the ith observation as $\ell_i = -\lambda_i + y_i \ln \lambda_i - \ln y_i!$ and specify the log link $\ln \lambda_i = X_i \beta$.

Straightforward differentiation of the log likelihood function yields $\partial \ell_i / \partial \beta = -\lambda_i X_i' + y_i X_i' = X_i'(y_i - \lambda_i)$ and $-\partial^2 \ell_i / \partial \beta \partial \beta' = \lambda_i X_i' X_i$. Note that these results are a consequence of operating on the Poisson log likelihood function. However it is not necessary to know the Poisson log likelihood as long as we recognize that this statistical model is a member of the linear exponential family. The only information required is knowledge of the link between the conditional mean and the parameter vector and the form of the conditional variance. So if the same log link, $\ln \lambda = X_i \beta$, is adopted and if $V(y_i) = v_i = \lambda_i$, then the formulas for the derivatives introduced above can be applied directly. That is

$$\partial \ell_i / \partial \beta = g_i = d_i' v_i^{-1}(y_i - \mu_i) = \lambda_i X_i' \lambda_i^{-1}(y_i - \lambda_i) = X_i'(y_i - \lambda_i)$$

because $d_i = \lambda_i X_i$ and $v_i = \lambda_i$.

Similarly $-\partial^2 \ell_i / \partial\beta\partial\beta' = H_i = d_i' v_i^{-1} d_i = \lambda_i X_i' X_i$ so that the equivalence of g_i and H_i to their corresponding derivatives of the log likelihood is established. Because g_i and H_i can be determined without knowledge of the underlying log likelihood when the distribution is a member of the linear exponential family, this result then will allow us to consider more complicated models and construct quasi-maximum likelihood estimators.

The mean-variance equality required by the Poisson distribution is frequently violated by empirical data. This problem of overdispersion does not affect the consistency of the Poisson estimates of the conditional mean. Further, the variances of the estimated parameters can be consistently estimated using the formula given above. A common measure of the degree of overdispersion is given by the scale parameter σ^2 which is defined as the average of the squared Pearson residuals (McCullagh and Nelder, 1989). For the Poisson model the scale parameter is calculated as

$$\hat{\sigma}^2 = N^{-1} \sum_{i=1}^{N} \left(y_i - \hat{\lambda}_i\right)^2 / \hat{\lambda}_i.$$

An approximate test for over(under)dispersion may be conducted by comparing $N\hat{\sigma}^2$ to the right (left) tail of a χ^2 distribution with N degrees of freedom (McCullagh and Nelder, 1989). It is important to recognize that both the GLM parameters and robust standard errors are invariant to the magnitude of the scale parameter since the scale parameter defines v_i (the conditional variance of y_i) as a constant multiple of λ_i according to $v_i = \hat{\sigma}^2 \lambda_i$.

9.5 MULTIVARIATE EXTENSIONS

Now consider the case that for each observational unit or individual more than one response (dependent variable) is measured. An individual's responses are assumed to be non-negative integers and may be correlated; however the responses across individuals are still assumed to be independent. In the biometrics literature such multiple measures on an individual are called longitudinal data (Diggle *et al.*, 1994). Prentice and Mancl (1993) have noted that longitudinal data analysis is a subset of multivariate data analysis. For our purposes this generalization to multivariate data manifests itself as resulting in possibly different scale parameters across the responses of a given individual. This distinction should become clearer as the model is developed.

Liang and Zeger (1986) first extended generalized linear modeling to the longitudinal case. Here we define $\mathbf{y}_i' = \left[y_{i1}, y_{i2}, \ldots, y_{iJ}\right]$ and $\boldsymbol{\lambda}_i' = \left[\lambda_{i1}, \lambda_{i2}, \ldots, \lambda_{iJ}\right]$ to denote that there are j=1, 2, ..., J different measures (in recreation demand modeling these would be the number of visits to each of J sites) on each individual and each has a corresponding expected value of the form $\ln \lambda_{ij} = X_{ij}\beta_j$ and β_j is of dimension k_j. The derivatives of the link functions are now matrices of dimension $j \times k$ for each observation as $D_i = \partial\lambda_i / \partial\beta'$ where $\beta' = [\beta'_1, \beta'_2, \ldots, \beta'_J]$ is a row vector having K elements such that

$$K = \sum_{j=1}^{J} k_j.$$

Particular interest focuses on $V_i = Var(\mathbf{y}_i)$. Specifying V_i as a diagonal matrix implies that the responses across an individual are uncorrelated and no efficiency gains can be obtained from system-wide estimation.

For the multivariate Poisson, we extend Liang and Zeger's (1986) class of estimating equations by representing V_i as the product $V_i = A_i R A_i$ where R is a "working" correlation matrix and A_i is diagonal matrix of dimension J having as its $[j,j]$ element $\sigma_j \lambda_{ij}^{1/2}$. In a typical longitudinal analysis $\sigma_j = \sigma$ for $\forall j$, but this constraint will not be imposed. Both A_i and R are permitted to depend on the vector σ which is related to a set of unknown auxiliary parameters contained in the vector α. Consequently the $J(J-1)/2$ unknown elements in R (note that its diagonal elements are unity) comprise part of the vector α. Additionally the J (square roots of) scale parameters are the other elements of α. From this setup it is seen that, when R is an identity matrix and the scale parameters are all unity, V_i is a diagonal matrix with $[j,j]$ element λ_{ij}—the Poisson variance of y_{ij}.

The first order conditions for the estimation of the β vector now become

$$\sum_{i=1}^{N} D_i' V_i^{-1} (\mathbf{y}_i - \boldsymbol{\mu}_i) = \mathbf{0}$$

which is the multivariate analog to the sum of the gradients, g_i, given above. Similarly, a set of first order conditions is required in order to estimate the elements in α. The elements of α are functionally related to the scale parameters and correlations between responses (equations) by another link function, $\sigma = h(\alpha)$. Clearly σ must be estimated from functions of the second moments of the sample data. Call these estimated functions of the sample data $\mathbf{s}$. Liang and Zeger proposed using functions of the current Pearson residuals to provide the estimates of scale parameters and correlations of responses which would comprise $\mathbf{s}$. First $\mathbf{s}_i$ is defined for the ith observation as the data-based vector of the scale parameters, occupying the first J elements, and the unique elements of the data-based correlation matrix, occupying the next $J(J-1)/2$ elements. Thus the ith data-based contribution to the jth scale parameter is

$\left(y_{ij}-\lambda_{ij}\right)^2/\lambda_{ij}$; and its contribution to the correlation between responses (equations) j and k is $e_{ij}e_{ik}/\sigma_j\sigma_k$ where $e_{ij}=\left(y_{ij}-\lambda_{ij}\right)\lambda_{ij}^{-0.5}$.

This representation leads to the generalized estimating equations for α:

$$\sum_{i=1}^{N} \not{D}'\not{V}_i^{-1}\left(s_i-\sigma\right)=0.$$

Here the strike-through provides a link to the previous notation because $\not{D}_i=\partial\sigma/\partial\alpha'$ and $\not{V}_i$ is the "working" covariance matrix of the $\mathbf{s}_i$. Prentice and Zhao (1991), among others, have considered different specifications of $\not{V}_i$. We will return to this topic once the full model is developed.

Estimation of the vectors α and β can be accomplished simultaneously by the generalized estimating equations:

$$\mathbf{g}=\sum_{i=1}^{N}\mathbf{D}_i'\mathbf{V}_i^{-1}\mathbf{f}_i=\mathbf{0}$$

where

$$\mathbf{D}_i=\begin{pmatrix} D_i & 0 \\ 0 & \not{D}_i \end{pmatrix},\ \mathbf{V}_i=\begin{pmatrix} V_i & 0 \\ 0 & \not{V}_i \end{pmatrix} \text{ and } \mathbf{f}_i=\begin{pmatrix} \mathbf{y}_i-\lambda_i \\ \mathbf{s}_i-\sigma \end{pmatrix}.$$

Then by defining

$$\mathbf{H}=\sum_{i=1}^{N}\mathbf{D}_i'\mathbf{V}_i^{-1}\mathbf{D}_i$$

and

$$\mathbf{M}=\sum_{i=1}^{N}\mathbf{D}_i'\mathbf{V}_i^{-1}\mathbf{f}_i\mathbf{f}_i'\mathbf{V}_i^{-1}\mathbf{D}_i$$

consistent estimates of the covariances of can be obtained by $\mathbf{H}^{-1}\mathbf{M}\mathbf{H}^{-1}$ (Liang and Zeger, 1986; Prentice and Zhao, 1991). A Newton type procedure can be used to update parameter estimates from the rth to the sth iteration according to

$$\begin{pmatrix} \beta_s \\ \alpha_s \end{pmatrix}=\begin{pmatrix} \beta_r \\ \alpha_r \end{pmatrix}+\mathbf{H}_{(r)}^{-1}\mathbf{g}_{(r)}$$

where the subscript **(r)** implies that the matrix or vector is evaluated using the estimated parameters from the rth iteration. All parameters are estimated jointly and the estimation method does not require explicitly deriving first or second derivatives. In fact these derivatives are an artefact of the generalized linear model specification and the estimation algorithm takes the form of an iterated method of moments approach. Ease of estimation comes at the price of not being able to specify a log likelihood for the multivariate system because the Pearson residuals from the count data model are essentially treated as if they are normally distributed.

The generalized estimating equations presented above are not necessarily efficient because they do not take into account the covariances of $\mathbf{y}_i$ and $\mathbf{s}_i$ in the construction of $\mathbf{V}_i$. However Prentice and Mancl (1993) suggest that to avoid incurring possibly inconsistent parameter estimates due to the misspecification of this covariance that $\mathbf{V}_i$ be block diagonal. They then demonstrate that the Liang and Zeger (1986) methodology, as detailed above, has broad applicability. A final consideration is the construction of $\yen_i$, the covariance matrix of $\mathbf{s}_i$. Prentice and Zhao point out that if primary interest is centered on estimating the parameter vector β, that efficient estimators of β can still be obtained if $\yen_i$ is specified as an identity matrix. Diggle *et al.* (1994) in fact suggest the use of an identity matrix for count data and support the use of a block diagonal $\mathbf{V}_i$ matrix. They state that under the generalized estimating equation approach that has been outlined above "$\hat{\beta}$ is nearly efficient relative to maximum likelihood estimates of β in many practical situations provided that $Var(\mathbf{y}_i)$ has been reasonably approximated....When regression coefficients are the scientific focus ..., one should invest the lion's share of time in modeling the mean structure, while using a reasonable approximation to the covariance (p.144)". Of course in recreational demand modeling we devote major attention to estimating the parameters which determine mean levels of demand since the second moments have no behavioral implications nor impacts on welfare calculations.

9.6 EMPIRICAL APPLICATION

The data used to provide an empirical example of a multiple site count data travel cost model were obtained from a subset of data collected using a mail survey of a sample of individuals who live in the Pacific Northwest. The larger data set was developed to examine water allocation policy issues (see Callaway *et al.*, 1995), the most important being related to flushing salmon smolts from spawning areas down the Columbia River. The survey questionnaire focuses mainly on reservoirs on the Columbia, and we select four such reservoirs as destinations for the analysis: Lake Roosevelt, Dworshak, Lower Granite, and Lake Pend Oreille. Only actual behavior data are used, rather than the actual and contingent behavior data used by Cameron *et al.* (1996). Because travel costs to the various sites constitute the prices of trips, the analysis falls under the rubric of the travel cost model of recreation demand.

Using data on 203 randomly sampled individuals who live in the vicinty of the four reservoirs, the mean number of trips and the percent of the sample not visiting the site were for Lake Roosevelt: 2.84 and 61%; Dworshak: 0.85 and 82%; Lower Granite: 2.26 and 76%; and Lake Pend Oreille: 0.93 and 88%. These sample statistics clearly indicate the visitation data are not continuously distributed and that a count data estimator should be adopted. To insure non-negative predictions, the expected level of demand for the jth site by the ith individual is specified as $E(q_{ij}) = \exp(a_{j0} + a_{j1}Age_i + \beta_j p_{ij} + \gamma \ln I_i)$. Here the price an individual faces is defined as the round trip mileage to the site multiplied by $0.25. The logarithm of household income (in $1000s) is used as it was found to give a better fit than its untransformed representation. Of course the specification above reflects the imposition of the restrictions required by integrability. A test of whether behavior is consistent with the incomplete demand system can be constructed by allowing for non-zero cross-price effects and different income coefficients. This was accomplished by first estimating the restricted system using the multivariate generalized estimating methodology outlined above. A score test (Lagrange multiplier test) of the restrictions embodied by the incomplete demand specification was then derived. The test statistic which is asymptotically distributed as chi-squared was computed to be 28.01 with 15 degrees of freedom. Hence a test that the restrictions imposed are consistent with the data generating process cannot be rejected at the 0.01 level. It should be pointed out, however, that a Wald test of the same restrictions led to rejecting the integrability conditions at the 0.01 level. Because the unrestricted model can not be used to derive unambiguous welfare measures, only the restricted model is presented.

Estimation results are presented in Table 9.1. Note that the income term enters the model in a highly significant manner. Own price coefficients are all significantly less than zero. The age variable enters three of the equations with a negative sign suggesting that visitation rates tend to decline with age. The (square roots of) scale parameters are all significantly greater than unity—over-dispersion appears to be a feature of the data. The estimated correlation coefficients are small relative to their associated standard errors, hence equation by equation estimation may be entertained. However a caveat to univariate specifications must be recognized: the estimation method focused on obtaining efficient estimators of the conditional means, not the higher moments. Thus the reported standard errors of correlations may actually be overstated.

Finally, the model can be used to obtain welfare measures from changes in the prices of the sites. This is accomplished by first calculating the utility for each individual by evaluating the quasi-indirect utility function (9.2) at observed levels of its arguments. Next these utility levels are substituted into the

Table 9.1 Restricted System

Equation	Variable	Parameter	Estimated Parameter	Estimated Std. Error
1—Lake Roosevelt	Intercept	a_{10}	1.698	0.648
	Age	a_{11}	−0.0165	0.0085
	Price	β_{11}	−0.0524	0.0051
	Income[a]	γ	0.5034	0.1361
	Scale	σ_1	2.721	0.4457
2—Dworshak Lake	Intercept	a_{20}	0.1577	0.9161
	Age	a_{21}	0.0051	0.0150
	Price	β_{22}	−0.0590	0.0077
	Income[a]	γ	0.5034	0.1361
	Scale	σ_2	1.702	0.291
3—Lower Granite	Intercept	a_{30}	1.716	1.023
	Age	a_{31}	−0.0283	0.0173
	Price	β_{33}	−0.0638	0.0105
	Income[a]	γ	0.5034	0.1361
	Scale	σ_3	2.779	0.611
4—Lake Pend Oreille	Intercept	a_{40}	3.556	1.142
	Age	a_{41}	-0.0404	0.0237
	Price	β_{44}	-0.0765	0.0126
	Income[a]	γ	0.5034	0.1361
	Scale	σ_4	2.677	0.653
Correlation Coefficients		ρ_{12}	0.0058	0.0218
		ρ_{13}	0.0170	0.0234
		ρ_{14}	0.0774	0.0593
		ρ_{23}	-0.0353	0.0694
		ρ_{24}	-0.0253	0.0375
		ρ_{34}	-0.0407	0.0327

[a] Logarithm of household income in $1000s.

corresponding expenditure function (9.3) to provide a base expenditure for each individual. Then the welfare consequences of a change in one or more prices can be calculated by comparing how expenditures change when utility is held constant at its base level. We consider both a \$5 and infinite increase in the price of site 1—Lake Roosevelt. The average compensating variations associated with these price changes are \$12.58 and \$54.59 respectively. These measures can be compared to the consumer's surplus per-trip from a straight multinomial logit model estimated using the same data and a single parameter on the price variable. The price coefficient was –0.0715 with a robust (White) standard error of 0.0070. This model gives surplus measures of \$2.60 and \$20.21 per-trip for the \$5 and infinite price changes, respectively. Here it is seen that there is no way to compare welfare measures since the multiple site travel cost model takes into account substitution and changes in the total number of trips; whereas the multinomial logit welfare measures do not reflect changes in the number of trips. If these numbers are scaled up by the average number of trips to Lake Roosevelt, then we observe values of \$7.38 and \$57.40 under the two price change scenarios. Note that the former underestimates the value from the multiple site travel cost model, while the latter overestimates it.

9.7 SUMMARY

This study has attempted to draw attention to methodologies for non-market valuation that have largely been overlooked by recreation demand researchers: incomplete demand systems and generalized linear modeling of multivariate count data. The incorporation of the incomplete demand system restrictions for exponential specifications of expected demand are seen to provide several critical benefits. These restrictions provide a test for optimizing behavior, reduce the number of free parameters, and permit exact welfare analysis. The incomplete demand system specification avoids the difficulty of having to scale up the per-trip consumer surplus measures that are obtained from a RUM analysis. While the incomplete demand system does suffer from arbitrariness in measuring welfare changes from non-market effects (LaFrance and Hanemann,1989), it appears to be the ideal tool for examining the loss of a site under the assumption of substitutability.

Of course the underutilization of incomplete demand specifications for multiple site travel cost models is likely linked to the lack of proper, feasible estimators. The generalized estimating equations approach to multivariate count data is relatively simple to apply. The resulting estimators are consistent under correct specification of the conditional mean and it is easy to construct standard errors robust to distributional misspecification. Together these methodologies provide a non-market valuation technique that could profoundly change how demands for multiple recreational goods are specified and estimated.

REFERENCES

Aitchison, J. and Ho, C.H. (1989), "The Multivariate Poisson-Log Normal Distribution." *Biometrika*, 76: 643–53.

Bockstael, N., Hanemann, W.M., and Kling, C. (1987), "Estimating the Value of Water Quality Improvements in a Recreational Demand Framework." *Water Resources Research*, 23:951–60.

Burt, O.R. and Brewer, D. (1971), "Estimation of Net Social Benefits from Outdoor Recreation." *Econometrica*, 39: 813–27.

Callaway, J.M., *et al.* (1995), "Columbia River Systems Operation Review of Recreation Impacts: Demand Model and Simulation Results." Final Report prepared for the U.S. Army Corps of Engineers, Portland, Oregon, by RCG/Hagler, Bailly, Inc. Boulder, Colorado.

Cameron, T.A., *et al.* (1996), "Using Actual and Contingent Behavior Data with Differing Levels of Time Aggregation to Model Recreation Demand." *Journal of Agricultural and Resource Economics*, 21:130–49.

Cicchetti, C.J., Fisher, A.C., and Smith, V.K. (1976), "An Econometric Evaluation of a Generalized Consumer Surplus Measure: The Mineral King Controversy." *Econometrica*, 44: 356–60.

Diggle, P.J., Liang, K., and Zeger, S.L. (1994), *Analysis of Longitudinal Data*. Oxford: Clarendon Press.

Englin, J. and Shonkwiler, J.S. (1995), "Estimating Social Welfare Using Count Data Models." *Review of Economics and Statistics*, 77:104–12.

Feather, P., Hellerstein, D., and Tomasi, T. (1995) "A Discrete-Count Model of Recreational Demand." *Journal of Environmental Economics and Management*, 29:214–27.

Gourieroux, C., Monfort, A., and Trognon, A. (1984), "Pseudo Maximum Likelihood Methods: Theory." *Econometrica*, 52:681–700.

Haab, T.C. and McConnell, K.E. (1996), "Count Data Models and the Problem of Zeros in Recreation Demand Analysis." *American Journal of Agricultural Economics*, 78:89–102.

Hausman, J., Leonard, G., and McFadden, D. (1995), "A Utility-Consistent, Combined Discrete Choice and Count Data Model: Assessing Recreational Use Losses Due to Natural Resource Damage." *Journal of Public Economics*, 56:1–30.

Hellerstein, D.M. (1991), "Using Count Data Models in Travel Cost Analysis with Aggregate Data." *American Journal of Agricultural Economics*, 73: 860–66.

Hellerstein, D.M. and Mendelsohn, R. (1993), "A Theoretical Foundation for Count Data Models." *American Journal of Agricultural Economics*, 75: 604–11.

Johnson, N., Kotz, S., and Kemp, A.W. (1992), *Univariate Discrete Distributions*, 2nd edition. New York: John Wiley.

LaFrance, J.T. and Hanemann, W.M. (1994), "On the Integration of Some Common Demand Systems." Staff Papers in Economics 83-10, Montana State University, October (rev.).

LaFrance, J.T. and Hanemann, W.M. (1989), "The Dual Structure of Incomplete Demand Systems." *American Journal of Agricultural Economics*, 71: 262–74.

LaFrance, J.T. (1990) "Incomplete Demand Systems and Semilogarithmic Demand Models." *Australian Journal of Agricultural Economics*, 34: 118–31.

Liang, K. and Zeger, S.L. (1986), "Longitudinal Data Analysis Using Generalized Linear Models." *Biometrika*, 73: 13–22.

McCullagh, P. and Nelder, J.A. (1989), *Generalized Linear Models*, 2nd edition. New York: Chapman & Hall.

McFadden, D. (1974), "Conditional Logit Analysis of Qualitative Choice Behavior" in *Frontiers in Econometrics*, P. Zarembka (ed.). New York: Academic Press.

McFadden, D. (forthcoming, September 1998), "Computing Willingness to Pay in Random Utility Models." *Trade, Theory, and Econometrics: Essays in Honor of John Chapman.*

Ozuna, T. and Gomez, I.A. (1994), "Estimating a System of Recreation Demand Functions Using a Seemingly Unrelated Poisson Regression Approach." *Review of Economics and Statistics*, 76: 356–60.

Parsons, G.R. and Kealy, M. (1995), "A Demand Theory for Number of Trips in a Random Utility Model of Recreation." *Journal of Environmental Economics and Management*, 29:357–67.

Prentice, R.L. and Mancl, L.A. (1993), "Comment on Regression Models for Discrete Longitudinal Responses." *Statistical Science*, 8:302–4.

Prentice, R.L. and Zhao, L.P. (1991), "Estimating Equations for Parameters in Means and Covariances of Multivariate Discrete and Continuous Responses." *Biometrics*, 47: 825–39.

Seller, C., Stoll, J.R., and Chavas, J.P. (1985), "Validation of Empirical Measures of Welfare Change: A Comparison of Nonmarket Techniques." *Land Economics*, 61:156–75.

Shonkwiler, J.S. (October 1995), "Systems of Travel Cost Models of Recreation Demand." W-133 Research Publication, 8th Interim Report, pp.3–20.

Shonkwiler, J.S. and Shaw, W.D. (1997), "The Aggregation of Conditional Recreation Demand Systems." *Applied Economics and Statistics* Working Paper, University of Nevada, 1997.

Smith, V.K. (1989), "Taking Stock of Progress with Travel Cost Recreation Demand Models: Theory and Implementation." *Marine Resource Economics*, 6: 279–310.

Smith, V.K. (1997), "Combining Discrete Choice and Count Data Models: A Comment. Unpublished manuscript. Duke University.

Smith, V.K. and Von Haefen, R. (April 1997), "Welfare Measurement and Representative Consumer Theory." Unpublished manuscript. Duke University.

White, H. (1982), "Maximum Likelihood Estimation of Misspecified Systems." *Econometrica*, 50: 1–25.

10. Can We Count On Count Models?

Daniel Hellerstein

10.1 INTRODUCTION

Within the last decade, the use of count models in travel cost analysis has become commonplace. The ability of count models to control for censoring and truncation in a natural fashion, the robustness of many of the simpler count models, and the ease of computation in the era of cheap computing have contributed to this acceptance (Creel and Loomis, 1990; Hellerstein, 1991). While certainly useful traits, these are essentially statistical niceties, and are not the result of a deep insight into how trip-taking decisions are made. While it is true that the "zero-bounded, integer-only" nature of count distributions does describe the possibility set available to even the most addled recreationist, in most applications this fundamental insight is of minor import.

Yet one might wonder if the adoptance of this modeling strategy necessitates, however implicitly, a set of assumptions about the how and why of recreational trip taking. Ideally, demand models should be the analytic expression of an underlying utility function (Pudney, 1989). So derived, one can test for adding-up, Slutsky substitution, and other normative requirements of well behaved demand functions. Furthermore, Hicksian surplus measures can be more readily divined when the underlying utility function is known.

In common practice, most demand models do not come packaged with this ideal derivation. Instead, various "integrability" assumptions are appealed to in a general way, often in the context of a partial demand system (though recent work has fortified the menu of explicit choices, viz LaFrance, 1985). Given the constraints of applied analysis, most critics will accept these appeals, and forego the requirement for a more strenuous proof. However, these integrability results apply to demand systems derived via constrained optimization of a continuous utility function. The non-continuous nature of count models may render this logic inappropriate.

This chapter attempts to address this issue by suggesting behavioral foundations that could generate "count" data. By and large, these motivations are based on count models as representing a constrained choice process, or count models as the limiting distribution of a repeated discrete choice process. But before delving into these details, it is instructive to consider the role of the random shock in count models.

Abstracting from questions regarding model specification, consider the semi-log model of demand:

$$\ln(Q) = \alpha + \beta P + \varepsilon\,, \tag{10.1}$$

where Q is observed quantity, P is observed price, α and β are demand shift and price coefficients, and ε is some form of random shock. In particular, ε accounts for unobservable factors that generate an individual specific demand shift term ($\alpha^*;\alpha^* = \alpha + \varepsilon$). Thus, granted knowledge of the components of equation 10.1 (including ε), one could work backwards from the demand curve and obtain a utility function containing an "individual specific" α term.

Now consider the simple Poisson model (Maddala, 1983; Johnson, Kotz and Kemp, 1992) with parameter λ:

$$E[Q] = \lambda = \exp(\alpha + \beta P)\,. \tag{10.2}$$

The Poisson model parameterizes a distribution of outcomes as a function of λ. Although stochastic, there is no explicit random shock term driving this distribution. Unobservables, which certainly are present, influence demand in some fashion that can not be concentrated into a simple (albeit unobservable) ε term.

In a sense, count models force us to consider demand curves as descriptions of potential behavior, rather then as exact models of demand but for our lack of ability to measure the elusive ε factor. This latter sense, that an exact model could be derived, underpins the intuition that permits applied demand curves (such as equation (10.1)) to be used in welfare analysis. That is, one could derive (or lookup) an exact utility function; if only one could overcome ignorance regarding the size of ε.[1]

In other words, much of applied analysis is marked by a "less than careful link" between estimating equations and utility functions. This oversight is justified on the basis of underlying (though perhaps unstated) integrability assumptions. The existence of a random shock (ε) complicates the integrability story, but doesn't change it fundamentally. In models that lack an explicit

---

[1] I abstract from the use of ε to account for mean-preserving model misspecifications. In such cases, the set of unobservable factors now includes unobservable (and individual specific) permutations in functional form. Although of a somewhat different flavor than "unobservable factors", the general result still holds: knowledge of ε allows one to obtain an observationally equivalent utility function.

(albeit unobservable) random shock term, one must wonder if the logic still holds.[2]

10.2 COUNT MODELS AS CONSTRAINED DEMAND

Perhaps the unspoken assumption of most count model practitioners is that classical optimization is occurring, but indivisibility forces people into solutions that approximate their true desires. That is, they might desire 1.56 trips, but the best they can do is two. Thus, λ (a continuous parameter) is informative about true (but unobtainable) desires. So conceived, count models are akin to the continuous demand curves economists are used to seeing; what with a deterministic portion that describes the representative consumer, and a stochastic portion to account for both unobservable factors and the need for rounding.

Unfortunately, it's not a satisfying story. Besides the heroic assumptions regarding the distribution of the ε terms (see Haab and McConnell (1996) for an example); such a story slights the fact that indivisibility is more than an inconvenience, it's a fundamental attribute. When faced with an infra-marginal choice as to further expenditure (albeit on dQ=1.0) the rational consumer must consider the benefit from consuming this extra trip, as compared to the benefits that might flow from alternative uses of the (infra-marginal) trip cost. Although in cases of a constant marginal utility of income this is readily computed, it still represents a departure from pure marginal decision making.[3]

As shown by Hellerstein and Mendelsohn (1993)[4], this indivisibility can be represented by an expenditure function (M) of:

$$M\left[P_1, P_2 \middle| \varepsilon, U_0\right] = \min_{X_1}\left[P_1 X_1 + \min_{X_2} P_2 X_2\right] \quad \text{s.t. } U(X_1, X_2, \varepsilon) = U_0, \tag{10.3}$$

where U_0 is a reference level of utility, X_1 is the indivisible good (recreational trips), X_2 are other continuous goods (in the simplest case, X_1 is a money

---

[2] One could argue that in the context of continuous models, the ability to pinpoint an ε contributes to an illusion of exactness; that all we have is a parameterized distribution of results. Under this interpretation, the same fundamental questions (regarding integrability issues) arise.

[3] That is, when faced with a constant marginal utility of income, it is fairly simple to compare the utility of an extra trip against the utility gained from increased expenditure on a "money numeraire" good. As an aside, the existence of such a constant-marginal-utility money- numeraire good is closely felt by anyone with kids facing college expenses (it's not just a lazy economist's simplification)!

[4] This is a simplification of their equation (10.3).

numeraire), ε captures unobservable factors, and P_i are prices.

The idea is simple: given a quantity of X_1, an optimization on X_2 (over remaining income) is conducted. This process is iterated until an optimal quantity of X_1 is deduced.[5] Since X_1 can only be changed in infra-marginal amounts, the expenditure function will be piecewise linear in P_1, and the compensated demand curve for X_1 will be a downward trending, stepwise function in P_1.

So what's the fuss about? If you have an expenditure function, then compensating variation (and other welfare measures) automatically follow. Ah, but what of the stochastic proclivities of ε? Recollecting the above discussion of the random shock, one can't just "add" ε to the expenditure function (or its derivatives); demand must follow a step function along an integers-only pathway. Rather then try to finagle some story featuring ε as some kind of fungible quantity, I would argue that it's better to think of ε as indexing a state-of-the-world. This line of reasoning allows one to make statements along the lines of: *as the level of ε grows (shrinks) the probability of observing quantities higher (lower) than the expected value increases (decreases)* This is not quite the same as saying "tell me ε and I'll tell you what you'll see".

If you are willing to accept this vision of ε's role, then the interpretation of a demand curve is straightforward—it parameterizes the distribution of what one might observe. In almost all cases, this parameterization is equivalent to uncovering an expectation of quantity (across observations in a sample of observationally equivalent individuals).

More formally, expected trip demand (E[Q]) is given by:

$$E[Q] = \mu(p, P_2, Y; \beta) = \int_{\Psi} f(\varepsilon) T(p, P_2, Y, \varepsilon; \beta) d\varepsilon \qquad (10.4)$$

where p is the trip price, P_2 is the price(s) of other goods, Y is income, β is a vector of coefficients on prices and income, ε identifies some state-of-the-world, Ψ is the range of support of ε, f is a probability distribution function over ε and $T(\cdot)$ is a "downward trending, stepwise" trip demand function. Note that T is a stochastic function of the "state of the world" (as indexed by ε).[6]

It's a simple matter to derive consumer surplus. Given ε integrating $T(\cdot)$ between observed price (P_{obs}) and some choke price (P_{max}; possibly equal to ∞), yields a "state-specific consumer surplus". Integrating this state-specific consumer surplus across $f(\varepsilon)$ yields the expected value of consumer surplus

---

[5] A similar, notationally complex, story can be told when multiple indivisible goods are available.

[6] No parametric assumptions are made about how ε influence choices.

($E[CS]$). Since Ψ, P_{obs}, and P_{max} are exogenous quantities, the order of integration can be reversed, and equation (10.4) can be substituted in:

$$\begin{aligned} E[CS] &= \int_{\Psi} \left\{ \int_{P_{obs}}^{P_{max}} \left[f(\varepsilon) T(p, P_2, Y, \varepsilon; \beta) \right] dp \right\} d\varepsilon \\ &= \int_{P_{obs}}^{P_{max}} \left\{ \int_{\Psi} \left[f(\varepsilon) T(p, P_2, Y, \varepsilon; \beta) \right] d\varepsilon \right\} dp \\ &= \int_{P_{obs}}^{P_{max}} \mu(p, P_2, Y; \beta) dp. \end{aligned} \quad (10.5)$$

In the simple Poisson model, where $\lambda = \mu = \exp(\alpha + \beta_p p + \beta_2 P_2 + \beta_y Y)$, this yields the familiar formula:

$$E[CS] = \frac{-\lambda}{\beta_p} \quad (10.6)$$

Equation (10.5) (and equation (10.6) as a special case) is a fortunate result, for it states that if you are willing to report *expectations* of consumer surplus, you can use a standard continuous formula. You do not need to consider the indivisibility of the good in question.

10.3 COUNT MODELS FROM REPEATED DISCRETE CHOICE

Although the constrained demand story is fairly uncluttered, the treatment of ε has an ad-hoc flavor. A more closely told story, with a clearer set of testable hypotheses and a richer set of implications, would be desirable. In particular, a goal is to derive count models from the linkage of an explicit utility function and a parametric distribution of random shocks.

Given that trips occur in non-overlapping "days" (or some other time block), and that individuals must choose what to do (on each "day") from a menu of possibilities, the notion of repeated discrete choice arises. More precisely, on any given day an individual must choose a consumption bundle; with "take a trip" being one of the choices. If the decision is irreducible (one can either take a trip, or not take a trip), this is essentially a discrete choice. Over many such choice opportunities (i.e., many days in a recreation season), the appropriate model is one of repeated discrete choice.

One might think that repeated discrete choice models are best estimated with multiple observations (over many choice opportunities) per individual (Bockstael *et al.*, 1984). Unfortunately, it is rare that such a complete dataset is available. Therefore, some sort of modeling strategy is used to make up for the analyst's inability to adequately measure behavior.

A common strategy is to adopt a two-stage model; where:

- Stage 1: a discrete model (i.e., a logit) is used to explain a single choice (over multiple alternatives)

- Stage 2: using a price index generated from the discrete model (i.e., the inclusive value) the quantity of trips taken is predicted.

Estimation of stage 1 requires information on the choice set (and choice) for at least one trip. Estimation of stage 2 (the "quantity of trips stage") requires information on the total number of trips taken (to all sites), and is often estimated with count models (Feather and Hellerstein, 1995; Parsons and Kealy, 1995; Hausman *et al.,* 1995).

Since these models can carefully account for site characteristics, they are often quite attractive. Furthermore, the creators of these models are careful to base the discrete choice stage on some sort of utility function (i.e.; linear with additive extreme valued random shock). Much attention is also given to the proper price index (Hausman *et al.,* 1995; Shonkwiler and Shaw, 1997). However, the choice of a count model in the quantity stage is usually based on econometric convenience, with no attempt to derive some underlying utility function that will generate this "count" demand curve.

An alternative to this two-stage model is to proxy for repeated choices. For example, Morey *et al.,* (1991). present a model that is useful when only a subset of the choice opportunities can be observed. One issue that their model endogenizes is the problem of "number of choice occasions". This can be quite important, since taking 5 trips on 5 choice occasions versus 5 trips on 100 choice occasions may imply different price and quality elasticities.

But what if you do not have information sufficient to construct a discrete choice model? That is, what if all you have is visitation information for a single site, consisting of quantity of trips, prices (including a suitable set of substitute prices), and demand shifters. In this case, does the consideration of discrete choice models shed any light?

Actually, it's fairly straightforward to link a repeated discrete choice model to a single site count model. A key insight is that a Poisson process (as the limit of binomial distribution) arises from the repetition of many small, independent probability events. Thus, given many events (say, days in a season), each with a small chance of success (say, a small probability of visiting a site), the net result will be approximately Poisson distributed.

Furthermore, the standard consumer surplus formula ($-\lambda / \beta_p$) approximates the compensating variation (Hellerstein and Mendelsohn, 1993). This can be shown by starting with a generic discrete choice utility function defined over trip cost (p_i), income, and "taking a trip":

$$V^* = \max\left(V(0, Y, \varepsilon_0), V(1, Y - p_i, \varepsilon_1)\right), \tag{10.7}$$

where 1 signifies "take a trip" and 0 signifies "no trip". The compensating variation for a single trip (CV_t) satisfies

$$V(0, Y, \varepsilon_0) = V\left(1, Y - (p_i + CV_t), \varepsilon_1\right). \tag{10.8}$$

Since ε is stochastic, CV_t is a random variable with expectation (Hanemann):

$$E[CV_t] = \int_0^\infty [1 - F(cv)]dcv, \tag{10.9}$$

where *F(cv)* is the cumulative distribution function of CV_t. Since *F(0)* is the probability of not choosing to take a trip at a given price and income, *1-F(0)* will equal $\pi_t(p, Y)$, the probability of taking a trip at the observed price. Similarly, *1- F(A)* is the probability of taking a trip at a price of *p+A*. Substituting these results into (10.9) yields

$$E[CV_t] = \int_{P_{obs}}^\infty \pi(p, Y)dp. \tag{10.10}$$

Repeating this over a *T* day season yields the total (seasonal) compensating variation (*CV*):

$$E[CV] = \sum_{t=1}^{T} \int_{P_{obs}}^\infty \pi_t(p, Y)dp = \int_{P_{obs}}^\infty \left[\sum_{t=1}^{T} \pi_t(p, Y)\right]dp. \tag{10.11}$$

Finally, if *T* is large and π small, the summation term will be approximately Poisson distributed with parameters $\lambda(p, Y)$. Therefore,

$$E[CV] = \int_{P_{obs}}^{\infty} \lambda(p, Y)dp. \tag{10.12}$$

Abstracting from the form of the λ function, this last result is essentially the same as obtained from the constrained demand scenario. In fact, it can be shown that when V is modeled as logit, the standard formula, $\lambda = \exp(X\beta)$, can be obtained.

10.4 ON INDIVIDUAL SPECIFIC COUNT MODELS

The preceding review of the behavioral underpinnings of count models has leaned on the notion of predicting expectations. While this is often desirable, there may be occasions where one is interested in making speculative statements about a known set of observations. For example, consider a simple linear demand:

$$Y = X\beta + \varepsilon, \tag{10.13}$$

where X is a vector of observable variables. Using OLS estimates of β (b), a consistent prediction of the ε residual can be obtained using:

$$e = Y - Xb. \tag{10.14}$$

Therefore, given a new set of observable variables for an individual (χ), and an estimated coefficient vector b

$$q' = \chi b + e$$

will be a "full information" prediction of an individual's demand, given χ.

As argued in the introduction, residuals don't have a place in the count model story. Therefore, the use of a simple additive (or multiplicative) residual may be inappropriate. Nevertheless, there are certainly systematic differences between observationally equivalent individuals, differences that should persist even when observable factors (such as prices) systematically change.[7] The challenge is to measure such differences in some *aesthetically pleasing* way.

To address this challenge, we need to dissect the notion that the demand curve *parameterizes a probability distribution*. That is; if $T(p, P_2, Y, \varepsilon; \beta)$ is the

---

[7] By observationally equivalent individuals, I mean individuals with equal values for all characteristics that are to be included as explanatory variables in a demand curve. This does not encompass the actual level of demand; which may be influenced by *unobservable* factors.

"step-wise" demand function for trips by an individual, then ε is an unobservable index into probability space; a probability space defined over "types of individuals".[8] One can say that ε indexes the *relative avidity* of an individual (Hellerstein, 1996).

Consider the case of Poisson distributed trip demand, parameterized by $\lambda = \exp(X\beta)$; with a probability density function over total trips (Q) of:

$$f(q;\lambda)\text{: Prob}(Q = q) = \frac{e^{-\lambda}\lambda^{q}}{q!}. \tag{10.15}$$

and a cumulative distribution function:

$$F(q;\lambda)\text{: Prob}(\mathrm{Q} \le \mathrm{q}) = \sum_{i=0}^{q} \frac{e^{-\lambda}\lambda^{i}}{i!}. \tag{10.16}$$

We define a two element vector κ :

$$\begin{aligned} \kappa_1(q,\lambda) &= F(q-1;\lambda); \\ \kappa_2(q,\lambda) &= F(q;\lambda); \end{aligned} \tag{10.17}$$

and with $\kappa_1(0,\lambda) = 0 \; \forall \lambda$.

κ_1 is the fraction of a population (of individuals all possessing identical values of λ) that have demand less than q. A fraction of $1-\kappa_2$ will have demand greater than q. That is, compared to an individual observed to demand a level of q; a κ_1 fraction of this population are less *avid* users of the resource, and a $1-\kappa_2$ fraction are more *avid*. This implies that the individual has an actual (but unobservable) level of "relative" avidity that lies between these endpoints. For example, consider the following table of Poisson densities (f) and distribution (F).

---

[8] The term "type of individual" should imply the same sort of meaning as "state of the world", with an emphasis on cross-sectional differences.

Table 10.1 Poisson Densities

	λ=2.6		λ=2.1		λ=0.6	
q	$f(q,2.6)$	$F(q,2.6)$	$f(q,2.1)$	$F(q,2.1)$	$f(q,0.6)$	$F(q,0.6)$
0	0.0743	0.0743	0.122	0.122	0.548	0.548
1	0.193	0.267	0.257	0.379	0.329	0.878
2	0.251	0.518	0.270	0.649	0.098	0.976
3	0.217	0.736	0.189	0.838	0.0198	0.996
4	0.141	0.877	0.099	0.937	0.003	0.997

An individual with λ=2.6 and an observed q=2 will yield:

$$\kappa_1 = F(1,2.6) = 0.267,$$

and

$$\kappa_2 = F(2,2.6) = 0.518$$

Hence, in a population of individuals all possessing λ=2.6:

- at least 26.7%, but no more than 51.8%, are *less avid* (than this individual);
- at least 48.2%, but no more than 78.5%, are *more avid* (than this individual).

The key point is that a permanent ranking of individuals exists. Given the constraints of count data, placement of individuals in this ranking is not exact. Instead, one can determine a "quantile of relative avidity", a quantity whose bounds are κ_1 and κ_2.

Adopting the usual assumption of zero correlation between random shocks and explanatory variables (e.g., Johnston (1984), pp. 172), it is reasonable to assume that κ is exogenous to changes in explanatory variables. That is, when λ changes as a result of changes in explanatory variables, the avidity rankings of a set of individual will remain the same (each individual's κ will not change). Therefore, given

- new values for the explanatory variables (λ), hence a new value of $\lambda = \exp(X\beta)$,
- and given an individual's observed λ and q,

it is possible to determine the upper and lower bound of quantity demanded (q'):

$$q'_{-} \leq q' \leq q'_{+}, \qquad (10.18)$$

where

$$q'_{-} = F^{-1}(\kappa_1(q,\lambda);\Lambda) = \text{the lower bound},$$

$$q'_{+} = F^{-1}(\kappa_2(q,\lambda);\Lambda) = \text{the upper bound},$$

and F^{-1} is an inverse CDF, which generates a quantity given a probability. For example, if q=2, λ=2.6 and Λ=2.1, then (using Table 10.1):

$$q'_{-} = F^{-1}(\kappa_1(2,2.6);2.1) = F^{-1}(0.267;2.1) = 1$$

and

$$q'_{+} = F^{-1}(\kappa_2(2,2.6);2.1) = F^{-1}(0.518;2.1) = 2 .$$

Note that some fraction of this "λ=2.6" population will continue to demand 2, but some will decrease their demand to 1.[9] By appropriately integrating over these bounds, an expectation of the "full information predicted demand" (η) can be computed:

$$\eta(\Lambda|\lambda,q) = \frac{1}{f(\lambda,q)}\int_{\kappa_1}^{\kappa_2} F^{-1}(\Lambda,r)dr . \qquad (10.19)$$

For example:

$$\eta(2.1\,|\,2.6,2) = [\,(0.379-0.267)*1+(0.518-0.379)*2\,]\,/\,0.251 = 1.55 .$$

Lastly, a "full information consumer surplus" can be generated by integrating η from observed price to some choke price.[10] This integration, which effects the Λ term, may require numeric techniques (F^{-1} routines for count models are not easy to find). Nevertheless, with modern computing power the repetitive computation of η (and of the consumer surplus) is readily accomplished.

Having accepted that these results make some sort of sense, the concerned reader may wonder as to the practical significance of the proposed means of

---

[9] More precisely, individuals with an avidity between 26.7% and 37.9% will decrease their demand to 1.

[10] Note that the choke price will be finite, since at some price $F^{-1}(\kappa_2;\Lambda) = 0$.

calculating consumer surplus over a survey sample. First, this is likely to be an interesting question when environmental (or other) changes may be distributed unevenly across a population, and you have a good measure of just how each respondent will be effected by such changes. It may be the case that the use of the "full information" predictions will capture non-linearities that would be missed in a more aggregated, expected-value based computation.

On the other hand, it's much easier just to use "expected-value" computations; and it's only a little bit of work to abstract from count-data-ness and use predicted residuals. Furthermore, it's possible that the heavy reliance on "predicted avidity" (which is the count-model counterpart to predicted residual) may exacerbate model misspecifications. In fact, some preliminary analysis (available from the author upon request) does suggest that in many cases, use of expected values, or of "naive" residuals, can outperform the more time consuming "full information" predictions. That is, these less rigorous methods can give more accurate results (with accuracy defined using "full information" predictions and known model coefficients).

Take your pick: are these (albeit preliminary) results good or bad news? Perhaps the gentle reader has just wasted her time contemplating a useless methodology. Or perhaps this provides proof that, in the messy world of less-than-complete models, our "naive" and "expected value" simplifications can work surprisingly well.

10.5 SUMMARY AND CONCLUSIONS

The goal of this chapter is to heighten the reader's appreciation for the nuances of what it means to indulge in count modeling. On a practical level, the main message is that for most purposes of applied analysis (where demand projection and average Marshallian welfare measures are sought), one need not worry about the non-standard behavioral models that count models imply. That is, standard expectation formulas (those derived from functionally similar continuous models) can be used without modification.

The careful reader may note that the Poisson has stood in for a bivouac of more sophisticated count models; such as the negative binomial, and various double hurdle models. For these, more realistic, models the stories remain essentially the same. In the constrained scenario, the key insight is that the count process used to describe individual behavior; in particular, that the mean of whatever model you choose is consistent. The repeated discrete choice model is somewhat more complicated, but the essential insight is similar: that some sort of repetition of a discrete choice opportunity yields an estimable mean.[11]

---

[11] For non-Poisson models this repetitionill not be strictly iid across individuals; hence the need for more sophisticated likelihood functions.

For individual specific demand, the case is less clear; given that the use of "predicted residuals" is unnatural when using count models. However, some preliminary analysis suggests that the naive use of residuals may yield adequate approximation to the more rigorous "full information prediction" outlined above.

REFERENCES

Bockstael, N., Hanemann, M., and Strand, I. (1984), "Measuring the Benefits of Water Quality Improvements Using Recreation Demand Models: Vol II", prepared for the Office of Policy Analysis, Environmental Protection Agency, Washington DC.

Creel, M. and Loomis, J. (1990), "Theoretical and Empirical Advantages of Truncated Count Data Estimators for Deer Hunting in California", *American Journal of Agricultural Economics*, 72: 434–45.

Feather, P. and Hellerstein, D. (1995), "A Discrete-count model of recreational demand", *Journal of Environmental Economics and Management,* 29:214–27.

Haab, T. and McConnell, K. (1996), "Count Data Models and the Problem of Zeros in Recreation Demand Analysis", *American Journal of Agricultural Economics*, 78:89–102.

Hausman, J., Leonard, G., and McFadden, D. (1995), "A Utility-consistent, combined discrete choice and count data model Assessing recreational use losses do to natural resource damage", *Journal of Public Economics*, 50:1–30.

Hellerstein, D. (1991), "Using Count Data Models in Travel Cost Analysis with Aggregate Data", *American Journal of Agricultural Economics*, 73: 860–67.

Hellerstein, D. (1996), "Quantile Methods of Using Count Data Models in Travel Demand Estimation", in *W-133 Benefits And Costs Transfer in Natural Resource Planning, Ninth Interim Report*, July, pp. 341–50.

Hellerstein, D. and Mendelsohn, R. (1993), "A Theoretical Foundation for Count Data Models", *American Journal of Agricultural Economics*, 75:604–11

Johnson N., Kotz, S., and Kemp, A. (1992), *Univariate Discrete Distributions: 2nd Edition*. John Wilen & Sons, Inc.

Johnston, J. (1984), *Econometric Methods*, 3rd edition. McGraw Hill.

LaFrance, J. (1985), "Linear Demand Functions in Theory and Practice", *Journal of Economic Theory,* 147–66

Maddala, G.S. (1983), *Limited Dependent and Qualitative Variables in Econometrics*. Cambridge University Press.

Morey, E., Shaw, W.D., and Rowe, R. (1991), "A Disrete-Choice Model of Recreational Participation, Site Choice, and Activity Valuation When Complete Trip Data are Not Available", *Journal of Environmental Economics and Management* 20:181–201

Parsons, G. and Kealy, M.J. (1995), "A Demand Theory for Number of Trips in a Random Utility Model of Recreation", *Journal of Environmental Economics and Management,* 29:357–67

Pudney, S. (1989), *Modeling Individual Choice: The Econometrics of Corners, Kinks, and Holes*, Basil Blackwell.

Author Index

Subject Index